SOLVED !

SOLVED !

HOW A BUSINESS LAWYER SOLVES CLIENTS' PROBLEMS STRATEGICALLY – WITH CREATIVITY AND IMAGINATION

Milton Bordwin

ISBN-13: 9780692832592
ISBN-10: 0692832599
Legal Risks Limited : Boston

To the woman who brought
music into my life,
and kept it there.

CONTENTS

Tenant Didn't Agree to Give Landlord a Windfall, But Still Has to Pay to
Avoid a Serious Risk. And You'll Appreciate the Important Distinction
Between a "Covenant" and a "Condition."

A Bonus **BLT:** What to Do? In Negotiations – When to
Interrupt and Talk,
and When to Be Still

and
If the other side's lawyer's instructions are the opposite of the
instructions your
client gave you, what then?

A tale from pre-Castro Cuba, 1957, tells of my start as a lawyer and
then, I recall a simple little case involving the Federal Rules of Civil
Procedure, more particularly, your right under Rule 15 to amend your
pleadings. As a young lawyer age 30 or so I took this case to the U.S.
Supreme Court and won a unanimous decision reversing the lower
courts. That Supreme Court decision appears to be cited in one or
more U.S. court decisions about every single working day since it was
decided in 1962 – at this writing almost 24,000 times. This case and
other experiences convinced me of a powerful approach when you ask
the judge up there on the bench to decide a case in your favor. It's
worked for me and may work for you.

APPENDIXES

ACKNOWLEDGEMENTS

Since the Tales span a 60-year career as a business lawyer, it's hard to pinpoint just when this book of Tales began and to whom I owe some thanks. So let's just say that the book began when I gave to my partner-to-be, Howard Rubin, that very first legal memo in August 1957, just as I was starting my Faculty job at Harvard Law School. That memo supported my conclusion that a contract for the sale of all the capital stock of a single-asset corporation (a factory building in this case) was still enforceable even after the destruction of that asset (the factory building had burned to the ground). The lesson from that experience is the title of Part III of this book: "Knowing 'The Law' Helps You to Win," nine cases which pay homage to my legal education at Harvard Law School and the memorable outstanding professors – all deserving to be acknowledged in this book. It is especially gratifying to publish my first book this year, 2017, the Bicentennial Year of the founding of Harvard Law School, my alma mater. And prior to law school, I had a wonderful educational experience at New York's CUNY system at Baruch College of the City College of New York, four years which have stood me in good stead ever since.

More recently, I am ever grateful to my colleagues, clients and friends who read drafts of *SOLVED!* and offered their valuable criticism : Partner (retired) and friend Jason Sokolov (who also was my Associate Editor for *The Bordwin Letter*); Rubin and Rudman partner and friend Ralph Rivkind; and my New York colleagues, Solomon Friedman, a securities/corporate lawyer with Moses and Singer and Richard Bertocci, a real estate and banking/international specialist with Gilmartin, Poster and Shafto. Clients and friends

Sheldon M. Woolf and Rory J. Cowan provided not only materials for the Tales, but offered valuable comments on the manuscript. And thanks to business/management consultant, Dan Ciampa, for his early, incisive comments. From my days in "Preventive Law," I am grateful to Professor Tom Barton of California Western School of Law for his thoughtful comments on the manuscript. And of course my gratitude extends to the lawyers, educators and judges whose kind words appear on the covers of this book.

At the top of the list of people important to any business lawyer are the clients – ah, those gutsy folks who started businesses, took chances, assumed risks and made a success of it all – the folks who kept coming back to me with their problems and giving me the opportunity to find a solution and enjoy the satisfaction of seeing those solutions work. Many of the real estate Tales and most difficult problems came from my twenty-five year association with the late Robert Leventhal, Norman Leventhal and Edwin Sidman and their business, Boston's Beacon Construction Company and later, The Beacon Companies. Other real estate work came from my long-term relationship with the now 50-year old firm, Leggat McCall Properties, a relationship that spanned three generations of owners (the founders Tom Leggat, Bill McCall and Fritz Werner; their successors Brad Griffith and Jay Walton; and the present owners, Mahmood Malihi and Eric Sheffels [and my direct report, Executive VP Eric Bacon]).

I am fortunate to have had over the years a most supportive family, who put up with a paper-hoarder (and sometimes organizer/filer). My good fortune extends especially to my daughter-editor, Malka Bordwin (a published author in her own right – *Toby's Tale – A Dog's Memoir*), who provided invaluable criticism as I wrote the Tales. And I'm grateful to my daughter-in-law, Gabrielle Bordwin, who created the cover of *SOLVED!*

My writing for a business audience in plain-English style took a formal shape during the 90s when I started my newsletter, *The Bordwin Letter – Preventive Law for Business.* With the tag-line, "Prevent Legal Problems – Stay Out of Court," it became a leading publication in the field. This could not have come about without the support of a distinguished group of lawyers and educators, all published authors in their own right, and so here's a copy of the newsletter masthead from the 90s listing this Board of Advisors to whom I express my gratitude and appreciation for their support during those years of my publication, *The Bordwin Letter*::

ADVISORY BOARD – *The Bordwin Letter* – **1990 – 1996**
Paul A. Allen, Senior Vice President, General Counsel and Secretary, VISA USA, Inc., San Francisco, CA and Author/Editor, *How to Keep your Company Out of Court.*

Louis M. Brown, Sanders, Barnet, Goldman, Simons & Mosk, P.C., Los Angeles, CA: Author, *Preventive Law*; Co-Author, *The Legal Audit*; and Consulting Editor, *Preventive Law Reporter.*

Edward A. Dauer, President, National Center for Preventive Law and Consulting Editor, *Preventive Law Reporter*, Denver, CO; former Dean, University of Denver College of Law.

Michael L. Goldblatt, Assoc. Gen. Counsel, Tidewater, Inc., New Orleans, LA and Author, *Preventive Law and Corporate Practice.*

Robert B. Hughes, Partner, Hughes & Multer, P.S., Bellingham, WA; Author/Editor. *Legal Compliance Checkups* (4 vol.)

Ronald L. Jones, Counsel, Occidental Chemical Corporation, Dallas, TX and Author, *Practice Preventive Corporate Law.*

J. Alden Lincoln, Chair, Preventive Law Committee, Massachusetts Bar Association, formerly General Counsel, GTE/Sylvania.

Joseph Murphy, Co-Editor, *Corporate Conduct Quarterly* and Co-Author, *Interactive Corporate Compliance*, Philadelphia, PA

Kenneth Ross, Partner, Bowman and Brooke, Minneapolis, MN; Co-Chair Practising Law Institute Annual Seminar and Co-Editor, *Product Liability of Manufacturers: Prevention and Defense.*

My thanks to Harry Arthurs, my Canadian classmate in the Masters' program at Harvard Law, 1958-59. Harry went on to become University Professor and then Dean of Osgoode Hall Law School and later President of York University. He generously shared his deep insights both as a law teacher and an administrator, insights that have opened new vistas of how *SOLVED!* may be useful in an academic setting and a classroom environment.

My brother, Moe Bordwin, over the years has given me the benefit of his acumen and ideas, both as a lawyer and a businessman. These have helped in producing *SOLVED!* and for that I'll always be grateful.

To my old Army buddy and long-time book retailer, Marshall Smith, my thanks for his insights in the business end of producing a book. At our advanced age, he's still running his flagship store in Brookline, MA, the Brookline Booksmith (and a few other stores!).

I cannot conclude these acknowledgements without saluting a group of some of the very best lawyers, finest minds and nicest people I know – my partners past and present at Rubin and Rudman LLP. Their support and encouragement and, indeed, friendship, over the years have been a blessing during the writing of *SOLVED!* – and for that I will be eternally grateful.

Milton Bordwin
July 2017 Boston, Massachusetts

———

INTRODUCTION

"You're the lawyer. Figure something out!" Clients would give me these "marching orders" after seeing my skeptical look on hearing their problem. One client, whose matters often took me out of town put it another way:

"Come back with this thing resolved, or keep going."

And so facing difficult problems and some seemingly impossible challenges became the direction of my business law practice. This book tells you what happened and how I managed to solve most (not all!) of the problems clients threw at me.

I wish I could say with full assurance (paraphrasing the words of Law Professor Charles W. Kingfield, Jr. in the movie, *The Paper Chase*): "You come to this book with a skull full of mush; you read it and leave thinking like a lawyer." I cannot say that, but what I can say is this: *SOLVED!* can get you inside the mind of this lawyer and maybe you'll better understand how we think our way through your business problems and how you ought to be working with your lawyer – working to both prevent and to solve your problems.

I've been a practicing business lawyer since 1957, when I started part-time while still a member of the Harvard Law School faculty. I wrote this book to tell the stories of how I solved clients' problems over a 60-year career – some problems were relatively simple to solve; others seemed insoluble. (One was solved ten years before it happened.) I tell you these Tales hoping that they will help businesspeople work more effectively with their lawyers and help lawyers solve their clients' problems. I'm also hoping that the Tales will help students of both business and law, once they graduate into "the real world," to gain an insight and a better understanding of how to work *together* to solve problems.[1] And as you'll see, the Tales span a broad range of legal areas and law school subjects.[2]

Reflecting back over my work as a business lawyer, I found that most of it fell into one of two categories:

(1) doing a deal – help negotiating and then documenting (a/k/a "papering") a transaction; or
(2) solving a client's problem.

Deals

"Yes, I do make things, son. I make things called deals."

(1) In deal-making, I tried to ensure that the client's goals were achieved, without disputes, misunderstandings or problems. The first step was always to learn the pertinent details of client's business and what they expected from the deal – their intentions. Then I'd weigh the client's strengths and weaknesses in the bargaining/negotiation stage. Next, I'd look ahead in time to identify client's bargaining advantages as well as any obstacles that might prevent the client from achieving those goals and meeting their intentions and expectations. This same theme – anticipating and preventing problems when doing a deal – shows up again in the Prologue and in many of the Tales in this book.

Problem-Solving

(2) When a client comes into my office with an existing problem, the ballgame changes: Something's already gone wrong; and that problem – sometimes a dispute – needs to be resolved. Some clients' problems seemed, on their face, insoluble – there was no way out. But that's an answer no client wants to hear and an admission of defeat I hate to make. The instructions I'd hear over and over again: "Look, Milton, you're the lawyer. Go figure it out!"

As you read about how clients' problems were solved, you'll also learn how to do better at that other crucial activity noted above – deal-making and documenting the deal you've made. And you'll learn that solving problems teaches how to prevent and avoid problems.

Preventing Problems

Preventing problems, avoiding that "next time," is an important byproduct of both deal making and problem solving. Having seen first-hand the cost, suffering and pain inflicted on clients who land in court, I've made practicing preventive law a hallmark of my law practice: "Prevent Legal Problems – Stay Out of Court." (Indeed, this was the tag-line of my plain-English style newsletter, *The Bordwin Letter – Preventive Law for Business*, which I published during the 90s for business readers.)

Strategy – Strategic Lawyering
At some point in writing this book I became aware that I had been using strategy to solve clients' problems – I realized I'd been practicing strategic lawyering.

Strategy is defined in detail in the brilliant article by Professors Lynn M. LoPucki and Walter O. Weyrauch, "A Theory of Legal Strategy."[3] Their explanation of how lawyers use strategy to solve business clients' problems – despite laws, regulations, judges' decisions, etc. – aptly describes the problem-solving process and style of law practice you'll see illustrated in many of the Tales.

What Is "Strategy?"
"Strategy" or strategic lawyering has been variously defined. For example, some years after the 80-page LoPucki-Weyrauch article, three lawyer-scholars came up with their own short-and-sweet definition. Deanne Siemer, Frank Rothschild and Paul Zweir, write in *Teaching Legal Strategy*,[4] that "Strategy can be taught"[5] and go on to define "strategy" as follows:

A strategy is a description of a process. It answers the question: How do we get from here to there within the available time and money.[6]

The authors then illustrate how to define the starting point of a problem ("here") and the goal ("there") and then go into the problem-resolution process intended to get the client from here to there. I was gratified to find how many of the points they make in teaching the subject of "strategy" are illustrated by various Tales in this book.

Yet another definition of strategic lawyering comes from some practicing business lawyers, whose definition combines these two elements:

(1) the viewpoint of the businessperson who sees legal strategies as helping them gain a competitive advantage and exclude competition in a legal way; and (2) the viewpoint of the lawyer on how to maneuver within the legal system. So with a steady focus on the

details of the client's business, strategic lawyering combines these two perspectives.[7]

Let me add my own view of "strategy" to this mix of definitions, but first, this redundant phrase capsulizes what you'll read over and over again: Long-term Strategy. Redundant because I view *all* strategy as long term – looking into the future and asking questions to determine whether your plan or deal will work for you. To expand a bit:

When I'm involved in negotiating and documenting a deal/transaction, I try to look ahead and focus on the future. I ask what could happen, what conditions might change (particularly market condition); and then try to respond to (or intentionally make no mention of) those changes, always with an eye on my clients' goals and expectations. This process requires that I learn all the pertinent facts about the client's business; that the client define their specific goals and expectations; and that I then clearly express those goals and expectations in the documents. You'll see these approaches to strategy and strategic lawyering in many of the Tales. And also remember that strategic thinking – looking ahead and asking those questions about what could happen, what could change and how should I deal with the situation – applies to many areas outside business and lawyering. For example, President John F. Kennedy dealt with the 1962 Cuban missile crisis in a way he thought would avert armed conflict and possibly a nuclear war with the Soviet Union.[8]

———

While I found many books and articles by practicing lawyers on both doing deals and preventive law,[9] I didn't find many by a practicing lawyer describing the kind of strategic problem-solving I'd done. With few exceptions, almost all the writing on problem-solving seems to come from legal scholars and focuses on pedagogical theory: how to teach problem-solving to law and business students. This was confirmed by Professor Phyllis Marion, who produced an ambitious 84-page bibliography on problem solving.[10] Responding to my question about other writings in the field by practicing lawyers, she replied that her bibliography "is mostly scholarly with a focus on pedagogy, not practice." Why haven't more practicing business lawyers explained how they used strategic lawyering to solve clients' problems?

Two legal scholars explain why those practicing lawyers who use strategy don't write about it. They note

> the understandable reluctance of lawyers who engage in strategy to admit that they do so. The use of strategy is often condemned as unethical,…and the articulation of strategy tends to destroy its effect …Together, these two factors remove practicing lawyers—the persons most knowledgeable about strategy—from the discussion of its role in the legal system.[11]

" I won't discuss the secret sauce . . . "

How true! I would not have written *SOLVED!* while still in active law practice for the reasons the scholars state. Nor did I mention at bar association seminars/presentations certain strategies clients and I had developed and used – that would "destroy its effect." Some readers reacted negatively to my use of strategy; one colleague called certain actions unethical (he was wrong, as explained in the Prologue); and the "articulation of strategy" would, indeed, tend to destroy its effect. But at age 86 with 60 years of practice behind me, I now feel free to describe the strategies I used to solve problems. And to repeat: In the process of *solving* problems, I learned how to *prevent* problems – and preventive law has long been my preferred style of business-law practice. The use of strategy (a/k/a "strategic lawyering") is explained in more detail in the Prologue and then illustrated in many of the Tales.

This Book Is Written Specifically For You

This book was written for businesspeople, their lawyers and students of both business and law, and the general reader who might find it interesting to get into the head of a business lawyer. This is how *SOLVED!* can help a wide variety of readers:

- **Business Lawyers** – Using strategic lawyering to respond positively to clients' business problems – even when those problems seem difficult, sometimes insoluble – with foresight, an open mind, creativity, imagination, and flexibility.

- **Businesspeople** – Learn about the kinds of results you should expect from your legal adviser and how you must educate them with the details of both your industry, your business and your particular situation so they can formulate a successful strategy and solution to *your* particular problem.

- **Law students and business students** – "Experiential learning" has become all the rage at law schools.[12] The same trend is appearing in the business schools.[13] *SOLVED!* can help you gain a real-world perspective to round out your academic studies. (Law schools are already getting deeply into clinical courses. Example: For several years I have participated in a business-law problem-solving exercise with a group of students at my alma mater, Harvard Law School.) Law students can learn some business basics from a book especially written for you, for example, an American Bar Association publication by Professor Bert Spector, *Understanding Your Business Clients*.[14] The other side of the coin – law for businesspeople – is the ABA's *Legal Guide for Small Business*.[15]

―――――

How This Book Began

SOLVED! began decades ago with an emotional encounter on a flight back to Boston. I had taken out my laptop and the younger man in the seat next to me noticed my business card pasted on the lid. He turned to me. "You're Milt Bordwin from Guterman Horvitz and Rubin? (our firm's former name). I said "Yes" and then he told me his name, Dave. He was the grown son of a long deceased partner and a most admired mentor when I started at the firm. He was just a young boy when his dad, Henry, died. We hugged, sitting there in those airline seats, and we cried. He pelted me with questions about his father.

I told him all I could and how much Henry had helped me to become a better lawyer. And then he said something I'd never heard before – something that has stayed with me over the years. At home Henry had told his family that "This new kid in the office is a genius problem-solver." (I was that "new kid," number eight in the firm of seven.) Not once had I thought of myself in those terms, but that "problem-solving" phrase set me off on the long road to writing *SOLVED!* (Indeed, Tales #16 and #23 were Henry's cases and maybe the basis of his dubbing me a problem-solver.)

Over the years, the "problem-solver" moniker stuck with me and I began recalling and writing about case after case of clients posing problems and expecting solutions. And as the writing continued, the theme of "strategic lawyering" emerged. This book tries to define with examples this approach to problem-solving and explain how "strategic lawyering" (the phrase I preferred to the others that scholars have used)[16] can both solve business clients' problems and in many cases teach how to prevent those problems from happening in the first place. The goal of this book is to provide useful information and guidance about both problem-solving and prevention to my target audience: businesspeople and their lawyers as well as students of both subjects and those general readers interested in my "Adventures in Lawyerland."

How This Book Is Organized

Part I begins with a short Tale that illustrates the importance of (i) looking ahead, a sort of crystal-ball exercise and (ii) *total* communication between the business clients and their lawyers, particularly about the details of a client's business. This Tale also contains the first "Business Law Tip" (BLT #1) – and who doesn't love a BLT? The BLTs summarize what I think you should be taking away from a particular Tale.

The other Tales in **Part I** illustrate what makes for "good" contracts, that is, ones that carry out the client's intentions and expectations. Bad contracts – e.g., those that leave important issues open and undefined or that use language open to misinterpretation – create problems that end up in court.[17] There, the judge will tell you what your contract meant and in almost all cases, the judge can go either way – and that way may not coincide with your own intentions. The lawyers who know their client's industry and business, *in detail*, who can get into the client's mind and understand both what they expect from a deal and what they want to avoid in a deal – those lawyers can produce a "good" contract" that doesn't later need a judge to fill in the missing material and tell the parties what they intended.

The Tales in **Part II** point out when you're most vulnerable in your deal and illustrate powerful strategies – creating incentives and risk-shifting. This approach is useful both when (i) making and documenting business deals as well as (ii) solving clients' problems should they arise later on. These strategies have worked for me – they ensured that the other side would perform their obligations; they would do what they agreed to do and not be tempted to act solely for their own advantage or to my client's detriment. Sometimes you've got to innovate, to invent those incentives; and I can tell you from experience, some unusual ones didn't go down easy with the other side or their lawyer. But using incentives to perform is well worth the fight. In the

Part II Tales you'll see how incentives and risk-shifting worked to achieve the clients' objectives.

Being a lawyer – and one who likes to keep current on The Law – I found it only natural that **Part III** should focus on different areas of The Law (ten to be exact) that helped solve clients' problems.[18]

But there's more to lawyering than just knowing The Law, as illustrated by the six Tales in **Part IV**. An experienced and effective business lawyer is one who works closely with clients and learns the pertinent aspects of their business. Getting involved in all kinds of situations, I accumulated some real-world business experience as well as a sense of how judges react to the cases that come up before them. With that experience you develop sensitivities that can alert you how both to prevent problems from arising and later resolve existing problems.

Part IV focuses on clients in diverse industries, from a commercial bakery to hi-tech computer components to canvas goods (tote bags, etc.). In each situation, the lawyer's business experience prevented (or could have prevented) or resolved the client's problem. That experience, coupled with the detailed facts about the client's business, is what leads to a successful strategy and a problem prevented or *SOLVED!*

Part V contains leftovers you might say, but no less important to businesspeople and their lawyers. I was fascinated by a 19th century business deal (not mine – I'm not *that* old!): It re-emerged in litigation in 1959 and may reach the courts yet again. It is one of the best illustrations of the "KISS" principle: **K**eep **I**t **S**imple, **S**tupid. KISS is illustrated by such diverse cases as Listerine trying to stop paying royalties for its mouthwash formula after more than 100 years; and the heirs of the creators of Superman trying to get royalties that were clearly relinquished decades ago. Other Tales illustrate how I convinced the other parties to a contract to assume my clients' obligations under that contract, followed by the other side of the coin: a Tale where I kept my client from taking on responsibilities which were intended for the other party.

Part VI was an afterthought, a couple of oddball situations brought about by some "interesting" clients and the other parties to their deals. One Tale is about a guru – my only guru client to date – and the second is about a Russian oligarch – and also my only oligarch client. Plus I've added a Bonus Business Law Tip (BLT) for good measure.

The Epilogue tells the strange tale – a memoir of sorts – of a U.S. Supreme Court case I argued (and won) as a second-year associate at my law firm and what has happened to that case since then and right up to the day you're reading this (and keeps on happening!). It might be dubbed "The Little Case That Could" – I warned you that it was a strange tale.

What I Learned Writing This Book and What You Might Learn from Reading It

Some lessons to be learned from the Tales are obvious and many of these are covered in the BLTs. But there are more elusive lessons to be learned. At one point while writing this book those lessons appeared because I began asking a question that I'd never asked before; there just was no occasion to ask this question:

How could the party who lost, who got hurt, have prevented that loss and that hurt.

In thinking through the answers and then generalizing them, applying them to other situations, I could formulate that lesson and what I'd learned from this process. Two examples stand out, so if you're curious about what I learned from this process and what you might learn, check out Tale #5 and Tale #9 under the heading, "What I Learned from Writing About This Tale." My hope is that the reader can, as I did, come away with something new and useful from this process of asking questions long after the fact and taking away a lesson from the answers, a lesson that can be useful in future deals.

What I also learned emphasized the paranoid tendencies I have to begin with, and so:

1. Never consider a transaction routine and never be satisfied just sticking with some standard form that you started out with.
2. Never be satisfied with a general or generic approach to a transaction without digging into the specifics, the details of the parties, their particular intentions and expectations from that transaction and some specifics of market and other conditions looking ahead.

~End of Sermon~

———

SOLVED! is organized so you don't have to go from front to back – feel free to skip around the Tales that interest you. The "Business Law Tips" or "BLTs" mentioned above may repeat material in the Tale, so if you feel you've learned the lesson from reading the Tale, just skip that BLT and move on. These BLTs are the lessons we learn from others' mistakes and, as the sage once said:

> Your experience can teach you not to make the same mistake twice. Other people's experiences can teach you not to make the same mistake once.

This book is about those other people's experiences.

The Cartoons

In *The Wall Street Journal's* "Portfolio of Business Cartoons" (1999), Editor Charles Preston's note on why that serious newspaper publishes its "Pepper … and Salt" cartoons is apropos: "[T]here was more than enough earnest gravity on the editorial page." And since most of the Tales discuss clients' serious business problems, I wanted to offset some of that seriousness with the wit and genius of some of the best cartoonists in the field. And so, in the words of Editor Robert L. Bartley, I hope these cartoons will be "bringing a moment of mirth, and often insight. In the midst of the weighty concerns of the world and daily life, any of us can welcome the chance to pause for a chuckle."[19] (All cartoons are reproduced in *SOLVED!* with permission of the artist or their agencies, CartoonBank and CartoonStock.)

———

Finally, a couple of business details FYI:

First: Most footnotes/end notes are not for the casual reader, but for the lawyer or student who might find them useful. They are all at the end of the Tale so as not to interrupt the flow or distract readers.

Second: Some legal terms are shown in **bold-face** type and are briefly defined in a Glossary, Appendix A, at the back of the book. When in doubt, check a dictionary, or go to Google to get the definition of the word *dictionary.*

———

Note to Readers: No Legal Advice Intended : Author's Sole Responsibility. This book and the Tales are intended to explain a particular style of strategic business-law practice; the book includes general information about legal issues and developments in the law. All such materials are for informational purposes only and may not reflect the most current legal developments. The book is sold with the understanding that neither the publisher nor the author is engaged in rendering legal or other professional services to readers. None of the statements in the book are intended, nor must they ever be taken, as legal advice on any particular set of facts or circumstances. If you need advice on any particular legal issues or problems, you need to contact a lawyer licensed in your jurisdiction. Furthermore, the author takes full responsibility for the events related in the Tales; none of the Tales involved any other lawyer in the author's firm. Indeed, since most of the Tales refer to events decades ago (some as long ago as 50 years); none of the author's law partners today, save one, were even in the firm at the time.

That's the book, 40 Tales to enjoy and learn from. On to the Prologue where I try to answer my critics; talk about the ethics involved in the strategic approach to lawyering; explain the zero-sum/win-lose situations we get into; and yet again emphasize problem-prevention.

Milton Bordwin   Boston, Massachusetts
July 2017

1 Former U.S. Attorney General Janet Reno, in her Law Day 1997 remarks at Capitol University urged students: "Become known for your ability to solve your clients' problems the right way, consistent with the law." (Reno, Janet Law Day 1997 : A Legacy of Public Service, 26 Cap. U.L. Rev. 227 (1997). Her essay contains the substance of her remarks at Capitol University on May 1, 1997 emphasizing the attorney's role as problem solver. (p. 227) See also Roy T. Stuckey, "Education for the Practice of Law: The Times They Are A-Changin'," 75 Neb. L. Rev. 648 (1996): "My thesis is that the primary objective of law schools should be to teach students to be competent problem-solvers. A lawyer's core function is problem-solving." (at p. 669) Available at: http://digitalcommons.unl.edu/nlr/vol75/iss4/3.
2 See Appendix B, "Some of the Law-School Subjects/Specialties Covered in These Tales."
3 Lynn M. LoPucki and Walter O. Weyrauch, "A Theory of Legal Strategy," 49 *Duke L.Jnl* Apr. 2000 No. 6.
(Available at http://scholarship.law.duke.edu/dlj/vol49/iss6/1). Professor LoPucki recently confirmed to me in an e-mail that some of my Tales unquestionably fit into his description of the use of strategy. I was gratified to find this rare piece of writing from academe that deals clearly and realistically with the challenges of a business-law practice and relates how practicing lawyers meet those challenges and succeed. This article is an important contribution to closing the gap between theory-pedagogy-academics and practicing law on behalf of business clients.
4 Siemer, Rothschild and Zwier, *Teaching Legal Strategy* (National Institute for Trial Advocacy "NITA" 2006).
5 Ibid. p.3.
6 Ibid., p. 4.
7 See Chanen, "The Strategic Lawyer," *American Bar Association Journal,* July 2005, a discussion of strategy with San Francisco business lawyer Michael A. Kahn and other lawyers plus the comments of Wharton Professor Richard G. Shell. (Available at http://www.abajournal.com/magazine/article/the_strategic_lawyer1.) [control + click] Practically

all the points made by the business lawyers interviewed for this article are illustrated by the Tales in *SOLVED!*

8 The Cuban missile crisis arose when U.S. surveillance planes spotted Soviet-Russian missile bases being constructed in Cuba and Russian ships bringing more missile-related materiel to the Island. Russia's response to Kennedy's objections was that these weapons were merely for self-defense, obviously a lie. Kennedy held meetings with numerous of his top advisors to decide on a course of action – invade Cuba; bomb and destroy the missile launch pads; or blockade Havana harbor. The final decision was to blockade, and that decision-making process showed Kennedy's strategic way of thinking.

After his naval advisors described the planned blockade, Kennedy asked, "What do we do if a Russian ship tries to get through, to run the blockade?" ("N:" is the advisor speaking.)

N: "We'd fire a shot across their bow."

K: "What if they kept moving? Would you destroy the Russian ship?"

N: "No, we'd just disable it."

K: "How?"

N: "A shot at the propeller and rudder aft of the ship."

K: "Okay, so now we've got a Russian ship, unable to move, and a couple of hundred sailors on board. Do we just let them sit there, run out of supplies and then starve?"

N: "No. We can supply them their needs. We then wait for them to tell us they're ready to turn back and at that time we help repair the damage so they can return to home port."

Kennedy was satisfied that a blockade was the best option, subject to a suggested semantic change – call it a "quarantine," a word that conveys America's message that missiles in Cuba were like a dangerous and contagious disease. Ah, the power of words! Kennedy then addressed the nation making seven points – just the first one will suffice for our purposes here; after describing the situation, he said:

I have directed that the following initial steps be taken immediately:

First: To halt this offensive buildup a strict quarantine on all offensive military equipment under shipment to Cuba is being initiated. All ships of any kind bound for Cuba from whatever nation or port will, if found to contain cargoes of offensive weapons, be turned back. This quarantine will be extended, if needed, to other types of cargo and carriers. We are not at this time, however, denying the necessities of life as the Soviets attempted to do in their Berlin blockade of 1948.

I hope recalling this historic moment and how it was handled provides you with a memorable example of what I mean when I use the words "strategy" and "strategic" and how important it is as you make your deals, agreements and contracts, to crystal-ball the situation, look ahead and ask what might change, what might happen that can affect your intentions and expectations in this deal? Will that effect be beneficial or detrimental to you? Do you want to provide for these future events or not? And if yes, how will you provide for them? And always remember external conditions, particularly the market in the goods/services your business deals in.

9 See Appendix C, Partial Reading List for examples of these books.

10 See the 84-page bibliography, "PROBLEM SOLVING: AN ANNOTATED BIBLI-OGRAPHY" 2nd Edition, August 2005 by Phyllis C. Marion (Western California School of Law) at https://www.cwsl.edu/-/media/files/library/problem_solving.ashx; and, generally, at the library website, http://www.cwsl.edu/library. This lists hundreds of mostly "how-to" books and articles on problem-solving, which seems has become standard fare at business and law schools. See also Note 12, below.

11 LoPucki and Weyrauch, *A Theory of Legal Strategy,* 49 Duke L. Jnl Apr. 2000 No. 6, n. 14. (Available at http://scholarship.law.duke.edu/dlj/vol49/iss6/1).

12 "Experiential learning is all the rage in law school, but legal educators are struggling to figure out how best to integrate such real-world training into their curricula and develop closer ties with the profession to advance the trend." *The National Law Journal* (Online), June 17, 2014, headlined "Legal Educators Plot the Future of Real-World Learning." *The New York Times* (February 10, 2013), headlined "A Call for Drastic Changes in Educating Lawyers," by Ethan Bronner, available at http://www.nytimes.com/2013/02/11/us/lawyers-call-for-drastic-change-in-educating-new-lawyers.html. And if you Google "Law Schools Experiential Learning" you'll see the 284,000 entries. Members of the Alliance for Experiential Learning in Law are affiliated with more than 100 law schools, firms and organizations. See also note 3, above; and Harry W. Arthurs, "The Future of Legal Education: Three Visions and a Prediction," Osgoode CLPE Research Paper No. 49/2013, available at https://papers.ssrn.com/sol3/papers.cfm?abstract_id=2349633 And see "Defining Key Competencies for Business Lawyers," *The Business Lawyer* (ABA Business Law Section), Winter 2016-2017, Vol. 72, Issue 1.

13 "Business Schools Tackle 'Real Life' Corporate Issues, *Wall St. Jnl.,* Nov. 3, 2016, p.B7: "Business schools are ... asking students to resolve actual corporate dilemmas in real time....

employers [said] "they wanted M.B.A.s capable of handling 'messy, real-life problems'." Available at http://www.wsj.com/articles/business-schools-tackle-messy-real-time-corporate-issues-1478102923.

14 Bert Spector, *Understanding Your Business Clients,* American Bar Association, ABA Fundamentals (2013).

15 American Bar Association, *Legal Guide for Small Business – Everything You Need to Know About Small Business, from Start-up to Employment Laws to Financing and Selling* (2nd Ed. 2010).

16 Writers have used other words for good business lawyering: "creative," "imaginative," "inventive," "flexible," etc., but I'll stick with "strategic," the term used by LoPucki and Weyrauch in their article cited in Note 2.

17 These faulty documents are dubbed "Incomplete Contracts" by the 2016 Nobel Prize winners – Economics – Professors Hart and Holmström. They were awarded the Prize for the work on "Contract Theory."

18 These are some of the areas of The Law used to solve problems in the Part III Tales:

- The mail-box rule (contracts);
- the constructive/resulting trust rules;
- environmental laws;
- workplace-safety laws;
- legally enforceable agreements to negotiate;
- the securities laws' margin regulations;
- product-liability law;
- The Rule Against Perpetuities;
- landlord-tenant law; and
- the rules of contract interpretation.

19 *The WStJnl Portfolio of Business Cartoons* (1999).

PROLOGUE

The Introduction tells you what to expect from the Tales in this book – how strategic lawyering and close cooperation between business-client and lawyer can produce solutions to clients' problems. This Prologue discusses the following three areas: (i) strategy (or strategic lawyering); (ii) the "zero-sum game" in business and law; and (iii) the ethics involved in business and law.

The practice of business law has changed over these past six decades, much of it due to the Three Horsemen,[1] namely Legislation, Regulation and Litigation. Solving clients' business problems in a business-law practice today must take into account the statutes coming out of legislatures and judges' rulings in decided cases. And don't forget that many areas of commerce are regulated by one agency or another – don't forget those state and federal "alphabet agencies" –

EPA	Environmental Protection Agency
DoL	Department of Labor
SEC	Securities and Exchange Commission
DoA	Department of Agriculture
DHS	Department of Homeland Security
DOT	Department of Transportation
DoE	Department of Energy
NLRB	National Labor Relations Board
FTC	Federal Trade Commission
	Bureau of Consumer Protection

"It's from the Consumer Protection Agency, demanding that we submit proof that the gates *are* made of pearl."

The Tales in *SOLVED!* describe how strategic lawyering, when combined with the business facts that only the client can provide, deals with these Three Horsemen to solve the clients' problems.

1. Strategy and Strategic Lawyering

(Repetitive and Important!)

My view of strategy: Look to the future and try to anticipate changes, risks, events – whatever can help or hurt in achieving clients' goals. In deal-making – just as in chess, in business, in war – "strategy" involves looking to the long term, projecting into the future. (Tactics are the immediate short-term steps you take to carry out your strategy.) Looking ahead and asking those "what if" questions, taking time to anticipate what the future may hold and what can change, will produce an agreement and a contract that meets your goals, carries out your intentions and satisfies your expectations from the deal you're making. (The cases in Tale #2 explore this notion of looking ahead in more detail, including both the **boilerplate** provisions that deal with the "what if" questions in standard-form contracts and those that the businessperson and their lawyer have to devise for their specific situation.)

One seminal scholarly article (noted in the Introduction) about strategy and strategic lawyering is *A Theory of Legal Strategy* by Law Professors LoPucki and Weyrauch.[2] Returning to that article, you will see how the authors' definition and descriptions of strategy are illustrated in many of the Tales. Although the authors' stated goal is to reduce the impact of strategy on legal outcomes,[3] I wonder if they share my skepticism of our ever reaching that goal. I think strategy and strategic lawyering are here to stay. Why? Because they work!

The authors write:

- "central thrust of legal strategy is to control legal outcomes despite the contrary intentions of legislators or judges." (See Tales ##4, 23 and 24.)

And this:

- "the legal process [is seen] as highly manipulable through legal strategy." The Tales in Part II (##6-14) involve structuring deals or resolving disputes to shift risk and create incentives for the other side to perform their contractual obligations to my clients. Readers will have to be the judge whether certain Tales involved manipulation, for example, ##4; 6; 9; 15; 18; 23; 24; 33; and 35.

The authors of *A Theory of Legal Strategy* make other points about strategy which are borne out by many of the Tales, for example:

Many Tales fit into these statements by the authors:

- legal strategy, not law, is the principal determinant of legal outcomes
- lawyers and parties construct legal outcomes in what amounts to a contest of skill
- lawyers can replace judges as arbiters.
- They note that "the belief that strategies often determine legal outcomes is widespread and generally consonant with the reality of legal practice." And "...the strategic view captures the reality of the legal process while the conventional view misses it."

———

Over 80 years ago, the great law scholar and teacher, Karl Llewellyn, addressed the use of strategy to achieve clients' goals despite laws and judges. In *The Bramble Bush*[4] (now in its 11th printing), which he wrote to help law students "think like a lawyer," Llewellyn describes a problem situation in the area of price-fixing or price-maintenance (a branch of the anti-trust laws), and he issues a challenge to his students:

If the judges say a contract with your buyer that he will not resell below a certain price will be illegal, and not enforceable, if they are likely to fine you or send you to jail for making such a contract, but you still want your goods resold throughout the country at a single price—what can you do? That is a problem for invention, for ingenuity; the problem of inventing a method of action which will keep you free of difficulty and will produce the results you want in spite, if you please, of what the judges in a case of dispute may be expected to do.[5]

My own Property Law teacher, Professor A. James Casner (Harvard Law School), would issue this challenge to his third-year graduating students at the end of the school year:

> "There's always a way to achieve the result that your client wants. It may not be direct, it may not be obvious, and if you're not smart enough to figure it out, give me a call – my consulting rates are reasonable."[6]

I've concluded that much of what's told in the Tales illustrates both strategic lawyering in action as described in the LoPucki-Weyrauch article, *A Theory of Legal Strategy* and "thinking like a lawyer" promoted by Llewellyn.

After some thoughts on these issues, I follow up on the LoPucki and Weyrauch's statement that "The use of strategy is often condemned as unethical." True – I've been criticized to the point where I had to contact the experts to confirm that my strategic lawyering was not only ethical but, under the circumstances, mandatory. But let me not get ahead of myself – I try to clarify this question of ethics in the third part of this Prologue. But first, . . .

2. In Some Business Negotiations, Transactions and Disputes, It's a Zero-Sum Game : One Winner – One Loser

"It's not enough that we succeed. Cats must also fail."

Many times, because of the situation and the parties' circumstances, the use of strategy in solving business-law problems results in a zero-sum game – one winner and one loser – and this holds true both when a deal is negotiated and later on, when disputes are resolved. I take a hard, realistic approach to my clients' problems, too hard, some people have remarked. Once it's clear to me that a deal or resolution is a zero-sum game – that there will be one winner and one loser – my hard, realistic approach is directed at having my client end up as the winner. (And that means the other party must be the loser.) And so I ask my critics the question that is the subtitle on the cover of an excellent business book entitled *Hardball*, written by Stalk and Lachenauer. They ask:

Are you playing to play or playing to win?

I play to win because that's what clients hire lawyers to do and that's what the rules of my profession – the Canons of Legal Ethics – mandate: Zealously represent the client's legal and legitimate interests. This is the rule in the zero-sum game that describes many business deals and disputes.

A win-win situation is, of course, most satisfying, but in my experience this is more common in business deals/negotiations than in most dispute situations (although a good, e.g., mediated settlement can, indeed, be win-win). For a win-win negotiation example, see Tale #25, a gratifying situation, where I used a common, garden-variety approach that pleased both the business owner and the employee whom he wanted to reward with some ownership in the company. Other Tales address ways to avoid the risks of American product-liability law, exposures so many companies face. Avoiding those risks can only help and not hurt – another good example of a win-win situation for the client-sellers and their customers. Risk prevention/management is always a win-win for the client.

But once there's a dispute that the parties don't settle, it's been my experience that the outcome usually becomes a zero-sum game: One winner and one loser. And I'm hired to make my client the winner. An amicable out-of-court settlement is usually the best for all parties – that's win-win – and I push hard for settling because I've seen the bitter financial and other costs of extended litigation. But disputes that don't settle usually end up as these zero-sum situations.

Here's the realistic description by one legal scholar describing two parties to a contract – each party has a reasonable, but different view of what their contract means:

> . . . it is possible for them [i.e., the two parties] to draw inconsistent conclusions, all of which are reasonable based on their individual situations. To place this into a contractual context, it is possible for one person to reasonably expect a contract term to be enforceable and for another person to reasonably expect the contract term to be unenforceable. If the law of contracts is to protect reasonable

expectations, to some extent anyway, how can both persons be protected? The short and irresistible answer is that they cannot. **One
person's reasonable expectations must be sacrificed to another's.**
[emphasis mine][7]

That's a zero-sum game.

The Tales tell how these more difficult problems arose and how they
were "SOLVED!" To the critics of my strategic lawyering approach, I ask
that they review our Code of Legal Ethics, which sets the high level of dedication and devotion we owe to our clients and to protecting their interests.

Perhaps the most important thing I learned early in my career is that
one party's unexpressed intentions and expectations get lost in the shuffle
if the other party's intentions and expectations are fully and clearly expressed by the words of the contract. Disputes arise (i) if the deal-makers
don't get it right when they make their agreement or (ii) if the lawyers
write contracts that don't clearly express what their client intends and expects. These disputes almost always end with one winner and one loser –
the typical zero-sum game.

I suspect that some negative reactions to certain Tales stemmed from
an understandable sympathy for the other side – the loser in that zero-sum
game, whether that is the opposing lawyer or their client. But sympathy is
no substitute for my obligation to clients under the Canons of Professional
Ethics to zealously protect their interests. The natural sympathies we feel –
me included – for the loser in these zero-sum games must always be overridden by my ethical obligation to my clients. So let's talk ethics.

3. Personal Ethics; Business Ethics; and Legal Ethics : Don't Mix Them Up

Ethics is not a unitary concept here – there's a different standard for different people in different situations. My focus as a business lawyer is the
role and the responsibilities a lawyer assumes when the client comes to call

and what that client should expect from us. The easiest way to understand the various ethical standards is to mention (i) my dear mother; (ii) two distinguished business-school professors; and (iii) the Canons of (Legal) Professional Ethics.

(i) *Personal ethics* came to me from my mother who taught my brother and me the difference between right and wrong. She taught us to be honest and "nice." I heed her admonitions when practicing law, particularly about being honest.

"I consider myself a passionate man, but, of course, a lawyer first."

But being nice comes into play only *before* I take on a professional engagement. And so, for example, I don't take cases against disadvantaged or weak or unrepresented parties. (Not nice!) Whether it's a matter of personal ethics or just personal preference and predilection or a matter of taste, I stay away from certain types of cases. For example: I don't do residential evictions or go against "widows and orphans" – there are enough lawyers to handle those cases. That's the "nice" part. But once I take on an engagement, that's when **legal ethics** kick in and "nice" takes on a different connotation. My clients hire me to solve a problem, and sometimes "nice" has to take a back seat.

Legal work for a business client typically involves company versus company, and it's usually about money. At that point I'm just a lawyer representing a client and I will zealously protect that client's interests. That client and protecting their interests then set my ethical standard and, within the limits of legality and legitimacy, I'll do what I can to further that client's interests. Once I offer the client the available choices of a course of action, it is for *them* to decide how they want to proceed, in accordance with their own business ethics. (Lawyers say to clients, "That's a business decision." You'll see this process in many of the Tales.) And I always make it a point to remind clients of the risks and possible negatives of a particular course of action, typically, landing in court where a judge might rule against them; and when client is the plaintiff who brings the lawsuit, they must be warned of the risks of a **counterclaim**.

(ii) *Business ethics* I take to mean the personal ethics governing the clients' actions when they make that business decision. Some business clients may choose not to take the approach that "If it's legal, it's ethical." Thus, I may give the client some legal and legitimate choices for a course of action – a way for the client to come out the winner. The client might reject that approach and reply, "Thanks, but no thanks. I don't want to do business that way." Whether it's fear of sullying a reputation or violating some personal ethical standards, the client calls the shots – it's their business decision. And once the client makes that decision, I am ethically bound to abide by it – "my work here is done."

Today, many business schools offer courses on Ethics where students are encouraged to follow paths that are morally right rather than wrong in how they will run their business and not blindly take a path that their lawyers dub as permissible and legal.[8] This point is succinctly made, for example, by Marc Lampe, Professor of Business Law and Social Responsibility at the University of San Diego- School of Business Administration:

> "Too often members of the legal and business community argue that if it's legal, it's ethical."[9]

"WHO GETS PRECEDENCE—OUR LEGAL DEPARTMENT OR OUR ETHICS COMMITTEE?"

Expanding on the shortcomings of that philosophy, Lynn Sharp Paine, Professor of Management Ethics at the Harvard Business School, writes:[10]

The law does not generally seek to inspire human excellence or distinction. It is no guide for exemplary behavior or even good practice....Law is a starting point or minimum for ethical behavior. But lawyers are trained to go to "the edge of the law" on behalf of clients. College faculty are not hired to be "zealous advocates" or to teach students to take a lawyer's approach to conduct when it involves questionable ethics. Business school law faculty must get beyond their own training to effectively incorporate business ethics in their courses. This means adopting the concept that just because something is legal doesn't mean it's ethical...A fundamental principle of business ethics is that to truly be ethical one must be willing to do more than the law requires and less than it allows...[A] lawyer may even advocate methods to dodge or circumvent the law or truth that are legal but unethical (e.g., tax "avoidance" schemes). Therefore, it may be up to clients to tell their attorney that they want to do the right thing. Clients don't have to follow advice that may be legal, but not ethical or socially responsible. We can encourage our [business] students to show such courage when they enter the professional world.

Let's take a detour to look at Tale #4, which deals with a successful tax-avoidance strategy. I acted under the legal ethics rules that govern my profession and offered the client legal and legitimate choices. It was then for the client to decide, governed by his own business-ethics standards, whether to take advantage of a poorly drafted tax statute – a "loophole" – in order to reduce his company's tax bill. That client chose to take advantage of the letter of the law and ignore the spirit/intention of that poorly drafted tax statute and, as you'll read, it worked (that is, until Congress fixed the statute).

This contrast between business ethics and legal ethics was also brought home in a 2014 lecture by a major high-tech executive.[11] He said that the corporate governance philosophy of his company is based on a set of simple principles, the primary one being:

To satisfy the spirit of the law and not just the letter of the law.

This speaker's business ethics are in sharp contrast to my legal ethics. Recall Professor Paine, above: ". . . lawyers are trained to go to 'the edge of the law' on behalf of clients." When I represent business clients, I go to that edge and will offer clients the choice of whatever routes best protect their interests, whether that route/solution satisfies the spirit of the law or the letter of the law. And if one of the legitimate, lawful possible courses of action goes against the spirit of the law, but satisfies the letter of the law, I am duty bound in zealously representing that client's interest to offer that choice to them. Then follows the business decision – and it's for the client to choose their course of action going forward. They've usually said, "Let's go for it." But it's always open to the client to decline: "No thanks, I don't want to do business that way." The client in Tale #4 chose the tax-saving route and we followed the letter of the law.

(iii) *Legal ethics:* These are the rules of my profession. A lawyer doesn't lose his personal ethics; they stay in play, but for me, only during the early stage – at the outset when I decide whether or not to take a case. An example from Case Two of Tale #23: I would not have represented the brother in his "adopting" two friends in their sixties so as to have "children" and thus deprive his sister of the inheritance their father intended in his will. I found that act wrong and distasteful and I would not have defended it. You'll also read in Tale #31 (from the 60s) about a case I'd never take on today – my conscience would not let me argue in favor of storing industrial chlorine in a residential neighborhood.

Some of my critics were concerned with my actions as they relate to opposing counsel, a subject covered in the legal ethical standards as set forth, for example, in the American Bar Association Model Code of Professional Responsibility, sometimes called the Canons of Professional Ethics. I certainly owe my opposing counsel the usual professional courtesies and a duty to engage in civil discourse. "The ethics rules focus on duties rather than on civil behavior."[12] And we don't take advantage of obvious mistakes. For example, if a typo in document favors my client – as it did in one situation – I must note and correct that typo; it did not reflect the parties' clear agreement and had to be corrected. But I am not obligated to teach opposing counsel the law or even assume that I know it better than they do. Nor am I obligated to be a mind-reader of what they have in mind if they fail to clearly state their intentions, or to clarify their language if I would have said it some other way. (Courts react similarly.[13]) I will not assume that the other party or their lawyer intend what I would intend in the circumstances. And if that counsel is lazy or ignorant or has other weaknesses that help my client, I'll accept that help.

One of the strongest proponents of the "zealous" dedication a lawyer owes to his clients' interests was the late Law Professor and Hofstra Law School Dean, Monroe Freedman. *The New York Times* called Freedman "a dominant figure in legal ethics whose work helped chart the course of lawyers' behavior in the late 20th century and beyond."[14] Freedman goes back to the beginnings of legal ethics and cites the words of Henry Lord Brougham when he represented the English Queen Caroline.[15] Probably at the extreme end of zealous representation, for example, is his 2006 article with this unusually brazen title: "In Praise of Overzealous Representation – Lying to Judges, Deceiving Third Parties, and Other Ethical Conduct."[16] I count myself an ardent follower of Freedman's "zealous" standard of representing my clients' interests, as you'll see in the Tales.

In any event, my conversations with Monroe Freedman and another nationally known legal-ethics scholar, Professor Geoffrey C. Hazard, Jr.[17], confirmed that my approach of (i) offering the clients the legal and legitimate courses of action available to them to resolve their problem; (ii) warning them of the possibility of litigation or other negative consequences of those courses of action; and then (iii) being guided by their decision was well within the ethical rules of my profession. Indeed, the legal-ethics experts told me that if I knew of a legal and legitimate solution and failed to disclose and offer it to the client, that might well constitute malpractice.

4. What About "The Golden Rule"?

As a practicing business lawyer with an ingrained moral drive, while recounting some of the Tales, I had concerns about this basic moral tenet: "Do unto others as you would have them do unto you." The Golden Rule is sometimes expressed as: "What is hateful to you, do not do to your fellow." Or "Do not do to the other what you would not have them do unto you." In a few Tales my actions violated that Rule in relation to the lawyer representing the other side: I admit I would not like have done to me what it may be said I did to that other lawyer. So the question that's been rolling around my brain is whether one can adhere to The Golden Rule and still practice as a business lawyer. I've had my critics and, while understanding their point of view, I still felt I was carrying out my ethical responsibilities to my client. But I needed an answer to the question, and I found it: Yes, you *can* adhere to The Golden Rule and still practice as a business lawyer.

In a relationship involving more than two people – as when practicing business law – there's "the other side" and their lawyer. In such a situation, the Golden Rule must be interpreted by asking, Who is "the other" mentioned in the Golden Rule? If it's the people on the other side of a transaction or dispute, then the Golden Rule won't work – the Rule is often incompatible with the use of strategy and strategic lawyering. No, the "other" is not the other side and their lawyer; my reading of the Golden Rule as a business lawyer is that my client is "the other." That works for me – it reconciles the moral aspect of lawyering with the ethical obligations the lawyer owes his client. "The standard conception of the lawyer's role, then, is that of a 'zealous advocate' who has little if any duty to third parties (i.e., non-clients). . . lawyers cannot be held accountable under common moral standards."[18]

Do you agree with my reading of The Golden Rule?

———

Note:

The 2016 Nobel Prize in Economics for Contract Theory. In *SOLVED!* Theory Meets Practice

When two disparate disciplines – Economics and Law – and two approaches to those disciplines – Theory and Practice – converge and look like two sides of the same coin, my interest is aroused. And so upon learning in October that the 2016 Nobel Prize in Economics had been awarded to Professors Oliver Hart (Harvard) and Bengt Holmström (MIT) for their work in Contract Theory, I looked into that work and was happily surprised. In addition to economic theory and arcane formulae (which I do *not* understand), they espoused principles I *did* understand. Indeed, many of the Tales involving contracts illustrate these scholars' principles (with but slight changes in our respective vocabularies). Some examples (their terms are in **bold-face** type):

Incentives – Part II of *SOLVED!* uses the phrase "Incentives and Risk-Shifting" – all nine Tales serve to illustrate Professors Hart's and Holmström's principle. And they exemplify my own conviction that sometimes the other party to a deal needs a special incentive for them to do the right thing (i.e., perform their obligations to my client under the contract).

Incomplete Contract – "Incomplete" because the contract fails to provide for some event that occurred. This failure to provide for some future contingency I refer to as the failure of "strategy." The use of strategy and strategic lawyering, as explained in the Prologue, above, means looking ahead and asking what might happen, what conditions might change; and, if goods are involved, how might market conditions and prices of those goods change? I was able to do this successfully, as you'll read, for example, in Tale #2, and managed to solve (read "prevent") a problem ten years before it happened. I avoided producing a fatally flawed, "incomplete" contract (a form office-space lease in that case). We should understand, however, that virtually *all* contracts must in the nature of things be "incomplete"—we cannot foresee everything and no one has perfect knowledge.[19] It's the *crucial* future conditions and events that you should try to identify and then decide whether and how to deal with them.

Asymmetric Information – This occurs when one side knows more, has more crucial information than the other. My term for avoiding being on the wrong side of this equation is "synthesis," which came up, for example, in Tale #19 and BLT 20: Synthesis is the joining of what the lawyer knows (applicable laws and regulations) with the detailed facts of the client's business, their intentions and expectations, the industry and dealings with the other side. (See Note 6 to the Prologue, second bullet • point from Chicago lawyer, Stuart L. Goodman.) And in Tale #1, my digging into the details of client's business, facts which the other side and their lawyer were not aware of, helped me solve client's problem (incredibly with the help of a non-compete covenant drafted by the other side!).

So there you have it: The relation of Economic Theory to Business Law Practice: Theories and principles propounded by academic scholars of economics are illustrated by real cases handled by a practitioner of business law.

———

On to the Tales!

1 You'll recall the Four Horsemen of the Apocalypse: War, Famine, Pestilence and Death. Factor in technology and you can understand that today we can produce more of these laws and regulations and also learn about and deal with the torrent of Legislation, Regulation and Litigation at the speed of light (except we're still stuck with the same old human brain we were born with). Strategy helps us deal with all these changes more effectively.

2 LoPucki and Weyrauch, *A Theory of Legal Strategy*, 49 Duke L. Jnl Apr. 2000 No. 6. 1405 (Available at http://scholarship.law.duke.edu/dlj/vol49/iss6/1) [Control + Click]. A Google check of "strategic lawyering" notes 128,000 entries and among those must be many other important writings – but alas, life is too short . . .

3 Ibid., at pp. 1483-84.

4 Karl N. Llewellyn, *The Bramblebush* 14 (1960) and later editions.

5 Llewellyn's view that strategic lawyering can often dictate judges' decision-making is echoed in the Introduction to the article cited LoPucki and Weyrauch, *A Theory of Legal Strategy*, p.1406:

> In a competing "strategic" view, lawyers and parties construct legal outcomes in what amounts to a contest of skill. Though the latter view better explains the process, no theory has yet been propounded as to how lawyers can replace judges as arbiters. This article propounds such a theory. It classifies legal strategies into three types: those that require willing acceptance by judges, those that constrain the actions of judges, and those that entirely deprive judges of control.

6 I was reminded of Professor Casner's parting words by Chicago lawyer Stuart L. Goodman's article, *The Fundamental Role of the Corporate Lawyer — And How to Succeed in It*, available at http://www.schiffhardin.com/Templates/media/files/publications/PDF/goodman-corporate_lawyer.pdf It's an almost mini-textbook that echoes the themes in *SOLVED!* Here's a sampling from that piece (and I commend it to lawyers and businesspeople in its entirety):

- "There almost always is a way to achieve the desired result. The challenge is to find it.."
- "Figuring out what the client needs is an important proactive piece of the corporate lawyer's role. To do that you must spend a lot of time learning about and understanding the client's business — understanding the industry the client operates in; understanding the business environment in which it operates."
- "Creativity is another critical aspect of helping the client achieve its business

goals. To be truly successful, you must be creative…to think 'out of the box.'"
- "The client ultimately has to make the decisions."
- "What I'm trying to show with these examples is the importance of being creative…having some measure of boldness to take risks to achieve a result."

"Good lawyers are not quitters," said Joseph F. Anderson Jr., a federal judge in South Carolina, quoted in a *Wall Street Journal* front-page article (3/13/17, p. A1) on the lawyer character in the movie, "My Cousin Vinny," reportedly a favorite among lawyers and some prominent judges. As the Tales illustrate, the author wasn't a quitter when faced with clients' sometimes intractable problems.

7 Professor Bailey Kuklin, "The Plausibility of Legally Protecting Reasonable Expectations," 32 *Valparaiso University Law Review*, No. 1 (*pp.*19-66) at pp. 45-46, Fall 1997.

8 A leading institution with a major focus on business ethics is Bentley University in Waltham, MA (www.bentley.edu/cbe) which celebrated its 40th Anniversary in July, 2016 and the renaming of the Center for Business Ethics for its founder and Director. The institution is now known as the W. Michael Hoffman Center for Business Ethics to honor this pioneer and leader in the field of business ethics education.

9 Marc Lampe, "A New Paradigm for the Teaching of Business Law and Environmental Classes," *Jnl of Legal Studies Education*, vol. 23 #1, pp. 1-51 March 2005 / IACCM & Turku University of Applied Sciences, 38 (2008); and see his note xliv.

10 Lynn Sharp Paine, "Managing for Organizational Integrity," *Harvard Bus. Rev.*, Mar.-Apr. 1994, at 106.

11 S.D. Shibulal, Co-Founder and Former CEO, Managing Director and Member of the Board of Infosys, delivering the Raytheon Lecture on Business Ethics at Bentley University, Waltham, MA on November 6, 2014 (p.9). (I wonder how he would resolve the dilemma between his stated dedication to the spirit of the law and his fiduciary duty to deliver value [e.g., increased net income after taxes] to his shareholders.)

12 Thomas E. Spahn, Esq., "Professionalism vs. Ethics?" in ABA's magazine *Experience,* Vol.24, No. 1, p 47 (2014).

13 "Although the Court can perhaps guess that Plaintiff meant to prohibit solicitation or contact for the purpose of employment elsewhere, the provision does not so specify. Particularly in light of New York's general hostility toward restrictive covenants in the context of employment, the Court will not redraft a poorly written, overbroad restraint in order to render it enforceable…" *Base One Techs., Inc. v. Ali*, 2015 U.S. Dist. LEXIS 5821; January 20, 2015, Civil Action No. 14-1520 (JEB). See also *IPS Electric Services, LLC v. Univ. of Toledo*, Case No. 15AP-207, 2016-Ohio-361: "…courts cannot decide cases of contractual

interpretation on the basis of what is just or equitable."

14 Obituary in *The New York Times (National)* Mar. 4, 2015.

15 2 The trial at Large of Her Majesty, Caroline Amelia Elizabeth, Queen of Great Britain; in the House of Lords, on Charges of Adulterous Intercourse 3 (London, Printed for T. Kelly 1821). Brougham stated:

> "[A]n advocate, in the discharge of his duty, knows but one person in all the world, and that person is his client. To save that client by all means and expedients, and at all hazards and costs to other persons, and, among them, to himself, is his first and only duty; and in performing this duty he must not regard the alarm, the torments, the destruction which he may bring upon others. Separating the duty of a patriot from that of an advocate, he must go on reckless of consequences, though it should be his unhappy fate to involve his country in confusion." (Quoted in Freedman's "Henry Lord Brougham – Advocating at the Edge for Human Rights," 36 Hofstra Law Review 311 (2007).

16 34 Hofstra Law Review, Issue 3, Article 6 (2006).

17 Conversation quoted with permission of Professor Hazard (Emeritus Thomas E. Miller Distinguished Professor of Law, UC Hastings College of Law, San Francisco, CA). He is author, with W. William Hodes and Peter R. Jarvis, of *The Law of Lawyering,* (2 volumes) Fourth Edition (Wolters Kluwer Law & Business, 2015).

18 For an examination of the moral component of legal ethics, see Anand, Rakesh K., "Toward an Interpretive Theory of Legal Ethics." 58 Rutgers L. Review 653, 665 (2006), available at SSRN: https://ssrn.com/abstract=975235.

19 "It is generally accepted by both economists and lawyers that almost all contracts are incomplete." *More is Less: Why Parties May Deliberately Write Incomplete Contracts*, Maija Halonen-Akatwijuka and Oliver D. Hart. NBER Working Paper No. 19001, April 2013, JEL No. D23, D86, K12. Available at http://www.nber.org/papers/w19001

PART I

The first five Tales illustrate "strategic" lawyering – a style of business-law practice that has served my clients well. How? By both (i) preventing problems and (ii) solving problems. You'll learn that the essence of this strategic approach is "crystal-balling" – looking into the future. You try to think ahead and project what might possibly happen, the changes that time can bring about. And then you provide for those scenarios or, in some instances, you intentionally omit referring to them at all. To put this another way, you're trying to avoid the law of unintended consequences.[1]

You'll also see how, by precisely expressing your intentions for and expectations from a transaction in the deal-documents/contracts, you achieve what you want and not end up with what some judges later decide they think you agreed to. Moving away from contracts into the area of statutes and regulations, we find that those governmental acts that lack precise wording will, in some cases, provide you with an opportunity to turn a losing cause into a winner (Tale #4). (You can read more about the prime importance of words – whether in a contract or a statute – in Tales #13 and #14 – and how strategic lawyering can help you come out on top.)

---

1 Google lists over 1.5 million items for The Law of Unintended Consequences. Some are virtually impossible to foresee. An example is Tale #9 – no one intended that Landlord enjoy a large windfall. The early-termination payment by Tenant was intended to reimburse Landlord (for unamortized tenant improvement work), but that's not what the provision said. I explain in that Tale #9 how the Tenant could have avoided paying the $250,000 early-termination fee by asking the right questions, for example, "what could change?"

TALE # 1

SELL THE BUSINESS; SIGN A NON-COMPETE; AND GO
BACK INTO THE SAME INDUSTRY.

B efore we get into the longer Tales about contracts that worked and
deals that failed, let's begin with a short story – a difficult and chal-
lenging situation that ended with a simple solution and a happy client
when she sold her business. And this Tale illustrates, as you'll read, "synthesis," one of the most important tools in business law problem-solving.

I. THE CLIENT'S PROBLEM
Hooray! Big Conglomerate Wants to Buy Client's Company
Client Charlene founded and successfully ran a company that was a dealer
in complex packaging machines; she sold them and also serviced and maintained them. She sounded excited when she called.

"We're having a meeting at your office with a potential buyer of the
Company. Next Tuesday, 2 pm – a giant multinational guy from Europe!
They're paying a good price, and in cash."

On Tuesday I met with Charlene and a rather large man, vest, watch
chain, and an attitude. Olaf's words, "We like you and your Company,
Charlene," he said "so we give you a choice – either we buy you or we destroy you." Wow! I'd never heard that kind of stuff from any prospective
buyer, or anyone for that matter. Despite my understandably not feeling
kindly toward Olaf, the deal moved ahead smoothly.

After Olaf left, I asked Charlene, then in her early 50s, what she intended to do after the sale with the multi-million dollar purchase money she'd be getting. Obviously she was too young and active to just retire. She told me that "Son Larry's going to run his own company, so I guess I'll be a kind of consultant, help with finances, y'know."

"Forget it, Charlene", I told her. "You'll be signing a non-compete agreement with the buyer, so there'll be no setting up Larry in business…". Charlene stopped me with some harsh sounding words: "Look, Milton, you're the lawyer. Figure something out. Larry's going into the business!" (Obviously, Charlene's plans ran counter to my expectations of what Buyer would require.) I knew we'd hit a stone wall when the draft Purchase and Sale Agreement came in from Olaf's lawyer – his expected "covenant not to compete" would surely prohibit what Charlene had in mind for son Larry – a new company that competed with the business she was about to sell. I had to know more, so I planned to visit Charlene's sales showroom. Any thoughts of this being a quick and easy purchase-and-sale quickly evaporated.

II. THE SOLUTION
"Synthesis" at Work: The Lawyer Learns About Client's Business in Detail

Charlene's plan for son Larry seemed impossible, but she was adamant – determined that he was going into the business; and with her backing and support. I reviewed her company's old sales catalog I had in my file and then called to arrange to visit the business, which I hadn't seen in years. I arrived at the Company for a tour and some explanations and was ushered into Charlene's office. After the initial greetings I asked her:

"Did Olaf ever ask you what I'd asked you, about what you plan to do after the sale?"

"Are you kidding, Milt, you saw what Olaf is interested in. Olaf!"

"So, Charlene, he never asked; and you never discussed with him your future plans for Larry, you know, after the sale?" Charlene confirmed that nothing of the sort had passed between them; all they discussed – with the business broker present at all these discussions – was price, terms and timing. So I proceeded to learn more about this company that Charlene was about to sell.

Charlene had built the Company as a sales agency for packaging machinery sold to frozen food companies. I asked for and got a demonstration of how these large and complex machines worked. The centerpiece of her line was a complicated 3-step piece of machinery that first formed a plastic TV-dinner type tray (an "extrusion"); the finished tray moved down a line where spouts filled the cavities with various foodstuffs; and then the filled tray would proceed down the line where a sheet of clear plastic would seal the tray once air was removed. And then off to the freezer. Charlene explained that although this was her business now, she considered it to be obsolete. I stopped her in mid-sentence: "Whoa! So you're selling a business you consider to be 'obsolete?'" She nodded, "Yeah." After some seconds of silence I just whispered, "Wow!"

She explained: "There's no need any more for this big hunk of complex iron to form-fill-seal these trays. I'm in touch with Chinese manufacturers who are now able to sell us pre-formed trays – to our spec with quick turnaround delivery, and the price is right – so Larry will be starting up a fill-and-seal business. A different and much simpler machine. No more headaches with 'form-fill-seal' for us."

You might ask why Olaf wasn't aware of this significant change in the packaging business? I believe in this age of hyper-specialization, very few people have "perfect knowledge."[1] Today, to be effective in certain transactions, specialists have to *combine* their knowledge; and a business-law practitioner must combine their knowledge of the law with the specific facts that only the client has – a kind of "synthesis."[2] Olaf should have had a person from Manufacturing with him. This coming change in the packaging business that Charlene explained was probably not even known to Olaf, whose job description was serving as his company's roving mergers/acquisitions person with limited knowledge of industry details and developments back home in the factories.

What to Do?

I was given the name of Olaf's local lawyer who would represent the Buyer acquiring Charlene's company. Since the Buyer typically produces the first draft of the Purchase and Sale Agreement and he had asked me for factual details, I sent Buyer's lawyer a rough term sheet (sometimes called a "Memorandum of Understanding" or MOU) outlining the basic deal and listing patents owned; corporate subsidiaries, domestic and foreign; corporate real estate; and a lot of other data he'd need to prepare the contract.

Since Charlene was *not* putting Larry into the business she was selling, maybe she could have her way if we specifically define that business she was selling – form-fill-seal – and limit the scope of the non-compete to just that business. I decided to take the initiative[3] and provide Olaf's lawyer with a detailed description of the Company's present business, namely, the "form-fill-seal" business as described above. "The machine forms a tray; then fills the tray; then seals the tray – the so-called "form-fill-seal operation." And, since we lawyers like to use defined terms, I followed the detailed description with the words "(hereinafter called the 'Business')."

Then the non-compete could simply provide that Seller/Charlene would not engage in the Business for a period of 24 months. This looked like the best way to achieve Charlene's wishes and I planned to submit it along with a lot of company data that Olaf's lawyer had asked for. I was hoping he'd accept my suggestion and draft the non-compete limited to the form-fill-seal business. But he never even got to see my draft. Olaf's lawyer's draft Purchase and Sale Agreement arrived before I could send my draft to him and, as you'll see, his draft was a big improvement over mine. He literally did my job better than I would have done it!

Here's what Buyer/Olaf's lawyer sent me – his draft non-compete describing what Charlene could *not* do: – She would not:

> "(i) engage in any manner in the sale, manufacture and distribution of the products *currently being manufactured, sold or distributed* by any of Charlene's companies…" [my emphasis]

I of course accepted the Buyer's lawyer's language without question. Charlene reconfirmed to me that she was totally abandoning the machines she was then selling and moving to the simpler "fill-and-seal" equipment. She had no intention that son Larry would be selling any of the "products currently being manufactured, sold or distributed" by the company she was selling – in her mind they were "obsolete." And so the deal closed on schedule, papers signed and passed, cash deposited in Charlene's bank account. My work here is done, or so I thought.

Side Excursion #1:
A Cash Deal or a Promissory Note : Client Could be in Trouble Either Way

Before we get back to how this Tale ends, let's focus for a moment on that word *cash* because it cuts two ways in this deal. First, if this sale had involved Buyer paying client with a promissory note, we might have had a different situation: Buyer would declare Charlene in breach of contract when she set up her son in the packaging industry. Buyer might then have stopped making payments on the note, claiming a breach of contract, and we'd have ended up in court. And then, depending on the judge – and judges have gone both ways on this issue of revising contract language to conform to the presumed clear intention of the parties[4] – Charlene would have been in an unacceptably risky situation. Realistically, she'd have to shut down son Larry's business rather than try to match the power of Olaf's giant multi-national in court.

But in this cash deal, what if Buyer had brought a lawsuit asking for money back for breach of contract. This would also have put Charlene in an unacceptably risky situation. Shortly after closing, Charlene invested the cash she'd received from Buyer in commercial real estate and securities. I doubt that she would have risked losing the case and having to undo investments and return the purchase price – and still own the business she wanted to sell! She would have had to cave and shut down Larry's business. But Buyer never did sue, just complained and complained, as you'll read, below. (This is what I suspect Olaf was thinking to protect his job and his pension: Competition from Larry's startup company was less likely to be noticed by Olaf's superiors than his starting a lawsuit against Charlene and thus, less of a chance that Olaf would be subject to criticism.)

Side Excursion #2:
What Are a Business Lawyer's Ethics and Duties to the Client?

Having represented buyers in this kind of deal, I knew well what *I'd* expect in that non-compete: I always started out requiring the seller, after the sale, to stay out of the business, in this case, the packaging-machine industry. (I later learned that this Buyer had the same expectation.) But being ethically bound to act in my client's interest, in this situation I am also *not* bound to inquire of the Buyer why his expectations don't match mine.

We lawyers do correct mistakes, for example the omission of some standard provision that all assume is in the contract; or some portion of the parties' mutual agreement that was inadvertently omitted. Those are mistakes, and as a business lawyer I would call them to the attention of the other side and we would correct them. (And I would expect the same from the other side.) But if the Buyer is not asking for a deal term that I think he should be asking for, that's no mistake and I have no duty to the Buyer or his lawyer to say anything, nor to teach them the law if their view disagrees with mine. To do otherwise would not only be arrogant, it would violate my duty to my client under the Canons of Ethics.

Back to the Tale – After the Closing of the Deal

After her brief vacation, I heard from Charlene that son Larry was setting up his business in a nearby town and, sad news for me, Larry's new wife was a lawyer and would be handling legal details for the new business. I heard no more of it until several months later when a letter arrived from Buyer's USA office objecting to Charlene being involved in the packaging-equipment business with Larry's company.

"Doctor, you're on the edge of violating
your non-compete."

I responded to that letter and the following two letters, explaining in detail why Larry's company and any involvement that Charlene had with it did not violate her non-compete covenant in the Purchase and Sale Agreement. (Remember, Larry was not selling the machines Charlene dealt with in the company she sold.) Larry and Charlene were clearly *not* violating her non-competition agreement. The letters stopped.

Then one day, another call from Charlene – Olaf was coming back for a meeting, again at my office. I wondered what nasty thing he might say this time, but he was all sweetness and light – until his exasperation began showing. The big, heavy guy was red and sweaty and obviously agitated. "What did we give you all those millions for Charlene? You were supposed to be out of the business…" he sputtered. "You were . . . you were supposed to stay home and . . . do knitting or something…"

Charlene gave me a mock-stern glare.

"Milton, was there a knitting clause in that Buy and Sell Agreement?" she demanded. I had to say no, there was no knitting clause. And so ended the meeting and our last less-than-delightful encounter with Olaf. I accomplished what my client wanted; but as Olaf made clear in his second visit, Buyer was *not* getting what it expected from the deal, namely that Charlene would stay out of the *entire* packaging machine industry. But that's not what *their lawyer* provided in the Agreement. And so, in effect, the very terms of the parties' Purchase and Sale Agreement – terms drafted by their own lawyer! – had defeated the Buyer's expectations. The lesson was clear: In most situations, reasonable expectations based on the clear wording of the contract will trump a party's unexpressed expectations based on other factors, such as, for example, industry custom and practice.[5]

What Went Wrong for Buyer?
Remember Side Excursion #2, above, about what I thought the Buyer expected from the non-compete? Olaf revealed it during that second visit: Olaf expected Charlene to stay out of the packaging machine business altogether – a most reasonable and legitimate expectation. But Olaf apparently never told his lawyer what he expected from the deal; maybe the lawyer just worked off some standard form he assumed would apply to this deal. And even if Olaf had read his lawyer's non-compete, if he had no notion of the dynamics and changes going on in the packaging machinery industry, his lawyer's draft provision would seem perfectly fine to him.

Again, I'm guessing that Olaf's job description was just to travel the world, make ugly threats and acquire businesses for his giant multi-national employer. He didn't know the inside workings of the packaging industry and what was happening. Charlene did. I'm also guessing that Olaf assumed this was just another routine acquisition and probably never even read his lawyer's draft of the Purchase and Sale Agreement.

As for Buyer's lawyer, he used standard non-compete language, a bit narrow for my taste by focusing on specific products and not the entire industry. But beyond that, he seemed not to know anything about the business his client was buying or the packaging industry. This was confirmed time and again when I asked questions during our working up the papers for the deal. He had never visited Charlene's place of business. But more to the point, he had not pushed his client with questions about the details of what his own client *expected* from the deal. The apparent lack of interaction between Olaf and his lawyer made this unusual situation appear otherwise, as just another routine non-compete focusing on the products rather than the industry. But as his second visit made clear, Olaf had expected that Charlene would totally stay out of the packaging-equipment business – the entire industry. But that expectation apparently never came up at the negotiations and deal-making stage.

BLT #1: Pardon the repetition, but this is the most crucial ingredient for a successful deal: If you're a business client, first, think through and identify, *clearly* and *in detail*, your goals and expectations from the deal. Then communicate all this to your lawyer, again clearly, expressly and in detail. When purchasing a business as in this Tale, the Buyer's lawyer should know *exactly* and in detail what his client, the Buyer, expects out of the deal. Look ahead, into the future, and project what might happen; and if you don't want it to happen, ensure that your contract says so. Buyers should read the early drafts of the contract they're about to sign to ensure that the lawyer's words express what the Buyer intends and expects. Lawyers' standard forms almost never do the specific/particular job you want done! Don't wait to learn this hard lesson, as Olaf did: Clear wording in the contract in favor of Party A almost always trumps the unexpressed, yet reasonable expectations of Party B.

It is up to the business lawyer to get *all* the facts about the business and the business client to ensure that this happens. The client-lawyer team in any deal/contracting situation must produce this synthesis. Otherwise, the lawyer is like a boxer going into the ring with one hand tied behind his back.

And if possible – as was the case here – if you're the Buyer or their lawyer, pay a visit to the Seller and chat and learn something about the business that your client is about to buy. Indeed it was my visit to Charlene's showroom that taught me how to help client achieve *her* expectations from the deal. That failure by the Buyer and its lawyer resulted in the frustration of this Buyer's expectations from the deal. Do your homework!

---

1 The term "perfect knowledge" comes from the field of economics. A short definition is "Perfect knowledge describes the state in which a consumer has all possible information in order to make a decision. This situation is ideal, not usual."

2 The need for "synthesis" is part of the bigger societal problem, hyper-specialization; and it goes far beyond the events in this Tale #1. A criticism oft made by Massachusetts industrialist/engineer and philanthropist Bernard Gordon is that we're learning more and more about less and less and missing the "whole." A book reviewer commenting on how the financial meltdown of 2008 happened to, e.g., The Bank of England, wrote: "No specialist saw anything amiss. Only a generalist could have looked at the whole financial sector and seen that it was skewiff." (Philip Delves Broughton reviewing Gillian Tett's book, *The Silo Effect. Wall Street Journal,* Sept. 4, 2015, p. A11.) The limitations of specialization are also noted in medicine, e.g., by Dr. Jerome Groopman, e.g., in his book, *How Doctors Think*, Houghton Mifflin (2007). Obviously, there are many areas that could use a dose of synthesis – a bringing together of the parts of the whole so that the whole can be truly understood and problems identified and then addressed.

3 Whenever possible, I try to produce the first draft of an agreement/contract -- that early document that will be negotiated, revised and end up being the contract for the deal between client and the other party. The lawyer who controls the document this way is really the only one who knows what is included and what has been intentionally excluded and, generally, what the document provides. In this case, the Buyer generally drafts the document, as turned out to be the case here.

4 This long note is to convince you that litigation is never a sure bet – judges have ways of "interpreting" language; they can focus on and follow the words, or they can chose to ignore the words and come to their own conclusion about what is "right" outcome. Some examples:

1. This court's decision is based not on the words of the contract, but what makes business sense to the court:

    But even if the language taken in the abstract is not decisive in the Trust's favor and even if the drafters never focused on the risk of negative royalties, only one reading of the contract makes any sense. No rational party in the Trust's position would agree to such negative royalties, nor would anyone in Engelhard's position demand such an option, because it would create an extraordinary perverse incentive for Engelhard to engage in otherwise irrational conduct and would create an unlimited risk to the Trust's legitimate general expectations. The point is so obvious as to require only brief explanation.

Later in their opinion, the court said:

    Even where courts are sure that the parties never thought about an issue, small wrinkles may be ironed out by interpretation where it is clear how the parties <u>would have</u> handled them.

(The case: *Rhode Island Charities Trust v. Engelhard Corp.*, 267 F.3d 3, 7 (1st Cir. 2001).)

2. Here, the U.S. Supreme Court claims to follow the intent of the parties which they believe is expressed by the plain words of the contract. The majority rules:

    …contractual 'provisions ordinarily should be enforced as written … In this endeavor, as with any other contract, the parties' intentions control. Where the words of a contract in writing are clear and unambiguous, its meaning is to be ascertained in accordance with its plainly expressed intent.'

The four concurring Justices agree with the majority's conclusions. Justices Ginsburg, Breyer, Sotomayor and Kagan write:

    Today's decision rightly holds that courts must apply ordinary contract principles, shorn of presumptions …When the intent of the parties is unambiguously expressed in the contract, that expression controls, and the court's inquiry should proceed no further.

(The case: (2015 *M&G Polymers USA, LLC v. Tackett*, 2015 U.S. LEXIS 759, 574 US xxx).)

3.   "The present agreement [not to make a will] is not in terms within the statute. Nor is it by implication. Accordingly, if the legislature meant by 'no agreement about making a will' or 'no agreement to make or not to make a will,' we think it is for it [i.e., the Legislature] and not for us, to say."

(The case: *Foman v. Davis*, 316 F. 2d 254 (1ˢᵗ Cir. 1963).

More of these examples show up in Tales #13 and #14, but for now, remember: Litigation is hardly ever a sure thing, almost always a gamble, and a costly one at that!

5 An English legal scholar addressed this question in "Leading a Life of its Own? The Roles of Reasonable Expectation in Contract Law", *Oxford Journal of Legal Studies,* Vol. 23, No.4 (2003), p. 639 at p. 656. Catherine Mitchell writes: ". . . contract terms can shape expectations and determine precisely what it is reasonable for one party to expect from the agreement. Provided procedural requirements are satisfied, chiefly that the party knows about and fully understands the effect of the term [*here in Tale #1, the non-compete provision*] and assents to it . . . *this negates any other expectation he may have which is at variance with the term.*" [my emphasis]

TALE # 2

THREE CASES

#1 Solving (read "Preventing") a Client's Problem 10 Years Before It Existed
(Of the 3 cases, this was the easiest to solve. The next one, not so easy.)

#2 The Movie-Deal Case
followed by

#3 The Impossible Case
All to Illustrate the Value of Strategy in Deal-Making and the Lawyer's Role.

We move further into contracts, because that's what we business lawyers do: We document or "paper" the deals, the transactions, our clients make. Contracts was my own favorite law school subject and I must agree with my First-Year law professor, Austin Wakeman Scott when in October 1906, then a law student, he wrote home that "Contracts is probably the most important subject we have."[1] Contracts are at the heart of most business activity and, indeed, at least half of all the Tales in this book involve a contract. Tale #2 begins with cases that illustrate a technique for writing a good contract and avoiding a bad one.

Despite the title, *SOLVED!*, my focus as a business lawyer has been to *prevent* problems from occurring; and there, the notion of strategy also comes into play. In deal-making, just as in chess, in business, in war, indeed, in life-planning, strategy involves looking to the long term, projecting into the future. Business people and their lawyers should be asking these important questions:

- What might happen?
- What conditions could change?
- How can I prepare for them, provide for them in the deal I'm making and the contract I'm signing in order to ensure that my intentions and expectations are carried out and not defeated?[2]

"And, while there's no reason yet to panic, I think it only prudent that we make preparations to panic."

"Standard Forms" and The Law Already Look to the Future

"Standard forms" already answer some of these questions by providing for future contingencies, for example: The office-space lease in the first (easy) case already provided for contingencies such as fire; eminent domain;

bankruptcy; **force majeur**; etc. The Law also offers some protection against certain unforeseen future events under the headings of "frustration of purpose;" "impossibility;" "destruction of the subject matter of the contract;" and the like. For example, a contract for selling or improving a house that's destroyed in a fire is typically nullified by that event – neither party is obligated under the contract to the other. You'll have to check the law in your jurisdiction to know what events excuse non-performance under a contract.

But you can't just rely on The Law or some standard-form **boilerplate.** Neither **boilerplate** nor The Law is strategy. You should be customizing *your* contract, *your* deal, by looking into the future and asking those three questions as they relate to *your* industry and *your* circumstances – and if the answers lead you to more questions, then get answers and use them in negotiating and documenting your deal.

Sometimes, parties intend that the contract be carried out without *any* excuse, no matter what happens. Such contracts usually contain what's called a "hell or high water" clause. For example, when a real estate loan is structured as a **ground lease** (sometimes called a **net lease**), and the loan payments are called "rent" under that lease, the obligation to pay rent is usually subject to a "hell or high water" clause. No matter what happens, that loan must be repaid and thus, that obligation to make "rent" payments (which are really loan repayments) is absolute and not subject to any exceptions, events or circumstances. But in most deals, you *will* want the contract to end if certain things happen – say new government regulations change the economics or some specified business conditions arise. It's up to the businessperson and their lawyer to identify those things that will excuse performance and in some cases, even terminate the contract.

Let's move on to the three cases: The first where looking into the future was a simple task; the second where the future was more cloudy and hard to predict; and the third, where it was literally impossible to predict what eventually happened.

Case One
Client Landlord Asks for a Standard Form Lease for His New Office Building – and I Deliver One that Deals With a Problem That Would Arise 10 Years Later

Developer Client asked me to produce a "Standard Form Office Lease" for a building then under construction. While working on the "Electric/Utilities" provisions I learned some local history. In past years, most existing office leases provided for a "master-metering" arrangement which worked like this: Landlords would buy electric current for the entire building at the lower "wholesale" rates from Edison Company. Each month, the building's total consumption was read off a single "master meter" which measured *all* the electricity coming into the entire building; and Landlord paid the electric bill for the building as shown on the master meter. Landlords then hard-wired each tenant's office space with its own sub-meter; and would bill each tenant off their individual sub-meter, but at the higher, "retail" rates, enjoying the markup profit. This was, of course, taking profits out of Edison's pockets, and so...

In 1956, Edison Co. took the matter to court and defeated this sub-metering arrangement.[3] In its place was a new Edison regulation that prohibited landlords from sub-metering. In the words of the Edison regulation, Landlords could no longer make a separate charge for tenant electricity which varied with use. (Sub-metering was dead!)

The result: By 1963 (the year I was asked to draft this Standard Form Office Lease) most landlords continued to provide electricity to tenant spaces, but under a different arrangement so as to comply with the new Edison regulation. The new arrangement was dubbed "rent-inclusion," which worked like this: Landlords would calculate the cost of electricity used by the average office tenant (on a kilowatt-per-square-foot basis) and then add to the tenants' rental this estimated cost of electricity which Landlord would be providing to the leased space. In this way, Landlords continued to provide tenant electricity while avoiding violating Edison's regulation: Landlords did not measure tenants' electric usage and did not make a separate charge for tenants' use of electricity.

But addressing the strategic question (What could change?), we knew that tenants could add equipment or increase their hours of operation. The form leases I checked already protected landlords against increased electric costs by billing tenants if they (i) made a change in their electric-consuming equipment and (ii) increased their business hours of operation. I followed suit in my own draft Lease. (And "just in case," the Lease gave Landlord the right at any time to end the rent-inclusion arrangement; reduce the rent accordingly; and install separate Edison meters for each Tenant's space. In that case each Tenant would pay its own electric bills directly to the Edison utility company with no further Landlord involvement.)

After dealing with an increase in equipment and hours of operation, I found one question still remained open, namely when electric bills went up because of an increase in electric rates charged by the utility. It was time for a visit to the Edison people.

When I asked them about this other component of the cost of electricity, namely electric rates, they seemed surprised. I clearly told them that we were not going near a tenant's increased *use* of electricity – a no-no under the Edison regulation. I was asking Edison only about that rate and whether they'd have a problem if my Lease provided for a rent increase if the electric-current rate increased. Could Landlord, in effect, pass on *rate* increases to the Tenants? They shrugged off the question:

"No problem, there hasn't been a rate increase in years." And there was no mention of rate increases in any Edison regulation. This gap was understandable since rates had been level for years, maybe decades, at pennies per kwh, if I recall correctly; no one I spoke to at Edison had any memory of any increase in electric rates. But still, the per kilowatt hour (kwh) rate was, after all a variable and, therefore, subject to *change*, the important word in one of those questions I urge *you* to ask – "what could change?"

The answer: Electric rates could change and so I had to cover that risk. I provided in this form Lease for Client's new office building that Landlord could impose a charge on his tenants if electric rates went up to compensate

Landlord for that increased cost. I then went back to the Edison people and met with them a second time to confirm that I wasn't stepping on any toes with this pass-through of rate increases. They had no problem with it. Then, before leaving, I asked if there were any other "pass-through" items that Landlord could collect from its tenants and to which they'd have no objection. They said it was fine for Landlord to add a "rent-inclusion service charge" somewhere in the range of 6% to 7% of a tenant's estimated electric-current usage. I added this to "Utilities" in the Lease and advised client Landlord of these provisions for future reference.

Ten Years Later the Unexpected Event!

Fast-forward to a surprise that came ten years after I drafted that Lease: The 1973 Arab oil embargo. The cost of oil and gasoline shoots up; shortages cause long lines at gas stations; and, of course, the increased cost of operating Edison's oil-fired electric generating plants caused a spike in generating costs. This was soon reflected in rate increases and higher bills to Edison customers including, of course, all those Landlords with their "standard-form" rent-inclusion leases. Under those leases, Landlords had to keep providing electricity, but without any lease provision for passing increased costs on to tenants, Landlords had to pay and themselves absorb these cost increases under their leases' "rent-inclusion" provisions. Many suffered financial hardships, but not Client Landlord. He was able to recoup the higher costs under his rate-increase pass-through provision. Problem *SOLVED!* Client Landlord was certainly among the few, maybe very few, who could recoup those cost increases under their Lease forms – all because of my asking that question, "What could change?" and then providing for that change. You can see why I call this the "easy" case: If the electric bill could increase because of increased use (which Landlord could *not* measure/meter and bill for) or an increase in the rate (which I could deal with), then simply provide for a pass-through of these additional costs of electric current resulting from an increase in the Edison rate per kilowatt hour. Problem prevented!

———

Let's now move on to Case Two in this Tale, a show-biz story from the newspapers, you'll learn how *not* asking the kinds of questions noted above can result in a movie mogul's contract that failed to carry out their intentions and fulfill their expectations in the case of Miramax versus Warner Bros.

Case Two
A Showbiz Deal in 2013-2014 – Not as Easy as Case One

Miramax and its owners, movie producers Weinstein Brothers, owned all film rights to J.R.R. Tolkien's *The Hobbit*, a work that Warner Bros. wanted to produce as a film. They agreed that Miramax would give the film rights to Warner Bros. in exchange for a royalty: Warner would pay Miramax 5% of the gross receipts from "the first motion picture" based on the book. The deal was sealed, the contract signed.

"Now, if you'll just sign right here, Mr. Hark, you'll make the biggest mistake of your life!"

Warner decided (and I'd love to know exactly *when* that decision was made) to divide and release *The Hobbit* in three installments. Warner paid Miramax for the first installment, that is, "the first motion picture" based on the book, but refused to pay any more royalties on the second and third installments. Miramax expected royalties from the *entire* book – all three installments and not just the first one released by Warner. Warner's position simply relied on the words of their contract: they would pay royalties only on "the first motion picture" and not the second and third: Their first installment was "the first motion picture" and the second and third installments were not, they argued.

Miramax then sued Warner Bros. in New York courts for $75 million additional compensation. Warner moved the case to arbitration and, in a decision we may never get to see, the arbitrator ruled in favor of Warner. (These arbitration proceedings are generally not made public and so we probably won't know the bases for the arbitrator's decision.) But it's pretty clear, don't you think – those four clear words ("the first motion picture") decided the case. A major method of contract interpretation is "plain meaning of the words.") Miramax didn't ask and answer the questions during contract negotiations: What could change? Or maybe how could the format Warner chose change in a way that would negatively impact royalties to be paid? But maybe that's a stretch to expect.

This case illustrates the power of the specific words you use in your contracts –words that are more powerful than the parties' specific unexpressed intentions, which the arbitrator could easily have discerned from the circumstances and pleadings in the case. For example, Paragraph 6 of the Miramax Complaint, originally filed in the New York court, makes this interesting point:

> Warner's position is inconsistent with the parties' intent, the terms of the parties' written contract, Warner's own director's statement that *each of The Hobbit installments was written and shot as part of a single motion picture...* [my emphasis]

(If Miramax expected royalties from a movie based on *The Hobbit*, why didn't they just say so? They were clear enough to exclude "remakes" from the royalty arrangement, so why did they end up with just this "first film made" language? Makes you wonder…

My theory is that Miramax intended "the first motion picture" language to describe and clarify the exclusion of "remakes." And maybe they had in mind so-called prequels and sequels, also intended to be excluded from the royalty deal. I envision Miramax's intention would have been more clearly expressed as follows:

> No royalties shall be due on any remakes, prequels
> or sequels, that is, only on the first film made.

I think that's what Miramax meant, but it's not what they said. And I'm frankly puzzled how such a multi-million-dollar deal gets done on these rather rudimentary and simple terms. This is a complex industry with lots of twists and turns to which, apparently, Miramax paid little attention. More particularly, why didn't Miramax say what they obviously intended, namely, "5% of gross receipts from the motion picture based on *The Hobbit*, except for remakes."

Another puzzling matter: If, indeed, the Miramax pleading, above ("each of *The Hobbit* installments was written and shot as part of a single motion picture") is true, then weren't the three "installments" a single motion picture, that is, "the first motion picture" based on *The Hobbit*? Why does it matter that Warner chose to split up and distribute the film to theatres in installments? (We must assume that the top-notch legal counsel representing Miramax strenuously pressed this point in the arbitration.) And why should it matter (to the arbitrator) how the *next* step following production – the release of that motion picture to theaters – was handled? What happens *after* the motion picture is made – whether divided/edited(?) into three, five or ten installments – doesn't seem to change the fact, maybe an irrefutable fact, alleged in the Miramax Complaint that "each of *The Hobbit* installments was written and shot as part of a single motion picture…?" Without seeing the entire record in this case, maybe I'm missing something. It's puzzling.

You can understand why this case is not as easy as the above Case One (electric clause in a Lease). Here it's not so easy to answer those forward-looking "what-can-happen" questions. Maybe I say that because I'm not in the business and anyone in the movie business would have asked the right questions. My guess is that Warner Bros. drafted the contract which, on its face seemed to state the parties' deal, and so there was no occasion for Miramax to ask *any* questions. But here is where my "paranoia" kicks in, based on my assumption that they *are* out to get me. So my question is, "How can Warner Bros. defeat Miramax's intention?" Given the way some film and television works are broken up into episodes or installments, maybe asking the paranoiac question – possibly in a brainstorming session[4] – would have produced an answer resulting in a clearer expression of Miramax's true intentions and expectations from the deal. Maybe – we may never know.

Should Miramax have foreseen the possibility that their *Hobbit* property could be split into several installments? And that Warner Bros. would pay royalties only on the first one? This division of a work into installments is not an uncommon a practice. For example, movie critic Kenneth Turan[5] said this about the movie *The Hunger Games* and its final installment, *Mockingjay Part 2*: "You know, splitting this last book into two films is such a naked commercial move. But, they did it. And it seems to be working." So maybe Miramax should have foreseen what Warner Bros. did, but hey, who am I to say. I'm just a business lawyer, so you be the judge.

Case Three
Some "Changes" Are Simply Unpredictable
I don't want to leave you feeling like you've failed if something happens that you didn't anticipate or provide for. You can never foresee all that can happen – some things are unpredictable and you cannot protect against those events. Here's the classic example we all read in law school, the saga of that good ship, *The Peerless:* This case was decided in the English courts in the mid-1860s; and notice the interesting ruling at the end.

The British Buyer contracted to buy 125 bales of a certain type of cotton from the Indian Seller at an agreed-upon price. The contract called for shipment of the cotton from Bombay, India to Liverpool, England aboard a ship, *The Peerless,* scheduled to sail from Bombay to Liverpool. With all the details settled, their agreement was done – or was it? As this case illustrates, sometimes the parties to an agreement really have no agreement – they have differing intentions and expectations.

What the parties didn't realize was that there were *two* ships named *The Peerless* and both were scheduled to leave Bombay for Liverpool; one left in October and the other in December. The Buyer expected his goods on the October ship, but Seller shipped the cotton on the later December ship.

When the goods arrived on the December ship, the Buyer refused to accept or pay for the late shipment; he expected his goods on the October ship. The Seller said the date difference didn't matter to their deal and brought suit against the Buyer for the purchase price of the cotton as stated in their contract. Buyer moved to dismiss the case and the court granted the motion – case dismissed; Defendant-Buyer wins and Plaintiff-Seller loses. Why? The judge ruled that the parties had never made a contract – there was no agreement between them.

The Court ruled that there hadn't been a "meeting of the minds," a requirement for the formation of a legally binding contract. Each party had a different (and not unreasonable) understanding and intention and thus there was no agreement for the Court to enforce in the famous case of *Raffles v. Wichelhaus*.[6] To all intents and purposes, the parties had signed a contract and appeared to be in agreement, but appearances can be deceiving.

For our purposes here, this case illustrates one of those situations where asking the questions noted above would *not* have helped. There are certain changes in circumstances that realistically, you cannot expect to anticipate and provide for. But there are others (like the easy Case One about electric rates) where asking and answering the questions did, in fact, prevent and solve the client's problem, and in that case, years before there even was a problem.

The wider afield you go in asking the "change question," the more possible changes of circumstances you consider, the better you're able to provide for those changes (and to your advantage!). When I suggest you look "wider afield," I'm referring to as many aspects of the transaction as you can think of when asking "What can change?" Typically, market conditions changing can convert a good deal into a bad one. Other possible considerations are the other side's interests and goals and the particular personalities involved. Might those people be replaced and could that affect your situation? But mainly remember these two words: *Things change*. Many, perhaps most, business disputes that land in court seem to happen because something changed; and that "something" was not anticipated and so not provided for in the parties' agreement. (Or maybe their contract tried to cover a change of circumstances, but failed to do so clearly.) And if you're in Warner Bros.' position, as in Case Two, above, you may intentionally want to conceal your plan to release the film in three installments and pay royalties only on the first.

For another Tale involving big changes that the parties did not anticipate, but which worked to the unexpected advantage of one of the parties, see Tale #9. There a drastic increase in office-space rental rates and other factors turned a payment intended as a reimbursement into a windfall for the Landlord. Things change.

To help you remember that things change, let's get away from The Law: Some words from the great science-fiction writer and science teacher, Isaac Asimov, from his 1981 *Asimov on Science Fiction*:

> "It is change, continuing change, inevitable change, that is the dominant factor in society today. No sensible decision can be made any longer without taking into account not only the world as it is, but the world as it will be. This, in turn, means that our statesmen, our businessmen, our everyman must take on a science fictional way of thinking."

How right he was, when we look at the thirty-plus years after he wrote those words! I hope you ask the right questions and get the answers that help you to resolve a problem *before* it even exists.

This show-biz dispute and others reported throughout this book should make you appreciate the importance of this next BLT (and I warn you, it's repetitive, so if you've learned the lessons by reading this far, skip this BLT). Otherwise, here it is:

BLT #2: First, determine what the client intends and what they expect that this contract will (i) provide to them and (ii) obligate them to provide to the other party. Say what you mean and mean what you say. Then ask these three questions whenever (i) negotiating and then (ii) documenting any deal or transaction:

1- What can change that can harm me? Circumstances? Parties? Markets? Other?
2- Can I and should I make provision for any change that could harm me?

3- How should I make provision for that future change?

- Appreciate the importance of brainstorming (gathered together in a group if possible) on what the future might hold in store that could help or hurt your deal. (See Note 3.) What circumstances could change that could affect your deal's succeeding or failing?
- Clearly and early on identify your near-term and long-term specific goals for the deal – what it is you really expect to get out of the transaction, expressed exactly and in detail. (I don't plan to deal with situations where you might intentionally want to keep your goals a secret – you may see this happening in some of the Tales.) But remember that if you're expecting something out of a deal, that something had better be expressed loud and clear enough for a judge to rule in your favor; that judge is the bottom-line arbiter and the real target of your words if there's ever a dispute with the other party to the deal. Remember this question (which is repeated in this book): What does the contract mean? And my answer:

Your contract means what a judge says it means!

- Early on pick out those issues you'll raise and which ones you're better off staying away from in your negotiations with the other party to the deal. My view on picking and choosing what you'll raise and what you'll skip over: If you know in advance you'll lose the point, then intentionally avoid raising the point (assuming your arguments will be futile).
- Convey to your lawyer, fully and in detail, your expectations from the deal and as much factual background as possible. Most successful deals are made when business clients and their lawyers work closely together as a team and the lawyers are fully briefed on the client's business and industry and his exact intentions and expectations from the deal. (Remember "synthesis" from Tale #1.)

- Switch your mindset: Put yourself in the other side's position and ask: Can the other side interpret or twist the language of the contract to their advantage and against your interests? If so then it's back to the drafting table (or is it drawing board?) with your lawyer.

Good Luck!

Bonus Feature : A Puzzle from the New York Real Estate Scene
A New York City real estate lawyer tells this tale: Her Building-Owner Client sends her a Term Sheet and asks her to prepare a lease for a prospective tenant. The deal describes the premises as "the entire top floor of the building consisting of 10,000 square feet of Rentable Area [later defined]." The lawyer drafts the Lease and describes the space, the "demised premises," as follows:

> The entire ninth floor of the building located at 1234 XYZ Street consisting of 10,000 square feet of Rentable Area (as hereinafter measured and defined).

Why did this lawyer change the wording of her Client's Term Sheet from "the entire top floor" to "the entire ninth floor" [of the nine-story building, which fact she never mentions in the Lease she prepared]. For a clue and another illustration of the need to ask that "What could change?" question, check out *The New York Times* story of October 24, 1999 in the Real Estate section, headlined "Adding New Floors atop of Old Buildings." (http://www.nytimes.com/1999/10/24/realestate/adding-new-floors-atop-old-buildings.html?pagewanted=all) As you can see, if this were a lease of the "top floor," tenant might well be able to prevent the landlord from adding any floors. But if this was a lease of "the ninth floor," what's to keep landlord from adding a tenth, eleventh, twelfth or more floors?

Say what you mean and when you read what you've said, mean what you say!

1 Austin Wakeman Scott, *Letters from a Law Student to His Family 1906 – 1908,* Harvard Law School (1974), p.4.

2 The same point with other words is made by business consultant Daniel Burrus in *Amazon's Secret Weapon: Being Anticipatory.* He notes that the lesson from Amazon's success lies in its understanding "the strategic importance of being anticipatory." Available at (control+click) http://insights.cermacademy.com/2016/06/142-amazons-secret-weapon-anticipatory-daniel-burras/ [not a typo]

3 *Boston Real Estate Board et al. v. Dept. of Public Utilities et al.*, 334 Mass. 477 (1956).

4 In his article, "The Fundamental Role of the Corporate Lawyer — And How to Succeed in It," Chicago lawyer Stuart L. Goodman stresses, in a business-law firm setting, "the importance of teamwork. I couldn't do it all by myself — not only because I was certainly not an expert in every area of the law, but because no one person can think of everything. It is so important to have teamwork and to be practicing in a law firm or legal department where there is a spirit of teamwork. For example, brainstorming often is the best way to solve tough legal problems." Goodman notes "how important it is to bring other minds to bear on difficult issues. " {Goodman's article is available at http://www.schiffhardin.com/Templates/media/files/publications/PDF/goodman-corporate_lawyer.pdf].

5 Critic Turan's statement was made in his review of upcoming movies on CBS' "Sunday Morning" TV show October 18, 2015.

6 *Raffles v. Wichelhaus,* [1864] EWHC Exch J19 (1864) 2 H & C 906; 159 ER

TALE # 3

IF THE EX-EMPLOYEE'S NON-COMPETE IS NARROW, IT LEAVES ROOM TO COMPETE.

Client, John, was a salesman for Copier Company, not the big Xerox, but a smaller national competitor. He sold supplies and copy machines, on commission, but his ambition was to go into business for himself. John was a true salesman, an affable personality who could talk to anybody with ease. He thought he could put these talents to use for himself in his own business. So he gave notice and rented a small office in the same downtown Boston area where he'd been working for Copier Company.

When his former employer learned of his move, they sued, dredging up an old agreement he'd signed way back when he started working for them. In it he agreed that he would not compete with the company's business for 24 months after leaving their employ.

A guy's got to make a living, and selling copier supplies and the like was what John intended to do at the outset of his new business. When he called me, I told John that some courts were resisting enforcing these non-compete agreements, moving in the direction of favoring employees, who should not be prevented from working in their field. And so it was worth a shot to contest this matter in court and not simply cave in to Copier Company's lawsuit. John's case ended up in an Equity Motion Session in Boston, with the Copier Company lawyer asking that John be enjoined from selling copier paper and supplies.[1]

I pleaded the matter to the court as best I could –the Big Guy versus Little Guy arguments. I sensed that the Judge was sympathetic and that the Copier Company was realizing that the case might be going against his client. Non-compete law involving a salesman and a large corporate employer was then in flux and the Judge, understandably, wanted to avoid having to make a decision. He "gently" suggested, "Why don't counsel talk this over and see if you can resolve the matter amicably?" Both lawyers mumbled "Yes, Your Honor" and we walked out the back of the courtroom. I tried hard to convince the Copier Company lawyer that John was a one-man operation that would not offer any competition worth talking about – he really couldn't hurt Copier Company with his one-man efforts. But he was under orders from his client, Copier Company, to take the matter to court. Finally, in desperation, I just blurted out, "What is it you want from this man? Be specific!"

The Company's lawyer answered, "We don't want him to solicit the same customers he sold to while employed at Copier Company." I said that if that's the best he could do, then let's go back inside and talk to the Judge. I reported to the Judge that Copier Company doesn't want John soliciting the same customers he served as a Copier Company salesman; and that my client was willing to agree to that. The Judge asked that the two lawyers fashion a court order that he would sign. So back out into the lobby we went and on a yellow pad, I spoke as I handwrote John's new agreement: For the next 24 months, John agreed "not to solicit any of the customers served by John during his employment by Copier Company."

I. The Solution
We returned to the courtroom, the Judge signed the hand-written sheet, his clerk date-stamped and filed it as the Order of the Court and we all left the courtroom. John was despondent, but I was more upbeat. "John" I said, "tell me about your relationship with your customers." John answered as I had expected:

"These customers like me – I'm sure of that. I've been doing business with them for lots of years, some of our families know each other. Sure, they like me." That was enough for me. "Let's get back to your office," and I almost pushed John out the door. Back at John's office I sat down at a typewriter (remember that antique writing instrument?) and typed the following:

Notice to My Old Customers

Having now left my job with Copier Company, I wish to thank you for your patronage and friendship over the years. Since I am under a court order which Copier Company has gotten against me, I am prohibited by the terms of that court order from soliciting your business, having been ordered "not to solicit any of my customers" of "Copier Company."

Accordingly I am advising you expressly that this Notice is not a solicitation of your business, as I do not wish to violate the Court Order.

Best regards and best wishes for happiness, health and success in the future.

John
John's Copier Supply Company, Inc.
123 Downtown Boston Street
Boston, MA 12345
Tel. 617-555-1212

Soon John's phone was ringing with messages of sympathy and support. Everyone understood that he was not soliciting their business, but hey, he was selling the same stuff and they all loved John. He was in business and nothing was ever heard from Copier Company again. They probably didn't even notice that there was a new kid on the block.

II. What Went Wrong?

My guess is that Copier Company's lawyer reported his success to his client – he'd gotten a court order against John's soliciting any of his Copier Company customers, and that ended it. But I doubt that Copier Company's lawyer ever even heard back from his client about all this. If he had, he would have learned that he should broaden his non-compete provisions beyond "shall not solicit." But you really can't fault him because when the two of us were in that courthouse lobby, the Judge was waiting for a quick, on-the-spot response to my question "What do you want from this man?" And he was stuck with his client's wording in the non-compete agreement – non-solicitation was obviously their main concern: They didn't want their former salesman to solicit his old Copier Company customers.

As an aside, it's sometimes possible for the ex-employer to deal with this problem by his informing his customer base about the salesman's departure. This must, of course, be done gingerly, maybe just informing them that their ex-employee had been enjoined by court order from soliciting/taking orders, and the like, from his former customers at the Copier Company. Tough decisions and maybe case by case. Sometimes the situation might call for a personal visit/talk from the ex-employer Copier Company with its important customers.

III. That Was Then, the Sixties – This is Now And "Now" Includes Social Medial, Linked-In, Facebook, and More
BLT #3:
Prudent employers today ask their employees to sign non-solicitation (of customers and other employees) in much broader terms than simply a promise not to solicit. If your non-compete is intended to prevent *any* contact with customers or other employees, then be specific and say so – that has become a well-accepted and routine provision. Use the word: *contact*. Two articles point out the case law and the broader, preferred wording of a non-solicitation provision in employment agreements and non-compete agreements.[2] The title of the first (which deals with non-solicitation of employees) hints at what happened when John sent his "Notice" to his old customers, above, in this Tale: "Nudge, nudge, wink, wink."

This can be a difficult and sensitive, but no less important matter to any business. As the Massachusetts Appeals Court stated in a case involving the alleged solicitation of customers, "as a practical matter, the difference between accepting and receiving business, on the one hand, and indirectly soliciting on the other, may be more metaphysical than real."[3] It seems clear from a 2013 Federal Appeals Court decision that the kind of contacts John made to his customers at his former employer, Copier Company, would today probably be enjoined as violating his promise not to "solicit"[4]

Social Media Changes the Picture!

In October 2014 a Connecticut trial court rejected the plaintiff's (BTS's) employer's claims against its ex-employee (Marshall) and his new employer.[5] During his time at BTS, Marshall had been active on LinkedIn. He'd had no discussions with BTS about this, nor did BTS have any policy/procedure in place restricting its employees' social media activities. Marshall's links, naturally, included his BTS clients and other contacts he'd developed while working at BTS. After he left BTS, Marshall continued to keep those links active; indeed, BTS had never asked Marshall to "unlink" from any of its clients when he left to take a new job. BTS lost its case at trial. Whether he appealed and if so, how that ended, we don't know (most cases settle).

The Connecticut Trial Judge noted similar situations in other states' courts, for example:

- An Oklahoma federal court ruled that an ex-employee's Facebook postings promoting his new employer's products did not violate an agreement not to recruit employees.[6]
- An Indiana appellate court ruled that the ex-employee's "non-solicitation" (of his ex-employer's employees) agreement was not violated when the ex-employee posted a job opportunity at his new company on a LinkedIn page – that was held not to be a "solicitation."[7]
- A Massachusetts trial court ruled that becoming "friends" on Facebook with former clients of his ex-employer did not, in and of itself, violate a non-compete clause.[8]

These cases seem to follow the trend against strict enforcement of a departing employee's non-compete agreements in some states. Non-competes work well in the context of sale of a business, but are less effective when an employee leaves their job.

BLT #4:

1. Remember that this area of law varies from state to state, court to court and even case to case within any one state. You will need your lawyer's guidance through this thicket.

2. One of the variations from state to state is how your state courts enforce such broad restrictions. Some courts merely reduce the scope of your language. For example, they cut down an over-long non-compete period (called "blue-penciling"). (And the time period courts will enforce may also vary from industry to industry – e.g., in parts of the fast-moving computer/software industry, six months has been held a sufficient time to protect the ex-employer's interests; elsewhere, a 12 or 24 month restrictive period is the norm.) Other states don't "blue-pencil;" they might simply rule that your entire agreement is unenforceable. Again, your lawyer's guidance is a must in this area.

3. If you're the employer, you should consider a broad and explicitly detailed definition of "solicitation" that includes a prohibition against *contacting*, as well as the solicitation and acceptance of business from customers.

4. Consider the same broad prohibition against the departing employee contacting, soliciting and facilitating the hiring of the ex-employer's other employees.

5. Courts generally don't like to restrict people's freedom as to where they work or whom they talk to unless it's really necessary to protect some important interest you and your business have – like protecting proprietary information or trade secrets, etc. from being disclosed. Therefore, include these facts in the "recitals," those "whereas" clauses at the head of your document and be prepared to explain to a court what that important interest is and why the restrictions you put on your ex-employees are necessary to protect your business. Remember, these overarching "public interests," such as the freedom of employees to work where they please and do business with whom he pleases are obstacles you'll have to overcome to convince a judge that enforcement of the restriction will not negatively impact those "public interests."

6. And don't forget social media contacts: Develop a policy for employees (i) during their employment and (ii) after they leave. A lawyer experienced in Labor and Employment law in your state is again, a must.

In this Tale #3, the employer's problems probably lay more in the restricted wording of his non-compete agreement. Today, the Copier Company lawyer could have gone back into court and argued for a broader reading of the agreement not to "solicit". And his client, Copier Company would have broadened their employee agreement to prohibit "contacting or communicating by any means with Copier Company's customers."

Good Luck, you ex-employers!

1 Check your own state's law. Some states will not enforce or severely limit employee non-compete agreements. Such agreements are routinely enforced against the Seller of a business to Buyer, but not in employer-employee situations. These states cite "public policy;" the parties unequal bargaining power; etc. California's statute is the prime example: BUSINESS AND PROFESSIONS CODE SECTION 16600-16607:

Section 16600. Except as provided in this chapter, every contract by which anyone is restrained from engaging in a lawful profession, trade, or business of any kind is to that extent void.

2 I am indebted to Boston Attorney Lee Gesmer for this insightful and practical advice, summarized above, in his July 2, 2013 article, "Nudge, Nudge, Wink, Wink – Are you 'Soliciting' in Violation of an Employee Non-Solicitation Agreement?" which can be found at http://masslawblog.com/employment/nudge-nidge-wink-wink-are-you-soliciting-in-violation-of-an-employee-non-solicitation-agreement/. [Control + Click] Another useful article is by Johnson, "The Parameters of 'Solicitation' in an Era of Non-Solicitation Covenants," *ABA Journal of Labor & Employment Law*, Vol. 28, No. 1 (Fall 2012), pp. 99-127.
3 *Alexander & Alexander, Inc. v Danahy*, 21 Mass. App. Ct. 488, 488 N.E.2d 22 (1986).

4 Corporate Technologies, Inc. v. Harnet and Onx USA LLC, 943F. Supp. 2d 233 (D. Mass. May 3, 2013); affirmed. No. 13-706 (1st Cir. Sep. 23, 2013).

5 *BTS, USA. Inc. v. Executive Perspectives, LLC and Marshall Bergmann,* Docket No.. x10CV 116010685, 2014 Conn. Super. LEXIS 2644 (October 16, 2014).

6 *Pre-Paid Legal Services, Inc. v. Cahill,* 924 F. Supp. 2d 1281 (E.D. Okla. 2013).

7 *Enhanced Network Solutions Group, Inc. v. Hypersonic Tech. Corp.,* 951 N.E. 2d 264 (Ind. App. 2011).

8 *Invidia, LLC. V. DiFonzo,* Docket No. MICV 2012-3798-H, 2012 Mass. Super. LEXIS 273 (Oct. 22, 2012).

TALE # 4

100-Store Retail Chain Enjoys Tax Benefits Intended for "Small Business"

I. The Problem the Client Didn't Even Know He Had

Sometimes good lawyering includes finding an opportunity the client may not know about because it involves The Law and not the client's business. This Tale is such a case. Let's set the scene: Client starts his retail discount chain-store business (called "Multi") in 1960 and in a couple of years, when he has ten stores, we discussed the corporate organization. We started out by forming a new **subsidiary corporation** to sign these store leases (each lease being guaranteed by Multi, the parent company). By the mid-'60s Multi had grown to almost 100 stores and **leased departments** within discount stores in 35 states.

During those growing years, as the business began to expand with stores and leased departments across the USA, this question came up: Should Multi's business be organized this way as it spread to cities and towns across the country? Obviously there was a cost in forming and maintaining all these subsidiary corporations, but beyond that, what were the advantages and disadvantages of such a multi-corporate structure?

Meanwhile, we continued in that direction: For each new location, Multi set up (under the laws of **Delaware**) a new subsidiary, which signed a lease (with Multi as guarantor in order to satisfy the landlords' need for a "credit-worthy" tenant). Time for me to do a bit of research and learn about this client's industry. That research included a meeting with Multi's accountant. From her I learned of a possible tax benefit – multiple surtax exemptions – and so I made inquiries about what the competition was doing; and this is what I learned: The competition uniformly used a different corporate structure from Multi's one-store/one corporation set up: They all used a separate subsidiary on a state-by-state basis. One corporation in each state ran *all* the stores in that state. (They apparently either hadn't been informed of the surtax-exemption advantage; or they thought it wouldn't work for them.) I already knew Multi's numbers such as inventory levels; sales; and bottom-line profits. The annual projected per-store profit number (which turned out to be an important detail) was $25,000.

Federal Corporate Taxes

*"For want of a better word, I call my idea
'taxes.' And here's the way it works."*

The federal corporate income-tax rate formula at the time (it has varied over the years) was a two-level arrangement: The first $25,000 was taxed at 22% and all income/profits over $25,000 paid an additional surtax of 26%. Congress intended this arrangement as a benefit for "small businesses," namely those with profits less than $25,000. Thus the larger corporations paid tax at the effective rate of 48% on all income over $25,000 per year. The smaller businesses that earned less than $25,000 were exempt from the second level of tax – they enjoyed a "surtax exemption." And then there was this happy coincidence: The typical projected profit at each Multi location was $25,000 – exactly the amount of the tax law break-point above which the surtax kicked. This coincidence was just too clear to miss.

Wouldn't it be nice, I thought, if each and every Multi location could be run by a separate corporation, just as Multi had been doing from the outset? Each subsidiary would file its own tax return; show the $25,000 profit; and be taxed at the 22% level. Multi's *entire* business could enjoy the surtax exemption. Yes, wouldn't it be nice! Although no competitor used this one-store/one-corporation arrangement, it was worth investigating.[1] And so I dove into the tax law – I became an instant, but amateur Tax Attorney and refreshed the basic stuff I'd learned in my law school tax courses.

Probably the most basic principle I was reminded of was this: Any business arrangement with the sole purpose of saving taxes would be disregarded by the IRS. In order to stand up to IRS scrutiny, your arrangement has to have a real business purpose unrelated to just cutting taxes. There had to be some "economic substance" to the arrangement beyond the benefit of tax reduction.[2]

The same theme is repeated in the tax law itself – I even got to a crucial section of the tax law, Section 1551. That was the section of the Internal Revenue Code that prescribed how to (and how not to!) set up these separate subsidiary corporations if you expected the benefits of the multiple surtax exemption, keeping each subsidiary at the 22% tax rate. Under Sec. 1551, to enjoy that exemption, Multi, the parent company, in setting up its subsidiaries, must not transfer "property." It could transfer only cash. That was easy!

Section 1551 then falls back on the above-mentioned "business purpose" requirement when cash is transferred into a subsidiary; Multi would lose the multiple surtax-exemption benefit unless it could establish by a clear preponderance of the evidence that the securing of such benefits was not a major purpose of such transfer.

There are, of course, other business benefits to having separate subsidiary corporations. The major one is the limitation of liability. In many instances Multi, as sole shareholder of its subsidiaries, would typically not be held liable for obligations of those separate corporations. Also, filing state taxes is much simplified if your corporation in each state files its own return, eliminating the process of allocating Multi's total corporate income among its subsidiaries to satisfy each and every state's allocation formulas and having to deal with all those states' taxing authorities and pesky audits, each one seeking an ever greater share of the parent company's taxable income. But apparently the chain discount store industry as a whole deemed these reasons for a store-by-store multi-corporate structure inadequate. They didn't consider those factors of limited liability and simplified state-tax filings as being enough of a real business purpose to justify a one-store/one-corporation setup. At least that's what the retail discount-store industry seemed to have concluded, since it appeared that they had uniformly organized their corporate business with a single subsidiary corporation in each state where they had any stores, and that subsidiary ran *all* the stores in that state.

And so the problem (which client was not yet aware of) and the challenge was to find a "business purpose" strong enough to justify that ideal, the one-store/one-corporation setup which could keep almost *all* of Multi's income at the 22% level.

II. The Solution "Magically" Appears!

If there were a good business reason for issuing stock in each subsidiary to the manager of that subsidiary's store, that should justify a one-store / one-corporation structure.

I asked Multi's President (and major shareholder) how he felt about issuing stock in each subsidiary corporation to the store manager – admittedly rather odd in a business where the manager was not a highly paid "executive" in some fancy office, but more of a hands-on supervisor and jack-of-all-trades on the sales floor. The President said he'd never seen it done.

"But we do hand out year-end checks," he reminded me. "A bonus for high performance by store managers." He urged me to attend the upcoming annual meeting of Multi Store Managers where I witnessed the annual Bonus Awards Ceremony. There I learned how Multi's Manager's Bonus Plan worked:

First, each store reported annually its (i) sales, increases in sales and sales trends, (ii) payroll costs as a percentage of sales; and (iii) "shrinkage" (shoplifting, other unaccounted for merchandise losses), also as a percentage of sales. From all these data, a "median profitability" figure was established for the entire chain. Managers whose data were above the line got a bonus, the amount depending on how far over the median they achieved. When I learned all this, that's when the light-bulb went off: Let's turn the Manager's Bonus Plan into a Cash/Stock Bonus Plan. After I explained the idea and the prize (multiple surtax exemptions), the President agreed to this new Plan. I cautioned him that we might go through all this work and planning (and expense!), it might not succeed in Multi enjoying a surtax exemption for each and every Multi subsidiary. There wasn't much hesitation – the President said, "I'll take that chance." And thus was born The Multi Store Managers Cash/Stock Bonus Plan, which worked like this:

1- The award formula (as outlined above) would stay in place.
2- A manager who earned a bonus would get shares of stock in his store's corporation for 60% of the bonus; and 40% would be paid in cash (to cover taxes owed on the bonus). And if the manager needed more cash, he could use his stock as collateral and Multi would make an interest-free loan against the value of his stock. (A very popular feature!)

For purposes of the Plan, each Multi subsidiary corporation created a special **Class B Common Non-Voting Stock** so as not to interfere with Multi's continued total management control over its subsidiaries. But other than being non-voting, this Class B stock had all the other financial features of the Class A Common, all of which Multi held.

Remembering those words in Section 1551 prescribing the "how-to" aspect of adopting the plan, the Multi Directors Meeting Minutes provided expressly that the major and sole purpose of the new multi-corporate structure was to enable the new Managers Cash/Stock Bonus Plan to operate – a genuine business purpose: Give each store manager an incentive to make his store more profitable and his ownership stake in his subsidiary corporation become more valuable. The important employee-incentive feature was emphasized. I hoped that those Minutes would also, by negative inference, make it clear to the IRS that tax benefits were not the motivation behind the multi-corporate, one-corporation / one-store structure. Nowhere in the tax statute did it say what was obvious: The tax break was intended to benefit small businesses, ones that earned less than $25,000 a year, and not a corporation that owned one hundred such small businesses – a prime example of a loophole in the tax law that violated the spirit of the law, what the Congress really intended.

" You need to stay within the spirit of the loophole. '

Multi's accountants had no problems and the store managers seemed pleased. Indeed, some of them piled up a six-figure net worth in their stock, which was paid out to them in cash when they left Multi. So everyone was pleased all around – everyone, that is, except the IRS, but we'll get to that.

But before we get to that, here's a little exchange I observed at another one of those Annual Managers Awards Dinners after the Plan had gone into effect; it showed that the intended incentive effect was working – evidence of the reality of this new Plan:

A nice young man – Manager of one of the Illinois stores – approached Multi's President, sitting next to me at the head table and he leaned in to say: "You know, boss, since I got that stock, things have changed. Before I used to walk the store and if I saw some damaged package, I'd toss it into the bin for discard or return, whatever. Now I feel like an owner and I carry a roll of Scotch® tape and I patch up those packages and put them right back on the shelf." I was pleased to hear that my suggestion, whose object had been to keep taxes down, was, in fact, creating positive incentives and serving Multi's business objectives. I felt comfortable that this would meet the requirements of Sec. 1551 of the tax law by providing a major non-tax related business purpose for a multiple-corporate-subsidiary structure.

III. The IRS Disagrees . . . At First

After a couple of years of each store/subsidiary filing separate tax returns and reporting as income only that store's income, Multi's total tax liability was very close to the base 22% rate – all as a result of enjoying the surtax exemption for each of its subsidiary corporations. Then the inevitable IRS audit of several past years occurred. IRS called the arrangement invalid and recalculated Multi's federal income tax at the 48% level for all Multi's income over $25,000.

At an IRS conference, I explained the situation to the IRS Agent: Multi absolutely needed the separate corporate setup in order to provide an additional incentive by giving each store manager a sense of ownership (with that stock certificate issued in his name) and to relate each manager's compensation to the bottom line produced in his store. All for naught; the Agent denied Multi's right to file taxes separately for each of its many corporations. I appealed up to the next level and again – Denied!

IV. The IRS Finally Backs Off and Multi's Tax Rate Stays at 22% !

I then took the matter to the next step, the IRS Appellate Division, atop the local Federal Building and met with a very bright, pipe-smoking IRS tax expert, (TE). TE reviewed with me – step by step – the company's need for multiple corporations for its Stock/Cash Bonus Plan to work and the process by which I had set up Multi's subsidiaries – all in accordance with every applicable section of the Internal Revenue Code and the Regulations. I pointed out that Multi had transferred no property, just cash to start up (remember Sec. 1551?) and that each subsidiary corporation maintained its own separate bank account and check book; each subsidiary had its own Board of Directors and set of officers and met all the formal requirements of a separate and independent corporation. Separateness was the order of the day!

But most important was Multi's independent, sound business reason for having all these 100 subsidiary corporations: It was the best way Multi could incentivize each manager by giving them not just cash or some abstract award or certificate to hang on the wall, but another kind of certificate, a stock certificate representing his direct owner's stake in the success of his store – a piece of equity ownership that could grow in value as long as the store was profitable. And I was prepared and could demonstrate the real, growing value of stock ownership that a number of successful store managers had already enjoyed since the Plan was put in place. Stock-incentive plans were coming into popularity with many large public companies, so why not at Multi. (I even tried to relate to TE that experience with the Illinois store manager I'd seen at the annual managers' meeting and how the Plan changed his attitude after he became "an owner." TE shushed me with a wave of the hand.)

I offered to show TE a copy of the minutes of a Multi Directors Meeting where they expressly recognized the value of having these store managers, geographically remote from the home office, become "owners," incentivized to give their best to maximize profit. I offered TE a copy of the corporate minutes of some sample subsidiaries adopting and ratifying the Managers Cash/Stock Bonus Plan. I asked if he wanted to see the sample Class B Common Stock Certificate. I was being, as we all must be in the presence of IRS people, respectful and cooperative. Again, TE waved all this aside, impatiently. "Naw, I don't need to see all that stuff," and he gave me a knowing half-smile. I put the papers back in my briefcase. Silence.

TE furrowed his brow and took a long draw on his pipe, leaning his desk chair way back and looking at the ceiling. More silence. Then he swiveled his chair and looked out the window, down toward a building on the other side of Cambridge Street and the ground-floor retail stores. I could swear he was looking directly at a Fanny Farmer Candy Store, a chain with over 400 stores. Then he mused, half to himself and half out loud – to me?

"So if someone went through this process as you've done, step-by-step, with the cash transfer and all these other things you've done, a gigantic chain-store operation of 300 or 400 – or more – stores would be paying tax at the 22% rate?" "Sure," I replied and then asked, "Don't you agree?"

TE suddenly speeded up a bit: He closed his file and, disregarding my last question, he said "I don't want to litigate this." He stood up, extended his hand for a goodbye hand-shake. Appeal Allowed. Yay!

––––

I drove back to Multi's office. I was drained after that session – I always am when my work is put to a "real-world" test. Time to talk turkey with the Boss, the President:

"I've got good news and bad news," I said. "We're okay on the multi-corporate subsidiary setup *today* with respect to those subsidiaries that were audited – the guy at IRS Appellate won't contest it – he's overruling his Agents and the first appeals level. That's the good news.

"The bad news: It can't last. A 100-store chain – a huge business – taking advantage of a loophole, a tax break meant to benefit small businesses is not what Congress intended. What you're getting away with, as long as it lasts, is called an 'abuse' by the tax people; and I'm sure that the law will be corrected as soon as the Congress gets around to it. In your favor is that there doesn't seem to be anybody else in the discount-store industry who's doing what you are with your Managers Cash/Stock Bonus Plan to justify a multi-corporate subsidiary organization. So enjoy it while you're still flying under the radar, but remember, it's only a matter of time. When this 'abuse' becomes a bit more public, it will end and you'll lose the surtax exemption."

Sure enough, some years later, Congress said what it meant in the first place but failed to express: They amended the tax-rate structure provisions so that if a corporation is a component member of a controlled group (like Multi), it would have only one surtax exemption (i.e., tax effectively at the 22% rate) which had to be shared by *all* the component members of that controlled group – no exemption for each subsidiary, as Multi had enjoyed for the past years. Translated into English: Under this amendment, Multi and its subsidiary corporations constituted a "controlled group" and each subsidiary constituted a "component member." This whole gang now had but a single surtax exemption, which had to be shared by *all* of Multi's subsidiaries. So from that time on, each Multi subsidiary lost its own surtax-free $25,000 taxable profit benefit; and Multi had to pay taxes, just like any other large corporation, on *all* the net profits of *all* its subsidiaries at the then 48% corporate rate.

P.S. The benefits of the Cash/Stock Bonus Plan lasted through Multi's initial public offering (**IPO**) at which time and because of the after-tax earnings formula for determining per-share price in the **IPO**, the multiple surtax exemption tax savings accounted for over 7% of the **IPO** stock price. Mission accomplished!

NOTE: This Tale also illustrates the risk-shifting strategy you'll read about in Part II of *SOLVED!* Recall the words of the IRS Appellate Division's TE when he cut short our meeting:

> "I don't want to litigate this."

What those six words told me was that he realized that Multi's case was strong enough for us to win and the IRS to lose and create a precedent that others in the industry would pick up on. And recall his glancing down at a Fanny Farmer candy store – a chain much larger than Multi's – and his thinking out loud: "So if someone went through this process as you've done, step-by-step, with the cash transfer and all these other things you've done, a gigantic chain-store operation of 300 or 400 – or more – stores would be paying tax at the 22% rate?" He did not want to risk losing in court and opening a Pandora's box for the IRS with other retail chain-stores adopting a multi-corporate structure. So he gave us a pass and left it to Congress to correct the faulty tax law.

And, indeed, some years later Congress corrected the tax law to eliminate this loophole and to say what they'd meant to say: "The legislative history of the new amendment made clear that its purpose was to eliminate surtax exemption advantages for large enterprises having multi-coporate structures.[3] Congress finally got it right!

"Now that we've agreed on the loopholes, should we start drafting the amendment?"

Some Thoughts on the Moral Aspects of Taking Advantage of Loopholes in the Tax Law, Cutting Your Taxes, Accounting "Tricks" and the Like

The oft-quoted words of the great jurist, Federal Judge Learned Hand:

> "Anyone may arrange his affairs so that his taxes shall be as low as possible; he is not bound to choose that pattern which best pays the treasury. There is not even a patriotic duty to increase one's taxes. Over and over again the Courts have said that there is nothing sinister in so arranging affairs as to keep taxes as low as possible.

Everyone does it, rich and poor alike and all do right, for nobody owes any public duty to pay more than the law demands."[4]

Those last three words, ". . . the law demands," is where these situations must be corrected. Just as parties to a contract must clearly and with particularity express their intentions and expectations in their business-transaction documents, so also must the legislatures and regulation writers write their laws and regulations with crystal clarity. The simple understanding that an intended beneficiary of some law or subsidy, etc., namely, a "small" company, can be owned and controlled by a giant company should not have been difficult for Congress to foresee. Indeed the correction of the surtax statute proved simple enough using the concept of a small corporation which is a "component member" of a "controlled group."

Another view of such situations comes from a moral and ethical standpoint, as exemplified in the title to an article in *Fortune* magazine[5]: "Just Because Tax Avoidance is Legal Doesn't Mean It's Right" (dealing with use of "shell companies in overseas tax havens" and the like). High on the list of solutions is the strategic draftsmanship applied in writing the law; the author's words: "toughen the existing tax code." But in the end, those moral-ethical issues in tax planning are for the client to decide. The planning lawyers do not, I believe, face any such issues so long as they follow the letter of the law.

Lawmakers Are Still Making the Same Mistakes : Case #1 – FCC Spectrum Sales . . .

Laws and regulations were still coming out of Washington in 2015 which are imperfect and do not work as intended, as illustrated by the opening line of a *Wall Street Journal* op-ed piece[6], similar in many ways to the Multi situation in this Tale #4:

Should the federal government hand out more than $3 billion from American taxpayers to a Fortune 500 company as part of a program to help small and disadvantaged businesses compete with large corporations? Of course not, but it's about to happen.

This piece focuses on a major telecom ($14 billion annual revenue) which owned the controlling interest in two companies. Each of these corporations reported to FCC that they were a "very small business" with no gross revenues. This enabled these "little" companies to bid at the FCC broadband spectrum auction (with the benefit of the Federal "small business" subsidy of 25%) and win in that auction by bidding astronomical sums. Maybe this administrative fiasco will be corrected, but the *Wall Street Journal* authors tell us "don't hold your breath." And "Congress should conduct oversight and put an end to this corporate welfare."

In defense of Multi's actions, they were already operating in a multi-corporate structure for sound business reasons; all I did was find an advantageous tax law; Multi did not form subsidiaries to avoid taxes. The giant telecom did just that to take advantage of Federal subsidies not intended for them.

This Tale and the spectrum-auction examples in the footnotes are not unique. Back in 2014 it was reported how "Older Firms Benefit From Startup Rules."[7] The Subchapter S rules, intended to let small corporations operate and be taxed like a partnership (avoiding taxes on the corporation) ended up also benefitting large corporations. A 1960 article explains it in detail.[8]

If the tax law dealing with surtax exemptions had contained a preamble – those "Whereas…" clauses I favor in contracts (see, e.g., BLT #32b, p. 267 in Tale 29) – I would not have been so certain of the outcome here. If the Congress had said right up at the beginning of the statute, for example, "In order to promote and benefit small businesses – those earning less than $25,000 annually – they are hereby granted an exemption from surtaxes and shall be taxed only at the base rate, all as hereinafter provided…," there would probably have been no Cash/Stock Bonus Plan. But, alas, Congress did not heed the words of Supreme Court Justice Joseph Story, who favored preambles in legislation.[9]

The lesson, oft-repeated in these pages: Say what you mean and mean what you say. Just as businesspeople and their lawyers must learn to make clear their intentions and expectations from a deal, those who write the laws for Congress must do the same. Otherwise, there are legal loopholes which it is our duty, as lawyers, to explain to our business clients and if the loopholes provide an opportunity for tax savings, to give clients the choice of taking advantage of those loopholes if they wish.

Case #2: A Judge Is Slapped Down for Going Beyond the Words of the Statute

This next story involves a case[10] that I appealed to the U.S. Supreme Court (and won!) back when I was a young lawyer, in the early sixties. (The story is set out in more detail in the Postlogue, but let me repeat the basics to make the point here about clarity of meaning and intention; and how judges look at these issues:)

Mother was ill; father asked daughter to care for her and made an oral promise to daughter that he would not make a will so that she would collect her intestate share of his estate under the state's **intestacy laws**. After mother died, father remarried and broke his oral promise to his daughter – he made a will leaving all to his second wife. The **statute of frauds** in Massachusetts provided expressly that in order to be enforceable, a promise to make a will must be in writing; it said nothing about a promise *not* to make a will.

In 1933, the Federal District Court in Massachusetts court ruled that the **statute of frauds** does *not* apply to a promise to destroy a will – it applies only to what is written in the law: a promise to make a will. One judge dissented, saying:

> I cannot doubt that what the [Massachusetts] Legislature *had in mind* by the expression, 'No agreement to make a will,' etc., was really, 'No agreement about making a will,' etc. . . . Where the object of a statute is clearly evident, but the language used is inappropriate, a considerable liberality of construction is admissible to support *the intended result.*"[11] [emphasis is mine]

That dissenting judge was going beyond the words of the statute and doing some mind-reading as to what he thought the Legislature intended; and then he would interpret the law to cover what he believed they intended – all this without any regard to the absence of any indication of such intent in the words of the statute. Sometimes lawyers can win making this "intent of the legislature" argument, but don't count on it without some "hard" evidence such as legislative history, committee reports, and the like.

When my case of the father-to-daughter promise was in the trial court, that court decided to follow the dissenting judge's opinion and dismissed the case because the father's promise not to make a will was oral; and under that trial court's view, the **statute of frauds** meant to deal with any "agreement about making a will" (per the old-case dissenting opinion). The trial court, in effect, disregarded the wording of the statute of frauds, which was limited to *making a will.*

After the U.S. Supreme Court sent my case back to the First Circuit Court of Appeals, it had to review that trial court's decision which looked to the presumed intent of the legislature; and they reversed the trial court, preferring to stick to the words of the **Statute of Frauds** and not get into mind-reading the Legislature:

> The present agreement [not to make a will] is not in terms within the statute. Nor is it by implication. Accordingly, if the legislature meant by 'no agreement about making a will' or 'no agreement to make or not to make a will,' we think it is for it [i.e., the Legislature] and not for us, to say.[12]

So let's end on this note: Although cases have been won by this mind-reading argument – "I know what you meant, although you didn't say it, ..." – more often than not you'll face the words of the judge like the one who found a contract unclear and incomplete and "so vague and ambiguous as to render it unenforceable." That court went on to say:

> Although the Court can perhaps guess that Plaintiff meant to prohibit solicitation or contact for the purpose of employment elsewhere, the provision does not so specify. . . . the Court will not

redraft a poorly written, overbroad restraint in order to render it enforceable. . . ."[13]

Don't depend on some judge assuming what you meant when you didn't clearly express what you meant – Say what you mean and mean what you say!

---

1 A multi-corporate arrangement was commonly used in other industries. Indeed, in the chain movie theatre business, they might have more than a single separate corporation covering the various business activities at each location such as 1-Movie ticket sales; 2-Advertising income; 3-Concessions, popcorn, etc.

2 U.S. Tax Court put it nicely:

> The tax law . . . requires that the intended transactions have economic substance separate and distinct from economic benefit achieved solely by tax reduction. The doctrine of economic substance becomes applicable, and a judicial remedy is warranted, where a taxpayer seeks to claim tax benefits, unintended by Congress, by means of transactions that serve no economic purpose other than tax savings.
> *ACM Partnership v. Commissioner*, 73 TCM at 2215

And then the Federal Court of Appeals wrote:

Business purpose doctrine

A common law doctrine that often is considered together with the economic substance doctrine is the business purpose doctrine. The business purpose doctrine involves an inquiry into the subjective motives of the taxpayer – that is, whether the taxpayer intended the transaction to serve some useful non-tax purpose. In making this determination, some courts have bifurcated a transaction in which activities with non-tax objectives have been combined with unrelated activities having only tax-avoidance objectives, in order to disallow the tax benefits of the overall transaction.

ACM Partnership v. Commissioner, 157 F.3d at 256, n. 48. Other expressions of this standard are the "substance-over-form" test and the "sham-transaction" test. This area is examined in detail in the context of the so-called "tax shelters" of the late 1990s and early 2000s. See "Tax Shelters or Efficient Tax Planning? A Theory of the Firm Perspective on the Economic Substance Doctrine" by T. Christopher Borek, Angelo Frattarelli and Oliver Hart, 57 *J.of Law and Economics* 975 (Nov. 2014).

3 See James E. Skeen, "Federal Income Taxation-Disallowance of Surtax Exemption to Brother-Sister Corporations-Stock Ownership Test Under Sections 1551 and 1563," 1976 BYU L.Rev. 1000 (1976). Available at: http://digitalcommons.law.byu.edu/lawreview/vol1976/iss4/1

4 *Gregory v. Helvering,* 69 F.2d 809, 810 (2d Cir. 1934), aff'd, 293 U.S. 465, 55 S.Ct. 266, 79 L.Ed. 596 (1935)

5 *Fortune* contributor and a *New Yorker* magazine staff writer, John Cassidy, in *Fortune* magazine, July 1, 2013, p. 42

6 "Ending Welfare for Telecom Giants" by Sen. Kelly Ayotte (*R., N.H.*) and FCC Member Ajit Pai, *Wall St. Jnl* February 5, 2015, p A13. Related is the April 28, 2015 headline in the *Wall St. Jnl,* p. B2: "FCC Looks Into Dish Bids," relating how the industry giant "claimed $3.3 billion in discounts aimed at small businesses" by bankrolling two tiny companies to place all the winning bids in the spectrum auctions.

7 *Wall St. Jnl,* September 25, 2014, p. B1: The JOBS Act, intended to help startups, was used by "an unexpectedly broad range of players" hoping "to gain an edge under the new law." Unintended consequences? But a noted authority on corporate law, Professor John C. Coffee Jr., Professor of Securities Law at Columbia, described the use of the new rules (intended to benefit startups) by publicly traded companies as "perfectly permissible."

8 William P. Cunningham, *Subchapter S Corporations: Uses, Abuses, and Some Pitfalls,* 20 Md. L. Rev. 195 (1960)
Available at: http://digitalcommons.law.umaryland.edu/mlr/vol20/iss3/2. Other laws providing for set-asides or preferences have also been abused and the abusers in some cases charged with criminal fraud. Google "women-owned small business contracting program abuse misuse" and "EB-5 program misused abused by developers;" and see *Fortune Small Business* magazine, "Preferential contracting made easy" available at money.cnn.com/2008/03/14/smbusiness/sba_set_asides.fsb/.

9 Joseph Story, *Commentaries on the Constitution,* 1:§459 (1833): § 459. "The importance of examining the preamble, for the purpose of expounding the language of a statute, has been long felt, and universally conceded in all juridical discussions. It is an admitted maxim in the ordinary course of the administration of justice, that the preamble of a statute is a

key to open the mind of the makers, as to the mischiefs, which are to be remedied, and the objects, which are to be accomplished by the provisions of the statute." (Now there's a succinct lesson in determining the intent of the legislature!)

10 *Foman v. Davis,* 371 *U.S.* 178, 182 (1962).

11 *Cleaves v. Kenney,* 63 F.2d 682 (1st Cir. 1933).

12 *Foman v. Davis,* 316 F.2d 254, 257 (1st Cir. 1963).

13 *Base One Techs., Inc. v. Ali,* 2015 U.S. Dist. LEXIS 5821; January 20, 2015, Civil Action No. 14-1520 (JEB).

TALE # 5

CHANGE "GROSS" INTO "NET" WITH THE STROKE OF
PEN –AND SAVE LOTS OF MONEY.

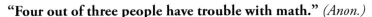

"Four out of three people have trouble with math." *(Anon.)*

I. The Client's Problem

Sometimes, clients make a bad deal and then need help to get out of it. I learned about this landlord client's bad deal long after he'd made it: He'd built and now owned a downtown office building with a large underground parking garage. The building was part of a city-sponsored redevelopment project and so Landlord made the typical redevelopment-project real estate tax deal with the city: he would pay the City

"in lieu of real estate taxes 22% of gross revenues received from the building."

A few years later Landlord refinanced the building with an institutional lender, not with a typical mortgage loan, but under a "ground-lease" (**sale-and-leaseback** arrangement), and his repayments were similar to the City deal:

"10% of gross revenues received from operation of the building."

And so it was that 32% of Landlord's gross revenues was going out to the City and the lender, right off the top. But after a few years, Landlord realized that he had a problem with these deals he'd made – that problem was the building's garage – a large parking facility under the building.

He asked me to come by to talk. I sat opposite him at his desk. He held his head in his hands. He was slowly shaking his head. "I wasn't thinking. I was ready to pay on the gross from this building – an *office building*! I didn't even think about the garage. It's like a separate business – and I forgot all about it." (And apparently, neither the City officials nor the lender had thought about the garage separate and apart from the building. No mention of the garage in any of the documents.)

I felt badly for this good guy, a very bright man. I said, "Look, you know what I always say, . . . " he interrupted me, "Yeah, yeah, I know. If you'll lose it, don't raise it."

"Right. If you'd raised the matter of the garage in negotiations, you know what would have happened." He looked up, this time nodding his head. "I'd have lost – they'd insist that gross is gross and the garage gross receipts would have been included. But what can we do about it now? Right now I'm paying out 32% of every penny that comes into that garage, and that's on top of the expenses – I'm also paying all the expenses! Payroll and benefits for a lot of attendants around the clock; tickets and supplies; cleaning; utilities; repair and maintenance and painting . . . See what you can do about it, please." I went back to my office to check the documents and see if something could be done.

Thinking through this situation, I saw that it had three components: (i) the tax deal with the City; (ii) the ground lease with the lender; and (iii) the operating deal with the parking garage operator. The first two deals were cast in stone. The deal with the garage operator was the only "moving part" I might tinker with. The first thought was to sublease the garage to the operator and, properly documented, he could "net out" parking receipts. (Under a sublease arrangement, the garage operator would collect all the parking fees; then pay all the expenses out of garage receipts (including his own operator's fee) and then pay Client the balance, which would be net of all expenses.) But this route was not possible; on checking the 80-page ground lease document, I found an express prohibition against subleasing any portions of the building. Was there another solution? How could client "net out" the garage receipts?

II. The Solution
I thought I had the solution – some arrangement I could offer Landlord – one with the same effect as a sublease, but not a sublease. Instead, a "license." I drafted a document, which I called "Parking Garage Operating and Management License Agreement." The license agreement approach should work as a way to net out the parking receipts number by deducting garage expenses *before* arriving at the amount paid to Client. (I understood that "calling a dog a cat doesn't make it a cat" – that's how courts look at the reality of a transaction.[1])

You should understand the similarity, but also the difference between a license – the way I was going – and a sublease, which was not permitted under Client's financing deal with lender. Let me explain:

In law, a "license" is different from a "lease" or "sublease." A license grants permission, for example in real estate, a license or right to use or pass over a piece of land or use a pathway is an **easement**. This legal device – the "license" – was definitely different from a lease or a sublease. The same concept is used in a patent license, for example, which grants permission to use the patented technology. A license arrangement is also sometimes used in hotel management/licenses and for in-building parking garages between the building owner and the garage operator.

In exchange for this license to operate the garage and earn his Fee under the License Agreement, the Garage Operator would pay Landlord a License Fee, "calculated per Schedule A." Schedule A (see p.67), was a simple Operating or Profit & Loss Statement. Top line, gross cash receipts from garage operations. Next, a list of all expenses (including the Operator's Fee). Next, the total of all expenses was deducted from the top line to produce that bottom-line figure. That amount (Landlord's gross receipts from the garage operation) was entered into Landlord's Cash Receipts Account; that cash was deposited in Landlord's bank account; and that amount was reported (along with office-tenant rental receipts) to the City and the Lender as "Gross Receipts." The City got 22% and the Lender 10% of that bottom-line amount. It was time to get the accountants' approval. To sum up:

"We are neither hunters nor gatherers. We are accountants."

Landlord already had a simple existing agreement with the garage operator (an old friend), who was being paid an operator's fee. My revision of their agreement would make no change in their financial or economic deal – garage operator would end up earning the same under the new agreement as he did under his existing agreement with Landlord. But the amount received by Client Landlord would be net of all those garage operating expenses. The new agreement provided that the amount paid to Client Landlord was "calculated in accordance with the attached Schedule A." The bottom line of Schedule A (a figure net of all these expenses) would thus become part of the "gross revenue" received by Landlord from the garage operation in his building. Remember, this was the figure he had to report to the City (and pay them 22%) and to the lender/ground lessor (and pay them 10%).

———

Since Client's books of account were subject to audit by both the City and the lender, I had to ensure that client's accountants would agree and this license fee figure would go into the "gross revenue" statement when calculating both (i) real estate taxes to the City and (ii) ground rent paid to the ground Landlord/lender instead of the total receipts coming into the garage. (Sample of the Schedule A form is set out at the end of this Tale.)

I submitted this new arrangement to Landlord for his review. From our years of working together, I knew him to be one of the most honorable and ethical businesspeople I'd ever dealt with, as he'd demonstrated over the years. I explained to Landlord that the new arrangement was changing the way he'd been reporting "gross receipts" to City and his lender – and asked if he wanted to go this route. I warned him that the City or the lender or both might object – this was no "slam-dunk." Landlord said he was willing to take that chance:

"This is a fairer deal and I'll stand by that. And what happens if they object? If I'm in breach of my ground lease, I get notice and a time to cure, right?" Landlord asked. I nodded "yes."

"And if the City has any problems, we can deal with those if and when they arise. I like this new arrangement; it's fairer. Let's go with it, but check it out with the accountants".

Landlord's chief financial officer said he had no problem. "Cash coming in from the garage operator would be cash deposit into our bank account and booked as the 'gross receipts' which we report to the City and the lender." I then went to Landlord's outside CPA auditors; they also gave their blessing. For income reporting purposes, the license fee received from the parking garage operator would simply be added to "gross receipts" from the rental income from the rest of the building in their financial reports to both the City and to the ground-lessor/lender.

Once the License Agreement was signed by Landlord and the parking garage operator, the matter was out of my hands. It never came back to my desk again. The new arrangement went into effect and nothing was ever heard from either the ground lessor or from the City real estate tax authorities or their auditors, who periodically reviewed Landlord's books. Looking back, my guess is that in the overall financial picture of the office building and given fluctuating office-space rental rates, the change in the amount of "gross receipts" reported was so insignificant that no one checked or noticed the changed numbers. And so for many years Landlord saved 32% of all those annual costs and expenses of running its garage. He'd made a bad deal, but didn't know it at the time, and was lucky to be able to get out of it and go forward under what he saw as a fair arrangement.

What I Learned from Writing About This Tale
In my original draft of this Tale I asked, "What could the City taxing authority and the Lender have done to avoid this situation." My answer back then, "Nothing," came too soon. I hadn't really thought it through at the time, but now, with the book completed, I've come back and I have a new answer. Whether it can used in other situations remains to be seen – I suspect it can.

"They presented us with an ironclad contract that we were able to totally reinterpret."

What the City and the Lender Could Have Done

They could have asked for a model or template for Landlord's reporting of Gross Sales and included that as an exhibit to their respective contracts. That model or template would be derived from Landlord's books of account, more particularly the Cash Receipts Book. Presumably that would show total receipts from the operation of the in-building parking garage – presumably a figure taken right off the ticket-spitting machine and confirmed by the daily bank deposits made by the parking garage operator.

Then next step: The tax agreement with the City and the loan documents with the Lender could have contained a provision something like this:

> For the purpose of reporting Gross Receipts under the herein Tax Agreement/Loan Documents, Landlord shall substantially follow the format of Exhibit X and certify to the City/Lender that he has done so and without any changes or alterations of any kind or nature whatsoever.

This approach, in effect, sets out an express example of the City's and the Lender's expectations and, it is important to note, an example with a high level of detail and specificity. But in truth, as a practical matter, one could not expect the City or the Lender to anticipate exactly what Landlord did in this case – in effect he produced a post-contracting unilateral amendment of the City's tax deal agreement and the Lender's loan documents. Indeed, since he was never questioned after he made his new arrangement with the parking garage operator, it would appear that neither the City nor the Lender were even aware of what had happened.

I'd love to hear from any readers whether they can discern a generalized lesson from this Tale #5. More particularly, what action should a party in the position of the City or the Lender take when they make their agreements with the Landlord in order to avoid what happened here, i.e., "gross" became "net."

But … if you think it through, my guess is that unless such a template or model Gross Receipts Reporting Form actually anticipated the exact changed arrangement as was done in this Tale, Landlord may still have been able to do what was done here and convert Gross into Net with the stroke of a pen – create, in effect, a unilateral amendment of their contract long after that contract was signed.

III. What Went Wrong?
Nothing…

…except that maybe Client-Landlord should have "run the numbers" in advance in his tax deal with the City and the mortgagee/ground-lessor lender. Ideally, you try to anticipate problems like these and deal with them during negotiations. But as noted above and as I told Client at our first meeting (and he agreed): If he had raised the issue during negotiations, the city and the ground-lessor/lender would not have agreed to netting out parking garage receipts. "Gross is gross," they would have said – what do you think? But this leads nicely into the . . .

BLT #5: A pointer on negotiating techniques

That last question – whether the City and the lender would have allowed garage expenses to be deducted from gross receipts – raises a useful point in negotiating techniques: Don't raise an issue that you're almost certain to lose on. Usually (I almost never say "always" and almost never say "never"!), you're better off leaving that "loser" issue unaddressed for decision another day. So if you think you'll lose it, don't raise it. Maybe deal with it later; or deal with it never. Let's leave it at that.

— —

Here's that schedule that converted "gross" into "net" and as accepted by all auditors:

Parking Garage Schedule A

Parking receipts: _____$_____

Less: Operating expenses:

    Payroll:

    Utilities:

    Repairs & Maintenance:

    Supplies:

    Parking Operator Fee: [Remember, this was unchanged from the existing arrangement between Landlord and the parking operator.]

    Miscellaneous:

Total operating expenses to be deducted

from Parking Receipts⁻..$_____

Gross receipts from garage operation_____- $_____

And it was just this last, bottom-line figure that the accountants included in their report of the gross receipts from the garage operation.

---

1 In some instances courts will disregard labels lawyers put on things. If a transaction in reality creates a lease or sublease (which in law is called an interest in real estate), a court will not be fooled by the parties' calling it a "license" (which is merely permission). Judges prefer to call a spade a spade, i.e. they will call a sublease a sublease, and disregard what they perceive to be a phony label. See, e.g. *Morrisville Shopping Center, Inc. vs Sun Ray Drug Co.,* 381 Pa. 576, at 584, 112 A.2d 183, 1955 Pa. LEXIS 517 (Pa. 1955):

> The device or subterfuge of calling a sublease a license or any other name cannot suffice to change its real nature or the real agreement which the parties entered into, nor relieve them from the legal consequences of their agreements.

But in Client's case, the essential element of a sublease – a transfer of an interest in land, namely a leasehold interest –, is *not* what happened. The garage operator got no interest in the real estate, just permission to operate the garage for a fee. That's clearly a license to operate, and thus, "License Agreement" was clearly a supportable characterization of the relationship. In Client's situation, he had nothing to lose and was willing to accept the risk that his "License Agreement" would be re-characterized as a sub-lease (and therefore in violation of the financing ground lease) or objected to by the City taxing authority or his lender/ ground lessor. Many garage operating agreements were and still are done as "licenses" and so this revised arrangement was well within the limits of typical business-law practice customs between building owners and garage operators. Remember: A sublease transfers an interest in real estate. A license is merely permission to – in this case – operate the parking garage.

PART II

USING INCENTIVES AND RISK-SHIFTING TO ACHIEVE YOUR COMPANY'S GOALS.

Our focus in some of these Tales is how to use incentives and risk-shifting, to avoid this common business situation: You've performed your side of a deal and all that's left is the other side's promise to pay. In the cases that landed on my desk, that money promised wasn't worth 100 cents on the dollar – realistically, it had to be discounted by the costs and expenses of collection efforts and possibly litigation against a recalcitrant party. These nine Tales illustrate some powerful tools to get the other parties to your deals to do what they promised – and without your having to take them to court. By (i) using incentives (and disincentives) and (ii) shifting the risk in any business situation to the other side – creating for them an *unacceptable* risk – you're forcing them to abide by their promise so that you achieve your goal and accomplish what you want done in your deal or relationship. And underlying this approach is always that strategic looking ahead so you can spot those risks; and then, in timely fashion, try to shift them over onto the other party.

A number of other Tales – outside this Part II – illustrate how risk-shifting as well as using incentives can help get your problem *SOLVED!*

"THE GOVERNMENT IS OFFERING US FINANCIAL INCENTIVES TO OFFER OUR STAFF FINANCIAL INCENTIVES TO OFFER OUR CUSTOMERS FINANCIAL INCENTIVES TO COME UP WITH SOME GOOD IDEAS FOR FINANCIAL INCENTIVES."

TALE # 6

WHEN ARE YOU MOST VULNERABLE IN BUSINESS?
AND WHAT CAN YOU DO ABOUT IT?
MONEY OWED ON A CONTRACT MAY NOT BE
WORTH 100 CENTS ON THE DOLLAR.
"WORRISOME" SELLERS AND BUYERS – HOW AN
INCENTIVE ELIMINATED THE "WORRY."

When You're Most Vulnerable to the Contract-Breaker

Almost every business person has experienced it – the hold-up of a nuisance claim or defense, particularly at the tail-end of a deal. Your contract has just about been performed and all that remains is for the other party to pay you money. It's at this stage that you are most vulnerable to a hold-up nuisance claim. And because business people are practical, what usually happens is that instead of receiving the full amount you bargained for, the amount you're owed, the payment is "discounted" – reduced to reflect the cost and risk of litigation if you're forced to go to court to collect.

Let's define the situations I'm talking about here; and also what I'm *not* talking about: Getting paid for an ordinary sale of goods is *not* what I have in mind here. In those situations, the seller typically protects himself, for example:

- You do a credit check on the customer – what's his record for paying in full and on time?
- If concerned, you ensure payment with money in advance; a letter of credit; COD, and the like.

My focus here is the larger deal/transaction, like the sale of a business (as you'll read about in the Tales immediately following). Or other business situations where it's in your interest to ensure that the other side fully and timely performs their contractual obligations. This approach is not rocket science, folks; it's been done routinely for years, for example:

Some Standard Incentive-to-Perform Provisions in Current Use

Certain types of contracts already routinely address this problem:

An installment promissory note contains an acceleration clause. If you miss a single payment, the entire principal balance of the note becomes immediately due and payable. A real incentive to perform on time!

A lease contains the same kind of acceleration clause: If you miss a rental payment, one of Landlord's rights under the Lease may well be to claim for *all* rent for the balance of the term. This may or may not be enforceable in court, but that's not the point. The tenant faces an unpleasant risk, which provides the incentive to pay rent in full and on time.

Another typical "boilerplate" contract provision intended to discourage nuisance or frivolous suits is the "Court Costs and Attorneys' Fees" clause. It provides that if the contracting parties get involved in litigation, the loser pays the winner's "reasonable court expenses, including attorneys' fees" – and these are not small numbers, like $100k+ in attorneys' fees where the case could have been settled for $7k.[1]

In those business situations where it may be hard to put a dollar figure on the injured party's damages (a number which is genuinely difficult or impossible to determine), we routinely insert an agreed figure which the parties may, in advance, put right into their contract in the event of a breach of contract – that number is called liquidated damages.

More About Liquidated Damages: A liquidated-damages clause is used where exact damages are difficult to ascertain and is enforceable in court if it is the parties' reasonable estimation of damages a party would suffer if the other party fails to perform their contractual obligations. The clause will not be enforced if it is disproportionate to the losses and expenses caused by the breach – that figure is dubbed a "penalty" and is unenforceable.

Example: In a typical case of selling your house, the contract may provide for a deposit by the buyer and a total forfeiture of that deposit if would-be buyer fails to close. Typically, a nominal $1,000 deposit would be lost if buyer doesn't close. But if the deposit were one-fourth of the purchase price (and particularly if the house sold almost immediately after buyer's default for seller's asking price), that oversized deposit might well be seen by a court as a penalty and, therefore, unenforceable.[2]

BLT #6: If you use a liquidated damage provision: State in your contract that the parties cannot fix the amount of damages; that the amount of the liquidated damages provided by the contract is the parties' agreed fair and reasonable estimate of what the innocent party would suffer if the contract-breaker fails to perform; and don't be greedy in setting that amount – a figure out of proportion to the numbers in the deal will generally be designated as a "penalty" and will not be enforced by the courts. If, for example, a promissory note called for five times the principal to be paid if one installment were missed, a court would probably not enforce it for the two basic reasons that these type of provisions fail: First, the amount of damages suffered by the holder of the note is fairly clear and can be precisely calculated, so there is no need to resort to liquidated damages; and Second, five times the principal amount of the note is grossly disproportionate. Ruling: This is a penalty and therefore unenforceable.

In this area, the law varies from state to state and sometimes from court to court within a state. If you're concerned about whether your contract will provide for enforceable liquidated damages or an unenforceable penalty, see your lawyer. This is not a DIY project!

Remember what your primary aim is here. It is *not* to provide extreme remedy provisions and risk them being characterized as penalties which courts will *not* enforce. Keep your focus on creating a real incentive for the other party to perform their obligations – they must be made to realize that not performing their obligations puts them at an unacceptable risk. Your object is to make them think twice before breaking the contract – and then not break it. You will have to do some thinking on this problem because each deal or contract will involve a different approach. Ask yourself, what would incentivize the other party to not break their promise and more, to perform their obligations as promised? Your lawyer should be able to help you formulate a provision that (1) the other contracting party will agree to include in the contract; (2) will provide a strong incentive to perform and disincentive to breach; and (3) is not so drastic as to be an unenforceable "penalty."

One Example of the "Self-Enforcing" Approach
A Variable Price Provision Creates an Incentive to Pay in Full and on Time

I. Client's Problem
Client Machinery Dealer Drops a Manufacturer/Supplier's Line
My client is a dealer who carries several brands or lines of machinery, and keeps on hand some machinery of each brand plus a large inventory of parts, all of which he has bought and paid for. Client was dropping XYZ Corp. products line and asked me to prepare "a simple contract" with XYZ Corp., which had agreed to buy back from my client all XYZ machines and parts. XYZ would make payment only after it had received these machines and parts and inspected them. Precisely the kind of situation we're talking about here – my Client would be vulnerable to some claim, real or imagined that would reduce the amount of the payment due. And waiting for payment after inspection is never a happy situation. Client had fully performed and was simply waiting to be paid – that is the vulnerable position we try to avoid.

II. The Solution

I thought I could build in that all-important incentive to pay. I asked Client, "Would you be willing to discount the price by 5% if you got paid in 10 days after XYZ receives the machines and parts?" Without hesitation, Client replied "Sure!" I knew that Client, if not paid, would not want to take back the XYZ machines and parts. All I had to work with was to give XYZ an incentive to pay.

And so I began to play with the price (something you'll see again in the following Tale #7): Lower the price for an early payment and increase it if payment is not received in the 30-day period the parties had agreed to. I explained to Client that I could give no assurance that such a provision would be enforceable in a court of law; certainly not if the bill remained unpaid for a long time and the price increase became so extreme as to become a "penalty," which courts will not enforce. But, as noted above, the primary object is not to create a clearly enforceable consequence for non-payment, but rather to incentivize the buyer, XYZ, to avoid the risks and pay early or on time. I knew that at the very least, Client would be entitled to an interest element on its unpaid money due. Indeed, this might even be cast as an increasing, or at least an increased post-default rate of interest – not uncommon in promissory notes, for example.

I suggested the following price provisions:

#1. The price of the inventory of XYZ engines, parts and tools shall be $100,000 and payable as follows: Payable in full ($100,000) within thirty (30) days after delivery of Inventory to XYZ.

#2. XYZ may elect to pay in full within ten (10) days after such delivery, at the reduced price of $95,000.

If the full purchase price in accordance with either #1. or #2., above is not paid within thirty days after delivery of goods to XYZ, the purchase price shall be increased by five percent (5%) of the unpaid portion of the purchase price for each ten days of delay in payment by XYZ.

If and to the extent all or any part of the Repurchase Price shall remain unpaid after such six-calendar-month period, the amount of the Repurchase Price shall thereafter increase at the rate of 10% of the unpaid portion of the purchase price, and at that rate, for each following 30-day period that the Repurchase Price remains unpaid.

I toyed with other approaches. Getting an irrevocable letter of credit, the kind used in foreign trade transactions, probably wouldn't work in this particular situation. Too much trouble for XYZ who wasn't really in need of buying more of its own type of inventory, machines and parts (despite the fact that he was getting a below-market price). Another possibility would be for Client to reclaim the unpaid for goods and then "dump" that inventory on the market at whatever he could get for it, then claim the difference plus interest in court. This might work, but again it meant further negotiations with XYZ – inappropriate in this situation; going to court; and veering off the incentive-to-pay approach that was my prime objective.

This is one of those areas where the applicable law might well vary, and so I had to think about providing a *choice-of-law* provision in the purchase/sale agreement between client and XYZ. Such a provision would mandate the law of a state – in this case, either Client's or XYZ's home office – whichever more clearly allowed my incentive provisions to operate and work in Client's favor.

Bottom line, XYZ took advantage of the 5% discount off an already low price by completing its inspection of the goods within the 10-day period and making payment in full: 95% of the contract price. The next few tales further illustrate this incentive-creating and risk-shifting strategy to avoid getting into the vulnerable creditor's position.

———

Your Author Creates a Risk and Has Some Fun Doing It . . .

. . . by giving the other parties an incentive to do what you need done and putting them at an unacceptable risk if they don't do what you need to be done. Let's begin with a fun "neighborhood tale" to illustrate the point before we get down to business:

Unclogging My Neighbor's Parking Area

Our friend, a widow, owned a large house in the neighborhood where she rented rooms out to students. She had paved the entire lot at the side of the house and therein lay the problem: First, the town's Post Office was right next to her own paved parking area; and Second, on-street parking was not to be had – all spaces were always filled with shoppers and delivery vehicles. And so those going to the Post Office were clogging her lot "for just a minute" while they attended to their business at the PO. Her tenants were complaining, and so was she. An electric gate was too expensive. What to do.

Having heard her complain to my wife so many times, I finally promised her a solution to her problem if she told me her favorite charity. Being a Christian Scientist, she named the Christian Science Church; and I made up the text for this large-size poster:

\/

K♥D♥L
THANK YOU FOR YOUR CAR AND YOUR GENEROSITY!

By leaving your car on our Kindness♥Donation♥Lot, you will be helping raise the funds needed to continue our good works.

Please follow these simple instructions:

- **Leave the keys in the ignition – our attendants check every few minutes.**

- **If you choose not to leave the keys, our towing service will simply remove the car to our annex Kindness Donation Lot, to prepare it for auction.**
- **Leave your business card or write your name and all contact information in this notebook. We will send you a receipt for your charitable contribution for tax purposes.**
- **Do not remove the license plate – we will remove and send you an RMV receipt. Also, we will use your registration number to identify you if you do not leave us your name.**

Thank you again for your kindness.
Mother Church, The First Church of Christ, Scientist
Boston, Massachusetts IRS TIN# 05-746-894

\/\/\/\//\/

Parking problem solved, wow! Remember the *risk* (however small) of not finding your car where you left it and the *incentive* to avoid "problems" that complicate your life (and take up valuable time to straighten out) helped my neighbor. I don't know how it all ended, but I stopped hearing her complaints about her clogged parking area.

---

1 *Diaz v. Jiten Hotel Management, Inc.*, 704 F.3d. 150 (1st Cir. 2012). The defendant is ordered to pay $104,626.34 in attorney's fees and costs in a case that could have been settled for $7,650. Don't poo-poo attorney's fees!
2 See, e.g., *LeRoy v. Sayers,* 217 A.D. 2d 63, 635 N.Y.S.2d 217 (1st Dep't 1995).

TALE # 7

TRANSFER YOUR BUSINESS NOW – GET PAID LATER AND TAKE THE RISK … (OR NOT)

Client Advertising Agency ("AA") was being sold to a large British advertising agency. But although the Buyer wanted to take over AA's advertising accounts immediately, the formal closing would have to be deferred. For some UK "tax reasons," they would immediately sign the contract, and put down a one-third "deposit" on account of the purchase price, but the balance of two-thirds would be paid, with interest, at the end of eighteen months.

AA would be taking a substantial step – a substantial "change of position" (as lawyers call it). AA could end up with only a promise of payment at some future date and, as noted above, that's when you are most vulnerable to a nuisance-suit claim: You have performed your end of the deal and all that remains is the payment of money to you at some later date. This was just such a situation. I explained my concerns to Client AA, but the owners said they were about ready to retire and welcomed this offer and the very favorable price the UK ad agency would be paying. "Let's just do the deal," they said.

My specific concern here was that Client AA would be immediately transferring their individual advertiser accounts (its *clients-customers*) to the Buyer, but would have to wait for 18 months to get be paid the substantial balance. Such a delay, to my paranoid mind, is always a signal of potential trouble. Since both the amount of money to be paid and the payment date were fixed, I wanted to build in an incentive to pay, which I tried to do, as follows:

> If full payment of the second and final installment of the purchase price due hereunder is not received by Seller when due and remains unpaid after a 10-day notice of default, Seller AA may **rescind** the Transaction by notice to Buyer. In the event of such rescission, (i) Seller shall automatically and without need of any further act or deed resume ownership of the AA advertising agency and so notify the affected clients; and (ii) any and all AA advertiser accounts previously transferred to Buyer would automatically, without any further act or deed, revert to AA ownership. In addition, in view of the uncertainty and difficulty in estimating the damages AA would sustain in the event of such a breach, as liquidated damages for such Buyer's breach of contract, Seller may retain as liquidated damages and as its own property and without any obligation to repay the same the one-third payment previously made by Buyer to Seller on account of the purchase price hereunder.

The message, therefore, to the buyer is this: Refuse to pay the full amount of the balance due and face a substantial risk: Losing the agency (and its accounts) that they wanted to acquire and forfeiting a substantial sum of money.

Surprisingly, I was able to get the Buyer to agree to this suggested arrangement – the buyer's lawyer said he'd been through these situations before and he "knew" his client would pay in full and on time. "No problem," as he succinctly put it. (It wasn't that easy with the lawyer in Tale #8, which follows.)

BLT #7: Analyze your own transaction, particularly where all that remains to conclude the deal is for the other party to pay you money. At that point you are most vulnerable to a hold-up nuisance claim. Devise a consequence for non-payment that puts that other party at risk if they don't pay, preferably a risk that they would not want to take.

If you are the client/businessperson:

- Work closely with your lawyer. It may well be that *you* and not your lawyer will have to devise and "sell" any kind of atypical provision. Be prepared – you may not be able to get the other party to agree – but your argument is, "If you intend to perform your promise, you should not be concerned about this provision. It only kicks in if you don't perform."
- Try to avoid anything that smacks of a "penalty." Your lawyer can assist on this. But even if the incentive to perform is not clearly enforceable, its function is to encourage performance and discourage breach. You're shifting a risk onto the other side and if that risk is sufficiently real, substantial and constitutes an unacceptable risk, that may well provide the incentive you want for the other side to perform per the contract.

TALE # 8

THE "DIFFICULT" SHOPPING CENTER SELLER –WOULD HE CLOSE ON THE DEAL IN TWO YEARS?

C lient Richard called to tell me that he'd made a deal to buy a shopping center from Seller, "But I've got to warn you," he said, "this guy is – how shall I put it – he has the reputation of being a difficult person to deal with – kind of a sharp trader, sometimes a little 'kooky,' if you know what I mean. A couple of the big chains have already tried and failed to buy this place. So be careful with this guy. But I really want this center."

The shopping center parcel was in an ideal suburban location and included a large and valuable parcel of vacant, undeveloped land. The "kooky" Seller had already added a condition to the deal: The sale could not close for two years because of what the Seller called his "tax situation," – no detailed explanation, just "my tax situation." And so the purchase transaction had to be modified into an alternate arrangement: A lease with an option to purchase – instead of a simple, straight-out purchase and sale agreement to close in 30 or 60 days. This is the deal they made:

Client Richard would sign a lease for the shopping center (including that big chunk of vacant [read "buildable"] land. The lease permitted him to develop the vacant land with additional construction. It also gave Richard an option to purchase the property at the parties' agreed price ($15 million) exercisable on the second anniversary of the Lease signing. At the end of this 2-year period, the rent would switch to a prohibitively high figure. This was the incentive the Seller needed to force Richard to exercise the option and buy the property.

Because of Richard's concerns about Seller, I did some checking on the Seller's background. He had, indeed been involved in a number of lawsuits in both the state and federal courts. A check at the Registry of Deeds showed that the property was held by a corporation, which raised yet more questions. It was rare, at the time, that anyone owned commercial real estate in a corporation; tax advantages accrued to those who owned their properties in the personal names of the owners or in a partnership.

Why a corporation? This seemed odd to me.

When I had my first meeting with Seller's lawyer, I told her I'd require a legal opinion on the "regularity" of this corporation and a copy of his title insurance policy.

Seller's lawyer was firm: "I don't know what he's got for title insurance. I suggest you just buy your own title insurance – I'm sure your mortgage lender will require it – and I'm not giving any legal opinions. We are not Seller's regular counsel – I doubt that he even has a counsel he uses regularly. We were engaged just to do this lease-with-option and the P&S – that's all, no more and no less – and we won't issue any legal opinion. We don't know this guy." This provided no comfort to me.

A few days later Richard and I went out to the site for a look-see. We stood on a rise overlooking the place. Almost knowing the answer in advance, I asked Richard whether he planned to just run the existing shopping center during the 2-year lease period or did he have some expansion plans for the place. Richard's eyes brightened.

"I'm not sitting still for any two years, not in this market. I certainly do have plans – I can show you the drawings – to develop just about all of that vacant land," he said, pointing to a meadow and wooded area. "This will almost double the size of this center. I've already got informal showings of interest from two major department stores and commitments from some chains that would love to have a store in this area. This is going to be big," Richard said excitedly

My mind leaped ahead in time, after that two-year period, when the closing date arrived to complete the sale, with the shopping center now worth maybe twice or more than the $15 million agreed purchase price, and my paranoid streak kicked in. The center would expand – maybe to the size of a small regional mall – as Richard had outlined, and I imagined a time after Richard's expansion plans were completed. The closing date is approaching and Richard is standing on that same rise not with me, but with the Seller, odd duck that he is. And I could just hear Seller's words in my mind:

"Richard, my boy, look at what I'm giving away for $15 million – a property probably worth $50 million today. Let's please add a couple of million to the price, maybe just $2 or $3 million."

I knew this Seller was not afraid to go to court; and what he would say on a witness stand was anyone's guess. Maybe his corporation had some "complications" that could spoil the deal. And who knows, protracted litigation with this odd man, the Seller, might eat up a million or more dollars. I knew that in documenting this lease-with-option deal I had to ensure that two years hence the sale would go through. I wanted none of Seller's possible shenanigans! I had to force Seller to go through with the deal – and no "tricks" when that closing date arrived. Thus was born my "Bargain Basement Price-Reduction Clause," (just the kind of incentive and risk-shifting we're talking about here).

Although it took some stubborn negotiating and overcoming strong resistance from Seller's lawyer ("I've never seen this kind of provision!") plus some encouraging convincing of the Seller by Richard's "comforting" words, the final lease-with-option-to-buy contract contained the following provision:

If the Buyer shall give due and timely notice of exercise of option to purchase and shall, on the closing date tender to Seller or Seller's lawyer [name] at their office a certified or bank cashier's check in the amount of the purchase price ($15,000,000.) and Seller fails to deliver a duly executed and acknowledged recordable deed conveying good, clear, record, marketable and insurable title to the Property, then and in such events the stated purchase price shall automatically reduce by the sum of $50,000. per month for each and every calendar month (and at that rate for a partial month) until such deed is delivered. If, for example, the parties engage in litigation with respect to the herein purchase-and-sale transaction, then such price reduction as aforesaid shall continue at the same monthly rate for the entire period of such litigation including, without limitation, time spent on discovery, depositions, production of documents, appeals, hearings, etc. Furthermore, the loser in any such litigation shall pay the winner's court costs and legal fees.

When I discussed this with one of my partners – more knowledgeable than me in conveyancing of real estate – he mentioned a device called a "title escrow." Under that arrangement, a trusted neutral third party holds the executed deed and at the future date set for closing, delivers it to buyer upon buyer's payment of the purchase price. "Not for this guy," I told him. "One of his lawsuits that I saw during my due-diligence search of court records was a suit he brought against a title insurance company. No. He might well go to court to enjoin delivery of the executed deed. I'm also concerned that a deed executed and dated when the Lease-with-Option was signed won't be acceptable to the Seller who had to defer title transfer 'for tax reasons'—no that wouldn't work either. All this Seller understands is money and if it's pure and simple and clear that any screwing around will cost him, then my 'price-reduction clause' should work."

Was that clause enforceable in a court of law? Maybe, but here (as in other incentive situations) I was less concerned with certainty that a court would enforce the price-reduction provision than I was with putting the Seller at some real risk – forcing him think twice before he took on the risk of losing money by engaging in holdup tactics and nuisance claims or forcing the client/buyer into litigation. Absent such a provision, I had a serious concern that, as a practical matter, Client Richard would be forced to come up with more money for legal fees and to buy off the nuisance claim.

As it turned out, the deal went off without a hitch and we'll never know if my price-reduction provision would have been enforced by a court or held to be an unenforceable penalty; or, indeed, if it even had any real effect on Seller's course of action.

BLT #8: This matter was another example of (i) creating an incentive for the other party to perform his obligations under the contract; and (ii) shifting the risk and costs (of not closing) onto the other party – risks and costs I believed would be unacceptable to him. Oh, and one more thing: I needed Client Richard to work in tandem with me to "sell" this price-reduction provision to the other side. Seller's lawyer made such loud objections and appeared to be on the brink of advising Seller not to sign on to this "unusual" price-reduction provision. And so our "script" read: Richard (with his arm around Seller's shoulder): "Look, Mr. Seller, you'll perform your part of the deal, as will I and this will never go into effect. Let the lawyer have his way, earn his money, y'know." Thank you, Richard, now the proud owner of a major (and successful!) shopping center.

TALE # 9

TERMINATE THE LEASE _AND_ PAY OR TERMINATE _BY_
PAYING MONEY?

T̶enant Didn't Agree to Give Landlord a Windfall, But Still Has to Pay
to Avoid a Serious Risk.

And You'll Appreciate the Important Distinction Between a "Covenant"
and a "Condition."

I. Big Consulting Firm's Problem
Big Consulting Firm ("BCF") occupied about five floors in an office building scheduled for demolition to make room for a bigger, better, nicer, more
modern office tower. BCF loved the location and so they agreed to move out
of the building and immediately sign a lease for space in the new, to-be-built
office tower. That new lease was set to begin five years after BCF vacated its
space in the old building, the time it would take to complete demolition and
construction of the new tower. But where to go during that 5-year period?

II. The Solution – a Short-Term Lease
BCF's CEO was personal friends with developer Client, who was then in the
process of signing up and moving tenants into his own new office building.
CEO asked Client about renting several floors for the 5-year waiting period
while the new office tower was being constructed.

"No dice!" was Client's response. "At this point in our leasing program, and particularly since you need so many separate offices to be built out in your space, I can only recoup my construction costs with a 10-year lease." A couple of weeks of talking back and forth and finally BCF and Client made their deal: A 10-year lease with BCF having the right to terminate at the end of five years.

But since Client could not **amortize** the cost of the expensive build-out in less than ten years, BCF would have to pay an "early-termination fee." This way Client/Landlord could recoup his **unamortized** costs of constructing all those BCF offices. The two agreed on a figure of a quarter million dollars – $250,000 to be paid by BCF to Client/Landlord in exchange for the early lease-termination right. I drew up a lease for the space and included the early-termination provision as the parties had agreed.

Now let's get back to the "vulnerability" concern described in Tale #6 and how you counter that weakness by creating incentives for the other party to do right:
In this situation, I didn't want Tenant BCF to be able to terminate the Lease and then end up owing Client/Landlord $250,000. Remember: If all that's left to be done is that the other side has to pay you money, that sum may not be worth 100 cents on the dollar, especially if circumstances change (as they surely did here!). I needed to draft a lease-termination provision that would avoid this vulnerability. How? Make the payment an intrinsic part of the "trigger" that caused the Lease termination. In other words, no payment, no termination. I would make the payment a "condition" rather than just a "covenant" – a mere promise to pay. And so the provision read:

> Tenant may elect to terminate this Lease effective on the Fifth (5th) Anniversary of the Term Commencement Date ("Effective Termination Date") by delivering to Landlord not less than 12 full calendar months prior to the Effective Termination Date the following:

1- A written notice of termination; accompanied by
2- A certified or bank cashier's check drawn on Boston Funds in the amount of $250,000.[1]

You see the effect: In order to terminate, BCF had to pay the money, right up front at the time when it gave its notice of termination. I thought this would eliminate client's "vulnerability." (I was prepared to pay the year's interest on the payment, but BCF never raised the issue.) To me it was clear that if BCF didn't pay, they lost their right to terminate the Lease; I hoped they saw it the same way. And to complete the picture, I tightened up the **anti-assignment/subletting** provision in the Lease (more about this later). Client would never be put in the position of having to sue BCF for the $250,000 *after* a lease termination: If BCF didn't pay when it sent Client the notice of termination, BCF would still be on the hook with a Lease that wasn't terminated, which BCF could not assign and for space they could not sublet – surely an unacceptable risk to BCF.

In due course BCF left its old quarters and moved its offices to Client's building. The five years that followed that relocation saw a wildly rising real estate (particularly office space) market. BCF's rent in Client's building was the then market rate, $5.00 per square foot. But by the fifth anniversary, when BCF was scheduled to terminate its Lease and move into their new office tower space, rents in Client Landlord's building were projected to triple, to $15.00 per square foot. But wait, there's more; something that made Client anxious to see BCF terminate its Lease:

A Lucky Turn of Events for Client : An Instant Tenant for BCF's Premises!

Client's own public accounting firm had expanded substantially and was looking to move into larger quarters – they needed an office exactly the size of BCF's space. And since that space was already fitted out with lots of offices and cubicles for a large staff of business consultants, it was just what Client's accounting firm needed. Client would have no major expenses in putting this new tenant in almost immediately, and at three times BCF's rental. All this brought a new meaning to the phrase "sitting in the catbird seat."

Tenant BCF Calls His Old Friend, Client/Landlord.

As the deadline date approached for BCF to give notice to terminate its lease, the old friend and buddy, the BCF CEO called Client. He recalled their long and wonderful "friendship" (they had served on the same charitable organizations' boards) and said something like "Look, Bill, you're getting an instant tenant into our space at three times the rent we're paying. You ought to be paying *me* to free up this space."

Client's response: "You're right, Hugh, that's what I'd do under other circumstances. But we have a deal. You can terminate if you pay. And you're making lots of money; I've read it in the papers. BCF isn't exactly a hardship case. So Hugh, a deal's a deal."

BCF's Lawyer Tries to Wiggle Out With Another Approach.

Hugh was not about to give up easy. Soon I heard from BCF's lawyer.

"We've decided not to terminate the Lease. We'll just sublet the space," he told me in a telephone call. I pointed out to him the limitations on subletting, namely this provision in his Lease:

> With Landlord's consent, not to be unreasonably withheld, Tenant may sublet a portion or portions of its premises, provided, however, that in no event shall the total sum aggregate of all such sublet space at any time during the term of this Lease ever exceed 7,500 square feet of premises area. [BCF's total premises area was almost 125,000 square feet.]

I had put this restriction in the Lease to prevent just such a situation as BCF's lawyer threatened; and since at the time we were negotiating the Lease, no one expected that BCF would ever need to sublet and would, in any event, be out of the space at the end of five years, this provision raised not a peep – no objection during lease negotiations. The parties' situation appeared clear and simple: BCF at that time had wanted an "out" so it could honor its lease in the new office tower when it was completed; Client gave him that out; and either BCF itself stayed in occupancy of its space in Client's building or it terminated its lease and paid the quarter-million dollar price.

Could Tenant "License" the Premises and Avoid Subleasing?

Let's recall Tale #5, where client changed payments for his parking garage operation from "gross" into "net" by *licensing* the garage to the garage operator. In that case, it was the client who faced a prohibition against leasing, just as BCF was facing here. So why couldn't BCF threaten to "license" its large office premises. Answer: Maybe they could have, but their lawyer never mentioned doing this. A license of leased office space would have been highly unusual and may well not have stood up in court. Here's what I wrote in Tale #5 and one judge's words from Note 1 at the end of that Tale:

> In some instances courts will disregard labels lawyers put on things. If a transaction in reality creates a lease or sublease, a court will not be fooled by merely calling it a "license." Judges prefer to call a spade a spade, i.e. call a sublease a sublease, and disregard what they perceive to be a phony label. [citation omitted]:

> "The device or subterfuge of calling a sublease a license or any other name cannot suffice to change its real nature or the real agreement which the parties entered into, nor relieve them from the legal consequences of their agreements."

As to subletting in general and especially given the then rising rental rates, no Landlord likes to see its tenants making a "profit" by subletting space in Landlord's building for more than the tenants' rental rate. Even the idea of sharing in any such profit with its tenants, given the market conditions, was something Client wanted to avoid.

As the Lease Termination Deadline Approaches, I Get Nervous.
I heard nothing back from BCF's lawyer after I made the point that BCF could sublet only a small portion of their multi-floor premises in Client's building. The target date for giving notice of termination was quickly approaching; and I was becoming more and more nervous by the day. On the Thursday before the deadline – Friday was the last day that BCF could give notice of lease termination – I had trouble sleeping. I've been in that spot a number of times, where some document I drafted was being tested in a real-life situation by a good lawyer on the other side. Self-doubt: "Did I screw up in some way? Will that termination provision work as I'd planned? Was there some technique or a law I hadn't fully considered?" The Friday deadline arrived and by noon I was visibly shaken, as one of my partners noticed. ("Is everything okay, Milt?")

That Friday afternoon, relief! My "Whew! moment" came at 3:45 pm when a messenger hand delivered an envelope. It contained BCF's formal "Notice of Termination of Lease" and a bank cashier's check (First National Bank of Boston, no longer with us under that name) for $250,000 payable to Client. I shakily signed a copy of the Notice and check to acknowledge receipt and then personally walked the papers over to Client's office. Client offered me a drink of some ancient Scotch – a singular (malt?) event for me, a non-drinker, but I accepted it.

BLT #9:
Remember : "Give 'em an Incentive, Put 'em at Risk and They'll Perform."
BCF was in a risky situation: It was legally bound to go back to its former location, into the new office tower; they'd signed that lease when they left the building that then was about to be demolished. And unless they effectively terminated their lease in Client's building, they risked being also bound on a second lease, one where they had no meaningful sublet rights. We cannot, of course, say how a judge would finally rule on any of the issues if a dispute arose that landed in court. But as I've said repeatedly in these Tales, that's not the point in these incentive/risk-shifting situations. BCF

was facing a serious risk that they could completely avoid by exercising the termination right as agreed –by paying Client the quarter million dollars. So my motto, above, worked well when I "Put 'em at risk."

BLT #9A: What I Learned from Writing This Tale:
What Might BCF Have Done to Avoid Paying this "Windfall" to Client?

Let's go back to the point made in Tale #1: Think strategically and ask questions at the time of the original negotiation. If BCF had looked ahead and asked itself "What could change?" over its 5-year lease term; if BCF had thought about one of the usual answers –market conditions could change – then the CEO of BCF could have tried to recharacterize the $250,000 payment, saying something like this, BCF speaking:

> Look, Landlord, I don't want to see you hurt and if you are hurt, you'll need and deserve the $250k payment. But if you're not hurt, then no payment.

Client building owner would, of course, have insisted on the same up-front timing for the payment: The money is due with the notice of termination and is an intrinsic part of that notice. Then BCF could have responded with something like this, BCF again speaking:

> "Fine. We'll pay the money up front, when we give notice of termination. But if you're not hurt by our early termination, then we should get our money back. I don't think you're asking us to make you a present of a quarter million dollars – you're protecting yourself against being unable to amortize the expensive fit-out of our space. Right? If, for example, market rents rise and you can immediately re-rent the space and not spend more to refit it for your new tenant, then you're not hurt and we should get our money back."

I can say all this now, years after the fact and with the benefit of hindsight. Maybe the more general "lesson" of this Tale is to stop and think and rethink whenever you're about to give one of those automatic, knee-jerk, routine responses with some "standard form." Maybe your actions and reactions need to be "customized" to the particular business situation you're in and not merely responding, as in this case, "Sure, we terminate the lease early and we pay you for unamortized premises-preparation expenses." It never hurts to ask those "What if . . .?" questions.

---

1 I was prepared with an alternative provision (e.g., **irrevocable bank letter of credit**) if Tenant was concerned about the time value of money, i.e., interest on the $250,000 during the 12-month period from the date of the notice of termination until the effective date.

TALE # 10

INCENTIVIZING SLOW-MOVING TENANTS TO LEAVE
WHEN THEIR LEASE ENDS

I. Client's Problem
The Office Tenants Who Can't Move Out On Time

Client Landlord complained to me about tenants not moving out when their lease expired – and it was wreaking havoc with his scheduling. Landlord owned an office building and used the usual overly long and detailed "Standard Form Lease." It already contained an incentive provision of the kind we've been talking about – one quite typical in many lease forms: If a Tenant failed to move out when his lease term ended, the rental jumped up to some higher amount. (In some leases I've seen, that amount is so high that it would probably be characterized not as legally enforceable **liquidated damages**, but as an unenforceable **penalty** – an amount so wholly disproportionate to the actual harm Landlord might suffer from the Tenant's holdover that courts would refuse to give it any effect. Courts generally do not enforce "penalty" provisions.

Client Landlord's plans for keeping his building fully occupied by rent-paying tenants go out the window when the departing tenants are slow to vacate their space – which starts a damaging domino effect, which happens like this: There's a new, replacement tenant waiting in the wings to move into the space, which usually has to be rebuilt for the new tenant. This may entail a total teardown and reconstruction with new wall partitions, doors, reconfigured electric wiring, air conditioning outlets, etc. – a time-consuming process. And that incoming new tenant has to be out of his old space by a certain date (and *his* Landlord is waiting for him to vacate that space). You see the domino effect working here, and that's what makes the exact calculation of damages almost impossible. That's where a **liquidated damage** provision has the best chance of surviving a court test.

Let's get back to Client Landlord's problem, office-space tenants "holding over," that is, staying on in their space after their leases had expired. They all had lots of good excuses:

- We can't get a mover.
- We just got notice of an unexpected audit.
- Our new premises aren't ready.
- We're in the middle of a big deal that cannot be interrupted.
- It's tax season – we've got client-return deadlines, and so forth and so on.

"Hell," the frustrated client said, "they're making their problems my problems. Y'know, I've really got enough problems of my own!"

Obviously, the old standard holdover provision was not having the desired effect. The departing tenant who remains in the space is willing to pay the extra rental charge for the convenience of moving out on *their* schedule rather than the expiration date of their lease. And so Landlord had two distinct problems: (A) Existing tenants whose lease term was expiring; and (B) prospective tenants who would be signing leases. Let's take one at a time:

II. A Solution
A. What to do About Existing Tenants?
I drafted a series of form "notice/warning" letters that would be automatically sent to departing tenants nine months; six months and 90 days prior to their lease-expiration date. Each letter would be sent by Certified Mail : Return Receipt Requested (no email back then!). After some friendly amenities from Landlord, the letters set out the above domino

effect – facts about the damages that would result if the departing tenant didn't vacate their space on time. The letter explained the risk of (i) Landlord losing the new, incoming tenant because of the departing tenant's delay in leaving and (ii) a claim for damages by the frustrated incoming tenant. All followed by a "gentle" hint that they check the matter with their attorney to fully understand the risks of overstaying their lease term. Why the "talk to your lawyer" hint?

Because the overstaying tenant should know they're exposed to substantial **special damages** – not just the additional rental amount already provided in their lease for failure to vacate their space on time. I assumed their lawyer would advise the expiring-lease tenants that, having been put on notice of these special circumstances and the substantial risks and costs of failure to vacate, their liability was expanded and they would be incentivized to get out when their lease expired. Since I didn't hear about the problem after that 3-letter plan was put into effect, I have to assume that this problem was *SOLVED!*

B. What About Future Tenants Signing Leases Going Forward?

The Standard Form Lease already had that incentive-to-move provision – a major rent increase for the holdover period – but it was obviously proving ineffective. Apparently tenants would gladly pay more for the convenience of keeping to their own, and not the Landlord's, time schedule. A stronger incentive to get out on time was needed. And I wanted to beef up the 3-letter notice plan outlined above for existing tenants.

Thinking about incentives and risk-shifting, I concluded that the last thing the departing tenant wants to happen is to be locked into the old space when he's already signed a lease for their new space they'll be moving into. Thus was born the "holdover = extension" provision, which I added to Client Landlord's Standard Form Lease to be used for all future tenants. It provided that if a Tenant overstayed the term of his Lease, Landlord had an option to extend the term for a full year at an increased rental. This is how this revised Lease provision now read:

Holdover by Tenant: In addition to and not in limitation of all of Landlord's rights and remedies under the herein Lease or otherwise available at law or in equity, the parties agree as follows: If after the term of this Lease shall have expired, Tenant shall fail to completely vacate the Premises and remove all of its property therefrom as required by Sec. XX of the herein Lease within 72 hours after Lease-term expiration for any reason whatsoever and without exception (and the *force majeure* provision of this Lease shall be of no force or effect and shall have no application to this holdover provision), Landlord may give Tenant a 10-day notice to vacate the premises stating the date by which the premises must be completely vacated. If Tenant shall fail to have so completely vacated the premises by the end of such 10-day period as required by Sec. XX of this Lease, Landlord shall have the option, exercisable by notice to Tenant, to extend the term of the herein lease for an additional term of up to one year at a rental equal to the greater of (i) 125% of the then prevailing rental rate under the herein expired Lease or (ii) the then current market rental rate. If Landlord shall so exercise such option to extend the term of the herein Lease then, notwithstanding anything to the contrary in this Lease contained, Tenant shall have no right to assign this Lease nor sublet all or any portion of the Premises during such extended term.

I picked a one-year period to avoid the provision smacking of a penalty. Tenants wouldn't just be paying for nothing – they'd have a valuable asset in the right to occupy the space for that one year. Also, any longer term might have allowed the departing tenant to sublease, removing the risk and incentive I was trying to create since a one-year lease is typically hard to sublease.

Would a court enforce this odd provision? Probably, but again, I was more concerned with the incentive effect of this provision than whether a court would enforce it as written. That risk was the Tenant's, not much of a risk for Landlord. I thought that the mere risk of being stuck on his old lease at an increased rent while bound by a lease of new premises he'd already signed would incentivize the tenant to get out on time.

Apparently that's just what happened, since I never again heard of that holdover problem as to any Tenant who'd signed the revised Lease. Client Landlord supplemented the new Lease provision with the end-of-term 3-letter "notice of **special damages**" (above). Facing these risks, somehow the outgoing tenants found a mover; relocated to temporary space while their delayed construction of new premises was finished, and so forth. In other words, they stopped making their problem the Landlord's problem. The previously existing incentive to perform – the rent increase in the standard forms of lease – proved too weak to do the job and had to be supplemented by a stronger incentive. It worked in this case.

BLT #10: Note that in these incentive/risk-shifting Tales, you're less concerned with how a judge would rule (unless your arrangement is obviously unenforceable, e.g, as a **penalty**). The effectiveness of this approach lies in the unacceptable risk the Landlord placed on the departing tenant. I was assuming, they would not accept the risks of (i) open-ended "**special damages**" under the 3-letter notice procedure, nor (ii) having an ongoing and substantial rent obligation if Landlord exercised his option to extend the term of their expiring lease. Those are strong incentives for departing tenants to solve their own "problem" and find a way to vacate the premises when their lease term was over.

TALE # 11

TECHNICIANS GETTING TOO "ENTREPRENEURIAL" – HOW TO STOP THE DEFECTIONS

I. Background

At its overseas headquarters, Client Tech Company ("TC") manufactured a highly complex (and expensive!) electro-mechanical-digital machine that all computer manufacturers had to use to test certain of their components. To service this equipment at their customers' sites all over the United States, TC had established a corps of service technicians specially trained on TC's equipment. These people came from TC's home country and were relocated from their homes to cities across the United States. TC had branch offices in some of these cities; the technicians worked out of those offices. Other technicians worked out of their cars.

Training these technicians on TC's equipment took almost a year and was obviously an expensive process. The home office Chief Technician would supplement this training with periodic updates and "Service Bulletins." Added to the expense of paying salaries during this lengthy training period, TC paid all the costs of relocating their technicians and their families to their posts in the United States, which included:

- Packing, crating and moving each technician's household to their new home in the USA for the minimum 5-year tour of duty.
- Air transportation for the technician and family, sometimes as many as six or seven people; and air transportation for a family return visit to their home country once each year.

- Provision of suitable housing, often subsidized by TC, located in the particular technician's assigned territory.
- Provision of a suitable leased car, plus payment of all car expenses.
- Meeting any "special needs" of any particular technician involving costs incurred because of his being away from his home country.

When I got involved as their lawyer, in the late sixties, TC's cost to train, move, house and otherwise provide for its crew of technicians across the United States was in excess of $50,000 per technician (exclusive of salary and benefits). But since TC's Service and Maintenance Division was a major contributor to its bottom line (about a third of revenues), these substantial costs of maintaining this Division were justified. These costs were just another necessary "investment" by TC in order to maintain its leadership in its line of computer-industry testing equipment. With that background, we can now get to "The Problem."

II : The Client's Problem : "Defecting" Technicians

An auditor spotted situations he considered suspicious – the numbers indicated something strange going on – billings for maintenance were down; but mileage and other expenses of visits to customers remained steady. This "tip of the iceberg" turned out to be caused by some technicians who were, in effect, moonlighting. Instead of putting their work through TC's forms and procedures and, of course, billing, they'd arrange with certain (smaller) customers to be paid in cash at rates below TC's published Schedule of Rates for Labor and Materials. Rather than accuse any particular technician of this practice, a stern broadside went out reminding all technicians of the rules that governed their activities and the consequences of disobeying those rules.

The second problem that appeared was more serious, because a number of technicians were actually quitting their jobs – resigning as TC employees – and opening their own "TC Equipment Repair & Maintenance" business. And these new competitors were charging TC equipment owners below TC's Schedule of Rates for Labor and Materials and beginning to draw business away from TC's own Service & Maintenance Division. That's when I got involved. I asked about the non-compete agreement these employees had signed, but TC management wanted to avoid possibly long and expensive litigation with doubtful chances of success in certain U.S. state courts.

TC's President said they would deal with the few technicians who had already left, either by threatening to enforce their Non-Competition Agreement or by denying all access to the software tools and data needed to properly service TC's equipment. The client needed some way to prevent any *future* breaches of company rules and, more important, the defections of employees going into business for themselves.

III. The Solution

Obviously, the incentives in place for these technicians not to leave the company and go into business for themselves were not working. I had to come up with a more effective incentive.

" Yes, we do have an incentive scheme. We call it 'continued employment'."

I suggested an "incentive-based" arrangement to address the problem directly. The arrangement was, as you'll see, rather simple, modeled on what investment-brokerage houses were already doing to keep their stockbroker employees from jumping ship. (My suggested arrangement was not as complex as that of the brokerage houses, some of which were ruled unenforceable in litigation.) My simpler suggestion apparently caused no problems; this is how it worked:

All TC technicians, when hired and before starting training, were told that they would be assigned for a 5-year period to a specific market area in the United States, to a European country or to a country in the Far East. If they weren't willing to take that assignment (by the way, most welcomed a stint in the U.S., away from their home country), then they should not join TC.

Each TC Technician was required to sign an employment agreement which (in addition to the typical provisions covering **non-competition; confidentiality/non-disclosure agreements; anti raiding; non-solicitation; non-disparagement**) noted the amount that TC would be expending in training and relocating them to an overseas post, say $50,000.00. Attached to the employment agreement was a $50,000 demand promissory note, which was an express promise to pay to TC on demand that amount, that is the amount of those presumed TC training costs. The promissory note included a reference to the employment agreement. The employment agreement activated the demand promissory note only if the technician at any time within the 5-year term of his U.S. assignment left TC or within the non-compete period undertook repair/maintenance of TC's or any competitor's similar equipment other than as a TC employee. There were other provisions about the employee leaving TC, but this demand-note arrangement responded to TC's major concern about the technicians who left to compete with TC. I helped TC implement this plan with other appropriate documentation.

IV. Another Related Problem and a Solution

During my fact-finding about Client's complex chip-inspection equipment, I learned that diagnostic software was built right into the equipment the customer had purchased. It could be accessed by the TC technician responding to a service call. TC customers' sales documentation included a prohibition against their accessing the built-in diagnostic software – but TC customers were not the problem. TC's problem was the buyers of used TC equipment from the original customer. These owners of second-hand equipment had no contracts with or obligations to TC. What to do?

Not rocket science, but I guess it was effective: I drafted a Notice to Customers which was sent to each owner/user of the equipment; and the text of that notice was printed as a non-removable (HA!) adhesive plastic label placed prominently on both the inside and outside of the access door to the "works" in the machine. This was the text of the Notice and that label:

IMPORTANT NOTICE TO USERS OF THIS EQUIPMENT WHETHER YOU ARE THE ORIGINAL PURCHASER OR YOU ACQUIRED IT ON RESALE.

This equipment is manufactured and sold by TC and is operated, and operating problems are diagnosed, by certain software, which is the property of TC and licensed pursuant to a non-transferable license granted only to its customers purchasing its equipment from TC. If you acquire this equipment from other than TC, you have no right to utilize this software. In the event its customer transfers this equipment to a new owner, TC reserves the right to remove or disable (in some instances remotely) all such software, which may be done on site or remotely, from TC's home office.

––––

I never heard about this client's problem again. As for their existing "problem" employees, I assumed they took appropriate disciplinary action against disloyal employees under TC's Rules of Conduct, Employees' Handbook, etc. And I assumed that not hearing from them meant that future TC Technicians stopped defecting to competitors or leaving to go into business for themselves servicing TC equipment and cutting into TC's lucrative repair/maintenance revenues. And buyers of used TC equipment were calling TC to sign up for a license to use the diagnostic software and, more important, to purchase a service contract. So, receiving no further calls, I assumed TC's problems were *SOLVED!*

... and in January 2016,

A California Court of Appeal ruled that employers may require an employee to repay the costs of voluntary educational benefits should the employee choose to leave within a reasonably defined time period, and compete, after receiving the benefit. And this despite California's well-known public policy against non-compete agreements.[1]

---

1 The statute is California Business and Professions Code section 16600); the case is *USS-POSCO Industries v. Case*, No. A140457 (California Court of Appeal, 1st App. Dist., Div. One; A140457; Super.Ct. No. MSC1102781 Jan. 26, 2016).

TALE # 12

CLIENT'S INSURANCE CANCELLED BECAUSE OF ACCIDENTS AND INJURIES – WHAT TO DO?

I. The Client's Problem
Losing His Liability Insurance!

This Tale involves client Bill's meat-processing machinery business, KS Machines. It started with a call I received from his comptroller:

"I just got a real scary letter from our liability insurer, a Notice of Non-Renewal! They say we have an unacceptably high accident record, injuries involving certain of our meat-processing machines."

Here's some background on this client's problem situation:

The large meatpackers who produce sausage and other processed meats use Bill's machines as a giant meat-grinder to reduce chunks of meat into small pieces which are then made into processed-meat products. These machines use huge razor-sharp blades, much like aircraft propeller blades, which whirl at near propeller speeds to cut up the chunks of meat fed into the machines.

The U.S. Department of Agriculture requires that these machines, made almost entirely of high-grade stainless steel, be shut off every few hours and washed down. The machines – imported from a West German manufacturer (this was at a time prior to unification of East and West Germany) – were manufactured under a very strict set of German government-mandated safety rules. One major rule required certain "safeties" to be engineered into the machines; these would automatically engage when a machine was shut down for cleaning. The safety feature prevented the machine from starting up accidentally until all parts of the machine exposed during cleaning were re-covered and shielded, which ensured that no person was anywhere near those whirling razor-sharp cutting blades when the "ON" switch was pressed.

The giant meatpacking companies using these machines had apparently found ways to disengage the safeties. This saved them time and allowed them to get the production line back up and running with shortened interruptions for the government-mandated cleaning. With those safeties shut off, workers cleaning the machines were being injured when a machine was accidentally turned on. Fingers, hands and even arms were injured or destroyed when this happened. Then these consequences would follow:

- An injured employee would typically collect on their employer's (the meat packing company's) workers' compensation insurance.
- The employees would then, in turn, assign/transfer their legal rights to the workers' comp insurance company that paid them the insurance benefits for their injuries. (The injured worker's employer – the meat-packer who was the real party at fault for bypassing the safeties – usually escaped liability under the Workers Compensation laws.)
- The workers' comp insurance company would, in turn, sue Bill's company, the seller of the machine that caused the injury, on the **subrogated** claim for personal injury based on product liability – the alleged faulty product that caused the injury.
- At this point, Bill's liability insurance carrier (the one that sent him that "Notice of Non-Renewal") would defend his company in a personal injury lawsuit that followed; and then that liability insurance carrier would settle or pay whatever amount the jury awarded.

When these claims and the payments began to proliferate and mount up in number and amount, the liability insurance carrier decided it would no longer insure Bill's company – it was just getting too expensive with those mounting injury claims. Insuring Bill's company had become a high-risk losing proposition for the insurance company. The worried comptroller who explained all this to me was at his wits' end; his telephone calls appealing to KS' liability insurance company had proved futile. And maintaining liability insurance is, as with most businesses and individuals, an essential part of surviving the risks of claims, litigation and money verdicts. What to do?

II. The Solution

I sent Bill and his comptroller a draft "Urgent Safety Bulletin" which I suggested they send to their customers. Bill's customer base consisted mostly of well-known large (and a few smaller) meat-packing companies. Before you read this Bulletin, here's some background on Bill's business:

A good portion of his company's revenue came from a maintenance and service operation staffed by expert mechanics on these machines strategically located around the United States (usually near the larger meat-packing centers). Since the processing of meat products is a "line operation" where the product moves along what is essentially an assembly-line, from station to station – from large chunks of meat at one end to the finished processed-meat-product at the end – any breakdown at any single station would stop the production on that entire line. And so any breakdown had to be repaired ASAP – the rest of the production line would be sitting idle waiting for these repairs to be completed so the line could get back in operation. KS' strategically located repair and maintenance mechanics/technicians were crucial to the meatpackers' keeping their production lines running.

Here's the "Urgent Safety Bulletin" I suggested KS send to all their customers who were using the particular "problem" machines that were causing these injuries:

URGENT SAFETY BULLETIN !

KS Machines are designed and manufactured to the highest safety standards, which are mandated by the manufacturer's home-country government regulations. One of the safety features prevents any machine from being turned on and operated while it is "open" for cleaning. You will understand that you must not have your personnel cleaning the innards of any machine which can be accidentally turned "ON" during the cleaning process exposing your employees to the machine's razor-sharp, whirling cutting blades.

It has come to our attention that a number of customers have by-passed the safeties built into these machines, resulting in severe injuries to your workers engaged in the periodic cleaning of the machines. As a result of these unfortunate accidents, we are now under notice from our Liability Insurance Carrier that we are about to lose that coverage. This would be a situation that, as you can understand, is untenable; it would literally put us out of the business to be without liability insurance coverage. **And so this bypassing of safeties must stop immediately!**

Enforcement of Our New Safety Policy – Effective Immediately !
Each of our regional Technician/Service People will be making unannounced surprise, random visits to your plant on a sporadic, unscheduled and irregular basis. This enforcement action is now being formalized by notices to all field technicians by our Service Manager. These notices include instructions and report forms.

If on any of these random surprise inspection visits it is found that any KS equipment is shut down for cleaning and the safeties have been by-passed or disengaged, serious consequences will follow, as explained below. We urge you to instruct your employees about this new policy, breach of which will result in the following consequences:

1. Your Maintenance Agreement with our company will immediately and automatically be cancelled and terminated; and the annual maintenance fee, paid in full in advance, will be forfeit and revert to our company. There will be no "second chance" or any appeal – you will immediately lose all rights under your Maintenance Agreement.
2. Our technician will no longer respond to future service calls and will not be permitted to visit the offending meat-packing plant; and we retain the right and may elect to terminate service calls to any or all of your other plants on the assumption that similar violations are occurring there as well.

I trust you understand that disengaging safeties now presents a life-and-death risk to your employees and to our company. So drastic a situation demands the drastic action we take today.

Going Forward: In order to continue our uninterrupted service arrangement with you, please be good enough to countersign the enclosed copy of this Bulletin and return it immediately. That countersigned copy shall have the force and effect of an amendment to the Service Agreement to which you and we are parties.

\/

If we do not receive the enclosed copy of this Bulletin, duly countersigned below by an authorized officer of your company by the 10th day after the date of this Bulletin, we reserve the right to immediately cancel your Service Agreement and send you a pro-rated refund of your fee, per the schedule in that Agreement.

\/\/\/\/\/\/\/\/\/\//\

―――――

The undersigned agrees that it will immediately take all necessary steps to put into effect and enforce this Safety Bulletin and agrees to the consequences, as above described, for any violations found by KS Machine's service technicians.

ABC Meatpacking Corp.

By_____
(name)   (title)
Hereunto duly authorized

Please mail this signed copy back to the following address immediately – preferably by Certified or Registered Mail

———

[end of service bulletin]

That was the last I heard about this situation from the client. I assumed that Bill's comptroller "made peace" with their liability insurance carrier, sending them a copy of this Bulletin – and I assumed their problem of injuries at their customers' meatpacking plants ended. As you may have noticed in Tale after Tale, when clients don't call, their problem is usually *SOLVED!* – no problems, no calls.

TALE # 13

WHEN WORDS DON'T MEAN WHAT THEY MEAN – IN CONTRACTS. A TALE OF HOPE AND A STRANGE LEGAL-OPINION LETTER

This may be the silliest of all the Tales, but it takes us into an area at the core of any business law practice: the meaning of the words in business contracts; and then, in Tale #14, we examine the meaning of words in statutes and even our United States Constitution.

Why This Tale #13?

Tale #13 is a tale of hope for businesspeople and their lawyers: Don't give up on a case or situation even when the "clear words" of a contract or a statute are against you. As the title says, sometimes those words don't mean what they mean and if you have an adequate explanation, some policy and some logic, then a court may, for example, rule that –

- "less" means "more"[1]
- "unlawful" means "lawful"[2]
- a state "Legislature" means "an independent commission established by citizen initiative"[3]
- "or" means "of"[4]
- "for public use" means "for private use"[5]
- "speech" means "money" and "people" means "corporations"[6] and
- "a police car" is not a "vehicle."[7]

See what I mean? When words don't mean what they mean.

"This is gobbledygook. I asked for mumbo-jumbo."

Some of the easier word-interpretation cases involve a clear **scrivener's error**, a "typo," you might say.[8] In others the cause for confusion of meaning is not all that clear. But since this is a Tale of hope, remember that sometimes – not often, just sometimes – all is *not* lost when the words in that contract or statute are clearly against you. Here's what happened to me and how I was able to leverage those crucial words to solve a client's problem:

It's No News: We Lawyers Copy from an Old Form to Make a New Form
We business lawyers use a lot of "standard forms" and "standard clauses." One of these is the Anti-Assignment provision, because parties to a contract like to know with whom they're dealing. And so if the other party to your contract is about to assign or transfer any rights under the contract, you want to know about it. Hence, the contract will include something like this standard piece of "**boilerplate**":

Neither party will assign, transfer, etc. this Agreement or any or all of its rights hereunder without the consent of the other . . .

A version of that simple anti-assignment provision helped me solve this Client's problem.

I. The Client's Problem
(Surprise! Some Lawyers Don't Read the Documents.)

Background: Many states have subsidized housing programs for low-income renters. I was working on such housing, a rental-apartment project in a city in Pennsylvania and, typical for these projects, construction costs are financed by the State's Housing Finance Agency. The State gets this money by selling its Agency's tax-free bonds to investors; and these state bonds, in turn, are legally authorized by the State legislature passing a Bond Resolution authorizing this funding transaction. And then even more and more papers are added to that already large Bond Resolution.

The Bond Indenture with that whole file of papers is about as big as a mid-sized city telephone book. The Bond Indenture and all that other stuff are the creation (not really!) of lawyers called Bond Counsel – usually a large, well-connected, big-city law firm. Bond Indentures are not exactly exciting reading and I doubt if that document or most of those other papers are read even by the lawyers who supposedly produce them. Just a copy machine at work, standard, routine, change a few names and dates and it's the same-old same-old.

The Client, a real estate developer, had a problem with something in the deal he didn't like and I agreed with him, I also didn't like it. Client insisted it be changed. I cautioned him that we were dealing with documents "cast in stone" – they're never amended, particularly that bond indenture. But with his typical force and candor, Client gave me the usual marching orders: "Don't come back without that change ..." And I most certainly wanted to come back. On the day before Closing Date, both on the flight down to the **Closing** in Pennsylvania and in the hotel room that night before the

Closing, I did the unthinkable: I read the Bond Indenture and all those other papers (fighting to stay awake!).

The next day, at the Closing, I asked for the change that Client developer wanted. The (expected) response from the State Housing Authority's lawyer was, "No dice. We cannot make changes." And when I pushed back and insisted that I had to have the change, they resorted to those old fallback positions: First, "This is a standard form and we cannot make any changes." Next, blame the guy who's not in the room – in this case, His Highness, the Bond Counsel. So, with the Client's final words echoing in my head, I asked to speak to the Bond Counsel. They called the large Wall Street law firm in New York.

The Bond Counsel was stern and negative: The change that Client needed was not to be, end of discussion.

II. A Solution to Client's Problem?
That's when I unholstered my weapon, something I'd read in one of those Closing documents (probably the Bond Indenture).

"I'm sorry," I said, "but then we cannot close. This deal is off!" Bond Counsel was surprised: "What are you talking about? Why can't we close?"

I asked Bond Counsel to turn to Page X of Document Y Paragraph Z, the **anti-assignment provision** (that common "boilerplate" provision in many contracts, as described above), which read in part:

(i) The Mortgagor [Client/Developer] shall be prohibited from selling, **leasing** or otherwise encumbering the Project . . . [my emphasis]

This prohibition is carried out in the mortgage document which Client was required to sign, where he expressly agrees "Not to sell, lease, or otherwise encumber the project . . ."

I reminded Bond Counsel (who probably had never read the Bond Indenture or most of those other papers) that the Project was rental apartments and without the right to lease apartments, it wouldn't be viable. And, with a straight face, I said: "I cannot allow my client to violate the Bond Indenture or the Mortgage or, indeed, any contract and, without this right to lease apartments, we cannot close." A long silence.

"That's not what we meant," said Bond Counsel. "Of course you can lease apartments. That's not what we meant!"[9]

"That's not what it says. We have to amend this document," I insisted, knowing full well that the Bond Indenture and many of the other documents are the result of legislation or government regulations and certainly not easily changed – just into and out of the good old copy machine. "So I'm afraid we can't close." I knew that bond counsel would not like to go back to the State legislature or the State Housing Finance Agency with this "**scrivener's error**" – maybe *his* error. A short silence.

Suddenly Bond Counsel recalled my request for the change that I'd asked for, the one Client needed. Bond Counsel seemed to soften considerably and said, hesitatingly, "Maybe we can talk about that change your client needs. How's that? Does that work for you?" I expressed my appreciation for Bond Counsel's cooperation in granting this most reasonable change, but on one condition: "I'll need your legal opinion." Mentally I pictured getting this kind of legal-opinion letter from this large New York Wall Street firm explaining the prohibition of leasing in the Closing Documents of a rental-apartment project. Again, a very short silence. Bond Counsel was thinking it through, and then, "Okay," he muttered.

Client was pleased that I was able to get the change he wanted. And resting comfortably to this day in my closing-document binder on this deal, on the letterhead of Bond Counsel's prestigious law firm, is their "legal opinion" and this statement:

the reference to leasing [in the Mortgage provisions of the Bond Resolution] is a prohibition against leasing the whole project and is not to be interpreted as a prohibition against the leasing of individual apartments.

So there you have it, a legal opinion to the effect that a provision that says it prohibits leasing is not intended to prohibit leasing.[10] And elsewhere in the documents is the change Client really wanted. Whew!

I Confess

Looking back, I wonder at the gall of that young lawyer (me) taking the position I took based on that provision in the Bond Resolution and Mortgage. If the documents had prohibited leasing the Project "or any part thereof," I would have been in a stronger position – but looking back I see that I was skating on thin ice. But I guess I took Client's orders more seriously in the 70s than I would today. And apparently Bond Counsel thought the situation too risky, and so he had to "buy my silence" by agreeing to my Client's requested change.

III. The Other Side's Mistake

BLT #11: This is mostly for lawyers who produce documents to paper a deal: If you're copying from some prior document – which is almost always the case when we paper a deal – read the *entire* old document to ensure that *all* the provisions in that old document apply to your current situation. I suspect that the same Bond Indenture and other forms that were used in my situation were also used for other rental-apartment projects, but nobody had ever noticed the wording of the **anti-assignment clause**. Lawyers rarely write business documents from scratch – that would be "reinventing the wheel." We generally start with some previous form. This is all the more true in the case of long, detailed and formal papers like Bond Indentures and related documents. So the lesson here is this: Read the documents! And make certain that the standard forms and *all* the boilerplate provisions coming from some prior transaction actually apply to your particular deal. Good drafting is more than just using a copy machine!

BLT #12: And on the same principle of BLT #11: When amending any existing contract to change just one or two items – say some date or some price/dollar amount or some other single item or detail. – same advice as above: Review the *entire* contract that you're amending. In my own experience, I've found that in addition to that one single item that client needs to be changed, other circumstances have changed, which requires that other provisions be reviewed, not just that date or amount. No excuses – no shortcuts: Read the documents!

Thought Question: Was the Client-Developer Really at Risk of a Breach of Contract When Leasing Apartments? What do *you* think?

I'm guessing that this **boilerplate** anti-assignment provision in the mortgage-financing documents that prohibited "leasing the Project" was never changed in many rental-apartment housing projects (just as it was not changed in mine in this Tale #13); and so there are probably many such projects around the country where the documents, because of this "standard" anti-assignment clause, can be read as prohibiting the leasing of apartments. Now let's suppose the state Housing Finance Agency tried to foreclose on its mortgage for breach of that anti-assignment provision. I'm guessing, again, that no court would allow the foreclosure. Courts would probably rule that from the circumstances – namely, a rental-apartment project – the parties contemplated that apartments would be leased to tenants and that the **boilerplate** anti-assignment/leasing provision was left in inadvertently; they might "interpret" it as in Bond Counsel's opinion letter; or courts might just dub it a "scrivener's error" and would disregard that "mistake." We now move into an area probably of more interest to lawyers, but try it – you may like it.

Another Contract Case Where Words Don't Mean What They Mean

Here's a contract case that illustrates the reasoning of a court – this court's addition to the "canons of interpretation" that courts use when they make words not mean what they mean. The court addressed this question:

Was Engelhard, a mining company, allowed to deduct certain amounts from the royalties it paid to a Trust.[11]

The contract wording was clear – Yes! It could do so. But the court overrides the clear wording and rules that no, it may *not* deduct those amounts from royalties, reasoning as follows:

> But even if the language taken in the abstract is not decisive in the Trust's favor and even if the drafters never focused on the risk of negative royalties, only one reading of the contract **makes any sense**. No rational party in the Trust's position would agree to such negative royalties, nor would anyone in Engelhard's position demand such an option, because it would create an extraordinary perverse incentive for Engelhard to engage in otherwise irrational conduct and would **create an unlimited risk to the Trust's legitimate general expectations**. The point is so obvious as to require only brief explanation. [**my emphasis**]

This court asked "What makes business sense?" It tried to fulfill what the court deemed to be the parties' reasonable expectations. And based on this approach, the court rules that the words the parties used in the contract could be overridden and disregarded. So if the alternative to *your* position is this bad and doesn't make sense, if that alternative would disappoint reasonable expectations of one of the parties, then, you could argue, *your* position must be the right one. The *other* one is irrational and goes against clear (even though implied and not expressed) intentions and expectations. This is a kind of interpretation by process of elimination (of alternatives).

Later in their opinion, the court said:

> Even where courts are sure that the parties never thought about an issue, small wrinkles may be ironed out by interpretation where it is clear how the parties **would have** handled them. [**my emphasis**]

But you should also know that many courts would not try to be such mind-readers about a situation that the parties didn't think about; those courts refuse to correct errors or fill in omissions – and that applies not only to contracts, but to legislation that's considered to be unclear.[12] This court, above, based its ruling on what the court thinks the parties *would have* meant if they *had* thought about it – what I call the mind-reader school of contract interpretation.

So here again we see the importance of your looking forward, into that crystal ball, when entering into deals and contracts; and avoid risking a court finding "that the parties never thought about an issue;" and then you beg the court to decide for you what you would have agreed to if you *had* thought about it.

Lest you think that the U.S. Supreme Court has abandoned the plain meaning of the words in the contract (and statutes, see Tale #14), let's read some words from a decision in early calendar year 2015[13] – the Court's comments on how a court interprets a contract (here resorting to the canon of interpretation sometimes known as the plain meaning of the words):

> . . . contractual "provisions ordinarily should be enforced as written . . ."
> "In this endeavor, as with any other contract, the parties' intentions control."
> "Where the words of a contract in writing are clear and unambiguous, its meaning is to be ascertained in accordance with its plainly expressed intent."

The four concurring Justices agree with the majority's conclusions. Justices Ginsburg, Breyer, Sotomayor and Kagan write:

> Today's decision rightly holds that courts must apply ordinary contract principles, shorn of presumptions . . .When the intent of the parties is unambiguously expressed in the contract, that expression controls, and the court's inquiry should proceed no further.

These same four Justices (together with Justices Roberts and Kennedy) in the Affordable Care Act ("ACA" or "ObamaCare") case described below did *not* take the words of the statute literally. In his dissent Justice Scalia complains that the words "established by a State" now means "not established by a State." (More about how courts interpret statutes below and in Tale #14.)

Are the rules different when interpreting a statute than when interpreting a contract? Maybe, to a degree. Or maybe my cynical view is the correct one: Judges interpret statutes (and contracts?) based on their own individual backgrounds, beliefs, politics, predilections and other personal considerations and common sense (see e.g., the *Kirby* case in Tale #14, text at Note 10) when they decide what words mean in the particular case before them. Once they've decided, they pull out the appropriate "canon of interpretation" that justifies their decision. (The quotations noted above illustrate what is probably the primary canon of interpretation – "the plain meaning of the words.")

Almost all the canons of interpretation are shot down by the cannons (experience and wisdom) brought to bear by 7th Circuit Federal Appeals Judge Richard Posner, so maybe my cynical (realistic?) view of the judicial interpretation process isn't far off base. At least it seems to jibe with Judge Posner's views.[14] He believes "that most of the canons are just plain wrong."[15] This is from a commentary on Posner's latest book:

> ... the Constitution and federal statutes rarely dictate precisely the outcome in a court case, so judges 'fall back on their priors – the impulses, dispositions, attitudes, beliefs, and so on that they bring to a case,' before they look at the facts and the law to be applied ... [16]

And a reviewer of Posner's book also states Judge Posner's views: ". . . judges must often follow hunches or intuition." And "Judges must frequently simply guess as to what the sensible answer to a legal question is." The reviewer notes Posner's suggestion that "Academics...should conduct scientifically grounded research into the role of ideological and other factors in judging."[17]

*"Don't spread it around, but on the really tough ones,
I just go with 'eenie, meenie, minie, moe.'"*

The late Supreme Court Justice Scalia had his doubts about the canons
of interpretation, particularly the hunt for the intent of the legislature. Here,
he talks about the courts giving deference to an administrative agency (like
EPA, FCC, etc.) in construing a statute passed by Congress:

> And to tell the truth, the quest for the "genuine" legislative intent
> is probably a wild-goose chase anyway. In the vast majority of cases
> I expect that Congress *neither* (1) intended a single result, *nor* (2)
> meant to confer discretion upon the agency, but rather (3) didn't
> think about the matter at all. If I am correct in that, then any rule
> adopted in this field represents merely a fictional, presumed intent,
> and operates principally as a background rule of law against which
> Congress can legislate.[18]

Judges may claim reliance on the intent of the parties or intent of the leg-islature (clearly a fictional notion about a multi-headed body of diverse opinions and operating largely by compromise); or the obvious intent of the legislation itself; and then they may conclude from this exercise in in-terpretation that the "intended" meaning of the words is not the literal, plain meaning. Or they might (as in the *Engelhard* case, above – Note 10) dismiss alternate meanings as absurd and then choose to avoid that result by selecting the meaning that "makes sense" or "business sense." Or what the court believes the parties would have intended had they thought about the question before the court. Maybe Emerson's old saw that consistency is the hobgoblin of small minds is applicable here.[19] One day words mean just what they mean, but on other days, when reading business contracts and public statutes, words may not mean what they mean. *Your* task, when you write *your* contract: Write it for the judge and write it to mean what *you* want it to mean.[20] Don't forget the answer to this

> Question: What does this contract mean?
> Answer: It means what the judge says it means.

Finally, as we near the end of our stroll down the path of the meaning of words in contracts, let's look at one specific example, namely the forum-/law-selection provisions of a contract. This typical **boilerplate** provision appears in almost every contract and provides that (i) a particular court will have jurisdiction (usually *exclusive* jurisdiction) over the parties' dis-putes; and then (ii) designates which state's law will apply. In this case, brought by limo drivers against the defendant, who brokers chauffeur ser-vices,[21] the contract expressly provided that any "disputes arising under this Agreement" would be resolved only in Iowa courts and only under Iowa law. But...

This dispute was about how the plaintiff drivers were classified by the defendant employer, namely, as **independent contractors** and *not* employees. The drivers thought that they should properly have been classified as **employ-ees**. As employees, they would be entitled to overtime – not so if they're in-dependent contractors. The Massachusetts-based Plaintiff employees charged LimoLink with violations of state and federal laws. LimoLink pointed to the forum-selection and applicable-law provisions in their contract and asked the federal court in Massachusetts to act accordingly and transfer the case to a court in Iowa.

The Court refused because the dispute did not "arise under this Agreement." The Court rules, quoting from cases it cites in its opinion:

> ...suits to recover payments due under the FLSA [Fair Labor Standards Act], such as overtime payments, are not dependent on the plaintiff's employment agreement." . . . where "FLSA claims do not depend on the existence of the employment contract, nor does the resolution of [plaintiffs'] FLSA claims related to the interpretation of the employment contract, the forum selection clause which is limited to claims which are derived from the employment contract does not apply." [Citing an earlier case:] The court found that the plaintiffs' FLSA claims were "not dependent on any provision of the employment agreement, and [thus] not controlled by the forum selection clause.

And so despite those "usual" forum-selection and applicable-law boilerplate provisions, which we lawyers take for granted, this defendant, who expected to litigate in Iowa, had to hire lawyers and defend the case in Massachusetts.

BLT #13: If your lawyer is drafting your contract or some "standard form" contract for you and you intend that *all* disputes with the other party be resolved in courts in your state and under your state's laws, then the usual **boilerplate** language has to be broadened out beyond just "disputes arising under this Agreement." Perhaps you need to ask your lawyer whether they ought to add to the standard language something like the following to the choice-of-law provision:

> ...including, without limitation, all other claims, whether based on tort, contract and howsoever based and any claims under any laws, regulations, public policies, etc. of any political subdivision (state, federal or otherwise), in any way involving the parties' relationships under the herein Agreement.

I'm suggesting you try this on for size with your lawyer – this book is not intended to advise anyone on any specific problem.

P.S. When Words Don't Mean What They Mean, a Fish Is Not a Tangible Object
(A Lesson in Common-Sense Interpretation of a Statute by Dissenter Justice Elena Kagan)

Yates, a commercial fisherman, caught and kept fish below the minimum size set by federal regulations. A federal inspector found these undersize fish and ordered Yates to keep them in a separate basket as evidence of his violation of federal fishing regulations. Yates destroyed that evidence when he threw the undersize fish back into the sea. He was charged and convicted under a destruction-of-evidence statute. Here are the words of the statute that need to be interpreted (cut down in size by me):

> The crime is committed by any person who "alters, destroys, mutilates, conceals, covers up, falsifies, or makes a false entry" if they do so "in any record, document, or tangible object."

Five Justices ruled that those undersize fish Yates tossed back into the sea are not a "record, document, or tangible object." My take: The crime was destroying evidence; the undersize fish were the evidence; Yates destroyed this evidence by discarding the fish. Sounds to me like the Court complicated a simple issue. The 40+ pages of opinions mention those "canons of interpretation" 25 times. They refer to the intent of the legislature (Congress in this case) over 60 times. If meaning is obscure, a court may have to resort to canons, legislative intent, etc. But here meaning is clear: A fish is *not* a "record" or "document." But it surely is a "tangible object." And that tangible object, that fish, is evidence; and the defendant did destroy that evidence. Justice Kagan's common sense approach should have decided this case:

> A fisherman, like John Yates, who dumps undersized fish to avoid a fine is no less blameworthy than one who shreds his vessel's catch log for the same reason.

So if Yates had burned papers or photos which recorded his catch of under-size fish, that would violate the law; but if he destroys the fish itself (the *best* evidence of the size of the fish is not the paperwork or photo, but the fish itself!), the Court rules this is *not* a violation of the law. Interpretation should begin (and it may often end) with common sense – a great starting point before falling back on the mind-numbing canons, legislative intent, and other "aids." For a catalog of 70 canons, check out *Reading Law: The Interpretation of Legal Texts* by Antonin Scalia and Bryan A.Garner (Thomson West 2012) and a non-canoneer's view, "The Incoherence of Antonin Scalia" by Judge Richard A. Posner (*New Republic,* 8/24/12). (*Yates v. U.S.,* 574 US _ **(***2015***)**.

1 *Amalgamated Transit Union* Local 1309 v. *Laidlaw Transit Serv., Inc.,* 435 F.3d 1140 (and the dissent!) (9th Cir. 2006).

2 *Scurto v. LeBlanc,* 191 La. 136, 184 So. 567 (1938).

3 *Arizona State Legislature v. Arizona Independent Redistricting Comm'n,* 576 US ___(2015).

4 *Stanton v. Frankel Brothers Realty Co.,* 117 Ohio St. 345 (1927).

5 *Kelo v. City of New London,* 545 U.S. 469 (2005), a 5-4 decision.

6 *Citizens United v. Federal Election Commission,* 558 U.S. 310 (2010). See one of many commentaries at:

http://www.slate.com/articles/news_and_politics/jurisprudence/2010/01/money_isnt_speech_and_corporations_arent_people.html

7 State Farm Mut. Auto. Ins. Co. v Fitzgerald, 25 NY3d at 801 (2015).

8 See, e.g., Robert Pear's "Four Words That Imperil Health Care Law Were All a Mistake, Writers Now Say," *NYTimes,* May 25, 2015.

9 These words showed up in a book review title, "Do What I Mean, Not What I Say," written by James Ceaser about *Philosophy Between the Lines* by Arthur M. Melzer. The book focuses on "esoteric writing," which has a "deeper meaning" and is the opposite of what good prose – and in most cases, a good contract – strives for: directness; clarity; lucidity; precision. Otherwise, a judge will tell you what you meant, and that may not agree with your intentions and expectations. Leave esoterica to the philosophers and in business, say what you mean and mean what you say. (The book review is at http://www.wsj.com/articles/book-review-philosophy-between-the-lines-by-arthur-melzer-1414181806.)

10 For a scholarly study illustrating the title to this Tale #13, see Professor Andrew S. Gold's "Absurd Results, Scrivener's Errors, and Statutory Interpretation," (75 *U. Cin. L. Rev.* 25 [2006]), which begins with these examples (some cases mentioned in the text, above) which

illustrate how "more" can mean "less"; "black" can mean "white" and "up" can mean "down" and, generally, the error of focusing exclusively on literal wording:

> ...[S]uppose that a statute makes it illegal to "draw blood" in the streets. Do its terms apply to a doctor who performs emergency surgery in the street? What of a prisoner who breaks out of prison because the building is on fire? Does his flight violate a law against prison escapes?

11 *Rhode Island Charities Trust v. Engelhard Corp.*, 267 F.3d 3, 7 (1st Cir. 2001).

12 Recent decisions suggest that the current Supreme Court does not endorse Justice Stevens' conception of the scrivener's error doctrine. *See, e.g.*, Lamie v. United States Tr., 540 U.S. 526, 542 (2004) ("It is beyond our province to rescue Congress from its drafting errors, and to provide for what we might think . . . is the preferred result.") (quoting United States v. Granderson, 511 U.S. 39, 68 (1994) (Scalia, J., concurring)).

13 *M&G Polymers USA, LLC v. Tackett*, 2015 U.S. LEXIS 759, 574 US ____ (2015).

14 Richard A. Posner, "Statutory Interpretation – in the Classroom and in the Courtroom," *U.Chicago Law School, Chicago Unbound* (Journal Articles, Faculty Scholarship 1983) p. 800, esp. pp. 805 ff.

15 Ibid. at p. 806.

16 See also Lincoln Caplan, "Rhetoric and Law – The Double Life of Richard Posner," *Harvard Magazine* Jan.-Feb. 2016, p. 49, and the above quotation (p. 50) from Posner's book, Divergent Paths: *The Academy and the Judiciary*.

17 Professor Kermit Roosevelt, "Judging the Judges," *NYTimes Book Review*, Jan. 31, 2016, p. 13.

18 Scalia, "Judicial Deference to Administrative Interpretations of Law," *Duke Law J.*, Vol. June 1989, No. 3, 511 at p. 517.

19 From the essay, "Self Reliance" by Ralph Waldo Emerson (Essays: First Series (1841)): "A foolish consistency is the hobgoblin of little minds.."

20 For an article on the subject by an expert in the field, see Bryan A. Garner's article, "Making Your Point – Tips on Organizing Your Table of Contents for Statutory and Contractual Interpretations," *ABA Journal* Oct. 2015, p. 24. This and Garner's other works are useful guides when you're arguing for a particular interpretation of a contract or a statute.

21 *Chebotnikov v. LimoLink, Inc.*, 2015 U.S. Dist. LEXIS 166367 (D.Ct. MA Dec. 11, 2015).

TALE # 14

WHEN WORDS DON'T MEAN WHAT THEY MEAN – IN STATUTES[1] AND THE CONSTITUTION. ANOTHER TALE OF HOPE

> "I have not read far in the statutes of this Com-
> monwealth [Massachusetts].
> It is not profitable reading. They do not always say what is true;
> and they do not always mean what they say."
>
> *(Henry David Thoreau, July 4, 1854)*

" The books on THIS shelf contradict all the books on THAT shelf. "

I n Tale #13, you'll recall the legal opinion letter I got from Bond Counsel to the effect that "the reference to leasing [in the Mortgage provisions of the Bond Resolution] is not to be interpreted as a prohibition against the leasing of individual apartments."

Translation: "You may not lease" means that "you may lease" – almost the very words of Justice Scalia's dissent in the U.S. Supreme Court ruling on Obama Care (Affordable Care Act or ACA). In that 2015 decision[2], the majority read the four key words, "established by a State" to mean and include "established by the federal government." Justice Scalia's scathing view of this interpretation:

> Words no longer have meaning if an Exchange that is *not* established by a State is 'established by the State.' It is hard to come up with a clearer way to limit tax credits to state Exchanges than to use the words 'established by the State.' And it is hard to come up with a reason to include the words "by the State" other than the purpose of limiting credits to state Exchanges.

In this ACA decision, Justice Scalia takes a literal approach and neatly avoids this point made by others: The words in question were actually a **scrivener's error** – a big typo.[3] But in other decisions he avoids the simple-literal approach of the majority. In *Smith v. United States*[4], criminal defendant Smith was arrested when he offered to trade his automatic weapon to an undercover officer for cocaine. He was convicted of numerous firearm and drug trafficking offenses. The Court's majority gave a literal reading to the Federal criminal law, which increases the defendant's sentence when a person

> during and in relation to any crime of violence or
> drug trafficking crime…uses or carries a firearm.

At his trial, Smith's jail sentence was increased because he'd used a firearm in a drug trafficking crime, just as it says in the statute. Smith appealed this increased sentence all the way up to the U.S. Supreme Court, losing every appeal including, finally, at the high court. The Court majority decided that an individual who traded his gun for drugs had, for the purposes of the statute, "used a firearm" and allowed the increased prison sentence to stand.[5] But here, Justice Scalia seems to depart from the apparently clear statute and in this 6-3 decision, argues about the meaning of the word "used" as follows:

> To use an instrumentality ordinarily means to use it for its intended purpose. When someone asks, 'Do you use a cane?,' he is not in-quiring whether you have your grandfather's silver-handled walking stick on display in the hall; he wants to know whether you *walk* with a cane. Similarly, to speak of "using a firearm" is to speak of using it for its distinctive purpose, i.e., as a weapon.[6]

Here's Scalia's bottom-line (tongue-in cheek?) "test" for determining the meaning of words:

> [T]he acid test of whether a word can reasonably bear a particular meaning is whether you could use the word in that sense at a cocktail party without having people look at you funny.[7]

Before we leave the U.S. Supreme Court's examples illustrating that "Words Don't Mean What They Mean," we look at another 2015 decision (80+ pag-es!)[8]. Here the words that needed interpretation came from the "Elections Clause" of the U. S. Constitution, Art. I, sec. 4, cl. 1. Those words tell us who can draw the lines of Congressional election districts, namely, "the Legislature." The Elections Clause reads:

> The Times, Places and Manner of holding Elections for Senators and Representatives shall be prescribed in each State by the Legislature thereof; . . . but the Congress may at any time by Law make or alter such Regulations.

Arizona citizens, on their own "citizens' **initiative**," took away the redistrict-ing right from the State Legislature and gave that right to redraw election district lines to an independent commission called the Arizona Independent Redistricting Commission (AIRC). The Arizona Legislature called this a violation of the U.S. Constitution's Election Clause (above) and brought suit against AIRC.

The question for the U.S. Supreme Court: Do the words "the Legislature" of a state include AIRC? The majority of the Supreme Court rules "Yes." The people of a state can perform the legislative function and the AIRC, a creation of the people of Arizona, results in this simple equation: "Legislature" = AIRC. The word "Legislature" is not limited to only the State's elected representative assembly, the Court ruled; and the plaintiff Legislature loses the case 5-4.

The four dissenting Justices give us a history lesson and see things differently. Before 1912, U.S. Senators were elected by each state's legislature, as per the U.S. Constitution. After a long amendment process, the 17th Amendment transferred the power to choose U.S. Senators away from state legislatures and gave it "to the people thereof." In his dissent, Chief Justice Roberts starts out describing the "arduous and decades-long campaign" to ratify the Seventeenth Amendment to the U.S. Constitution. He continues:

> What chumps! Didn't they realize that all they had to do was interpret the constitutional term "the Legislature" to mean "the people"? The Court today performs just such a magic trick with the Elections Clause. [U.S. Constitution, Art. I, §4, above]. That Clause vests congressional redistricting authority in "the Legislature" of each State. An Arizona ballot initiative transferred that authority from "the Legislature" to an "Independent Redistricting Commission." The majority approves this deliberate constitutional evasion by doing what the proponents of the Seventeenth Amendment dared not: revising "the Legislature" to mean "the people." . . .

> Nowhere does the majority explain how a constitutional provision that vests redistricting authority in "the Legislature" permits a State to wholly exclude "the Legislature" from redistricting.

My own explanation: Sometimes words don't mean what they mean.

Let's look at another approach and argument in this case, where the Chief Justice makes the point that merely performing a function does not change the nature of the thing: The fact that the people and the AIRC may legislate (by **referendum** or **initiative**) does not make them "the Legislature" of Arizona:

> As a matter of ordinary language and common sense, however, a difference in function does not imply a difference in meaning. A car, for example, generally serves a transportation function. But it can also fulfill a storage function. At a tailgate party or a drive-in movie, it may play an entertainment function. In the absence of vacancies at the roadside motel, it could provide a lodging function. To a neighbor with a dead battery, it offers an electricity generation function. And yet, a person describing a "car" engaged in any of these varied functions would undoubtedly be referring to the same thing.

Sounds convincing to me: The words "Legislature thereof" certainly seem clear – they mean the State's representative assembly (usually a senate and a house of representatives); yet the majority here rules that "Legislature" includes a body that is clearly and definitely *not* a "Legislature." But hey, sometimes words don't mean what they mean.

The next example again illustrates how a group of smart federal judges can differ as to the meaning of a simple word like "less" – the majority rules that Congress really intended it to mean "more." The dissenters say no: "less" means less.[9] The question is a fairly simple time-limitation provision in the statute: A party to a lawsuit has certain rights after the court issues an order –

> if application is made to the court of appeals not less than 7 days after entry of the order.

The court rules that in this statute, "less" means "more." The dissenting judges consider this an "abuse of our judicial power." The losing party in this case filed the application to appeal 43 days after they lost in the lower court. As the dissenters point out, this was "a period that was plainly within the terms of the statute – 43 days is clearly 'not less than 7 days after entry of the [lower court's] order.'" And of course, each set of judges – the majority and the dissenters – provide sound justifications for their totally opposite conclusions. Surely, when "less" is ruled to mean "more," words don't mean what they mean.

Listen to the desperate tone of the judges in the dispute between these parties:

> Though 'troubled that, in contrast to most statutory construction cases where we are usually asked to construe the meaning of an ambiguous phrase or word, we are here faced with the task of striking a word passed on by both Houses of Congress and approved by the President, and replacing it with a word of the exact opposite meaning,' the panel did just that…The panel's confession was forthright: We have construed the statute to require a procedural framework that is not readily apparent from the statutory text or its legislative history, and have changed the statutory deadline for seeking to appeal to the opposite of what the plain language of the statute says…Thus, the panel declared, a statute that reads 'not less than 7 days' must henceforth be read to mean 'not more than 7 days.' … The text of 28 U.S.C. § 1453(c)(1) is unmistakably clear, and the panel should have applied the statute as written. In its decision, the panel conceded that the language of section 1453(c)(1) is unambiguous. Once it recognized that the statute is unambiguous, the panel should have stopped, for it is a paramount principle of statutory construction that '[w]here [a statute's] language is plain and admits of no more than one meaning the duty of interpretation does not arise, and the rules which are to aid doubtful meanings need no discussion.'

Finally, before we conclude with the true "mistake" – the "scrivener's error" – here's an illustration of Charles Dickens' words, "The law is an ass" – a patently stupid decision by a lower court requiring the U.S. Supreme Court to correct the situation.[10] Mr. Farris is indicted for murder and Sheriff Kirby is ordered to arrest Farris. Sheriff Kirby forms a posse and locates Farris on a steamboat. The lawmen used necessary force to arrest Farris but, it turns out that in the process, they delay the steamboat, which was carrying the U.S. mail.

Here comes the statute in this case: It is unlawful "to obstruct or retard the passage of a carrier of the mail" – and based on that statute, a U.S. Attorney indicted Kirby (and his posse?) for impeding the U.S. mail. I found it incredible to read that the good Sheriff was indicted for violating that law; and that this matter went through lower courts and ended up in the U.S. Supreme Court. The high Court set things straight: It was clear that the lawmen

> acted without any intent or purpose to obstruct or retard the mail, or the passage of the steamer. But the prosecuting U.S. Attorney responded, 'That doesn't matter.'[11]

Fortunately for Sheriff Kirby, the U.S. Supreme Court chose the route of common sense:

> The common sense of man approves the judgment mentioned by Puffendorf that the Bolognian law which enacted, 'that whoever drew blood in the streets should be punished with the utmost severity' did **not** extend to the surgeon who opened the vein of a person that fell down in the street in a fit. The same common sense accepts the ruling, cited by Plowden that the statute of 1st Edward II, which enacts that a prisoner who breaks prison shall be guilty of felony does *not* extend to a prisoner who breaks out when the prison is on fire – "for he is not to be hanged because he would not stay to be burnt." And we think that a like common sense will sanction the ruling we make that the act of Congress which punishes the obstruction or retarding of the passage of the mail or of its carrier does *not* apply to a case of temporary detention of the mail caused by the arrest of the carrier upon an indictment for murder. [my *emphasis*]

Kirby was found not to have caused an obstruction of the mail "within the meaning of the act of Congress" making that a crime; nor was Kirby's arrest of Farris "obstructing or retarding the passage of a carrier of the mail within the meaning of that act." A good instance of where being literal is being wrong – where words *should not* mean what they mean! (Maybe that prosecuting U.S. Attorney should have been indicted, or maybe just awarded The Stupidity-in-Law-Enforcement Award.)

Sometimes, a simple clerical/typographical error creeps into a statute unnoticed at the time by the legislature or the executive signing the bill into an act or law. That was the situation in Louisiana[12] where the court easily found that the word "unlawful" in the statute was supposed to read "lawful":

> ...in copying Act No. 126 of 1908, as the first section of Act No. 115 of 1934, the writer of the new statute, inadvertently, substituted the word "unlawful" for the word "lawful," and thus made the law declare that a party litigant may impeach the testimony given by his opponent on cross-examination, "in any unlawful way." We take cognizance of the fact – which is obvious – that this substitution of the word "unlawful" for the word "lawful" was an accident;. . .

Conclusion

To repeat, let hope spring eternal! Don't give up when those words in a contract or a statute go against you. Sometimes words don't mean what they mean, but...

Yes, There's Always a "BUT" in The Law Because There *Are* Occasions When Words Mean What They Mean ... No Changes Allowed !

Plaintiff "Ali" made a portrait of Minister Louis Farrakhan and right on the painting appeared "Ali ©." In 1983 Farrakhan bought the painting for $5,000 and hung it in his home. Ali registered his copyright in 1986. Later on, Farrakhan began selling materials that included copies of the painting and when Plaintiff Ali learned of this, he sued for copyright infringement.[13] There was no disagreement as to who owned the copyright – Ali – but ...

There was a disagreement as to whether Plaintiff Ali had authorized Farrakhan to make copies/prints. Plaintiff had written Defendant a letter in March 2008 and a question was asked in relation to this letter at a **deposition** in the infringement lawsuit. Plaintiff Ali was asked:

(Q) "Were you aware at the time of the March 2008 letter that lithographs [i.e., copies] of the painting had been made?"
(A) "Yes."

Ali wanted to change that answer and when you testify at a deposition, you get a chance to review the written transcript and make corrections. This is done on an "errata sheet" and Plaintiff Ali, claiming he misunderstood the question, tried to correct his answer from "Yes" to "No."

"No" was the Judge's ruling: Absent a transcription error, errata sheets may not be used to change deposition answers in a way that would contradict the original testimony – and nothing contradicts "Yes" more than "No." So in some circumstances, words *do* mean what they mean and "Yes" cannot mean "No." (For you legal scholars, note that the Judge did tell Plaintiff Ali that he could change his answer later, when he testifies on trial and offer his explanation at that time.)

———

Just Before *SOLVED!* Went to Press, on March 17, 2017, a Federal Court Decided What Words in a Maine Statute Mean (And Beware the Oxford Comma!)
Let's start with the words in a Maine statute dealing with overtime pay. More particularly, they describe who does **not** get overtime, namely those who work with certain kinds of perishable food products (like dairy, produce, meat and fish, etc.). Those workers do **not** get overtime if that work involves

the canning, processing, preserving, freezing, drying, marketing, storing, packing for shipment or distribution [of those products].

If there were a comma after "shipment," this case would not exist – read on and see why. The workers in this case are truck drivers who deliver dairy products and their employer denied them overtime under this statute claiming that they are involved in the "distribution" of dairy products. Sounds good to me – what do you think? If that comma appeared after "shipment," the word "distribution" would stand alone and, since truck drivers *do* distribution, they would *not* be entitled to overtime pay.

The drivers, however, say no, that's not what those words mean. The word "distribution" does not stand alone (as it would if that magical comma appeared). The drivers contend that the last phrase should be read as "packing for shipment or distribution" and, as drivers, they don't do *any* packing. So, again, what do you think the Maine statute means? What did the legislature intend when they wrote this law describing the workers who do *not* get overtime?

It was surely the $10 Million in overtime pay at stake in this case that led to a 30-page opinion by the Court. The Judge tries several approaches to answer the question – what do those words mean? Are the drivers right or is their employer company right? The Court struggles, but doesn't find an easy answer.

Searching for the intention of the legislature that created this law about who does *not* get paid for overtime, the Court looks to state legislative drafting manuals, which expressly deal with the missing comma: The manuals "expressly warn that the absence of serial commas can create ambiguity concerning the last item in a list." And sure enough, it's that last item –"distribution" – that's the problem here. The absence of this "serial comma" – also called the "Oxford comma" – is the problem in this case. The Court then starts to dig to discern the meaning of the statute and whether the company-employer is right (and drivers are not entitled to overtime) or whether the drivers are right in their claim for overtime pay.

Following the first canon of interpretation – "plain meaning of the words," – the Court concludes that "The text has, to be candid, not gotten us very far." And "the text turns out to be no clearer on close inspection than it first appeared. As a result, we turn to the parties' arguments about the exemption's purpose and the legislative history." That also seems to lead the Court nowhere:

> "Thus, we do not find either the purpose or the legislative history fully clarifying. And so we are back to where we began. . . .To be clear, none of this evidence is decisive either way."

The Court then returns to Maine's legislative drafting manual, noting that "under Maine law, ambiguities in the state's wage and hour laws must be construed liberally in order to accomplish their remedial purpose ..." Again, not helpful. But the Court pushes on: The default rule of construction under Maine law for ambiguous provisions in the state's wage and hour laws is that they "should be liberally construed to further the beneficent purposes for which they are enacted." And since those purposes are intended to protect and benefit the employees, the drivers. And so the Court decides in favor of the drivers.

I don't agree with the Court: Your author humbly sides with the company and without much deep analysis – just a simple, common-sense interpretation based on the English language and the way I read that provision – I come away with a strong feeling that "packing for shipment" is one separate category and "distribution" is another. But if we have to take a more lawyerly approach, then let's:

Since "shipment" and "distribution" are fairly synonymous, "distribution" becomes surplus – two words that mean the same thing. But such an interpretation violates a prime canon of interpreting a writing: Each word or phrase in the statute is meaningful and useful, and thus, an interpretation that would render a word or phrase redundant or meaningless should be rejected. So shipment and distribution stand apart and distribution has meaning only under the employer company's interpretation: The two phrases are (i) "packing for shipment" and (ii) "distribution." (see e.g., Tale #23, Case One where a term is repeated in a regulation and the consequences of such repetition). And so my simple-minded approach tells me that the company is right and these employees are not entitled to overtime under the Maine statute. But I'm no federal judge, so this ends the English language lesson – and we go on with our lives knowing a bit more about what can happen when the Oxford or serial comma – the last comma in a "series" of words – is missing.

1 The basic multi-volume text on interpretation of statutes is Norman J Singer and Shambie Singer, *Sutherland Statutes and Statutory Construction*, Clark Boardman Callaghan (2008-16).

2 *King v. Burwell*, U.S. Supreme Court No. 14-114, 574 U.S. _____(2015) (Scalia, J. dissenting).

3 See, e.g., Robert Pear, "Four Words That Imperil Health Care Law Were All a Mistake, Writers Now Say," *NYTimes* (Politics) May 25, 2015.

4 *Smith v. United States*, 508 U.S. 223 (1993) (Scalia, J. dissenting).

5 I wonder why no one focused on the word "carries" in the statute; Smith obviously carried his firearm. What am I missing? (Maybe the Justices would have read "carries" as meaning "carries with intent to use.")

6 Justice Scalia appears not to have addressed the word "carries" in the statute; Smith was clearly carrying a firearm.

7 *Johnson v. United States*, 529 U.S. 694, 718 (2000) (Scalia, J., dissenting).

8 *Arizona State Legislature v. Arizona Independent Redistricting Commission,* U.S. Supreme Court No. 13-1314 574 U.S. _____(2015)

9 *Amalgamated Transit Union Local 1309 v. Laidlaw Transit* Serv., Inc., 435 F.3d 1140, 1146 (9th Cir. 2006).

10 *United States v. Kirby*, 74 U.S. 7 Wall. 482 482 (1868).

11 Technically, as the Supreme Court notes, the U.S. Attorney "demurred." Under the old-style of formal pleadings, filing a "demurrer" means you're admitting the facts pleaded (i.e., no intention to obstruct the mail, etc.), but it doesn't matter – in effect, Sheriff Kirby still violated the letter of the law. (Was the U.S. Attorney when he indicted Sheriff Kirby in this 1868 case an early version of what we would today call a dumb robot?)

12 *Scurto v. Le Blanc*, 191 La. 136, 184 So. 967 (1938).

13 *Ali v. The Final Call, Inc.*, No. 13 C 6883, Slip Op. (N.D. Ill. Jun. 19, 2015) (Feinerman, J.).

PART III
KNOWING "THE LAW" HELPS YOU TO WIN!

W hy do most people go to a lawyer? Because we're supposed to know "The Law" and be able to apply it to the case (the facts), to solve their problems – and to do so within the law. Here are nine Tales showing how legal doctrine and principles – the stuff we learn in law school – were put to use to solve clients' problems. Some of these turned out to be ancient principles (like the Rule Against Perpetuities or the notion of a "Resulting Trust"); others focus on more modern rules, like the environmental and workplace-safety regulations and the margin regulations in the securities business. Knowing the law certainly helped these nine clients.

"You seem to know something about law. I like that in an attorney."

TALE # 15

THE LEASE THAT ALMOST DIDN'T HAPPEN – BUT IT DID BECAUSE OF "THE MAILBOX RULE."

I. The Client's Problem
"The Cave"

This Tale starts with a description of "The Cave." That's what Barry, the Client (Landlord) and I called the unusual office space on the street level of his downtown office building. The building lot sloped upwards toward the rear and during excavation for foundations, Landlord decided to expand the excavated area – extend it under that elevated area (a kind of hill) and create some more "rentable area." So although The Cave's entrance was at street level with other retailers along the front of the building, the space going back inside the Cave had a low ceiling, no show windows – just a nice glass double-door entry at street level. Not the easiest "retail space" to lease. And so it was that client Landlord, having leased out the entire building except for The Cave (and this was six years after completion of the building!) was left with this vacant space, beautifully finished but unrented. Broker after broker had tried – no luck. Landlord was beginning to wonder why he had finished the space with a nice floor and ceiling, lights, air conditioning, plumbing and electrical connections – the whole shebang, but no tenants. Finally the day came...

Broker Bill Finds a Tenant!

Real Estate Broker Bill walked in with a signed Offer-to-Lease form from a major stock brokerage house. Hallelujah! I spoke with their lawyer, we agreed on some changes to our standard form Lease and I mailed off four copies to the Stock Brokerage House main office with instructions to sign all four copies, return them and I'd get Landlord to countersign and return two copies to them.

Client Landlord called almost daily to see if the signed leases had come back. I counseled patience: "It's been almost ten days, they should be here any day now," I reassured him.

The Market Crashes – Dow Cut by Half!

Then came a day, Thursday, January 11, 1973, the start of a major stock market crash that ended with the Dow dropping from about 1050 to about 578 (remember, this was 40+ years ago!), losing about 45% of its value. I returned from lunch and my secretary handed me those pink telephone call slips commonly used back then. Among them, a call from someone at the new tenant for The Cave, the main office of the Stock Brokerage House. My immediate reaction was to pick up the phone and call him back. But I hesitated – I shuddered to think that after all this work, after 6+ years of effort, the only lease to materialize might be in jeopardy. I knew from past experience that stockbrokers froze – stopped in their tracks when such a major drop happened. (I also knew that as time passed, the Dow recovered and all went back to business as usual.) I did not want my Client Landlord to lose out because of the panic re-action I expected. The pink call-slip said nothing – just a name and a telephone number (remember this for later on).

I asked my secretary what message the caller had left. She replied, "No message, he just said to call him."

"But what did he *say*," I asked again. "Did he say *anything*?"

My secretary was quite clear and impatiently replied: "He said to call him. That's all he said," she replied. I asked her to please memo all the calls she'd noted on those phone slips and the messages people left – even if all they said was to call them back.

What to do? Stock Brokerage House had received the Lease some time ago and I had just told Client Landlord Barry "It's been almost ten days; the signed Lease should be back here any day now." I decided I needed an after-lunch walk – two blocks down to the local Post Office. I asked the postal clerk for any undelivered mail addressed to me. (In those good old days there was a second, afternoon mail delivery.) The clerk gave me a bundle and there it was, a fat envelope addressed to me with four copies of the Lease of The Cave, which the Stockbroker had signed two days earlier. I walked over to Landlord's office in a nearby building.

I showed Landlord Barry the contents of that fat envelope and told him he had a decision to make. He asked his secretary to "assemble the team" in the conference room, and I explained to Barry about the call I'd gotten from the prospective Tenant and that I hadn't yet called him back. I told him that the caller's only message was to call him. Barry led me into the conference room. The company executives were sitting around the table.

I repeated to the group what I'd told Barry about the "call-back" message I'd received from the Stockbroker's New York office and showed them that fat envelope that would have been delivered with the afternoon mail. Then I explained "The Law" in such a situation:

II. The Solution : The Law and Client's Decision

"When you give a tenant prospect your form Lease, that's an invitation to deal. When a tenant signs it and sends it to you, that signed lease is an offer; and your countersignature as Landlord and delivery of the countersigned Lease back to Tenant is an acceptance. Once you have an offer and an acceptance, a legally binding contract is formed."

Then I explained the law in more detail, namely "the mailbox rule:"

"When a contract is negotiated through the mails – as was the case here – then once the acceptance (the Lease countersigned by the Landlord) is deposited in the U.S. Mail, that constitutes delivery of the acceptance and the Lease becomes a legally binding contract."

I confirmed to the group that I hadn't returned the Broker's call and had no definitive knowledge of why the prospective Tenant was calling – he didn't leave any message other than "Call me back." He could have been calling for any number of reasons, but the coincidence with the sharp stock market drop gave me concern that Client Landlord's deal was in jeopardy.

I asked Barry, the Client's President/CEO if he was ready to make a decision on how I should proceed. He wanted to get his top management group together. He seemed to react positively to getting the deal done and I thought the whole team would quickly agree, but I was surprised.

"Barry, you've got a great reputation in this town and I don't know if going in this direction is going to help," said their public relations VP. "Your name is important . . ."

Her words were hardly out when the Treasurer interrupted: "You know how much money we've got invested, sitting there, in the Cave! And it's doing nothing."

One of the construction people chimed in: "What are we supposed to do? Let this go and wait another six years?"

Another officer spoke: "I'm concerned about this reputation thing and we ought to think this through."

Things were getting a little chaotic. Barry glanced in my direction:

"Milton, can we have a few minutes?"

I left the room, got some coffee and waited. After about ten minutes they called me back to the meeting. Barry said, "There's some concern about this reputation thing. If we follow your "mail-box rule," who's going to know about it?"

"Just the people in this room," I replied. Barry was quick with his instruction: "Then let's go ahead. Let's get the damn Cave leased! And, oh, when you call that guy back in New York, let me know what he called about."

I told them I'd follow their instructions, but it was possible – not likely, but possible – that the Stock Brokerage house would sue Landlord to invalidate the Lease if, indeed, that was what they were calling me about. Everyone agreed that they would deal with that if and when it happened. (It never happened.) And so, Client having made the business decision, I was then bound to carry it out, which I did.

Client countersigned the four copies of the Lease that Tenant had signed two days earlier; and I put two copies into an envelope with a cover letter. Landlord's secretary brought them to the Post Office and put them in the mail, Certified Mail. She brought back the time/date-stamped receipt of the mailing, and I went back to my office to pick up all those pink-slip telephone calls.

The first call I returned was the one from the person at the Stockbroker's main office. He told me that the Board of Directors had held an emergency meeting that morning and in light of market conditions, voted to stop all expansion, so they were calling off their Lease for The Cave. I replied, "But that deal is done. The signed Lease, your two copies, are in the mail back to you." Silence, then an "Oh . . ." and "I'll get back to you." But I never did hear from him again.

Stockbroker moved in, maybe a couple of weeks late and operated its office for years – and, of course, the Dow stock market numbers bounced back up and life returned to what passes for normal.

BLT #14: What Went Wrong? What Should Tenant Have Done?
And what should *you* be doing when faced with this kind of situation? The deal is half done, you've signed the contract and mailed it out. But suddenly you've got to get out of it. What to do?

- First, contact your lawyer immediately! Explain the situation – *all* the facts – and what you want to happen. Make it clear that you want to get out of a deal that's already signed up and in the mail, and you've got to get out of that deal.
- My guess is that your lawyer would say to first create your message ("Disregard the signed documents we mailed to you. We are withdrawing from this deal, *now!*").
- Then, send that message by the quickest means of communication, which today is typically an email, a text message, a cell phone call or a regular telephone call. If possible, also use fax (available back in 1973). And if you can have a messenger service, Federal Express or other such courier service deliver a hard copy immediately, do so, and get a signed receipt (with the date and time of delivery noted).
- When you call by telephone, be sure you get to some person "in authority" or an assistant or secretary to that person. If they're unavailable and you have to leave a message, then…
- Don't just leave a "call-back," as the Stockbroker did in this situation. That was a mistake under the circumstances and under his Board's instructions. Today we have voice-mail, so leave your message, loud and clear. "This deal is terminated. Disregard any prior communication, signed agreement, etc."
- Try to get proof of your call and the message – you're typically permitted by some states' laws to record your own side of a telephone conversation (but not the other party without their permission). Proof of receipt of an email is also possible today – use all technologies available to produce hard evidence that (i) you sent the cancellation message; (ii) that it was received; and (iii) when. And make a memo of the call.
- Don't make the mistake the Stockbroker made in this situation: Tenant had signed the Lease two days earlier and then simply left a call-back message with my secretary. (Remember, there was no voice-mail and no e-mail back in 1973.)

Suppose caller had left the same message he gave when I called back, namely: "Mr. Landlord and Attorney: Our Directors voted to stop all expansion immediately. The lease deal is off." If that had happened, I would have had to notify Client Landlord that under those circumstances, this tenant had withdrawn and there is no deal. "Start looking for a new tenant."

What Could Brokerage Have Done *After* Hearing "The Deal Is Done!"

There is a doctrine in law called "willful blindness" or "willful ignorance." Was I being "willfully blind" by deferring my return call to the Stockbroker? Although this doctrine comes up mostly in criminal cases, some courts have applied it to civil cases as well.[1] As the U.S. Supreme Court has described this doctrine in a criminal-law setting:

> The doctrine of willful blindness has two basic requirements: (1) the defendant must subjectively believe that there is a high probability that a fact exists and (2) the defendant must take deliberate actions to avoid learning of that fact. These requirements give willful blindness an appropriately limited scope that surpasses recklessness and negligence. Under this formulation, a willfully blind defendant is one who takes deliberate actions to avoid confirming a high probability of wrongdoing and who can almost be said to have actually known the critical facts.[2]

And so Brokerage might have taken the position that I "knew" what they were calling about when they left the "Call back" message and, knowing that (they would argue), I should have concluded and so advised my Client Landlord that The Cave Lease deal was off. Or, they could argue, that I was bound (which I was not!) to return the call immediately, or at least *before* strolling down to the Post Office. The message said nothing about "Urgent!" or "Call back immediately!" Instead, I took steps – by *not* returning the call until later – to avoid learning from Brokerage that the deal was off.

Come to think of it, Brokerage had no idea of the scenario of my trip to the Post Office. So I leave with the reader the question: What would have come of a claim of "willful blindness" if Stockbroker had made it? We'll never know.

Notice also the conflict between this doctrine of willful ignorance and the point made in the Judge's ruling quoted at the end of this Tale. To paraphrase, "I can guess what you meant, what you intended, but you didn't say it in the contract. I will not correct your mistake; I will not fill in the omission you left in your agreement." Notice how close that Judge's actual words – "the Court can perhaps guess that Plaintiff meant to prohibit solicitation" – are to the first element of willful ignorance, namely: "the defendant must subjectively believe that there is a high probability that a fact exists." That's the thin line that often makes it hard to predict just how any particular judge will come out in these cases of unexpressed intentions.

NOTE: Electronic Signature Contracts – Is There a Mailbox Rule?
At the time of this writing, the law is still developing and becoming refined in its details. But ask yourself as you whip e-mails back and forth: Do I intend to get into a binding contract? If not, say so. If yes, say so. If these matters are not expressly provided for, you leave it open to some judge to tell you, "Yes, you have entered into a binding agreement." And judges may well rule that, "Yes, Virginia, there is a mailbox rule in on-line contracting." And they may rule that the deal is done when you press the "Send" key. Ask your lawyer what the current state of the law is if you're starting down the road of emails which may lead to a legally binding contract.

BLT #15: Some "doubts" to share with those who also may have some "doubts" and a bit on the risks of litigation in many of these business situations.
Once the business lawyer has given his client the choices of alternative courses of action, before deciding, the client should consider the likelihood that this situation could end up in court. Here, I warned the Client that they could be sued – end up in court on this lease deal; and that they might lose. I might explain to them the doctrine of willful blindness (sometimes, "ignorance"), discussed above. But more generally, a judge might well consider what I did here to be a "sharp practice." The practical downside of *any* such "close-to-the-line" action is that many judges don't like sharp practices. If they think you are over the edge, they can rule against you and write their opinion in such a way that

you will never get it reversed on appeal. (A judge's ruling and opinion based on his findings of fact reached after his seeing and hearing the witnesses and based on adequate evidence is often practically immune to reversal on appeal.) So there can be consequences for going too close to the line of ethics as perceived by some judge.

Other judges see things differently and generally will not enforce unexpressed intentions and expectations; nor will they generally correct poor draftsmanship or insert omissions in contracts. One judge put it clearly in a case noted a number of times in other Tales; from this 2015 case[3], with **my emphasis:**

> [T]he proper interpretation of Section 3(B) calls attention to a more fundamental problem: its wording is **so vague and ambiguous** as to render it unenforceable. The provision prohibits soliciting or contacting Base One employees and independent contractors. But solicit or contact for what? The Agreement never says. Is an employee prohibited from contacting another employee about health insurance? From soliciting another employee to attend a political fundraiser? **Although the Court can perhaps guess that Plaintiff meant to prohibit solicitation or contact for the purpose of employment elsewhere, the provision does not so specify.** Particularly in light of New York's general hostility toward restrictive covenants in the context [18] of employment, the Court will not redraft a poorly written, overbroad restraint in order to render it enforceable…

But there's that risk of litigation, of angering a judge who takes the approach, "You, Mr. Lawyer, must have known or at least had a strong hunch what Tenant was calling you about on that day the market crashed." Such a negative view from the judge doesn't help you win cases. So there was the chance that if a lawsuit ensued, client risked losing in litigation, something the client should think about before deciding which way to go: Always ask: What's the likelihood that we'll be sued? And if so, what's the likelihood that we'll lose?

Finally, Some More "Doubts" from Readers – I Wasn't Being "Nice"

My nature, as I noted in the Prologue, derived from my dear mother, was to be "nice" which, as I explained in the Prologue, works for me as a lawyer only at the beginning, when I'm engaged by a client. If the nature of the client or the case doesn't meet my personal "nice" test, I just don't take on the job. But once I accept an engagement, the Canons of Legal Ethics take over and "nice" takes a back seat to my professional obligation to that client: To zealously promote the client's interests.

This Tale #15 brought a lot of criticism from friends, relatives and colleagues. Why? Because I didn't immediately return that call from the Stockbroker when I was handed the pink call-back slip. I agree that the nice, polite, and courteous thing to do would have been to call him back. But under the circumstances, in the hierarchy of values in play, my professional obligation to the Client Landlord trumped those personal values. I was obliged to follow the Canons of Legal Ethics and zealously protect my client's interests, even if that meant violating my personal values of being nice, polite, and courteous (and immediately returning a "call-back" telephone call). And, as noted in the Prologue, when I later checked with the nation's two experts on legal ethics, both confirmed that I had acted properly: I gave the Landlord Client choices that were lawful/legal and legitimate. It was then for the Client and not me to make the business decision of how to go forward. And once made, I must be guided by the Client's decision, as I was in this matter. Simply stated, the other side made a mistake, as noted in BLT 13, above, and I took advantage of that mistake for the benefit of my client. I was not nice, polite or courteous, but I believe I did right. Enough said!

---

1 *Gowan v. Patriot Grp., LLC (In re Dreier LLP)*, 452 B.R. 391 (Bankr. S.D.N.Y. 2011)

2 *Global-Tech Appliances, Inc. v. SEB S.A.*, 131 S. Ct. 2060, 2061, 179 L. Ed. 2d 1167, 1167 (2011)

3 *Base One Techs., Inc. v. Ali*, 2015 U.S. Dist. LEXIS 5821; January 20, 2015, Civil Action No. 14-1520 (JEB)

TALE # 16

DEPARTING "GENIUS" SPORTING-GOODS BUYER
NEVER SIGNED A NON-COMPETE AGREEMENT,
BUT EMPLOYER STOPS HIM FROM OPENING A
COMPETING BUSINESS – HOW?

I. The Problem
Sonny, The Hot-Shot Sporting Goods Buyer, Gets Ambitious

Client Jim owned a downtown department store with suburban branches. Jim's stores were known for great sporting goods "deals" – ski and tennis equipment, and more – all due to the "genius" of Sonny, their Sporting Goods Buyer. But Jim sounded nervous when he called us for a meeting – "Right away, the sooner the better!" This was back in the early sixties, shortly after I'd begun at the law firm and was working with our litigator, Henry.

Jim looked distressed when he told us the bad news: Sonny had given notice – he was quitting. With a group of five investors, Sonny was planning to start up a new 5-store, free-standing sporting goods specialty retail store to be called "Five-Star Sports." And worse, their five prospective locations were in the very suburban towns where Jim's department store had a suburban branch. What to do? It's a free country. No **non-compete agreements** back in the 60s, at least not in the department store business. Sonny was free to quit his job and go into business for himself. There was no secret or proprietary information being stolen. But a big chunk of Jim's business was about to walk out the door.

Henry, a seasoned commercial litigator with a background as a prosecutor, initially could not see that any law was being broken or any of Jim's legal rights violated, but there had to be a hook somewhere, so we began to dig. Henry and I met with Jim at the main, downtown store; he provided us with a lot of background about Sonny and the department store.

We learned that Sonny, the stores' "powerhouse" sporting goods buyer, had an unusual job description. Sonny was highly-paid and had no fixed hours – he came and went as he pleased. He had a hefty expense account and a company car, a red Thunderbird. Jim had given him a free hand in running the sporting goods business for Jim's chain of stores – no supervision by upper management needed. Sonny was able to select the most desirable merchandise; and he would organize informal buying syndicates based on his contacts with buyers from similar stores in other (non-competing) cities, get extremely low prices from manufacturers – sometimes even buying out a manufacturer's whole season's production for a particular syndicate. Sonny was also a big help in setting competitive retail prices. Jim's cost of goods was the lowest possible! And so it was that Jim's stores had become *the* sporting-goods leader in the area. I recall going down the escalator after an early morning meeting at the main store, which just then opened the doors. I was almost trampled by a mob rushing up the escalator to the major ski event. All because of Sonny's astute buying abilities.

Although Sonny was important and highly compensated under a written Employment Agreement, under that contract he was expressly designated an "at-will employee." This means that he could quit at any time and Jim could fire him at any time for any reason or no reason. But this Agreement had no formal **non-compete** provision. The United States was still a free country and Sonny was free to pursue his ambition to be in business for himself – the American Dream! But Sonny's dream was Jim's nightmare.

What to do? How to stop this potentially powerful competitor from setting up in Jim's backyard, and based on the business model and valuable contacts that Jim had incubated and paid for?

II. The Solution
An Ancient Equitable "Trust" Remedy – of All Things!
The more I dug into the facts of how Sonny operated in his job for Jim, the clearer it became that this was no ordinary employee. He had complete and unsupervised freedom to come and go on his own hours, to select merchandise, to negotiate deals for Jim (and to enter into written contracts he was authorized to sign on behalf of the Store), to take trips and use his generous expense account. He appeared to have no real "boss" and worked without any oversight, as long as he "delivered the goods" and kept making deals that helped Jim's stores remain the acknowledged leader in the region's retail sporting goods market. It could be said that Sonny ran a sort of "business within a business." He was almost like an owner of the business more than what we think of as an "employee" (although an employee he surely was).

What to do? It was clear that Sonny was ungrateful for the opportunities Jim had given him and that his 5-Star venture would be hurting his employer. But there was no theft, or fraud or breach of contract. How could Sonny's conduct be classified as a wrong for which Jim could ask a court for relief? There is, after all, a lot of reprehensible behavior, bad actors who talk too loudly on cell phones in crowded spaces or the guy in the seat next to you on the plane who apparently hadn't heard of underarm deodorant or sharing an arm rest. Annoying, but behavior for which The Law offers no relief. Not being a nice guy is not what is termed "actionable," meaning that a legal action can be maintained in court to stop it.

I finally came up with this theory and a claim I thought Henry could take to court:

> Sonny had in fact misappropriated some of Jim's property. That property was the series of valuable networks of contacts, relationships with suppliers, other dealers and the buying syndicates of non-competing department stores which Sonny had created – and which Sonny had been handsomely paid to create. It was not the same as a situation in which, say, Sonny was a test cook who created a valuable secret recipe while on Jim's payroll. That might belong to his

employer as a trade secret or a work-for-hire, and those can usually be protected. There was nothing secret about what Sonny created. Sonny was legally free to build another network, a *new* roster of suppliers and a buying syndicate, but that was obviously not what he was planning to do. The chink in Sonny's "armor" – his freedom to go into business for himself – was that he was leaving and taking the very network that he created for Jim, and "on Jim's nickel." Jim had paid for what Sonny was about to take away from him!

OK, so now I had a hook—a wrong for which a judge could grant Jim some relief. Clearly, it would not be a slam-dunk – judges don't like to restrict employees' freedom to leave their job and go into business for themselves. Not a sure thing, but enough to get us into court.

Next problem: What relief could Jim get for this wrong? Courts award actual damages, not speculative damages. Most courts look askance at a claim for loss of future profits – they're usually designated as "highly speculative." So a claim for damages didn't hold much promise. Now what? Could we get an injunction? Highly unlikely; judges do not like to restrain free commerce and certainly would not make Sonny, in effect, a slave or deprive him of his right to make a living as a shrewd sporting-goods buyer. And Jim certainly wasn't about to pay legal fees for getting some judge to rule that Sonny was not nice, but only owed Jim six cents in **nominal damages**.

Enter the remedy of a constructive trust, more particularly here, a "resulting trust." Let's explain a bit of law: Here's a textbook definition:

A Resulting Trust is a trust implied by law (as determined by a court) imposed on a person who holds title or possession to some property. If from the circumstances it is clear that the parties' intention –which is inferred from the circumstances – is that the "property" is held for the benefit of the intended owner, the court may impose "resulting trust" status on that property.

Given the breadth, the broad scope of Sonny's job and his freedom to pursue all sorts of directions, why wasn't this planned venture of his just another aspect of his job for the Store? Why doesn't this newly planned venture belong to his employer, Jim's store? Under this "resulting trust" theory, Sonny (I could argue) is considered a trustee of a resulting trust for the benefit his employer, the proper owner of his planned venture. Jim's Store was beneficiary and Sonny's venture was really, in law, the property of his principal or beneficiary. Jim's Store owned Five-Star Sports! Although a legal fiction, the "resulting trust" forces the holder or "trustee" (Sonny) to honor the parties' intention and prevents **"unjust enrichment"** (another legal phrase). Back to the books:

> **A Law Textbook Example:** Mahalia leaves $100,000 with her friend, Albert, while she is on a trip to Europe. She asks him "to buy the old Barsallo place if it comes on the market." Albert buys the property, but has title put in his own name, which the court will find is held by him as trustee of a resulting trust for the benefit of Mahalia.[1]

Sonny was going to exploit the networks that Jim paid him to create. It is right and just that Sonny not be able to keep the profits of his misbehavior—judges call this "unjust enrichment." I felt I had my case—a wrong, misappropriation, and a remedy, a constructive trust. Was this a clear winner? Nope. A palpable threat that could not be **motioned** out of court at the outset on the basis of just the Complaint? Probably.

But wait – there's more: Sonny had spent the past two years, it appeared, assembling his group of four or five other investors, finding locations and setting up store leases for his new business – all that while taking salary and expenses from his employer, client Jim's store. Sonny's plan was for each investor to take over a suburban sporting-goods specialty store under the corporation that Sonny had already formed, "Five Star Sports, Inc." I was able to learn the investors' names and also that each one was represented by his own lawyer in his negotiations with Sonny.

I spoke to Henry about my idea. He thought it was worth a try – after all, this was a hopeless case otherwise. I drafted a Complaint, ostensibly to be filed in court. It was captioned "Petition for Declaratory Judgment," a judgment by the court that would declare the rights of the parties. A "courtesy copy" of the Complaint was, per the custom among local lawyers, sent to each of the lawyers who represented Sonny's five partners in his proposed new venture. All the partners were named as Defendants in the Complaint.

The thrust of the Complaint:

- Sonny's entire effort at the new business fell within the broad scope of his job description and duties for Jim's Store and, therefore, belonged to Jim's, the Store that employed him. Sonny, with his broad-ranging and free-wheeling job description, was running, in effect, a business within a business. And that business belonged to his employer. Citing legal authority in an accompanying legal brief, the Complaint asserted that the planned new 5-store business was rightly the property of Jim's Store, relying on the theory of a "resulting trust." The Store, the party plaintiff in the Complaint, asked the court to declare that Jim's Store owned Five Star Sports, Inc. and whatever income it generated.
- Furthermore, for his disloyalty in trying to divert a "corporate opportunity" (see BLT #16 at the end of this Tale #15 for an explanation) away from Jim, his employer, Plaintiff Jim was asking for a return of salary, bonuses and certain expenses paid to Sonny in the two prior years. While still employed and being paid by the Store, he was in fact, during that time, working for himself and Five Star Sports. This calculation produced a tidy six-figure sum.

An important practical consideration that made this situation work out for Jim: Nothing "chills" a new investment situation so much as "problems" or troubles – and this draft Complaint pleading, ready for filing in court, clearly spelled trouble for the venture. It was authoritative and credible enough to be of concern – to communicate to the investors that their investment was at risk from the get-go.

After they received the "courtesy copy" of my draft Petition for Declaratory Judgment, the investors and Sonny asked for a meeting. The question on the table, from this group to Jim, came down to a simple "What do you want?" Obviously the deal would go forward only on Jim's terms.

Jim wanted Sonny out of the sporting goods business, but we told him it was unlikely that any court would order that. Courts do not lightly deprive people of their careers.

"Then keep them out of my neighborhoods," shouted Jim at his meeting with us. So when we all met with Sonny and his investors, Jim asked for, and received, a written commitment that Five Star Sports would not locate a store within a given radius of any of Jim's existing downtown or suburban stores. A "meaningful" **per diem liquidated damage** provision, as a practical matter, ensured that Jim would not have to go to court if his new competitor, Five Star Sports, violated the restriction. And so the matter was settled to Jim's grudging satisfaction without the draft Complaint ever having been filed in court.

Before we leave for the BLTs, notice that this Tale #15 would also fit well into Part II, where we talked about risk-shifting as a strategy to resolve a problem situation. Whether my legal theory was weak or strong, it was good enough to worry Sonny and his 5-Star investors. The risk that some judge would make Jim's business the owner of 5-Star was real enough and unacceptable, even more so at this sensitive point in time *before* the investors had put in any big money. Jim's business got the protection he wanted, but clearly, Jim was still angry at Sonny for his disloyalty and ingratitude.

"Upset at you for breaching the non-compete? Of course not."

BLT #16: From Different Points of View

1- Employees: If you're ever in a "Sonny Situation" – ambitious to go into business for yourself and realize the American dream – don't do it on company time or using company assets, supplies, copy machine, telephone, computer or anything else that belongs to your employer. This is a clear no-no while you're still taking salary, bonus, expense account, etc. from your employer. An employee owes a duty of loyalty to his employer – a fiduciary duty not to act in his own interests when those go against the employer's interests.

2- What you may do under some states' laws – and these vary from state to state – is to *prepare and plan* your venture, but do it on your own time and without using your employer's personnel or assets (office supplies; equipment; other employees, etc.). But then, I believe it's safest that you resign *before* these plans mature into as fully developed a plan as Sonny's: He had four partners, store locations selected and store leases under review. Clearly, Sonny was working for himself on his employer's time.

3- If you're a lawyer, this situation illustrates that you have to remain keenly aware of "The Law" – in this case, this ancient "resulting trust" doctrine. And how did I dredge up this rarely used doctrine? By getting all the facts of Sonny's employment – "Synthesis" I call it: The combining of a lawyer's knowledge of The Law with the facts, which only the client can provide. In this case it was crucial to learn the details of Sonny's unusual job description. You'll read in some other Tales how knowing all the facts can turn a weak case (and sometimes no case) into a possible winner.

BLT #17:- Whether you're an owner of a corporate business or only an officer or employee, you should know about another legal theory – the doctrine of "Corporate Opportunity" – something I could have used in Sonny's case, but I felt that claiming ownership of Sonny's venture under the "resulting/constructive trust" approach would be more powerful and more effective (and it was!). But here's the doctrine of corporate opportunity:

If you are an employee – and remember, even the major owner/shareholder and CEO is an employee – and particularly if you operate in a corporate setting, be alert and distinguish between (i) what is YOURS and (ii) what belongs to your employer, the CORPORATION. In this Tale #15 situation, I was able to characterize Sonny's new venture as something he was doing for the corporation, his employer, something that The Law doesn't permit him to do for his own account (at least not without his employer's consent). These kinds of situations fall under the heading of "Corporate Opportunity."

Here's another mini-tale of a corporate opportunity – something that belongs to the corporation and must be offered to it before the individual can take advantage of that opportunity. This mini-tale of one of my retail chain-store clients should help you remember to avoid these conflict-of-interest situations:

The chain store's founder, major shareholder and CEO found a parcel of land in his home town that he wanted to own and told me it would make an ideal site for a new store. I suggested that this might constitute a "corporate opportunity." This meant that he had to disclose his personal interest in the land, the opportunity to buy it and then offer to lease it to the corporation. As I advised, he disclosed the opportunity to his Board of Directors. They all agreed and so voted: The company should not own land or get into the real estate business, but rather continue to operate stores in buildings leased from their owner/Landlords. This board action (properly recorded in the corporate minutes of the meeting) recognized and gave up the company's corporate opportunity, which freed the CEO to buy the parcel of land for his own account.

---

1 For a relatively modern reference to the ancient resulting-trust principles, see the U.S. Supreme Court case involving a real estate financing/purchase, *Oyama v. California*, 332 U.S. 633 (1948).

TALE # 17

LOOKING FOR A NEW SITE? WHY YOUR LAWYER MUST VISIT IT FIRST!

. . . *Before* You Buy the Property or Sign the Lease

I'm sure I've admitted elsewhere in this book to having a paranoid streak. I believe just a bit of paranoid concern can serve lawyers and their clients well[1]. This is particularly so when they call, all happy and excited about "a new place." I learned early on not to just sit at my desk and produce papers. Never! There's too much of value to be learned by meeting with the client at the place of business and if they're planning to move, I want to see *both* the new property and their existing space; and that latter is usually my first visit. Here are the stories of six such visits and the problems that were avoided by what I learned. Ah, paranoia!

Case No. 1: Client-Printer Expands and Finds a Great Building for His Plant

This is not a tale of today, when we have some strict environmental controls in place. Concern about what we are dumping in the ground and into our rivers and oceans was in its infancy and we business lawyers were just starting to become aware of the regulations and the legal risks some of our industrial clients would be facing. That was then and this is the story of the expanding printing plant:

It was a hot July day when I drove out to a distant suburb of Boston to look at the proposed new location for client's printing plant. A discreet sign announced that it was occupied by XYZ Auto Parts. I went to a nearby coffee shop to get some "local color" and learn what I could. I even jumped in a cab standing at a taxi stand and chatted up the driver about the area. I bought a town newspaper and one item caught my eye – something that was mentioned both in the coffee shop and by the taxi driver. Apparently after a recent heavy rain, a number of local wells were showing signs of contamination – again. More to the point, those wells were at houses in the neighborhood of the building Client wanted to buy. The coffee shop proprietor filled me in: These post-rain situations were a mystery and "folks don't seem to know what to do about it. Or even where it comes from." I went back to the building client intended to buy.

It was almost high noon and hot as hell. Along the curving driveway from the back delivery gates to the street, XYZ Auto Parts workers were sitting along a curb, in tank-tops or shirtless in the heat. They appeared to be washing auto parts. I approached and was told, as I could see, that they were cleaning carburetors for resale to auto repair shops. They were using what smelled like one of those volatile solvents that dissolves grease – like super cleaning fluid. I could understand not wanting to work indoors in an enclosed space with that stuff – at least not without a gas mask. Then I saw "The Problem" – a couple of workers dumped the spent solvent, loaded with dirt and grease, right at the curb where they sat; and the liquid ran down to a drain at the end of the driveway. When I asked one of the men whether that was "okay," he assured me: "Oh yeah, the stuff evaporates fast." But I was seeing liquid reach and run down the drain.

And so, being a "Defective Detective," I concocted a theory (actually, we'll never know the true facts): I suspected that the dirty goo was landing on whatever was in that drain and hardening up into a solid. Then when it rained, that solid gunk, with rain water running over it, began to dissolve and get into the earth somehow and then migrate into those water wells in the neighborhood.[2] I drove to Client Printer and told him he'd better not buy this place, at least just yet – it might be so contaminated as to impose massive cleanup costs on him as the new owner. I gave him a little chapter-and-verse of the then-new state and federal environmental laws and regulations. Client Printer was so in love with the place that he decided to take a lease with option to buy. Needless to say, that lease (from the Landlord, XYZ Auto Parts) took some careful work to protect Client Printer against claims for pre-existing contamination conditions.

I advised another precaution because of the then new environmental laws: Since the printing plant itself also used solvents in cleaning presses and equipment, a system had to be installed to track everything that came in and everything that went out; and a licensed hazardous chemicals disposal company had to be engaged to take away rags and other waste that might have these cleaners/solvents in them.

End of story: Client Printer did lease the building, and a year or so later his company was bought out by a larger national outfit, which operated there for a while and then consolidated into another Boston area location. No harm, no foul. And since no related pollution sites are listed for the town, I assumed that the problems with the nearby wells ended soon after the carburetor-cleaning I'd seen on that hot July day had come to an end.

Case No. 2: Chain-store Retailer Finds Ideal Warehouse Location – <u>Whoopee</u>!

The location was, indeed, ideal – almost equidistant from many of client's chain of retail stores – and we drove out for a look-see. The large building certainly met client's needs: lots of space and loading docks and a fairly young structure. It was located in an older, well-maintained office/industrial park. BUT, on a small hill at the back of the building and not too far from the building was an old red brick industrial structure with smokestacks puffing away and the sign: "Silver-Plating and Jewelry Manufacturing Company, Founded 1931" – apparently the first building in this park, nicely set high up on that hill and behind my retailer-client's choice for his warehouse.

Having learned something about environmental problems from other situations, I explained to Client Retailer about "migration" and "plumes." This is what happens when substances – like hazardous chemicals – are dumped on or into the ground. The stuff migrates deeper into the ground and will frequently, because of pressures and other conditions, start to spread laterally instead of just sinking farther down into the earth. Most frequently, the up-gradient property (Silver-Plating Company) will contaminate the down-gradient property (Client's "perfect" building lot).

I told client that he should not even consider this location without some very extensive testing over the entire lot and extending up the hill toward that silver-plating operation. Since that silver-plater had been at this same location for so many years – starting long before there was any concern about the metallic wastes produced and dumped on site – chances were high that this "ideal" warehouse site was already severely contaminated; and that would show up only after some test borings were made. Client quickly learned what I had then only recently learned about the risks of buying real estate and becoming a PRP – potentially responsible party – responsible under the environmental laws for cleanup costs even when the polluted condition of his land originated off the property – it came from elsewhere through migration and plumes.

Client retailer decided not to spend money for environmental testing and instead continued his search for another suitable location. I agreed with his decision – a prudent course of action under the circumstances.

Case No. 3: The Art at the Ad Agency Must Be Preserved!

I revisited Client Ad Agency when they sent me a lease form for new offices. I wanted a tour of the entire place. Although I'd previously met with the owners in their office, I hadn't seen the entire floor they occupied. But now I needed to see their present space to make my lease review of their new premises more meaningful and effective. On the walk-through, we passed a large art department with people busy at drawing tables and then came to a door with a sign posted: "Do Not Enter! No Matches or Cigarettes! Danger!"

When I touched the door handle to go in, Client put his hand on mine. "You don't want to go in there." I did and was frankly horrified. The room was dense with fumes and two men, no masks or gloves, were spraying some wicked stuff on large drawings. I began to choke and cough and got out immediately.

"They're spraying fixative," the Client explained. When I finished coughing, I asked how they could stand it in there and why the room wasn't vented.

"There was no place for a vent in that little inside space. Beside, those guys are used to it." I was appalled!

"You'll get used to sitting in a jail cell if something happens to them," I almost shouted. I told the Client the sad story of the father-and-son photo-finishing company in New York. They used a cyanide solution in their work, and workers without gloves were putting their hands into vats of this solution. Some got sick and one died, resulting in manslaughter convictions of the father and the son. "We'd better make sure the new premises are vented and the air is breathable. I'd hate to have to visit you in jail." I looked Client in the eye, looking down and shaking my head – "They're used to it." How lame![3]

Sure enough Client, in its new premises, was able to include a chase (inside-wall channel) for a vent; and as soon as the lights were turned on in the fixative room, a powerful exhaust fan automatically went on. I urged client to get an air-test done in the room and keep the "clean" report for future use – I hope they took my suggestion. I was pleased to have seen all this in time and always believed that my "paranoid" visit to this ad agency made life a little better for those two guys spraying fixative in that little room, even though "they were used to it." (And if you don't already know, fixative keeps a chalk, charcoal or pastel drawing from smudging – it "preserves the art.")

Case No. 4: Same Situation, Other Chemicals, But Just as Risky/Costly

This client was also moving – this time a high-tech electronics firm manufacturing equipment with lots of circuit boards, chips and the like. And again, I went for a walk-through with the client at their existing location before I tackled a lease of new, enlarged premises. Wouldn't you know it – almost the same door sign, except this time bigger, more colorful and with a large skull and cross-bones over the "Do Not Enter!" warnings. Of course I had to enter.

A large white porcelain sink stood in the corner, and hanging on the wall over the sink were three tanks or cylinders. Each had a little hose running from the top of the cylinder down to a spigot at the end of the hose, which lay in the sink. And each cylinder had its own frightening label: Concentrated Sulfuric Acid, Concentrated Nitric Acid, and Concentrated Hydrochloric Acid. Plenty of rubber gloves lying around that sink!

Client explained: "We use the acid to wash certain chips and circuit boards and other equipment."

"What happens to the spent acid," I asked. Client replied that they use just a little bit and that it's flushed down the sink with water from the faucet. I informed client that flushing acid down a sink drain is a violation of law in Massachusetts. "This 'little bit' is no defense – you're breaking the law!"

I insisted that they find a way to handle this acid, and they did. I later learned that in their new premises, a plumber installed a bicarbonate-of-soda filter cartridge onto the waste line under the sink. This chemical would neutralize acid going down the drain. Changing the filter periodically cost them about ten cents per change.

Shortly after that visit, I sent Client a newspaper clipping reporting on a nearby firm in the same business as theirs and in the same town. That company was fined $475,000 for "pouring acid down a common drain," in violation of Massachusetts environmental safety regulations. Client got off cheap!

Case No. 5: The Big Office Tower Mortgage Loan That Didn't Happen

This is a goodie that my partner, Larry, experienced and it belongs right here, to emphasize the message of this Tale: A visit to the site pays off! Larry was engaged by a major bank client to document a proposed mortgage loan transaction – Bank was lending a hefty eight-figure sum and taking back a mortgage on Big Building located in a major West Coast city. I don't know how he managed it, but Larry wangled a trip to Big Building where he conducted a sort of "lawyer's inspection." He got the facilities manager to take him through portions of Big Building, starting in the basement.

Larry was a real estate lawyer and knew a lot about construction, engineering and mechanical details of these office towers that he and I had worked on. As Larry tells it, an odd feature of the basement was the absence of equipment, like boilers and air handlers, but there were some major size pipes or ducts coming through the wall into (or maybe out of?) the basement. Oh well . . .

Up on the roof, Larry noted the absence of any cooling towers – those large structures we see from the air, big fan blades and piping – all an intrinsic part of the building's air-conditioning system. But on this Big Building, no cooling towers. However, on the adjoining building – a sort of twin – that one *did* have a huge cooling tower.

Larry made inquiries and was referred to the Building Engineer. Larry explained who he was and that he was there on an inspection visit. Then he asked about this strange situation – no HVAC equipment in the basement or on the roof of the Big Building on which Client Bank was about to make a major loan secured by a mortgage. Big Building appeared to have no heating, ventilation, air conditioning system – no on-premises HVAC of its own. The engineer explained that Big Building depended on the building next door, which *did* have a large-capacity system, large enough to service *both* buildings. That accounted for the big pipes and ducts coming through the basement walls – they were coming from the equipment in the building next door.

This unusual situation was an economical way to heat and cool a building, utilize the equipment in the abutting building since they're both under the same ownership. But this presented an unacceptable risk for a lender/mortgagee whose rights did *not* extend to that building next door, which housed the HVAC equipment. A mortgagee who doesn't get his loan repaid and has to foreclose on the mortgage and sell the collateral – the Big Building – would find himself with a structure that was not an independent, stand-alone structure and could not be operated commercially without the HVAC service from the next-door building. Possibly both buildings, adjoining properties, were under common ownership at one time, maybe when they were built. Or different owners might have a written agreement to ensure (in the weakest sense, that is, contractually) a continued supply of HVAC service to the Big Building without any of its own equipment. But Larry knew that he had to inform client Bank immediately of these facts, facts that would surely cause them to "rethink the deal."

They rethought their way out of that transaction – defective collateral, they called it. So Larry's visit paid off for the Bank – amazingly everyone had taken for granted up to that point that the Big Building could serve as good mortgage security/collateral, and could operate as a stand-alone commercially leasable structure. Oops!

P.S. Can you imagine the conditions inside the offices at that building if the next-door building *with* the HVAC equipment fell into the hands of a new owner or was itself foreclosed on by another mortgage lender – and they cut off service to their neighbor? Sealed tight, windows don't open, no heat and no cooling and no ventilation. In the words of my trusty smoke alarm: "EVACUATE! EVACUATE!"

Case No. 6: A Residence – But the Same Message: Visit the Place!

This final case involved Ron, a son of Client John in Tale #3. I'd known him since age eight and he'd grown into a mature businessman and one of the most effective and successful executives I'd ever met. He was looking for a house in the beautiful and historic suburb of Concord, Massachusetts and asked me to come out and walk the property with him. It was, indeed, a wonderful, bucolic setting with a fine old house and lots of land. Everything I saw was positive – but not things I heard. Airplanes.

After ten or fifteen minutes of exploring the site, Ron asked, "So what do you think?" I told him it looked great and just right for his family, but . . .

"Ron, I counted eleven airplanes flying right overhead during this brief time. You ought to check it out, unless you like a lot of planes going by."

Ron called the next day to report that he'd told the broker to find another house. Seems that Hanscom Air Force Base in nearby Bedford also extends into Concord and nearby Lincoln. Hanscom is a joint-use civil airport/military base with Hanscom Field which serves the private executive/corporate jets of general aviation and charter air services. Definitely, as was clear from our brief visit, a very busy facility – meaning a takeoff or landing every minute. The runway layout caused outgoing and incoming planes to fly directly over the house we'd visited. This particular site visit taught me that you have to use *all* your senses. The footnote deals with the sense of smell, a very disgusting smell that came up (literally!) in one case – check it out.[4]

Ron didn't need a lawyer here, just another set of eyes and ears. The BLT for this Tale is right there in the title. Check it out. Oh, and by the way, if you don't take these Tales seriously, check out the next story where apparently *no one* visited that new location:

**What if You *Don't* Thoroughly Check Out
the Premises and Environs and Zoning?
How a Warehouse Lease Brings New Meaning to the Word
"Morass!"
and
Be Sure to Check the P.S. to this Case – a Whole New Lesson!**

I'm guessing that the national fresh-produce company executive, in need of a warehouse in a distant city to store farm products before shipment to customers, found an ideal location; size; truck docks; highway access, and so forth – but he was too busy to pay a visit. And "neighborhood" doesn't matter – after all, it's just a warehouse to store boxes (of food!). And so the lease was signed and operations began. Shipments of produce in followed by a period of storage and then shipments out. The company executive, knowing his business, began a program of air quality checks to be documented – something federal regulators "recommend." The reports starting coming into the executive and the pattern became clear from the high levels of "bad stuff" (starting with lead, mercury, a bit of asbestos and a lot of other pollutants in the air in that warehouse).

The executive called my partner, Lawyer One, who contacts Lawyer Two, a colleague located in the same city as the warehouse, who visits the place. What does he find? The warehouse is next door to a busy 24/7 recycling plant. Let's just stop right here and make a guess: If that fact had been disclosed by a site visit and inspection *before* the Lease was signed, would the deal have gone through? Would some kind of testing have been done *before* the lease was signed if the executive knew he was next to this 24/7/365 operating recycling plant?

This company is about to have an active legal dispute with its Landlord, a fight that it may win or lose. It may face a costly product recall and even some product-liability claims from injured consumers that they may win or lose. But generally you don't win against government regulators/agencies which may shut you down and fine you. Was I right about a new meaning to "morass?"

So remember to heed the title of this Tale: **Your Lawyer (or someone else who is knowledgeable of the risks!)** *MUST* **Visit Your New Premises Before You Buy the Property or Sign the Lease.**

P.S. – When I Asked My Partner, Lawyer One about This Problem Situation…
I learned that when the food warehouse was leased, there was no recycling plant next door. The plant was built *after* the food warehouse lease was in operation. And when I asked about zoning laws, I learned that they specifically permitted a recycling plant. So, do you see the next BLT coming?

BLT #18:
Before signing up for that nice new space, check the zoning ordinance and map and ensure that you can live with the "worst" permitted use of adjacent or nearby premises. This was especially true in this case, where the adjacent lot was vacant, waiting for a building (a recycling center!). And if you can, as part of your leasing deal of your own warehouse, get some rights or limitation on the use next door, try it. In this case, a zoning search would have turned up "Recycle Center" as a permitted use – and the food-warehouse would have probably have sought out a "cleaner" location elsewhere.

---

1 *Only the Paranoid Survive* by Intel founder Andrew Grove is a good business book on issues related to "strategy."

2 More recently, "Water Contamination Found in Vermont Wells" was a headline in *The Wall Street Journal*, p. A2, March 16, 2016. Here, the culprit was PFOA or perfluorooctanoic acid and interestingly, the nearest plastics plant operator, the article notes, "said none of its facilities now use PFOA." And the beat goes on.

3 In April of 2016 the Massey Energy (Coal) CEO was fined $250,000 and sentenced to a jail term for conspiracy to violate mine-safety laws after an explosion which killed 29 miners. *Wall St. Jnl* 4/7/16, p.B3; and *NYTimes*, p.A17..And then, *The New York Times* headline read: "Construction Company Guilty of Manslaughter in Immigrant Worker's Death." And you can add to that charges of criminally negligent homicide (a felony) and reckless endangerment (a misdemeanor). (6/10/16, p.8)

A 2015 English case also teaches the need for corporate executives to be mindful of employee safety: A young apprentice at an engineering company died from serious head injuries sustained when he became entangled in a metal lathe he was cleaning (while the lathe was still running!). On July 14, 2015, the employer company was fined £150,000. The company's director was sentenced to eight months in prison and was disqualified from working as a company director for 10 years. A senior supervisor received a four-month suspended sentence, 200 hours of unpaid community work and a £3,000 fine. Even the employment agency that placed the apprentice at the engineering company was fined £75,000. They all had acted in disregard of applicable health and safety rules. Although these rules may not be as stringent in your jurisdiction as the UK's Health and Safety at Work etc. Act 1974, company executives should take seriously their responsibility for on-the-job risks to their employees' health and safety. (Reported by the law firm DLA Piper in its paper of 7 September 2015, "Corporate manslaughter charge following death of apprentice – White Collar Crime Update.")

4 Not to extend this Tale even more, here's a place that didn't pass "the smell test." This property was intended for client's warehouse and truck terminal. Walking about I smelled something – an odd and unfamiliar odor; disgusting is the nicest word I can think of. When some test borings were made and then some minor excavations, this land turned out to be the site of an old leather factory where waste products from hides, etc. had been buried for many decades. As the ground was opened up, the smell became stronger and it spread quickly. Finally, the State Attorney General had to order the site permanently sealed as a major "public nuisance." Use your eyes, ears and nose when you check out what may be your new home, whether for your business or your family.

TALE # 18

CLIENT WANTS HIS SON TO TAKE OVER THE
BUSINESS – BUT SO DOES AN IMPORTANT SALESMAN

Part I : THE CLIENT'S PROBLEM
In Desperate Need of This Ace Salesman, But . . .
The Salesman Has a Demand

Client Tom owned a sizeable and successful printing business which he'd started years ago. Tom was an active and energetic initiator. But although he could start up and run a good business and was an excellent salesman, he was now overseeing production and had to remain on site, at the printing plant. That's where I visited him and learned of his concerns.

"I can't go out on the road to sell any more," Tom told me. "I've got to stay here and make sure production gets done, right and on time. But dammit, I need some ace salesman out there beating the bushes." Tom was in desperate need of an experienced "outside" salesperson. I knew that the printing business was becoming increasingly competitive and it was clear that Tom felt under pressure. And he had to move fast. Finally, he found the ideal candidate, "Ace" – many years as a successful salesman in the business and lots of contacts. But (there's always a "but"…)

Tom called one day shortly after my visit with the "good news and bad news" message: Ace was entrepreneurial and, noting the age of the owner, said he wanted a right to buy the business when Tom was ready to retire or when he died. Tom said, "I really need this guy, but you know, I always had hopes that Tom Jr. would take over the business." Tom Jr. was then in graduate business school. I knew that Tom's wife had worked in the office as the bookkeeper and their four kids helped out after school and during summers. Understandably, Tom felt this was a family business and he wanted it to stay that way. But with his son's plans uncertain, reluctantly Tom decided that his immediate need for the ace salesman trumped other concerns. Tom called me:

"I want to talk to you about us negotiating a buyout by Ace, y'know, if I retire or when I'm gone. I'm just not sure about Tom, Jr., who hasn't made up his mind yet about coming into the business full time."

Tom and I met to discuss the situation and then we set up a meeting with Ace and his lawyer. The triggers for the buyout, retirement or death, were pretty straightforward, as were the salary, benefits and other terms of Ace's employment as Sales Manager. Indeed, most aspects of the deal were agreed upon except for one crucial item: the price or price-formula for Ace's buyout of the business. Tom was becoming increasingly desperate to get Ace into the company and out on the road, selling and generating revenue. But that price issue remained unsettled; Tom seemed unusually stubborn. The meeting dragged on without much progress on the price issue.

Tom and I stepped out of the room and I expressed my sympathy at his dilemma:

"I know how important it is to you to get Tom Jr. into the business. But you've got to decide or you'll lose this guy – and from what you said, you need to get Ace into the company and out on the road selling – now!"

It didn't take a sage to sense the conflicts tugging at Tom. But there the two men were, clearly at a stalemate on the price issue, and Tom was becoming more anxious by the minute to get Ace into the company.

II. THE SOLUTION

Ace had already given notice at his job that he was leaving, or he may even have already left his old employer. What to do? Then, out of the blue a thought came to me, something I remembered from labor law and the words of the great Professor Archibald Cox,[1] namely, the duty to negotiate is a labor-management technique of getting past a tough issue and moving on to get the rest of a collective bargaining (labor/management) agreement done. That thought was a way to move this deal forward, not yet to conclusion, but forward. And since Ace was a free agent and about ready to start, they could, indeed, move forward and get him into the company. My suggestion, after more than an hour in that meeting, was for the parties to sign up what they'd agreed to – a kind of partial Memorandum of Understanding – and then meet again to negotiate the buyout-price issue. I made this suggestion when Tom and I went back into the meeting room:

"Look, I don't think we're getting anywhere on this price issue today. We've got a couple of businessmen here champing at the bit to get back to business. So let them each do that. Maybe after some time together they will come to agreement on a buyout price. It's not rocket science, after all. Let's finish off the draft buyout agreement, which the parties can sign, and add a provision that they agree to negotiate the buyout price beginning in 60 days."

Now it was Ace's turn to confer with his lawyer. They excused themselves from the room and when they came back: "You've got a deal." Tom and Ace shook hands; they signed the Buy-Sell Agreement / partial Memorandum of Understanding[2]; and Ace started work almost immediately.

As the meeting was breaking up, Ace spoke to me, first out of Tom's hearing: "Understand, Milton, that I will never end up working for any of Tom's kids." Tom heard Ace repeat this at later meetings, and I could see him clenching his fist and tensing his jaw at those remarks. As time passed, both Tom and Ace became increasingly busy selling and producing printing jobs, money flowed in and it wasn't until a few months later when I heard from Ace's lawyer:

"Let's please meet and finish off the price negotiation." And so once again we four gathered in a conference room, but after more than an hour, it became clear that they were still not near agreement – they were still far apart on the price Ace would pay for the business. Ace made it clear: "Look, Tom, I'm not going to overpay – get real!" I suggested we meet and try again, which we did.

After that second meeting, Tom called with the happy news that Tom Jr. was completing his MBA and decided to get into the family business. Seems he even had plans for expansion of their product line and market. Tom was excited. He resisted my urging that they schedule another negotiation meeting with Ace.

"What's the point? My son's coming in and I won't sell out to a stranger."

I put my hands on Tom's shoulders and looked him squarely in the eyes. "Tom, I remind you that you're under a legally binding obligation to negotiate. You *must* meet with Ace and at least try to reach agreement!" And even as I spoke those words, it had become pretty clear to me that this was not going to happen.

"Tom," I almost scolded, "you're under a legal obligation to negotiate in good faith or you'll be in breach of your agreement. That's not a position I want to see you in. You'll meet and you'll negotiate!"

"Can't you see? This isn't a real offer! They're just tossing us a bone!"

And so we met two more times over the course of a year, but to no avail – they could not reach any agreement on price. No surprise! They stuck to their guns and the numbers Tom and Ace each had in mind were just too far apart. Eventually, Ace, the salesman left for greener pastures, but by that time Tom Jr. had taken over the company. Tom Jr. brought his new energy and creativity to the company and transformed it into a successful business based on the then newly emerging software industry and the need for manuals and packaging of CDs. The company was eventually sold to a large public company, where Tom Jr. was given a high post befitting his MBA status and experience in the business.

This simple approach of deferring and agreeing to negotiate a difficult point in the parties' agreement had accomplished Tom's goals: It (i) solved his immediate problem; (ii) deferred an issue that could not be immediately resolved; and (iii) ended up fulfilling Tom's other wish – to have his son take over the business.

> **BLT #19:** As events played out, it became clear that Tom, so long as Tom Jr. remained undecided, intended to stretch out negotiations until Tom Jr. made a firm decision one way or the other. But this stalling tactic can be costly to the staller, particularly when the other party acts in reliance that the negotiations will lead to a deal. A 2015 Delaware case illustrates the risks facing Tom, in that case to the tune of almost $200 Million.[3] Ace's lawyer should have told him that an agreement to negotiate is nothing more than a promise to sit down and talk – it is not an agreement to come to a final enforceable contract. (In some states, pre-agreement negotiations do not even include an obligation to negotiate in good faith.) And if Ace had felt as strongly as he'd expressed to Tom – that he would never work for any of Tom's children and that he must own the business at some point – then he should have stuck to his guns and not left his job until that crucial price in the buy-out agreement was set. Agreeing to negotiate is a good tool in the right circumstances, but parties have to beware when it becomes, as it apparently did for Tom, just an opportunity to stall for time. You've got to make a judgment as to what the other side's real intentions are and remember, those intentions may change over time.

> Remember the old saw: An agreement to agree is no agreement – it binds neither party. But a promise to negotiate is generally recognized and if you're under that obligation, then go ahead and negotiate in good faith. Failure to come to agreement if you in fact do negotiate in good faith should not give rise to a breach-of-contract claim, but don't forget that Delaware case in Note 3.

1 Cox is remembered not only as a Harvard Law School Professor of Labor Law and Constitutional Law, but also as Special Prosecutor in the Nixon Presidency / Watergate scandal and as the U.S. Solicitor General in the Kennedy administration.

2 At this point in the deal, I intended that the Tom-Ace draft buyout agreement be a non-binding letter of intent which lacked the all-important price component, which was left open to be negotiated later. This agreement to negotiate is not uncommon in letter-of-intent situations, where the parties should know that although their deal is not yet a legally binding contract, they *are* under a legal obligation to negotiate in good faith toward reaching agreement on the open item(s). And in some of these negotiation situations, questions arise: Is one of the parties *not* negotiating in good faith? Do they have another agenda? Or are they just doing some hard bargaining? In this situation, it appeared to me that Tom was just stalling to give his son more time to decide whether or not to join Tom's company. The parties' motives and intentions are central to these situations and to answering these questions. A 2011 7th Circuit (Federal) case is a good illustration of this question of the parties' "real" intentions during this negotiation stage – *Trovare Capital Group, LLC v. Simkins Industries, Incoporated, et al.,* No. 10-2778 (7th Cir. July 20, 2011). (For an extensively researched article on these issues, see "Precontractual Liability and Preliminary Agreements: Fair Dealing and Failed Negotiations," 87 Columbia L.Rev. 217 [1987]). Trovare, interested in buying the assets of Simkins Industries, signed a letter of intent in what would be a complex transaction and they began negotiating the many open items. During those negotiations, an email from Simkins' controlling shareholder to his negotiators said he "definitely does not want to go through with the Trovare Transaction. He has intentions of operating with his children in charge." (Familiar?) Negotiations were set to terminate by a fixed date at no cost to either party. But if one of the parties backed out before then – e.g., if Simkins sent Trovare a formal termination, Simkins would have to pay Trovare a $200k **breakup fee**. It appeared that Simkins continued to "negotiate." The Federal Appeals Court sent the case back to the trial court to determine whether Simkins was just engaging in hardball negotiations or a pretext by delaying in order to avoid having to pay the breakup fee. The trial court ruled that he was just negotiating hard and wasn't stalling for time. The appeals court affirmed that decision.

3 *Siga Technologies Inc. v. PharmAthene, Inc.* --- A.3d ---, WL 9591986 (Del. Dec. 28, 2015). Although the only document that the parties had signed was a Memorandum of Understanding (MOU) expressly noted as being "non-binding," the Delaware Supreme Court affirmed the almost $200 Million verdict rendered by the trial court. The message of this case is clear: The trial court found that, but for defendant's bad faith negotiations, the parties would have reached an agreement. Based on that finding, the trial court was not limited to reliance damages but could award expectation damages, namely the same amount of damages that would be awarded for a breach of contract. And so the old-fashioned approach of using these preliminary MOU's, Letters of Intent, etc. as in the Tom-Ace situation may carry substantial risks for any party who has no real intention of ever reaching a binding agreement. The courts' opinions spent many pages dissecting the parties' discussions/negotiations and finally concluded that there was, indeed, an enforceable deal, that one of the parties was in breach and should pay contract damages. (I'll leave you with the homework to check examples of "reliance damages" – Google is always a good start.)

TALE # 19

BORROW $375,000 AND REPAY WITH $10,000?
GET SERIOUS!

I. The Client's Problem

It was the early '70s and the stock market was moving up steadily – it reached over 1,000 for the first time in 1972. That's about when Dr. A (for anonymous), a physician, looked jealously at investors making "a fortune" (as they say) in the rising stock market as he worked by the hour, "Like a day laborer," he'd complain to friends. So he went to his stock broker for some advice on buying stocks.

"We know stocks will go up but we don't know which ones or when."

The stock broker advised that he borrow the money he needed to get into the market. So the good doctor went out and borrowed, and borrowed and borrowed – $375,000 before he was done, and in 1970-dollars. And then he bought and bought and bought – stocks that, he later told me, were recommended by one of his patients (whom he described as a very ill and unstable person – maybe it was Dr. A who needed to see a doctor!).

Jump ahead to 1974 – and the stock market loses almost half its value, dropping into the 500s. It was then when I met an old friend and fellow lawyer, Pete, in the law library. Pete was Dr. A's lawyer at the time and frankly, he looked like a lost soul. His client, Dr. A, now had to pay back the money-lender and was being sued for the entire amount of his note, $375,000 plus interest; and the stocks he'd bought (collateral for the loan) were now worth less than half of that amount. What to do? I asked Pete for some details and then volunteered to take the matter over if Pete didn't want to handle it.

Pete shrugged: "What's to handle? He owes the money." So I promised to look into the situation and maybe take it over, as Pete wished – he had other pressing cases that he had to deal with.

I met with Dr. A to get as much background as I could – otherwise this would just be a "You Borrow : You Pay Back" case. I asked how he got to this money-lender. He explained that his stockbroker, seeing A's frustration at being left behind in the rising stock market, had told him he could borrow the money to invest and then sent him to a money-lender.

"Yes, I can help you with your loan
questions. I'm the loan arranger."

A bit of law: You can't just go to your bank and borrow money to buy stocks in the market – there are laws against that – the margin regulations. And margin loans – money you borrow from your broker leaving the stocks as collateral security – are a highly regulated area. What to do? Dr. A called the money-lender recommended by his stockbroker; and ended up borrowing and buying stocks; by the time he was done, he had borrowed $375,000.

At my meeting with him, Dr. A was nervous and in desperate straits in fear of "losing everything!" I pumped him for details and learned that the money-lender to whom the stock broker had referred him was the stockbroker's cousin. So the broker had, in effect, helped to arrange for this loan to buy stock – a financial arrangement that seemed to have something to do with margin regulations.

II. A Solution to Client's Problem of Inability to Repay His Loan

Research into those regulations revealed language in Regulation T of the Federal Reserve's book of regulations that made it a crime to lend money to be used to buy stock beyond the lending limit allowed by the margin regulations. Under the regulations at that time, a stockbroker could lawfully lend up to 50% of the purchase price of the stock to be purchased. But, and this is a big BUT, here the broker arranged for Dr. A to borrow 100% of the purchase price of the stock he was buying through the broker by sending Dr. A to a cousin, the money-lender. The broker was breaking the law. And the cousin money-lender, a family-related party, I could argue, was "in cahoots" with the law-breaking stockbroker, aiding and abetting him in the commission of a crime, namely, a violation of the margin regulations and Federal Reserve's Regulation T – a federal crime.

The money-lender had sued Dr. A in the U.S. Federal District Court demanding repayment of the loan. In response, I filed a Motion to Dismiss the money-lender's collection action on these grounds, as I argued to the Judge:

This is a suit based on an illegal loan and the law is clear: Courts do not enforce repayment of an illegal loan. Why illegal? Because the loan was, in effect, arranged by the stockbroker who was subject to the Federal Reserve's margin regulations (the 50% limit mentioned above). The stockbroker and his cousin money-lender, were in cahoots. The plaintiff money-lender had aided and abetted his cousin, the stockbroker, in the commission of a crime, that is, making the unlawful loan and thus making the loan transaction an illegal act. And, I argued, the law will not allow you to enforce an illegal loan in court. (Two other examples of unenforceable illegal loans are (i) a gambling debt incurred in a state where gambling is illegal; and (ii) a usurious loan, that is a borrowing at an interest rate above the maximum permitted by a state's usury laws. Those debts cannot be collected by suing the borrower because courts will not enforce the illegal loan.)

Despite the valiant arguments by the money-lender's lawyer, the judge ruled: Motion granted – case dismissed! Yep, right there in open court at this hearing on my Motion to Dismiss. In post-hearing discussions, the money-lender's lawyer hinted at taking an appeal. And so, after consulting with Doctor A, I offered to settle the matter. Negotiations ended up at a figure of $10,000, which was all the client could afford at the time. (Remember, the collateral – the stocks Dr. A had bought with the borrowed money – had already been sold, but there remained a substantial six-figure balance due and owing on the note.) So although the lender recovered the value of the depreciated securities plus the $10,000 he got in settlement from Dr. A, this was still a big loss for the money-lender, but certainly not a *total* loss.

— —

An Afterthought: Was my motion to dismiss the money-lender's collection suit moral and righteous? After all, if you borrow should you not repay? Was I doing "the right thing" by helping Dr. A get away without repaying the loan he made?

Wrong question! I was doing my duty under the rules of my profession – the Canons of Legal Ethics. I was zealously promoting the client's interests, which is what I was hired to do and which as a member of the bar I was sworn to do.

Was the client's choice not to repay his debt moral and righteous? You be the judge of that, not me. Maybe the stock broker and his money-lender cousin were playing a "shill" game with a lot of other investors – all in violation of the securities laws and margin requirements. Maybe they got what was coming to them. Surely, as a matter of morality, a borrower ought to repay his debts. But that choice is for the client and *not* his lawyer to make. My job was to give the client advice – offer him the choice of legal and legitimate actions available to him – and then carry out his choice and otherwise perform my obligations to my client, to protect his interests, which I did. So no apologies.

— —

BLT #20: This Tale is a good example of what should happen whenever a lawyer is called on to solve a client's problem – I call it "Synthesis" and this comes up in many other Tales. Synthesis is the joining of what the lawyer knows (in this case, Federal Reserve Margin Regulations – The Law) with the detailed facts, namely that the stockbroker subject to those Rules sent his doctor client to his cousin, the money-lender. Knowing those facts was enough of a wedge for me to make a legitimate claim that the loan was il-legal and therefore uncollectable by court action. The stockbroker is subject to strict securities laws, which include margin borrowing regulations/limits. I learned that the stockbroker had the wherewithal to himself make the loan, but, under the margin regulations he could not. I concluded that the stockbroker thought he could circumvent the legal restrictions that he was subject to by sending Dr. A to the broker's cousin. He was being "cute" and in many cases, cute loses, as it did here.

TALE # 20

A LAWYER REDESIGNS A "WORRISOME" COMPONENT
OF A MEDICAL DEVICE.

I first got into the product liability area when I was engaged to do some corporate and real estate work for a new client, OMT. Client had designed and was manufacturing and selling a complex surgical-assistance device for cranial operations. It had worked successfully with a growing number of patients and the hospitals in increasing numbers were buying the equipment. To understand the problem that came up, you should know about this low-tech/non-tech aspect of the high-tech equipment: In most head surgeries, the patient's head must be *totally* immobilized. This is accomplished, in part, by a "head-holder," a common accessory manufactured to OMT's design. This was a metal ring with three or four screws that would be tightened to the point where they pressed down on the scalp sufficiently to hold the ring in place. Linked to other devices connected to the operating table, this held the patient's head totally immobilized during the surgery. Now, on to The Problem:

I. The Problem

One day I received an urgent call from OMT's President, Edgar: An "incident" had just occurred at a hospital in the mid-west. In the operating room, just before the surgery was to start, a nurse noticed blood on the patient's scalp. That was not supposed to happen! It turned out that one of the screws in that the head-holder ring had penetrated the scalp and the skull of the patient. (There was no harm done and the surgery later went forward and was successful.) But that "incident" was unsettling and OMT President Edgar called me – he was concerned about legal exposure and liability.

II. To Solve the Problem, I Visit OMT

I visited OMT's office to examine the head-holder ring and understand the how and why of this mishap. I asked a technician, "How do they know when to stop turning the screws so they just compress the patient's scalp, but don't break the skin or penetrate?" The technician showed me a special screw-driver. "See, this is a torque screwdriver which prevents overtightening. It's set to just the pressure needed to press down on the scalp and no more."

I noticed that the head of the torque screwdriver, unlike any screwhead I'd ever seen – matched the odd notch at the top of the head-holder screws. The technician then demonstrated how the torque screwdriver fit into the four head-holder screws. I asked: "Why is there this straight line in the screw head? I thought that only your special torque screwdriver could turn these head-holder screws."

The technician looked puzzled. "I really don't know. Maybe…" I interrupted him: "Maybe a surgeon wants to use a regular screwdriver and not rely on the torque tool working properly. And maybe that's what happened at that hospital. I think I've seen enough." I returned to my office, did a little reading up on product liability law[1] and called Edgar.

First I asked whether the torque screwdriver operated accurately. Did it stop at the correct pressure. Edgar said they had a torque-check device which was on the pre-op checklist. We assumed that the hospital had followed that procedure and I moved on. That might be another issue later for OMT to check on. The talk returned to the straight-line screw head in the head-holder device.

I said to Edgar, "I checked the OMT head-holder and there may be what in product-liability law they call a 'design defect.' It's quite possible that this straight line in the head-holder screw head led to the scalp-penetration incident. That straight line in the screws appears to be an invitation to the surgeon *not* to use the OMT torque screwdriver, but rather to use a regular straight-blade screwdriver and rely on his own 'feel' of when to stop turning the screw. That may well have happened here – and the surgeon went too far. I can just hear a personal-injury plaintiff's lawyer pointing to that 'invitation to disaster' to a jury."

Edgar asked what they could do about this risky situation. Without hesitation I replied: "Ideally, I'd get rid of that straight line in the screw heads. I'd get rid of that invitation to avoid using the OMT torque screwdriver and rely on 'feel.' Unless you can come up with a good reason other than 'Some surgeons like to rely on their feel when they tighten the head-holder screw,' I'd get rid of that straight line." That was my legal advice; this was an occasion for a lawyer to suggest the redesign of a medical device component to avoid product-liability exposure. Sounds unusual![2]

Edgar replied that he'd take it up with his people and call me back if they needed more assistance from me. They never did call back on that issue, except when I asked to see a copy of the instruction manual, particularly the portion relating to the head-holder. I explained to Edgar, "Another basis for product liability is inadequate warnings or instructions. So I'd like to have a look at your manual on this head-holder."

I found the Manual to be pretty well done from a product-liability vantage point and made only a few suggestions for improvement. But when done, these instructions made some points that might be helpful in the event of another such "incident" in the future that might land OMT in court:

- Note that medical personnel using the head-holder must receive and satisfactorily complete hands-on training and testing of their capabilities.
- OMT must provide medical personnel with detailed instructions on the sequence of installing the head-holder and the stabilizing connection to the operating table.

- The medical personnel must never allow the use of *any* non-OMT parts.
- Use the standard red "Warning" octagonal symbols, yellow triangular "Caution" symbols, distinctive and conspicuous typography/design and any other tools that will draw attention to the important points made in the Manual.
- Repeatedly warn of the dangers of scalp and skull penetration and the absolute requirement that *only* the torque screwdriver be used to install the head-holder.
- Take into account that skull-bone thicknesses vary from patient to patient and must be taken into account when affixing the head-holder. On this and other decisions, emphasize the continued responsibility of the surgeon in charge to monitor all aspects of head-holder use.
- Perform the prescribed test of the continued accuracy of the torque screwdriver and the condition of the head-holder screws prior to actual surgery. Maintain written reports of these tests and the results for each torque screwdriver (which should be identified by a serial-number system).

Aside from the obvious salutary safety considerations, from my product-liability viewpoint and as OMT's lawyer, the object of all these Instruction Manual provisions is that they (i) anticipate mishaps; (ii) provide precautionary procedures to avoid them; and (iii) shift responsibility for any mishaps that may occur away from Client OMT. I indicated that invariably, when almost *any* mishap occurs in a hospital and lands in court, *all* parties connected with the situation become named defendants. And it would then be up to OMT to present evidence that nothing it did in (i) the design, (ii) the manufacture or (iii) providing required instructions and warnings for its device contributed to the mishap.

"Great little product, but liability could eat you up."

BLT #21:

I included this Tale because of the pervasiveness of product liability risks to the American business community. Every business – maybe *your* business – which makes or sells a product in the United States should give at least some thought, pay some attention, to their product-liability exposure. An active trial bar is out there, with some looking for so-called "mass torts" and class actions that can bring them huge legal fees. I've represented various lines of business and they all have varying degrees of exposure to product-liability lawsuits. I was surprised when a marine-engine manufacturer was sued by a yacht builder, but pleased when we were able to show that the engine malfunction the customer (yacht-builder) complained of he had caused himself by tampering with a "do-not-touch" sealed component. Back packs / knapsacks seems like a line of products that can't cause injury; but read Tale #27 and see how a "benign" product can suddenly become risky – one requiring the manufacturer to suddenly become interested in product-liability exposure.

If your business is high-risk – as is the medical-equipment manufacturer in this Tale #20 – then you need to be on the alert at all times to that risk. "High risk" in this instance comes from the likelihood that anything going wrong medically, in a doctor's treatment room or at home or in a hospital frequently ends in a courtroom. A lawsuit against a hospital will typically name everyone in sight of where the injury took place. (I probably wouldn't be surprised if the janitorial worker who mops the floor in the operating room where the injury took place would be named as a co-defendant.) And it's a guess and only a guess, but I suspect that very few accidental deaths or injuries in a medical/hospital setting don't involve some claim for compensation. That's what I call a high-risk business. And so although you may not be in the medical-device industry, think through whether *yours* is a high-risk business. If so, you should remain keenly aware of those risks and take appropriate precautions to prevent and defend yourself against product-liability claims.

---

1 For an overview of product-liability law and a discussion of "design defects," the issue in this tale, see, e.g. The Restatement of the Law, Torts (Third), Products Liability, (Philadelphia: American Law Institute, 1998).

2 For a peer-reviewed article on this point, see the author's article, "Factoring the Law into Medical Device Design," March 2005 issue of the industry's trade magazine, *MDDI* (Medical Device and Diagnostic Industry) available at http://www.mddionline.com/article/factoring-law-medical-device-design. (control-click)

TALE # 21

THE 400+ YEAR OLD RULE AGAINST PERPETUITIES? YOU GOTTA BE KIDDING!

Caution: First, you should that know that some states have modified this ancient doctrine; others have repealed it altogether. On rereading this ancient doctrine I was reminded how hard it was in law school to get a real grasp and understanding of this Rule Against Perpetuities in all its varieties. So feel free, if you're not in a mood to "work" reading this piece, to put it aside. But do remember the moral of this Tale and this Part III: It pays to know The Law.

This Tale deals with one of those old English real estate rules that most of us never have to deal with in practice. It had never come up in my practice before and never came up since, but it was a great help in this one and only case to solve a client's problem.

I. The Client's Problem

It all began long before I got involved. Landlord owned three adjoining parcels of vacant land, Lots 1, 2 and 3. Big Tenant, needing more and more office space for his growing organization, had **ground leased** Lot 1 from

Landlord for a long term – 100 years, and built his building on Lot 1. In order to provide for future expansion, Big Tenant's lease contained a **right of first refusal** to buy Lots 2 and 3 if they ever came up for sale. After a couple of years, Lot 2 did come up for sale; Big Tenant exercised the right, bought Lot 2 and built another building on it. That left Lot 3 still owned by Landlord.

Some years had passed when Landlord was approached by Builder, a friend of the family who wanted to construct an office building on Lot 3 and get into a hot real estate market leasing office space. But when they discovered Big Tenant's **right of first refusal**, they knew that if Builder were buying, Landlord would first have to offer the property to Big Tenant. So Landlord and Builder decided that it was best if Builder just took a long-term lease on Lot 3, which he did – plus options to extend, for a total of 70 years. They signed the lease and Builder began to construct his building.

When Big Tenant saw what was happening he hollered "Stop!" That protest came by way of a letter immediately followed by a lawsuit. That's when Landlord called me to help his friend, the Builder. Big Tenant's lawsuit asked the court for an injunction to stop Builder's construction on Lot 3 and for damages for breach of Big Tenant's **right of first refusal**. Big Tenant argued that Builder's long-term (70 years potentially) lease was the equivalent of a sale, legally speaking, and was, in effect, a violation of his **right of first refusal** to buy Lot 3. That's when I first met Builder; he became the Client who wanted to complete his real estate project with Landlord without interference or interruption from Big Tenant. What to do?

II. A Solution to the Client's Problem

I read through Big Tenant's old lease of Lot 1, the potentially 100-year lease that contained his **right of first refusal** to buy Lots 2 and 3. That long 100-year term triggered a thought from law school days. "The Law" doesn't like arrangements that go on for too long. And the basic document here – that old lease of Lot 1 – made no mention of time. More precisely, that **right of first refusal** didn't end by any date certain; rather, it lasted for the entire 100-year term of the lease. That's when "The Rule Against Perpetuities" popped into my head. So now we take a side trip to explain the rule which is both simple, yet complex, with many books and articles devoted to this ancient English rule.[1] Let me oversimplify:

Big Tenant's **right of first refusal** is a future interest in real estate – an as yet unvested interest. "Unvested" means that Big Tenant, at the present time, owns no interest in the real estate. All he has is the *possibility* of getting an ownership interest sometime in the future (by exercising his right of first refusal). And that can happen if (i) the "trigger" event occurs that gives rise to his right of first refusal to buy Lot 3; and (ii) Big Tenant exercises that right. But since the "trigger" event (Landlord offering Lot 3 for sale) may *never* occur, that right to buy Lot 3 may *never* arise. Thus, all Big Tenant has is an unvested interest.

But if and when Landlord offers to sell Lot 3, that offer would trigger Big Tenant's first-refusal right – only then does Big Tenant have a vested right in Lot 3. But until then, all he has is an unvested interest in Lot 3 – just a right to buy it sometime in the future, contingent on that trigger event occurring (i.e., when Landlord decides to sell Lot 3). (I really wish this were simpler, gentle reader.)

What the Rule Against Perpetuities does is to set a time limit within which such an unvested right must either (i) ripen into a vested legal right (to buy) or (ii) terminate. The old English time limit, which is still the law in some places, is that a right (such as Big Tenant's right of first refusal) must vest within a limited time, described as follows: "a life in being plus 21 years." A "life in being" refers to a named or described person alive when the right (of first refusal) was first created. Importantly, the document (i.e., the Lot 1 Lease containing Big Tenant's right of first refusal) that creates that unvested right must contain that time limitation in order to avoid the nullifying effect of the Rule Against Perpetuities. But without that time limitation, that right of first refusal is of no effect – void from the outset under The Rule.

In this case, for example, the draftsman who wrote Big Tenant's Right of First Refusal should have added (using the old English time formula, above) something like this:

Big Tenant's Right of First Refusal under this Lease to purchase Lots 2 and 3 shall end twenty-one (21) years after the death of the last survivor of such of the Landlord's descendants (e.g. children, grandchildren, etc.) as are living at the date this Lease is executed, as herein noted, by Landlord and Tenant.

(Any other "lives in being" could have been used as the measuring stick; "Landlord's children" is just one example because, in this case, Landlord did, in fact have several young children when this Lease was signed. In some states, the time limit might be set by a statute as, for example, 30 years. And some states have abolished the Rule Against Perpetuities altogether. But whatever that time period may be, if it is possible that such future interest in real estate could vest *after* the applicable Rule Against Perpetuities' time period, then that future interest (here, Big Tenant's right of first refusal) ceases to exist: "Void as a violation of the Rule Against Perpetuities.") And it is void as of the date it was created, i.e., when that 100-year ground lease of Lot 1 was signed.

Big Tenant's right of first refusal was created in that Lease, where *nothing* was said about when that right would end – just an open-ended right to buy anytime during the Lease term, triggered by the landowner's desire to sell. And (i) that 100-year Lease term was, of course, a lot more than 21 years; and (ii) the Lease provision made no mention of any "life in being." Therefore, Big Tenant's right of first refusal could possibly vest beyond the period permitted by the Rule Against Perpetuities. As such, it was void and of no effect at the date they signed the lease for Lot 1.

Time to check the applicable law – Massachusetts law in this case. The Massachusetts Rule Against Perpetuities appears in a Massachusetts statute,[2] which refers to both (i) lives in being and (ii) a fixed (90 years) period of time. But since there was *no* time limit at all mentioned in Big Tenant's Lease and right of first refusal, it was possible that Big Tenant could exercise the right more than 90 years after the Lease was signed (remember, the Lease term was 100 years). And so under the Massachusetts statute, Big Tenant's right of first refusal was invalid, unenforceable, as of the date that Lot 1 Lease was signed.

That's what I argued in court and won. Big Tenant did not get its injunction against Builder constructing his building on Lot 3 and lost its right of first refusal to buy Lot 3: The court's ruling: "The right of first refusal to buy was void as a violation of the Rule Against Perpetuities."

BLT #22: Just remember the theme of this Part III: Know The Law! Be sure your lawyer knows the law and ask them to explain it to you. And I'm referring to whatever law, municipal/city, state and/or federal law that will govern your particular situation. And especially in the real estate area (where some laws go back to feudal times in England), keep an open mind to the possibility that some ancient (here, a 400+-year old) legal doctrine can still apply and win or lose you your case in the 21st Century. The Rule's all-important time limitation varies from state to state and doesn't even exist in others; and so an experienced real estate practitioner in the state where the property is located should review your deal.

---

1 For a law school professor's explanation, see Leach, "Perpetuities in a Nutshell," 51 *Harvard L. Rev.* 638 (1938) and by the same author, "Perpetuities: The Nutshell Revisted," *Harvard L. Rev.* Vol. 78, No. 5 (Mar., 1965), pp. 973-992. For an odd 2011 case which illustrates how the Rule Against Perpetuities was used, see this article: "Perpetuities Rule Finally Ends $100M Waiting Game for Lumber Baron's Heirs, 92 Years After His Death" by Martha Neil, available at http://www.abajournal.com/news/article/perpetuities_rule_finally_ends_100m_waiting_game/.
2 See Sec. 251, Acts of 2008, Mass. GL Sec. 2-901. [Statutory Rule Against Perpetuities.]
(a) A non-vested property interest is invalid unless:

(1) when the interest is created, it is certain to vest or terminate no later than 21 years after the death of an individual then alive; or
(2) the interest either vests or terminates within 90 years after its creation.

TALE # 22

WHEN THE TENANT GETS MORE IN CONDEMNATION AWARD THAN LANDLORD – INTENTIONAL OR ACCIDENTAL? WE'LL NEVER KNOW.

———

Q. Can the Tenant of a Building Taken by Eminent Domain Ever Get a Larger Portion out of the Taking Award Than the Building Owner?

A. Sometimes (Hint: It all depends on the Lease.)

This Is Not Really My Tale, But Rather My Senior Partner's, and it's About a Lease He Drafted in the '40s.

> This is a Tale of Eminent Domain.
> It happens in sun. It happens in rain.
> The City comes in, takes your land away,
> But then compensation the City must pay.
> **Anon. [old English ditty]**

———

Client Department Store was the sole tenant of an entire building in "Suburb," a city north of Boston. The potential term of the 1940 Lease (the work of my senior partner) was long: 10 years, with four additional 10-year extension options. And as often happens with these old long-term **net leases**, Client-tenant's rentals failed to keep up with infla-tion:[1] Rentals either stayed flat or were subject to small increases at each renewal period. This Lease was still in effect when I joined the law firm in the late '50s, when a "situation" came up:

I. The Problem
The Leased Building is Taken by the City – "Eminent Domain"

Suburb was about to take the leased building by **eminent domain** as part of a downtown urban renewal plan. Apparently the blocks surrounding the build-ing had been upgraded, improved, rebuilt – all the good things that increase real estate values (and taxes paid to the city). My senior partner dropped a copy of the Lease on my desk with the warning that a dispute was probably brewing with Client's Landlord. That dispute might involve the determina-tion of how much the City would be paying as the eminent domain award, but more to the point, how would that amount be split between the Tenant (our Client Department Store) and the Landlord, who owned the building.

II. Some Law on the Subject
Eminent Domain is an "Orphan" Subject in Most Lease Negotiations

In my experience with lease negotiations, the eminent domain provision gets very little attention. We rarely spend much time on the "Eminent Domain" pro-vision because a condemnation/taking happens only rarely; maybe the cities just don't have the funds to pay for property they'd like to take. In any event, I can't re-call it ever being a point of contention during lease negotiations. But lawyers and businesspeople renting space should know something about the applicable law, so let's first look at the questions raised when a governmental unit like a city, state, sometimes a government agency or even a public utility company, using its emi-nent domain powers, makes a taking of some real estate occupied by tenant(s):

> Question One: How much will the taking authority pay?
> Question Two: How will that payment be divided up between the Landlord/owner of the property and the tenant occupying the prop-erty under a lease?

The answer to Question One is that the payment for a taking is supposed to fairly compensate the owner for the loss of his property – owners should receive fair compensation, sometimes referred to as the "fair market value." That phrase is usually defined as what a knowledgeable, willing, and unpressured buyer would probably pay to a knowledgeable, willing, and unpressured seller when both are in the market to buy and sell. Question Two is the focus of this Tale because of the eminent domain provision which (I assume) my senior partner had put into the Client/Tenant's Lease of the Landlord's building.

Client Department Store's Lease – The Eminent Domain Provision.
This is the crucial portion of the Client's lease provision dealing with eminent domain:

> ## Eminent Domain: (a) In the event of a taking by eminent domain of the leased premises by Suburb or any other governmental agency or taking authority during the term of this Lease, the proceeds or award for the taking shall be dealt with in accordance with the provisions of applicable law.

Sounds innocent enough, right? After all, what could go wrong when the Lease refers to the "provisions of applicable law?" Pure "vanilla" and harmless, right? Wrong! A lot can go wrong, as Landlord learned. That's because the applicable law (unless the parties otherwise agree) recognizes that a tenant under a lease owns an interest in the property, called the "leasehold interest." This interest is considered "property" – a lesser interest than that of the title holder / owner to be sure, but still a legally recognized and protected property interest. This entitles the tenant to be compensated for the loss of his property, namely, his leasehold estate. Here's what the Massachusetts high court ruled in 1810, and it appears still to be the law today [and FYI, "estates"means land, real estate]:

> [T]enants under written leases . . . own interests in the estates. If such estates are seized in whole or in part by exercise of eminent domain, the owner [the tenant] is entitled to damages. His interest is protected by the same constitutional guaranties as are other kinds of property. It cannot be appropriated to a public use without the

payment of reasonable compensation to the owner [the tenant].. . .
The holder of such an interest was early held to be an 'owner' within
the meaning of that word in statutes conferring a right to petition
for damages caused by the laying out of highways.[2]

Although a tenant is legally entitled to compensation for loss of his "leasehold estate," that tenant's interest is not taken into account by the city or
other taking authority when it sets out to value the real estate – they don't
take into consideration that there exists a leasehold interest held by a tenant.
That valuation determination takes into account only the loss suffered by
the owner of title to the real estate (and generally without any regard to the
existence of such lesser interests as a tenant's leasehold estate or an option-
holder's option to purchase the real estate). Nevertheless, these lesser interests may come into play when answering Question Two: How is the taking
award to be divided between Landlord and Tenant?[3]

Splitting the Taking/Condemnation Award between Landlord (Owner) and Tenant

Remember, in the case of our Client/Tenant, the eminent domain provision
provided for division of the dollar award "in accordance with applicable law."
The effect of this provision was the same as if there were no lease provision at
all dealing with eminent domain; and the effect of no eminent-domain provision is that Tenant would be entitled to be compensated for loss of his interest
in the real estate, called the leasehold estate, out of any taking award.

To sum up: Tenant's leasehold estate would *not* be factored into Question
One (what is the amount of the award?). That would be the fair market value of the real estate – a sum that should "fairly compensate" the landowner
for the loss of his property. But when we get to Question Two – how is that
amount to be divided between the Landlord property owner and the Client/
Tenant – the law generally gives Tenant a piece of the award as compensation for the loss of his leasehold estate.

In this particular situation, a professional appraiser came up with an unusual result: He put an exceptionally high valuation on the Client/Tenant's

leasehold estate. Why? Because the Lease still had many years left to run and the rental was so far below market. This was a very valuable lease! And given the age and physical condition of the Landlord's building, that property value came in comparatively low, saved only by the worth of the underlying land, which was located in a comparatively expensive downtown location. In fact, in this peculiar situation, oddly enough, the Client/Tenant's lease-hold estate was given an appraised value about equal to or greater than the Landlord's property, land and building.

When the respective numbers of the Landlord's ownership interest and the exceptionally high value put on the Client/Tenant's leasehold interest were reviewed to determine how the taking award dollars would be divided, Landlord had literally to beg Tenant to let him keep some more of that award. The parties settled the matter "amicably." It was too long ago for me to remember how it came out – but clearly Landlord emerged a big loser.

Such a situation would *never* happen under the standard eminent domain lease provisions in general use today, so let's take a look at to-day's "standard form." Here's a sample of the typical "standard form" lease provisions:

##. **Eminent Domain.** Landlord reserves for itself all rights to any damages or awards with respect to the Premises and the leasehold estate hereby created by reason of any exercise of the right of emi-nent domain, or by reason of anything lawfully done in pursuance of any public or other authority; and by way of confirmation Tenant irrevocably grants and assigns to Landlord all Tenant's rights to such damages so reserved, except if and as otherwise provided herein.

[The exception refers to those condemnation awards which may specifically provide benefits to tenants for such costs as relocation/moving expenses; certain fixture costs; etc.]

BLT: #23: If you're Landlord, the matter of eminent domain *must* be ad-dressed in the lease. Leave it out and you'd be stuck like the Landlord in this

Tale. And today, it is in fact covered in all "standard form" leases. If nothing is said about eminent domain, The Law would generally give the tenant some portion of the award to compensate him for loss of his leasehold estate. The general practice for many years has been for property owners, that is Landlords, to avoid having to share the taking award with anyone. They do this with a "Landlord-take-all" eminent domain provision, as in the above example; and such a provision is, indeed, uniformly found in all modern "standard form" Landlord-oriented leases.

How Should Client's Landlord Have Dealt with the Eminent Domain Provision?

A natural question is why the Landlord's lawyer let this language "in accordance with applicable law" get into the Lease and dictate the distribution of an eminent domain award. My guess is that the subject of eminent domain in lease negotiations was not thought of as important enough to be worth much time. As noted above, a condemnation event is a kind of "orphan" subject that rarely comes up in any law practice. Indeed, this Tale was the only eminent domain matter I'd worked on in all my years practicing law. And so my guess is that the Landlord's lawyer simply didn't know that unless negated in the lease, the tenant has a right to be compensated for the loss of his property (his leasehold estate) if the leased premises are taken by eminent domain. I've got to assume that in 1940, my senior partner (then a young lawyer), in drafting the Lease, did know the law.

Assuming he did know the law, was his lease provision "in accordance with applicable law" subject to criticism? Or was he just doing the best he could for his client? As noted in the Introduction, he had no obligation to teach the law to the Landlord's lawyer. You be the judge: Good lawyering or something he should not have done? My senior partner gets my vote for good lawyering.

BLT: #24: If you are the Tenant, then always reserve any rights tenant may have under the taking authority's action. This may include relocation expenses and compensation for certain personal property or fixtures. To be perfectly clear, tenant should expressly reserve at the very least those rights, if any, given to tenants by the terms of the eminent domain taking statute or order.

---

1 See other examples in Tale #24 and Tale #35.

2 *Ellis v. Welch*, 6 Mass. 246, 4 Am. Dec. 122 (1810).

3 For an scholarly article on option holders' rights to a portion of a condemnation award see *Compensability In Eminent Domain Of Lessee's Option to Purchase,* 25 Wash. & Lee L. Rev. 102 (1968), http://scholarlycommons.law.wlu.edu.wlulr/vol25iss1/11. See pp. 104ff dealing with an option to purchase which is *not* contained in a lease. See also CONDEMNATION OF LEASED PROPERTY: DIVIDING THE PIE BETWEEN LANDLORD AND TENANT by Gary L. Birnbaum at http://www.lawseminars.com/materials/07ACLAZ/birnbaum.pdf.

TALE # 23

IF APPLICABLE LAW DOESN'T WORK, TRY ANOTHER LEGAL THEORY AND WIN!

Two Solved Problem Cases and a U.S. Supreme Court Goodie

<u>Case One</u> : How to Win a Legal Argument When "The Law" Is Against You;
or
When Theory "A" Doesn't Work, Switch to Theory "B."

I. THE CLIENT'S PROBLEM

There an old joke among trial lawyers on how to win a case:

> If your case is weak on the law, pound on the facts. If it's weak on the facts, pound on the law. If it's weak on the law *and* the facts, pound on the table! I was handed one of these "beauties" where "the table" seemed to be the only alternative. The client had no case – it was a loser! And I knew that "pounding the table" would not make it a winner. So I had to do something with The Facts or The Law. Let's start with The Facts.

Client Construction Company ("CCC") was building housing units for the U.S. Army at an Army Base in Kansas when a tornado hit. Storm damage had to be repaired, so the parties agreed to an extended completion date, an

213

additional 56 days, which ran into the Fall and Winter, with certain costs added to the contract price. But CCC incurred three costs that were not covered in the time-extension documents: Additional (i) heating; (ii) mortgage interest; and (iii) bonding and insurance premiums – all costs associated with that 56-day extension period – about $25,000 in 1961 dollars. The extension was covered in the standard "Change Order," which amended The Contract Documents to provide for an increase in contract price, extend time of completion, description of additional work to repair tornado damage and other details. But when the contract was completed and CCC's accountants checked the numbers, they confirmed that certain cost increases were not accounted for in the Change Order. Client decided that it wanted to make a claim against the U.S. Army.

The "problem": The Army could find no specific authorization in The Contract Documents to pay CCC's additional costs for heating; interest; and bonding and insurance premiums. The Contracting Officer denied the claim and CCC asked me to take it to the next level, which was the United States Armed Services Board of Contract Appeals ("BCA") in Washington, D.C.

The Army's position was probably correct: In accordance with its own procurement regulations and standard forms, only those costs that were specified in The Contract Documents could be claimed by the contractor. There was nothing in The Contract Documents that covered this situation. Nevertheless, I filed an appeal to the BCA. Although I felt strongly that it was right and fair that CCC should be compensated for costs incurred because of this weather-related delay, I understood the Government's position: The Contracting Officer had to "go by the book," and "the book" simply did not allow this particular claim. This claim, this case, was a loser on the law issues. What to do?

II. THE SOLUTION
I suspected that I'd have the sympathy of the BCA. After all, CCC's losses were not its fault – they'd been caused by winter weather conditions and the problem lay in those Contract Documents. I had to find a "hook" for the

BCA to use to decide to come to a fair result: Pay CCC its losses despite the absence of any specific provision for paying them for the additional insurance, bond premium and heating costs. I set out to find that "hook."

I began by reading the Contract Documents – those pounds of paper you sign when doing business with the United States, in this case the U.S. Army. And while reading (and probably fighting to stay awake), somehow I managed to recall seeing words I had already read elsewhere in the papers. I checked and Bingo! I found two nearly identical paragraphs, once in the body of the contract and once again in the "standard form" General Conditions. This could be the key to solving the client's problem and getting him the money he was due for those unreimbursed expenses following the tornado. This duplication of contract provisions – two near-identical paragraphs – suggested the way forward. This was an unexpected "gift."

I was excited because I remembered these textbook principles of contract interpretation:

If ambiguity exists within a contract [*like whether these extra costs were recoverable*], consider the following rules of construction to resolve the ambiguity in the document:[1]

- Construe the contract as a whole.
- Construe the contract so as to give meaning and effect to **all** its terms.
- Do not construe a contract in a way that disregards or effectively writes any provision out of the contract.
- Construe the contract so as to avoid leaving any term being unreasonable or unconscionable.
- Construe ambiguities against the drafter.

My argument even went back to a U.S. Supreme Court case decided shortly after the founding of the United States: *Marbury v. Madison*[2]. Chief Justice John Marshall wrote on interpreting the U.S. Constitution in terms similar to those that apply when a court interprets a written contract. Marshall said:

"It cannot be presumed that any clause in the Constitution is intended to be without effect."

And so, I would argue, if there are two near-identical clauses in a document – whether it be a contract or the U.S. Constitution – and they were construed to mean the same thing, then one of them would be without effect – mere surplusage. And that violates a major rule of contract interpretation.

Putting all this "jurisprudence" together with those two nearly identical provisions in the same U.S. Army contract helped me formulate a winning argument both in a brief and at oral argument before the U.S. Armed Services Board of Contract Appeals (BCA). The obstacle I had to overcome – as noted above – was that the Army Procurement Regulations made it clear again and again that a contractor (like CCC) had no claim against the Government for any payment unless the Contract Documents contained a *specific provision* authorizing such a payment – and remember, there was no such provision authorizing the payment for these particular added costs of heating, interest and insurance and bond premiums incurred during that 56-day extension following the tornado. I went back to those principles from Contracts 101, and here was my argument to the BCA:

Here are two nearly identical provisions in this contract (i.e., The Contract Documents). No doubt about what one of these means. But the other, nearly identical, could reasonably be read to provide reimbursement to CCC for its expenses due to weather-caused delays. But these two nearly identical provisions cannot be interpreted to mean the same thing, because then one of them is without meaning. This Board cannot and should not excise a provision of the contract; rather you should determine what it means by giving it a proper interpretation, which I suggest is as follows: When a Change Order extends the time for completion, *all* costs caused by that extension are properly awarded to the Contractor, CCC. The principles of contract interpretation further state that a contract should be construed against the drafter. In this case, the Government produced The Contract Documents. Except for the building/construction specifications, Government contracts of this type are all on pre-printed "standard forms" which don't change. They were Army forms and CCC had nothing to do with them. It would be manifestly unfair and unreasonable to expect CCC to agree to extend the time for completion and not be compensated for the costs it actually incurred because of that extension; and this Board should make a ruling that produces a fair, equitable and reasonable result. I pleaded: "Don't make this Contractor give the Government an undeserved windfall." I relied heavily both on the "**Restatement of the Law of Contracts**" and on a major contracts-law authority, Professor Samuel Williston, whose text I quoted from.

The Good Guys Win !

CCC's appeal to the BCA was sustained and they eventually collected their $25,000 (plus interest). Here's the key quote from the decision, even citing the *Restatement of Contracts* that I'd cited in my brief:

In determining the intent of a contract one must seek to give effect to all its provisions and to avoid a result that would make some provision meaningless. See [case citation] in which the Board held as follows:

The contract, together with its drawings and specifications, must be given that meaning which would be attached thereto by reasonably intelligent persons acquainted with all operative usages and knowing all the facts and circumstances prior to and contemporaneous with the drafting of the contract. In so doing the contract must be read as a whole and all specifications and drawings forming part of the contract must be interpreted together. No part or parts of the drawings or specifications are to be rejected or treated as a redundancy or as meaningless if any meaning which is reasonable and consistent with other parts can be given them, or if the specifications and drawings are capable of being construed with the part or parts left in them. *Restatement, Contracts*, Section 230, 235 (c).

III. What Went Wrong for the Army?

… and maybe there's a lesson for you in your own contracting practices. Things went wrong in two places: First with the Contracting Officer and Second, at the appeal before the BCA.

The Contracting Officer Could Have …

First, understand that many of the papers in The Contract Documents are pre-printed forms, especially the "General Conditions" attached to each and every contract relating to the subject – here, construction of housing units. Other than the specifications of the job, much of an Army Contract I'm guessing is produced with a staple gun. This is a far cry from the bargaining and negotiation that goes on between the parties to a contract; and that's the "typical" kind of situation which contract law is designed to address. The **Restatement of the Law of Contracts** and Professor Williston's text and the rules they espouse come out of this kind of back-and-forth negotiation leading to the final agreement the parties sign. But these legal principles, if you understand the Army contracting model, have little application to a bunch of forms taken off a shelf and stapled together. That process, with the usual "General Conditions," almost ensures that provisions in the contract will contain some repetition. The Government should have argued that Williston and **Restatement** principles are valid when parties negotiate – like the buying and selling of a cow in old English cases. They make no sense in the Army contracting process.

In this case, the Contracting Officer, in drawing up the contract, repeated almost word for word paragraph 5(a) from General Provisions and put those same words into the Specific Provisions, Article II. As this case illustrates, identical language is two places in the contract leaves open the question of what that repeat means. The rules of interpretation push a court to give the repeated provision a meaning different from its meaning where it's first used, especially if it appears in some other context. And that different meaning is usually not something the parties even thought about. The Contracting Officer should have checked when he drafted the Specific Provisions that he was not repeating anything already contained in the General Provisions.

The Board of Contract Appeals Could Have …

Legal Counsel for the Army, JAG Colonel X, could have pointed out how the Army's method of assembling a contract was almost guaranteed to produce duplicate provisions. Pages were taken from various sources and stapled together and it was inevitable that those pieces that came together would to some extent duplicate each other. He made no such argument – he argued on the legal grounds that I had chosen and that guaranteed that he would lose, as he did.[3]

Although "wrong" on its face, I later (older and wiser?) became convinced that the BCA did right and if the only reason they could come up for that right decision is a "wrong" reason, then so be it. The problem lay in the contract documents, which should have provided for a contractor to be reimbursed for *all* such legitimate extra costs that CCC incurred from weather-related delays. BCA's decision corrected the error in the Army's contracting process and, in the end, did justice to this claim.

———

So there you have it, an example of how a lawyer can find a legal principle or concept – albeit one not the most appropriate one for his case; and make a good and strong argument based on that principle/concept to a court. And if the other side and the court accepts that legal principle as applicable to the case, a lawyer can win a decision based on that argument, *but* although this was a good decision judged by its fairness and equity, the decision may technically be wrong – bad law. Good argument, a fair result because the Client CCC deserved to be reimbursed for these costs it incurred. But it was, in the end, a bad decision on the law of the case.[4]

BLT #25: Avoid repeats in your contracts unless you have a good reason to say the same thing twice, in two places in the contract. Sometimes repeats are used for emphasis, but the drafter should preface the repeat with something like: "To ensure that the parties' mutual intention on this point is perfectly clear, they repeat…" Otherwise, one of those repeats may come back to haunt you with a judge's interpretation that you never intended. This means you must read any contract you, as a lawyer, prepare and if you can possibly make the time, any contract you sign as a business client.

Case Two: This Tale, Set in Probate Court, is about a "Phony Adoption": The Importance of the Notion of "Intention" Determines the Outcome

I. The Client's Problem

Case One, above, illustrates how courts faced with a contract dispute look for the meaning of the words of that contract; that search for "meaning" is another way of describing the court's job in a contract dispute: Finding the intention of the parties to the contract. Case One then goes on to illustrate that a basic intention of the parties to a contract is that they presumably intend *everything* in the contract to have a meaning; nothing appears in that contract without having some intended meaning. Here, in Case Two, you'll see how I argued intention – in fact "Three-Barreled Intention" – to win a decision from a court that I knew (and the Court knew!) from the outset had no **jurisdiction** over the matter that I argued – but more about that later. First, the story of sibling rivalry gone wild:

Brother hates sister, probably something from early childhood, but we'll never know. Brother has had emotional problems and is not gainfully employed; he lives mainly off a trust created by Dad. Dad's Trust designated the sister and a lawyer to serve as the two trustees for Brother. Under the trust document, Brother could use the trust fund only for himself or his children; and he could leave it to his children in his will. And failing that, his trust fund would go to his sister and her children. But Brother was aging, not married, had no children, and no relationship or marriage prospects.

The "trigger" event or boiling-point between Brother and sister was a dispute over the amount of Brother's monthly "allowance" from his trust. Sister and the co-trustee had increased that amount twice, but Brother wanted still more. The trustees were concerned that he'd run out of money and told him so; but they also said that if he had some one-time special need, the trustees would take care of it. This did not satisfy Brother, and he threatened to do something about it. His threats included this: "Neither you, sister, nor any of your children will ever see one penny from my trust fund!" Sad, but such is the way of some failing family relationships. What to do!

Brother Gets an Idea, But Then the Fickle Finger of Fate Intervenes…

Brother found a lawyer willing to "cooperate" in his plan, which was to adopt two friends, a man and a woman in their sixties. They became his legally adopted "children" and, under Dad's will, he could leave them his trust fund in his will. Brother then proceeded to make a will leaving his trust funds (as he is permitted to do under the Trust document) to his two newly adopted "children." Fate strikes: Brother suddenly gets sick and dies and sister learns of what he's done. His will is about to go to **probate** in the county Probate Court. Sister objects to her Father's money going to these two strangers – her brother's recently adopted "children." She engages us as her lawyers to "correct" this situation.

I explained to Sister the limited jurisdiction of the County Probate Court: "Their only function is to authenticate the will. What happens next has to be dealt with in the state's trial court." My words fall on deaf ears. "You've got to do something to stop this joke, this phony adoption, from having Dad's hard-earned money go to these…" she sputtered…"strangers!"

Citing the phony adoption and working with a probate associate in the law firm, I filed an objection to the will in the probate proceeding. The deceased Brother's lawyer filed a motion to strike my objection and a court hearing was ordered for us to argue his **motion to strike**. The issue being argued: Could the sister intervene in the Probate Court at this early stage to begin invalidation of the phony adoption? I knew I was on the losing side of that argument – the Probate Court simply did not have jurisdiction to invalidate the phony adoption; only the state's trial court could take on such a case.

My probate-law associate confirmed that the Probate Court had only limited jurisdiction – to authenticate the brother's will – and had no jurisdiction to get into the matter of the phony adoption; that was for the trial court, the County Superior Court.

I explained to my colleague that I wanted something in the judicial record noting this phony adoption, and I wanted it in at the earliest stage and the earliest date possible. "Anything this judge might say could well provide us with ammunition in a later proceeding – if we get that far – in the proper court or in settlement talks. I have been with this family for decades and I want to make a statement to the court." I told my associate to introduce me as the lawyer for the family when Dad established his trust (drafted by a Probate/Estates partner at the time). And so, with the court's permission, I made this statement:

"Your Honor, the law here is all about intentions and how this court should carry out people's intentions. First, when a will or trust is before you, it's the intention of the testator or grantor [*the person who made the will or trust in question*], in this case, the Father. He was totally family-oriented and clearly intended that half his money to go to his son and any children he might have. And if he didn't have any children, then that money would go to his daughter and her children. A decision in favor of these adopted so-called 'children' would defeat that all-important intention of the Father, who established this trust for his children and grandchildren, not for some strangers, like these so-called adopted 'children.'

"Second is the intention of the State legislature in passing adoption laws, and we all know what that obvious purpose was: To allow young children without parents to become children of an adoptive mother and father and be raised in a normal family setting. The legislature did not intend their law to be used to foil and subvert the intention of a Father who simply wanted his money to go to his own children and grandchildren – and *not* to strangers!

"Third: What was the intention of the deceased in this proceeding, the brother? His intention was to get more money from the trustees. That intention cannot possibly be carried out – he's now deceased.

"If this or any other court in this State gives effect to these phony adoptions, the only intentions that still matter – those of the Father as expressed in his will and trusts and those of the Legislature in passing adoption laws – will be defeated. If this court or any court in this State chooses to go along, to partner with the brother's shenanigans and trickery and legitimize the illegitimate, so be it. But I urgently plea that the courts of this State not become party to this fiasco, this perversion of the law. Thank you for your attention."

The Judge is Convinced!

This little speech apparently roused the judge's ire. He denied the deceased brother's lawyer's motion to strike my appearance for the sister and allowed me 90 days to elaborate on my objections to the brother's will. Here are the judge's words from his opinion on the points I'd made in his court; first, addressing the point about Father's intention when he set up trusts for his two children, brother and sister:

> The intent of the settlor [Father] must override a subsequent tactical decision, albeit cognizable in the law, by a trust beneficiary [brother] which subverts an intended inheritance scheme [*Father's estate plan for his family*].

Next, the judge addressed my point about the intent of the State Legislature when it passed adoption laws:

> In this case, it cannot be inferred that the Legislature envisioned protecting sixtyish adoptees with no discernible connection to decedent [brother] to be lineal descendants for whom statutory protection is conferred.

I was obviously pleased to have in the record this judge's opinion restating my argument in a way that could be used in later court proceedings (or settlement talks) to make his point: Brother's adoption of two elderly friends defeats the clear intention of both the Father when he set up trusts for his children and the intent of the Legislature in passing adoption laws.

This matter did not end in court, but as is the case more often than not, at the settlement table. All parties decided – after the case was filed in two other courts – that the expense of litigation would waste valuable trust assets, and so the parties settled. But this situation provided yet another example of trying to get out of a losing situation – here, by getting a ruling from a court without jurisdiction over the adoption issue, a ruling for possible use in a future proceeding before another judge in another court and a judge who *would* have had the power to deal with the phony adoption.

So there you have it: Solving a client's problem by knowingly arguing an inapplicable (in the Probate Court) legal theory to win a fair and just claim; and trying to solve the client's problem by asking a court for a ruling I knew (and the Court knew!) was beyond its jurisdiction, just to get some strong words on the record at the earliest possible date. Ah, the ways of The Law!

BLT #26: When a judge adopts your argument as their own by a judge in a judicial opinion, even if that judge and his court has no jurisdiction to make a binding ruling on the validity of your position, I believe carries more weight than just your argument in a brief later on, when the case reaches a court that *does* have the jurisdiction and power to make a definitive ruling. We'll never know in this case – it settled – but I'll always believe this to be a useful strategy.

And how can we leave Part III, "Knowing 'The Law' Helps You to Win" without Leo Cullum's classic:

1 See a recent statement of these Willistonian principles in a 2014 paper by Martorana, "A Guide to Contract Interpretation," which cites and quotes from *In re Lehman Brothers Inc.*, 478 B.R. 570, 2012 WL 1995089, S.D.N.Y. (2012) (at p. 21): "Divining the parties' intent requires a court to 'give full meaning and effect to all of [the contract's] provisions." *Katel Ltd. Liab. Co. v. AT & T Corp.*, 607 F.3d 60, 64 (2d Cir.2010). "Courts must avoid interpretations that render contract provisions meaningless or superfluous." *Manley v. AmBase Corp.*, 337 F.3d 237, 250 (2d Cir.2003). This paper is available at http://www.reedsmith.com/files/uploads/miscellany/A_Guide_to_Contract_Interpretation__July_2014_.pdf

And see "Contract Interpretation and the Parol Evidence Rule" by Richard J. Sankovitz, available at http://marketplace.wisbar.org/Documents/Products/SampleChapter/AK0040_SampleChapter.pdf

2 5 U.S. (1 Cranch) 137, 174 (1803)

3 Legal wordsmith Bryan Garner makes a related point in his piece on the late U.S. Supreme Court Justice Antonin Scalia, "A Tribute to Nino," *ABA Journal* April 2016, p.24, at p. 71. Garner describes the search for a proper adjective for the Constitution for this "originalist" Justice. If he adopted his opponents' favored term, a "living" Constitution, then Scalia would have been forced to express disagreement by favoring a "dead" Constitution. So for Scalia's purposes he'd dub his opponents' position as favoring a "morphing" Constitution; and then Scalia could assert the opposite: He favors a "stable" Constitution. Garner writes, on the point I make in the text:

"Naming rights are powerful. If you use your opponent's terminology, you're probably engaging in futility."

4 Appeal, ASBCA No. 6849 ; Armed Services Board of Contract Appeals; CONTRACT: 1962 ASBCA LEXIS 946 February 19, 1962.

PART IV

These six Tales illustrate how a seasoned lawyer's experiences with business clients – and not necessarily involving The Law – become useful when trying to prevent or later, solve problems that clients encounter. We start with a mixed-bag situation of knowing how judges react to certain situations and then move on to the product-liability exposures most businesses face in this litigious United States of ours. And we finish in the areas of unfair competition and the other side's intention to engage in unfair competition. Sometimes clients should listen to their lawyers' hunches and concerns about the other party to a proposed deal. Not listening in one situation proved costly to the client.

*"Look, I'm not saying it's going to be today. But someday—someday—
you guys will be happy that you've taken along a lawyer."*

TALE # 24

A SINGLE BRIEF $100-FEE-CONSULTATION AND
THEN A NEWSPAPER STORY (ONE BILLION DOLLARS
LATER!) LOW-RENT TENANT FORGETS TO EXTEND ITS
LONG-TERM LEASE – OOPS!

I. THE CLIENT'S PROBLEM
Those "Pesky" Long-Term Leases at Fixed Rents

At some point in the past, long before I got involved, Client had acquired an investment property – a **net leased** parcel of land on which stood a highly specialized fitted-out science/office building and a large paved parking lot. The building was leased to a science-based company under a long-term, let's say a *very* long-term lease, with a low fixed rent, and that was Client's problem – a rental way below "market." (Normally, long-term leases provide for upward rental adjustments over time. Sometimes we use the Consumer Price Index [a "CPI adjustment"] or some fixed percentage or dollar amount which would kick in on an annual or other periodic basis.) But in this situation, Client had for some reason acquired this real estate – land and building, maybe in a trade – subject to a long-term **net lease** at a fixed dollar rental. And that was their problem: Real estate values in the area had skyrocketed and the rent from this building was but a small fraction of the current fair-market-value rent, to wit: $6.16 per square foot versus the then current market rate of about $40.00 per square foot. An "opportunity" suddenly arose when the first 25-year term of this potentially 100-year lease was about to end. At that point, Tenant had three more 25-year extension options remaining.

The Tenant was a major research Laboratory and I'm guessing that Tenant, at its own cost, had built and fitted out this very specialized and expensive building on the property. I got involved on the day the client Landlord's Leasing VP came to see me with the news – he was excited, agitated:

"The date for Laboratory to exercise their first extension period has come and gone, but we've haven't gotten any notice exercising their option to extend." He explained that the fixed net rent in the Lease was $6.16 per square foot, but the area was now so desirable that Landlord could rent space in that building for more than over six times that number – about $40.00 a foot!

"The Lease term is set to end in nine months; and they never sent a notice to exercise the option to extend the term. So what do we do?"

II. A Solution (Maybe)

I said, "I assume you'd like to renegotiate the rent to a more current figure. I can't tell you what to do – that's a business decision for you to make. But let me spell out a couple of projected scenarios." I explained the legal situation they were in:

"You could send Tenant an immediate wake-up call and take the position that their Lease ends with the current term, in nine months. At that point, Tenant would probably send a belated Notice of Exercise of Term Extension Option with a 'Sorry we're late' cover note. You would deny the validity of the Tenant's Notice and then maybe end up in court.

"As a matter of law, you'd be correct, but you should know that in a court of **Equity**, that branch of the law that tries to reach results that are fair and equitable and to avoid unreasonable resolutions of problem situations, you stand a good chance of losing. Equity courts have their own little maxims, like 'Equity abhors a forfeiture.' That means that a few days' delay in sending in its Notice to Extend Lease Term would probably not result in Tenant losing its Lease.[1] My guess is that if this Tenant petitioned the court asking to be excused for its being just a little late in its exercise of its option to extend the Lease, the court would excuse this lateness. After all, Tenant had clearly sunk a fortune into building this specialized and expensive structure to house its research facility; and it's unfair for Landlord to get this improved real estate because of this little slip-up.[2]

"The Landlord could, of course, also argue fairness to the judge: 'Tenant is paying just a small fraction of what this property should rent for.' And if Laboratory/Tenant said, 'But that's what the Lease provides for,' Landlord would counter with 'And the Lease also provides for a timely notice of exercise of option to extend, which you, Tenant, failed to give. So let's, indeed, follow the terms of the Lease.'"

"So where does that leave us?" asked the client Landlord's Leasing VP.

"My guess," I said, "and again, it's only a guess: Tenant would win in this proceeding. The court would rule that on balance, the 'equities' of the situation favor Tenant. They've put in a lot of improvements; Landlord is not really harmed, he hasn't changed his position in reliance on the Lease not being extended, so let's just forgive these few days of delay in Tenant sending out its Notice to Extend Term."

Client's Leasing VP was obviously not happy with my response – "So what can we do to get a rental closer to market?" he asked.

"The legal term I just used, 'change your position.' You take some actions that would put the Tenant at such an increased risk of losing the lease that they come to the bargaining table. I'm not saying you'll win in court, but if you put the Tenant at some unacceptable level of risk, they might be willing to renegotiate the rent. You'll have to make the business decision as to what to do." I explained that Tenant could be put in a weaker and riskier position before a judge if the Client/Landlord "changed his position," a phrase out of the law books. And I explained what it means in these circumstances for the Landlord to "change his position;" and I made it amply clear that this would entail Landlord spending some money.

"How? What do we do?," the Leasing VP asked. I ticked off a few actions Landlord could take, sort of "scripting" events going forward:

- Wait to contact the Tenant until about a month before the current 25-year term is to end, which would be about nine months away. Get to the point in time where the Lease is about to expire and you have never gotten a notice to extend the term. If you get a late Notice of Exercise of Option to Extend in the interim, we can deal with it then. Chances are that if they missed the deadline date in the Lease, you won't be hearing from them. (Client Landlord did not, in fact, hear from them.)
- When you visit them at that later date, come in with your "people," maybe carrying some rolls of plans, clipboards, and ask for (i) permission to walk through the building and (ii) the timing and their moving plans. (Bring smelling salts!)

- Next, you'll have to do something to "change your position," meaning incurring expense and "doing things." So be prepared to spend some money. For example:
- Hire a fee-based appraiser or real estate broker to do a survey and give you a confidential report on the market for the re-leasing of this specialized property. You might even research possible new tenants with brokers, again on a strictly confidential basis; and try to deal in generalities of neighborhood/location; type of building; etc., without identifying the specific property.
- Engage an architect to do some preliminary sketches and give you some thoughts on some economically feasible uses for the building; possible expansion by adding floors; expanding the "footprint" of the building – that huge parking lot seems to leave room for that. In other words, actively make plans to alter the building. This would certainly be a prudent move if the realtors tell you there's a strong rental market in the area.
- You might engage our law firm to check zoning and building code issues and report back to you in writing on the limits of alterations; expansion; etc.
- Engage a contractor for a review of the site; ideas on materials, construction issues and the like for the development of the building and any possible expansion, added parking areas, all with cost estimates and other financial details. And again, on a strictly confidential basis.

"If that's what it takes to win," the Leasing VP said, but I stopped him short.

"Let me repeat: There is no guarantee that you'll win in court – there's no 'win,' as you put it. This is not a slam-dunk case in any court and that's not my point. What you're doing by Landlord's actions is putting Tenant, maybe, in an unacceptably risky position. What I'm saying is this: If you do all these things, Tenant may see itself at risk of losing the Lease in a court case. I doubt that Tenant will do nothing and take its chances with litigating the case with that kind of a risk hanging over them, especially given how much they have at stake in that specialized building. A tough and strict judge could well rule against them and they'd lose their lease. This should at least bring them to the table. What you can negotiate for a rental at that point is then up to you. But my guess is that they'll negotiate a new rental with you." (I was wrong on this last point, as you'll see.)

Client took my advice, spending a not inconsiderable sum, doing much as I'd outlined. A couple of weeks before the expiration of that first 25-year term Tenant was, as Client later told me, shocked when Landlord's Leasing VP came by with his contractor's representative carrying a set of tentative plans (to "take a quick look at the building") and inquire about Tenant's moving plans "next month." Shocked is a mild word for their reaction, as he reported, when they heard that what they considered their 100-year lease was about to come to an end.

That was the last I heard of this matter – nothing from Client or anyone else – usually a good sign, as in so many of the Tales. Apparently Tenant was more risk-averse than I had imagined because, after a "quiet" period, I read in a business journal that Tenant was buying the building – the parties had negotiated a purchase and sale agreement –. (Result: Landlord would get rid of a non-producing asset, receive a more current, market value price for its property and Tenant would now own its custom-built structure without future worries about exercising options to extend the term and giving timely notices.)

———

Note: Here's an interesting statistic to give you an idea of the magnitude of the dollars involved and how "cheap" a simple long-term land lease can become as decades pass, real estate values increase and inflation takes its toll; more particularly, what a genuine "bargain rent" Tenant was enjoying: The current market-rate rent projected for the balance of the 75-years left on the lease (if options had been properly exercised) exceeded the low $6.16 per square foot Lease current rent by well over one billion dollars. And the legal fee for that brief consultation – maybe $100. So, you see, there's not always a direct correlation between the cost and the value of legal advice.

And this: One of my partners tells me that, in his experience, when an institution (such as a city, large bank, financial firm, etc.) has a lease-extension option – particularly if it's a long-term lease – say over 15 years – chances are 50/50 that they will forget about it. And this is regardless of their reminder system, computerized or otherwise.

Decades ago, before the computer age, when a chain-store client missed such an extension option deadline (and ended up with a rent increase), I developed a business model for a reminder service. In researching the situation, I recall visiting the headquarters of a major U.S. insurance company on some deal and, just out of curiosity, asking their real estate chief how he ensured not missing these dates (this company had hundreds of branch offices all over the United States). The executive smiled confidently and patted a small tin box of index cards on his desk. "It's all right here," he said. I wasn't overconfident that this was as foolproof a system as he could use, given the magnitude of his responsibility.

BLT #27: If you're a tenant under a long-term lease with options to extend, never count just on your calendar notation or some index-card file or somebody remembering when to exercise an option. Don't depend on even the computer; and this refers to *any* option calling for some action in the future, whether it's to extend the term, expand the premises, reduce the premises, whatever. I don't believe even computers provide really fool-proof reminders over these long terms of many years, personnel changes, offices are moved, loss of data and the like. And so if I'm representing such a tenant, I insist on a "Wake-Up Clause" in the Lease, which works like this:

If Tenant misses the option-exercise date, they don't lose any extension rights until 30-days *after* they get a reminder notice from Landlord. Shifting this burden onto Landlord is the best way for a tenant not to lose out on valuable option rights.

---

1 **"Equity abhors a forfeiture."** A **Forfeiture** is a total loss of a right or a thing because of the failure to do something as required. A total loss is usually a rather high price to pay. And so unless the consequence is reasonable in relation to the seriousness of the fault, it may be

viewed by a judge as too harsh. In fairness and good conscience, a court of equity will refuse to permit an unreasonable forfeiture. This maxim has particularly strong application to the ownership of land or, indeed, any interest in real estate (such as a leasehold interest) for which the law shows great respect. Title to or an interest in land should never be lost for a trivial reason— for example, a delay of only a few days in closing a deal to purchase a house. See *The Free Dictionary by Farlex available at* http://legal-dictionary.thefreedictionary.com/ %22Equity+abhors+a+forfeiture.%22

2 A case illustrating my concern is *135 East 57th Street LLC v. Daffy Inc.* NY Slip Op 8497, 91 A.D.3d 1, 934 N.Y.S.2d 112 (App. Div. 2011): "…in some situations, principles of equity have softened the often harsh results of common-law rules of strict contract construction … equity will intervene to avoid a forfeiture." The law is clearly in the tenant's favor where it has made substantial improvements to the property – precisely the facts in this Tale. Indeed, if memory serves me, the Tenant in this Tale built the building and equipped it for their high-level scientific/engineering work (mostly for the government). In this NY "Daffy" case, the notice was just a few days late; and tenant there had made no improvements to the premises. Nevertheless, the Court ruled that the Landlord was not hurt by the few days of delay in getting the tenant's notice to extend the term.

TALE # 25

GIVING AWAY A PIECE OF THE BUSINESS, BUT KEEPING TOTAL CONTROL

This is probably the easiest problem I *SOLVED!* Businesses routinely do what Hal did here for his deserving employee. Hal's story exemplifies many "American Dream" food-product startups, for example, Pepperidge Farm products (see http://www.pepperidgefarm.com/margaretrudkin.aspx):

- "Invent" something new in your kitchen;
- share it with a few friends;
- word gets around about this delicious "good stuff" you make;
- others want to buy some; you step up production;
- you do a "test run" at a local store and your product is snapped up;
- the market gets bigger;
- and then you cross that threshold into a genuine commercial enterprise: You're in the food business!

Hal Finds a Grrreat Bread Recipe – a Business is Born!

That's what happened to Hal, a physician/scientist/researcher by profession. On a European trip he'd found a recipe for a new kind of bread and then he improved on it. The product caught on and it was time to formalize his business and so we formed Bakery Corp., which bought and fitted out a bakery out in a small rural town. The business grew rapidly. In a few years Hal had a fleet of vans delivering to supermarkets in four states, but – yes, there's always that "but" that comes up again and again. The business was consuming all his time and he felt he was losing precious hours away from his science and research interests. Then, along came Mac, an experienced commercial bakery manager who wanted to live out in the country and was looking for a job.

Hal "Is Thrilled" With Mac – the Ideal Commercial Bakery Manager Who Wants "a Piece of the Action"

Hal was more than pleased with Mac, who freed him up so he could get back to his science and research. Hal told me about Mac in a phone call later that year:

"I want you to issue 5% of the company shares to Mac – he's asked to become an part-owner of the business and it's okay with me." Hal was that much thrilled with this guy who was doing such a good job and freeing up Hal for what he really wanted to do.

I Didn't Want to Issue Stock to Mac – and Why

"Let me give you some advice," I cautioned. "First: It's too soon to be giving anything away; Mac has only been with you for less than a full year – it's just too soon."

I suggested that the ownership interest be phased in at say 1% a year. Just as Mac had left his prior job, he could just as well "jump ship" and leave Hal back where he started – but now with Mac owning a piece of Hal's company. "Of course we would provide that the stock interest is not vested irrevocably (meaning Mac doesn't own the stock) for a number of years. And the unvested portion of the stock is forfeited (i.e., reverts to the company) if Mac leaves the job for any reason before some set/target date." And maybe most important, I explained to Hal that an owner's life can get "complicated" by minority shareholders, especially when those shareholders start disagreeing with Hal about his business decisions. Hal thought that this phase-in would probably be acceptable to Mac.

I spelled out some details of an arrangement equivalent to, but not involving, ownership of any actual shares. For example, if the company were sold, Mac would get the full 5% of the net proceeds of sale; that should make this arrangement more palatable to Mac.

Second, I explained to Hal from my own past experiences the real problems a minority shareholder could cause him and how having even a 5% shareholder could severely cut down Hal's freedom of action. The control a 100% shareholder has over his company is a wonderful, delicious feeling; and that's gone once you're down to 95%. I explained to Hal my standard alternate approach: Give Mac the full *economic equivalent* of what he wanted, but no stock interest or voting rights. (This was not something I invented; as far back as the 1950s some major corporations had so-called "**Phantom Stock Plans**" for their executives.)

"Give him 5% of any dividends paid (usually none in a typical **close-corporation** situation); 5% of any bonus that you, Hal, might take at year-end (a kind of profit-sharing arrangement); and promise to give Mac 5% of net sales proceeds if the company is sold."

Mac's response was generally favorable: He asked that he be consulted when management decisions were being made, like changes in the bread recipe; sales, marketing and distribution issues and other management matters. Hal didn't have a problem with that – he was doing that anyway and always huddled with Mac on all business decisions. Indeed Mac, as an experienced commercial bakery manager, would probably come up with better decisions than Hal would on his own. So no problem on the management-decisions question – Mac would be consulted (and probably listened to). But bottom line: Final decisions were, of course, left to Hal, the 100% shareholder, the owner of Bakery Corp.

The Deal Is Done, and a Buyer for Bakery Corp. Appears

Mac agreed to the suggested approach to his getting "5% of the company" and, with his own lawyer's review and approval, signed the Agreement I had prepared. Less than 24 months later (Mac now had the economic equivalent of a 3% interest in Bakery Corp.) a large regional bread company offered to buy and Hal told me he was ready to sell out. I didn't like to lose a client, but was pleased for Hal; and, of course, Mac would get his full 5% of the net proceeds of sale, as their Agreement provided.

I pointed out to Hal that even this decision to sell might well have been made more difficult (maybe even impossible as a practical matter) if Mac were a 5% shareholder and decided he didn't want to see *any* changes. The deal went through; Hal and Mac got their money; Mac stayed on as general manager of Hal's Bakery Corp. as a division of the buyer, a much larger firm. Hal was free to do his science work and "they all lived happily ever after."

BLT #28:

1- The client shouldn't "practice law" and the lawyer should not be sidetracked by the client's request to take this or that legal action – in this case, "Issue 5% stock to Mac!" Client should set out his practical business goals to the lawyer ("Just the facts, ma'am") and let the lawyer recommend the legal steps to accomplish those goals. Here, Hal wanted to respond to Mac's request and give Mac the incentive of being an "owner" of Bakery Corp. How to accomplish that goal is for the lawyer to recommend, as I did here.

2- The sole owner of any **close-corporation** should be very slow to give up any of his 100% voting control by issuing a stock interest to a valued employee or a relative. In many instances, even a non-voting class of stock can prove to be an obstacle to what the owner wants to do.[1] In some states, certain corporate actions may require a supermajority level of consent, possibly near unanimous from *all* shareholders and including those owning non-voting shares. So go slow in issuing stock; look for other ways to provide the "economic equivalent." You don't want to be subjected to what I've seen in some instances, which amounts to "corporate blackmail."

Business owners should remember that minority shareholders and their "rights" can prove a major nuisance to you. Note that as far back as 1987, the leading scholar on the rights of minority shareholders wrote:

The amount of litigation growing out of minority shareholder oppression – actual, fancied or fabricated – has grown tremendously in recent years, and the flood of litigation shows no sign of abating.[2]

1 In Tale #4, the solution to Client's problem was to create and issue to store managers a new class of non-voting common stock in each subsidiary corporation that operated a store in the chain. But before I took those steps, I had to check the law of the state of incorporation and then tailor the detailed terms and conditions printed on those stock certificates to ensure that store managers could not interfere in the management decisions (made by the parent company) relating to the subsidiary corporation that operated each manager's particular store.

2 F. Hodge O'Neal, *Oppression of Minority Shareholders: Protecting Minority Rights*, 35 Clev. St. L. Rev. 121 (1987) available at http://engagedscholarship.csuohio.edu/clevstlrev/vol35/iss1/7. See also the late author's 2-volume loose-leaf treatise text published by West USA: O'Neal and Thompson's Oppression of Minority Shareholders and LLC Members, Rev. 2d By: The Late F. Hodge O'Neal, Robert B. Thompson - See more at: http://www.carswell.com/product-detail/oneal-and-thompsons-oppression-of-minority-shareholders-and-llc-members-rev-2d/#sthash.TwloGFs0.dpuf

TALE # 26

WHEN LAW COURTS ARE NOT THE ANSWER TO A COMPETITOR'S FALSE ADVERTISING

Sometimes "The Law" is too Slow.
Here, Time to Switch to the Industry Trade Magazine.

A large envelope from Client Bill landed on my desk – in it, a copy of the trade magazine serving his industry – meat-packing and processing machinery. The accompanying note: "Call me ASAP!" Bill called first and I told him I'd received the magazine and "so what?"

"Turn to page 68, in the back pages, *that's* what. Check out the ad from Zombie, Inc." (Zombie was Bill's local direct competitor). Bill was the exclusive U.S. sales agency that sold ABC's meat processing equipment; Zombie, Inc. sold XYZ's competing equipment. The ad was ingenious; it looked something like this:

For Immediate Sale !
Used ABC Meat Processing Equipment

Meat Packers are changing over to Zombie's new XYZ equipment in such numbers and we have taken in trade so many used ABC machines that we're running a sale on these used ABC machines. Some customers have also indicated concern with ABC's relationship with the manufacturer of ABC machines. Call this number – 999 123-4567 if you're interested in a used ABC machine – we have taken lots of them in trade and need to sell them.

Now, is that cute or clever or what? A back-handed way of telling customers that the competitor's machine is inferior to yours, which is selling off the charts. And the "cute tricks" continue: There's a rumor – just a rumor, mind you – that the competitor, my client ABC, may be in trouble with the ABC manufacturer (to make the customers worry: Will I still be able to get ABC parts?)

Bill assured me that this whole thing was false, a fabrication from start to finish. Indeed, he had an out-of-town friend call Zombie and ask them about ordering one of these used ABC machines. No luck, just shipped out the last one. "But while you're on the line, are you in the market for a brand new XYZ machine?" Bill was now shouting: "I want you to sue the bastards. They're a bunch of lying thieves." I rarely heard this from clients, and certainly never from Bill, usually a cool customer.

Bill calmed down after I explained what a slow and costly process a lawsuit would be, how difficult it would be to prove actual damages, how his potential customers would be alienated by possibly getting involved (e.g., as witnesses) in this messy situation. Even going through a government agency to complain about this false and deceptive advertising takes time. I said, "Let's try something first, Bill. Cool it while I make a call."

At that time I represented one of the most successful public relations agencies in the city. The woman who founded it decades ago – call her Jen – had connections to media I didn't even know existed, so that's what I did; I called Jen. She asked me about the client, his sales-agency business for ABC equipment, and more; we spent about half an hour on the phone. She wanted to meet with Bill and so I arranged for a meeting at her office the next afternoon.

At the meeting she reported that she'd spoken to an editor (maybe *the* editor-in-chief) of the industry's trade journal where the offending ad had appeared. The editor knew and admired Bill's company and he was prepared to do a cover story on Bill's company. And he could squeeze it into his publishing schedule – it might be out within 60 days. (In litigation terms, 60 days is like ten minutes of "normal" time.) Bill and Jen agreed on the fee for her PR agency and Bill and I left. I thought he was starting to feel better.

While waiting for the cover story to come out in the trade magazine, I worked with Bill and drafted a note to his customers to go out with the next regular mailing of invoices for service or parts or just as a separate mailing. It noted XYZ's ad in the magazine and brushed it off lightly as a fabricated piece of false advertising, motivated by desperation because of competition from the superior equipment Bill was selling. Bill was uncertain whether he wanted to call attention to the ad which, after all, may not even have been seen by many if not most of his customers.

"That's your call, Bill," I told him and left the draft mailing piece with him to decide whether he wanted to use it or not. "But I sure think you ought to get reprints of the cover story coming out in two months and mail those to your customers." Bill agreed.

The next call from Bill a couple of months later was an invitation to lunch at his salesroom, where I was greeted with a pile of the latest issue of his industry's trade magazine. On the cover was a color photo of Bill and his Sales Manager together with the President of the overseas manufacturer of ABC machines standing in front of the latest model ABC equipment. Their three smiles lit up the page! A headline right on the cover said something about "Sales of ABC machines going through the roof throughout the meatpacking industry." The story inside quoted the President of the ABC machines manufacturer: "We are so pleased with the sales performance and the excellent service organization of ABC's U.S. Sales Agency that we have just renewed their exclusive contract with us for another five years."

Bill then showed me a pile of reprints of the cover and cover story and the letter Jen had drafted for him to send to all customers and sales prospects. Copies were now in the hands of all his salespeople for distribution. The "message" of that letter to customers was clear: Readers should not be taken in by the "cute, but desperate" ad from Zombie about non-existent "used ABC machines." Jen had nicely avoided (sometimes narrowly, like a

245

skillful toreador) a possible trade defamation claim from Zombie, but she clearly succeeded in getting across Bill's message and his outrage at Zombie's ad. Needless to say, Zombie's "cute" ads never reappeared.

So you see, sometimes your business lawyer has to think outside the box of the law and courts and judges – some answers lie elsewhere.

BLT #29: Here, just as in the preceding Tale #25, the client should not practice law; and "Sue the bastards!" is as much a lawyer's decision, practicing law by a client as "Issue 5% stock to Mac." STOP! Don't "sue the bastards." Take a deep breath and maybe a sip of water (or something stronger?) and remember this: Litigation is a S-L-O-W process and often takes years. And it's very expensive and risky, with risks of losing and facing a **counterclaim**. Define your goals sharply and clearly early on and see if there isn't some way of achieving those goals more quickly than in a courtroom (or series of courtrooms!). Get some estimate – the best you can get even if it's only a "guestimate" – of the costs in time and money and consider the emotional drain of any planned litigation. And don't discount the negatives of time spent away from running your business. In the words of a few of my older and wiser clients decades ago, "Life is too short ..." Enough said.

TALE # 27

WHEN A LAWYER'S BUSINESS ADVICE IS WORTH MORE THAN LEGAL ADVICE

Two Cases
Case One : The Product That Was Too "Risky" to Manufacture

Client was in the "canvas goods" manufacturing business and called me about an order they'd received. They didn't want to fill the order with their standard sales forms; clearly this was not run-of-the-mill business for just another tote bag or knapsack. Client was concerned and, as it turned out, rightly so.

The order was from a would-be new customer ("PROMO"), a sales/promotions company that wanted to market a "bullet-proof school backpack." Their move was obviously prompted by the school shootings in the news and, naturally, parents' concerns about their kids' safety. This backpack was designed with a sleeve or pocket the size of the backpack. PROMO explained that they intended to insert a plate of Kevlar® into that pocket – that's the stuff the police and military use for their bulletproof vests. Client thought they needed "some extra protection" in the sales documentation in case of any "problems." I shared their concerns, but my worries went beyond getting indemnifications and making disclaimers. I immediately imagined how a "failure" of this product could expose Client to a product-liability lawsuit of unknown proportion. "I want you to imagine," I said to Client, "the publicity your company would suffer

just from being connected with the product if there were another shooting and this product failed to provide the protection promised." Her look
showed she was taking this concern seriously.

"There's more," I told Client. "Once you get into products for children,
you'll face the CPSC, the federal Consumer Product Safety Commission.
They've shown big interest over the years with children's safety, lots of regulations on baby carriages, cribs, and who knows about knapsacks, especially
'bullet-proof' knapsacks. If you go forward with this order, I'll have to check
those regs…"

Client interrupted: "Just do the documentation. I'll call you back after
we've talked it over at the company."

I moved ahead to respond to Client's request for documentation – the
usual lawyer stuff for the Purchase Order and Acknowledgement paperwork
plus some other thoughts:

- A disclaimer of liability and a limitation of warranty.
- A generic **indemnification** agreement (i.e., not focused on this particular product) including attorneys' fees and court costs.
- A suggestion that Client confirm the financial capacity of PROMO
  to stand behind the indemnification.
- A review of Client's liability (including products) insurance policies
  as to date/term of the policies; the face amount; scope of coverage
  and exclusions.
- An inquiry to Client's liability insurance carrier about PROMO's
  proposed product; maybe even pricing a rider to cover this specific
  product (if necessary) at some "realistic" premium level which could
  possibly be charged off to PROMO.
- An inquiry of PROMO's liability insurance coverage as to date/
  term of the policies; face amount; scope of coverage and exclusions.
- Requiring PROMO to name Client as an "additional insured"
  on their liability insurance policy and produce a "Certificate of
  Insurance" as evidence that this had been done.

- Client should complete and ship *only* the backpack, manufactured exactly to PROMO's order, measurements, specifications, etc.; but Client should have nothing to do with the Kevlar® insert. Ship the canvas piece and leave it to PROMO to insert whatever they wished (or nothing). And be sure these facts are documented in the sales paperwork.
- Client's name should nowhere appear on the finished product on any label or otherwise. All source identification should be limited – if at all possible and if legal (which I did not know) – to "Designed and Distributed by PROMO." I reminded Client that it could well be subject to state laws wherever PROMO chose to sell the product.
- Client should consider adding another "layer of protection" or insulation against liability: A separate corporation for this (or any similar "risky" products). (More detailed planning would be required if they chose to take this step.)

Maybe there was more, I don't recall. But the horror of a scene of a product-failure in some school shooting was so burned into my mind that I had to call the Client.

"How important is this order to you? What's the amount of this order from PROMO?" I was surprised at how small this order from PROMO was, compared to the typical orders that Client processed. And so I stuck my nose further into their business telling them this:

"If I ran your company, I would not risk getting into a potentially horrendous exposure if this Kevlar® thing fails and some kid is injured or killed somewhere. I would not want my name and my company name publicly associated with any such horrific event. And I'm sure that the cost of avoiding liability will eat into what must already be a small profit from this sale. But hey, it's your company and you're running it – not me." (I thought that some good accountant's cost-benefit analysis would support my concerns that the bad publicity and product liability exposure made accepting this order uneconomic.)

I later heard that Client turned down the order, with an invitation to come back "and do business when it's got nothing to do with bulletproofing a backpack." Mission accomplished! As noted above, a (paranoid) lawyer's business advice is sometimes worth more than their legal advice, especially when the client is asked to manufacture a product that carried more risk – much more! – than it was worth.

Case Two: The "Little (Marine) Engine That Couldn't" : a $15 Million Claim!

Client Marine Engine Manufacturer (MEM) called in a panic. "I'm sending over some papers; looks like some lawsuit in Italy. Call me back!" Sure enough, MEM was being sued in an Italian court and we deciphered the documents; this was a product-liability claim for two faulty engines that failed to produce the required level of horsepower. Plaintiff, an Italian luxury yacht builder, claimed he'd lost an order and was suing MEM for $15 Million. "I just don't understand it," the Client, owner of MEM said. "Those engines worked perfectly." I asked to come out to his plant and told him to immediately send a notice of claim to their product-liability insurance company and we'd talk the next day.

By the time of our meeting the following morning, we'd already engaged an Italian lawyer in the city where the court was located. What we learned about the legal process over there made one thing clear: This was not going to be a walk in the park – we were facing an unfamiliar judicial system with procedures and complications unknown to American lawyers.

At MEM's plant the owner told me he was manufacturing another three engines of the same type as the ones he'd sold to the Italian yacht builder and they were testing fine. I asked for all the facts and I accompanied the Plant Manager and a designer to the shop where the engines were assembled and tested. Remember that word, "tested," because it turned out to be crucial to solving this problem. I was shown the three engines in various stages of assembly and completion. One of them was ready for a bench test, which happened in a separate building with exhaust ventilation, cooling water – a "real" environment.

The engine was fired up and began running, then revved up to full power. "We run them for enough time for us to take all the measurements we need. One of those is the power output – is the engine putting out our rated HP, horsepower? – which is what this customer yacht-builder is complaining about." He showed me the gauges which record all these operating data. I asked if they keep a written record of the bench test.

"Of course. Some of the data prints out automatically right on our testing machine." I asked, "Can you show me those printed bench test results on the two 'problem' engines that went to Italy?" He pulled them out of a notebook he was carrying and showed me that all tests – including meeting the horsepower rating – were satisfactory. "We sent him perfectly operating engines. He must have done something that screwed up the performance that cost him that lost horsepower," the designer said.

That sounded promising and when I asked what the customer might have done I was told, "Very little. In fact he's not supposed to do *anything* to the engines we shipped him – when they leave here, they're ready to go!" This was puzzling and I asked to see what the guts of the engine looked like. We went back to the assembly area where an exposed engine was being worked on. Indeed, it was hard to see what a customer could tamper with; everything was neatly covered and shielded.

"This is big money," I said to MEM's owner. "I think you'd better send your best engineer over there for a look at the 'problem' engines. Maybe he can find something we can use to defend this lawsuit." The owner said he already had his man packing a bag and he would be leaving for Italy that evening. And, indeed, he did find something.

The engineer found that on both engines, a sealed unit that MEM bought from a major Japanese engine manufacturer had been opened and the innards tampered with. Some buyers have been known to try to soup up their engines to increase the rated horsepower. That may have been the case here. Not only was there a warning right on the sealed unit itself, but in the book put out by MEM, their, "Instructions for Installation," there in bold red letters was this warning:

NEVER OPEN ANY SEALED UNIT COMPONENT OF THE ENGINE OR ATTEMPT TO MODIFY OR IN ANY WAY TAMPER WITH IT. ANY EVIDENCE OF SUCH TAMPERING BY THE PURCHASER SHALL IMMEDIATELY VOID ANY AND ALL WARRANTIES ON THIS ENGINE.

"Can you get the Japanese manufacturer of that sealed unit to send someone to Italy and check into that piece?" I asked MEM's owner. After a series of telephone calls, "All set; he'll be in Italy by the end of the week."

Final result: We gave our Italian lawyer all these facts and, working with the Client's product-liability insurer, the case was settled on relatively favorable terms. That big exposure that Client was facing was shrunken down because of strong proof supported by written reports both from Client's bench tests and its supplier of the sealed component that the customer yacht builder had tampered with.

BLT #30: First, know something about the **product liability** exposure for the goods and services you sell. Understand that the United States, probably the most litigious country in the world, has the most active tort trial bar ready to take you and your product to court without much hesitation.[1] If you have an inkling of such exposure to a product-liability lawsuit risk from a product you're thinking about, notify your insurer and check with your lawyer or a product-liability law specialist. And if you're uncertain of the end use (remember the Kevlar® backpack?), ask about it. Shutting your eyes to some obvious risk may not get you off the hook if someone is injured or killed and your product is involved. Sometimes just the publicity of your innocent involvement/connection with some horrendous incident can cause severe harm to your business. And, as in my back-pack case, check whether the risk is worth it – is the dollar amount of business you're getting worth the risk you're incurring. And if you decide to take the risk, try to get as many protections in place as possible (some are noted in the back-pack case, above, especially your insurance coverages). But remember, sometimes the risk of damage to your reputation, if it happens, is often not as easily cured as a money-damages claim.

Also remember, your product may be as harmless as a knapsack, as in Case One, above in this Tale #27; or a marine engine or some "harmless" component of a medical product – almost *any* product has the potential to cause harm in one way or another; and that means exposure to a product-liability lawsuit.

I recommend a dose of paranoia when you smell product-liability exposure – that mental state is already manifested by the ladder manufacturers' warning label:

Always use and climb on the outer side of the ladder as it leans against the structure or house. Never climb on the underside.

And check out these and more at http://www.mlaw.org/wwl/photos.html:

Warning: Shin pads cannot protect any part of the body they do not cover.

Toilet sign: Warning! Recycled flush water unsafe for drinking.

On a Novelty Rock-Garden Set (called "Popcorn Rock"): Warning: "Eating Rocks May Lead to Broken Teeth!"

No, I'm not joking! Or how about this tag on an electric steam iron:

Never use on clothing while it is being worn.

A little dose of paranoia about product-liability exposure is surely justified in our litigious United States.

---

1 The Italian car maker, Ferrari was cautious before installing a certain piece of new equipment on Ferraris going into the U.S. Market. Their lawyers advised them against it. As reported in the June 2006 *Car and Driver* magazine at p.43: "Ferrari's legal department decided that the liability potential in the litigious U.S. market outweighed any benefit, and we [*Car and Driver* editors] find it hard to disagree."

TALE # 28

FOREIGN COMPANY ALREADY MAKES T-SHIRTS. WHY DO THEY WANT TO SELL YOURS?

Lawyer and Client Put Their Heads Together to Foil a Competitor's Scheme
The Case of the "Worrisome" Would-Be Customer

Client ("Sporty") manufactures sportswear with a focus on specialty printed and decorated T-shirts. Over the decades, Sporty had built up an excellent marketing structure – chain-store retailers and independents that sold his goods in malls and shopping centers in almost every state in the United States. Remember this factor, because it comes into play later in this Tale.

One day Sporty asked me to "check out" a Central American company that had sent in what appeared to be an inquiry asking Sporty for a quote on some specialty T-shirts. From the little I knew about Sporty's industry, I found this odd: A company in Central America, an area where so much T-shirt merchandise is manufactured, was asking about this very same kind of merchandise from the higher-cost USA manufacturer. The inquiry, more like a precursor to a formal purchase order, came with a letter signed by the President of "El Comprador" (my made-up name) and made mention of his interest in buying product in the United States. This made an odd inquiry even stranger: Why would a company that already manufactures a product in its own Central American country want to buy the same goods from a USA manufacturer? And then sell those goods in the U.S. when, obviously, it was already selling into the U.S.

market? My paranoid tendencies came to the fore. The Client, much more versed in "the business" was equally perplexed. I asked for some time to check some questions I had and promised to get back to Sporty with what I found out.

First I researched the President of El Comprador and the Central American country where his company was located; and also a bit about the city and province. The President's last name appeared throughout the governmental setup of both the city and the province where they were located. The Chief of Police, the Judge and various other officials – all apparently were relatives of the President. (I must add that the family name was not an Hispanic name, but an unusual European name – they must surely all be related.)

Further research revealed that this country has the highest per-capita murder rate in the world. And "the rule of law" was not – how shall I put it – as "strictly observed" as we like to see if we're intending to go into a country to do business. And with all those family members of El Comprador's President being the police, judicial and other officials, as I told Sporty, don't expect much legal recourse if you have "problems" with this prospective customer.

But the "why" question remained and at a meeting with Sporty's management, I left them to find an answer. "Why would a company that manufactures a product in its own Central American country want to buy the same goods from a U.S. manufacturer? And then sell those goods in the United States?" A few days later on a phone call with Sporty's CEO, he suddenly blurted out, "I have a thought. Call you right back." And when Sporty called back, he did, indeed have the answer to the "why" question.

The CEO had called the President of El Comprador to "chat about his possible order." He asked the President about his current sales in the USA and was told that his company was selling in other countries and was just now beginning to look into the USA market. And this telling statement: "Maybe you can help us with selling the goods you make for us." This meant that he had no relationships at present with any retail outlets in the USA. Any order to Sporty for T-shirts to be sold by El Comprador in the USA would, in effect open the USA market for El Comprador. That would make El Comprador a direct competitor for the goods that both Client and El Comprador manufactured. And the Client knew that El Comprador had much lower costs and could undercut Client in his own market. He almost shouted over the telephone: "He's trying to steal our marketing outlets! He doesn't need our American T-shirts any more than an Eskimo needs to buy ice. He's not buying goods – he stealing our marketing outlets!"

Client's concern was that once they got a toehold with U.S. retailers, El Comprador would start peddling its own, lower-cost merchandise to them – El Comprador could become a lower-cost competitor to Sporty – something Client did not want to see happen, much less help it to happen.

This major concern, together with my comments on "the rule of law" in El Comprador's home country and the family's pervasive presence in city and provincial governments resulted in the Client's response to the purchase order: "No, thank you."

Sometimes a simple and routine business event is neither simple, nor routine; and a little paranoia doesn't hurt. Sometimes they really *are* after you. So here's another example of a business client working closely with their lawyer to uncover a potential problem before it became a serious problem. No, thank you, Mr. President of El Comprador.

TALE # 29

A Lawyer's Hunch: Avoid a Long-Term
Relationship With a "Difficult" Person.
Sometimes the Client Should Pay Attention to
the Lawyer's Hunch

A **term sheet** landed on my desk from a tech company, Client, which manufactures a complex electronic device. A crucial component of the device relies on a **single-source** piece of copyrighted software, which Client agreed to **license** from the developer/owner of the software, an Eastern European ("Igor") who lived in London. Client asked me to formalize their deal with the inventor – a simple task: A **License Agreement** per the term sheet – that's the assignment, with the usual request from Client: "Keep it short and simple." A pause, hesitation, and then, "Igor can be, well, difficult." How true.

I called Igor to get to his lawyer, but Igor told me gruffly that he doesn't need a lawyer. He knows the deal he made with the Client:

"I send you my form. Just put it down on paper, Mr. Lawyer, and not too long! You hear me?"

I had occasion to call Igor a few more times as I was drafting the License Agreement. Each time he left me with a distinctly unpleasant taste – clearly, this gruff guy was going to be a big pain in the butt. I called Client and told them about my concerns. First, as a lawyer, I don't like working with a party or principal who is not represented. I'd had unhappy past experiences dealing with a non-lawyer on legal matters – the deal always took longer; dealing with the businessperson directly puts a whole different "spin" on negotiating a document and I always try to avoid it. But I was stuck with Igor. Periodically Igor would make threats; he urged strict performance by Client or he'd sue – and this during contract negotiations!

I sent Client an email urging them to consider buying the software and not getting into a long-term relationship where they'd be dependent on Igor and his "difficult" personality. I repeated this at a meeting with Client that same week.

"We already tried to buy," Client said. "He wants $600,000; it's too much."

"If this guy is as difficult to deal with as he seems, and has no lawyer to explain things …" Client put up his hand to stop me: "We're not overpaying for this software – period! Just do the license agreement and let's be done with it." That closed the subject and, since Igor's was a **single-source component** for Client's product, I included a provision that Igor had to supply the component and support it for five years *after* termination of the license agreement for *any* reason. This single-source vulnerability gave me even more concern about going this route with Igor; and I said so to Client. They just repeated their position: "He wants too much money for us to buy his software." And so I finished the license agreement based, necessarily, on the form that Igor had sent me. It was signed and put away, but Client was not done with it, nor were they done with Igor.

The **non-exclusive** license agreement contained a standard "**boilerplate**" provision, a typical **anti-assignment provision** (which was to cause Client trouble later):

Neither party may transfer or assign the Agreement without the consent of the other; and such consent shall not be unreasonably withheld.

A few years into the term of this license agreement, Client entered into **merger** negotiations with a **publicly listed** software vendor, New-Tech – a so-called reverse takeover/merger. Client, a privately owned company, had its share-holders purchase control of New Tech, a publicly listed (on the NASDAQ Stock Exchange) company. Client then merged itself into New Tech, which was the surviving entity after the merger. Thus, Client became a public company without the time, money and effort required for an initial public offering (IPO). Client's shareholders received a substantial majority of the shares of New Tech, the public company, and took control of its Board of Directors. Such a transaction can often be accomplished within weeks as compared to the usually more lengthy IPO process.

The parties' business relations did not pose any problem: New Tech's software was used by Client on its other products, that is, the ones not using Igor's software. In other words, Igor and New-Tech were not direct competitors for Client's business; Client needed Igor's software for some of its products and New-Tech's technology for other of its products. Negotiations with New-Tech concluded with Client acquiring all the stock of New-Tech. Client made a slight change in its corporate name to reflect the merger with New-Tech; and after the merger, client became a publicly listed company.

Igor seized on this occasion. He called to say he considered this merger to constitute an assignment and asked that Client request his consent as required by the license agreement. Client refused, replying that the merger was not a transfer or assignment of its rights under the license agreement – it was merely the acquisition of another company. New-Tech owned the same type of software Client got from Igor; but they reminded Igor that New-Tech's software worked with Client's *other* products, not the ones served by Igor's software. The two were not in competition with each other, Client explained. This didn't change Igor's mind or his response.

It was clear to all of us that if Client asked for Igor's consent to its acquisition of New-Tech as Igor had requested, he would then refuse it and terminate or renegotiate the license agreement (and, of course, increase the license fees he was being paid). And so Client stood its ground and maintained its position: No assignment had taken place and, therefore, this acquisition was not an occasion to ask Igor for his consent.

When all this became clear to Igor, he simply sent a notice terminating the license agreement for breach of contract. Igor immediately stopped providing any product, service and support to Client's customers. And worse, he began contacting Client's customers, directly informing them of his termination of the license agreement and offering to serve them with product and support, but no longer through Client. It was instantly obvious that Client had no choice but to begin legal action against Igor to ensure its ability to provide continued support to its customers. Client brought suit against Igor in Massachusetts, but Igor won the **race to the courthouse** – he had already brought suit against Client for breach of contract in another jurisdiction, a mid-western state. He charged that Client had violated the license agreement by assigning it to a new company (i.e., the merger with New-Tech) without his consent.

I had to hire special litigation counsel to defend Client in the Midwest city Federal court where Igor had begun his breach-of-contract lawsuit. For a time both Client's lawsuit in Massachusetts and Igor's lawsuit in the Midwest proceeded, until it was agreed that Client's lawsuit would be suspended while they first defended against Igor's lawsuit.

Subpoenas began to fly back and forth and the **discovery** process got underway. A number of Client's executives had to take time off to sit with the mid-west trial defense lawyers preparing for depositions. Those trial lawyers, likewise, sent subpoenas to Igor's company executives. And this process began to grind on and on.

Something else was grinding away: the monthly legal bills for all this pre-trial activity. And they weren't for small amounts. In a few months Client's total fees were well into the six figures; and they continued to pile up. Then came the **motions** by Client and hearings before a judge. As a result, the judge in Igor's lawsuit dismissed that lawsuit. Client's lawsuit continued. Client saw the legal-fee numbers mounting and they well knew that Igor was in no financial position to pay back Client's legal fees, even if the court awarded them. After about six months of spending, the parties began to talk settlement; and that's how The Igor Affair ended.

Client bought the software and other "tools" it needed to service its customers without having to deal with Igor any further. For this Client paid Igor almost $300,000; but the mounting monthly legal fees stopped. By the time of settlement, the total cost to Client exceeded by far the price Igor was initially asking for his software back at the beginning of their relationship. And I'm guessing Igor didn't profit – or at least not by much – from his tactic of terminating the license agreement and forcing the matter into court. So, as is so often the case when litigation is involved, "The game is not worth the candle, as that old saying goes.[1]"

BLT #31: If litigation is on the horizon for any reason, for example, an "Igor-like" personality in the picture – then think ahead. Factor in the cost of litigation if the feared dispute arose. And do that early on – in this case, Igor's initial asking price of $600,000 for an outright sale of his software would, as things turned out, have been a bargain. In this case, if Client had considered the number of lawyers needed to work on this case, the time that would be devoted by them and the hourly billing rates for those lawyers, my guess is that simple arithmetic would have indicated the wisdom of pressing for an outright purchase of Igor's software as soon as he began "making noises" about breach of contract. Maybe negotiate down his asking price, but certainly avoid getting into an ongoing relationship with such a character in the first place, particularly when you're so dependent on this single-source for a key component of one of your own major products. And when litigation seems inevitable, push for *early* settlement, especially when what's looming ahead is a complex case in a distant city.

Another cost: A number of Client's major officers and executives had to be absent from their desks while being prepared for and then attending depositions and spending time producing documents. Another "invisible" cost, but a real one nonetheless.

I recognize that there are occasions where you must resist and fight out your case, in court if necessary. If, for example, a matter of principle or precedent-setting is at stake, then you may be forced to take the litigation route, with all its costs. This is sometimes the case when a departing employee fires off a false claim of harassment or discrimination. If you settle/pay off, this might set a bad precedent by encouraging other employees to file similar claims. But unless there's such a good reason for litigation, amicable settlement should always be seriously considered as early as feasible under the circumstances.

---

1 This old saw says that what we would get from this undertaking is not worth the effort we would have to put into it. The saying alludes to a game of cards in which the stakes are smaller than the cost of burning a candle for light by which to play.

PART V

A MIXED BAG OF TRICKS AND TALES – AND SOME IMPORTANT LESSONS

Here we have eight Tales that may be more "fun" than deeply serious, but useful nonetheless to businesspeople and lawyers and students of both business and law. I return to the opening theme: Look into the future. Then provide for any changes you foresee and do it in a way that clearly spells out your intentions and your expectations from the deal. The "KISS" principle – "Keep It Simple, Stupid" – has become a basic tenet of how to do business, make deals and paper or document those agreements. Then I take on other roles – Vocational Counselor and Detective. And finally we return to the subject of the meaning of words – here, where the same words can have different meanings. I hope you'll enjoy reading about these adventures in business-land as much as I enjoyed living them and writing about them.

TALE # 30

"KEEP IT SIMPLE, STUPID" = K-I-S-S.
THREE CASES ILLUSTRATING THE "K-I-S-S" PRINCIPLE

#1- Listerine®
#2- Superman®
#3- *The Hobbit*

Some Opening Thoughts...

The thing about "simple" contracts whenever possible (which is not always!) is that in many, if not most business deals, they best express the true intention of the parties (or at least *one* of the parties – see Case #3, below – *The Hobbit*.). A good, simple contract should leave little room for disputes about meaning or interpretation, although disputes (as you'll read) certainly do arise! We lawyers try to cover all possible contingencies, which makes most documents long – and not simple. But simplicity remains a worthy goal.

In many contract disputes the loser usually complains, "But that's not what I meant!" As noted back in Tale #1, unexpressed intentions almost always lose out to the clear (and often simple) words of the contract. Furthermore, long and complicated contracts risk repetition of a provision; and if you want to see the mischief *that* mistake can cause, read Tale #23 (Case One), where my winning argument was based on *my* interpretation of a provision that showed up *twice* in a lengthy Army procurement contract.

Keep It Simple, Stupid #1

Today's big brand of mouth-wash and related oral-care products is the Listerine® name. When he first formulated the product, Dr. J.J. Lawrence made a deal with a businessman, J.W. Lambert. The "final" agreement was made in 1885 and succinctly provided for a revised royalty to Dr. Lawrence. Here's their first (1881) royalty deal contract:

> Know all men by these presents, that for and in consideration of the fact, that Dr. J. J. Lawrence of the city of St Louis Mo has furnished me with the formula of a medicine called Listerine to be manufactured by me, that I Jordan W. Lambert, also of the city of St Louis Mo, hereby agree for myself, my heirs, executors and assigns to pay monthly to the said Dr. J. J. Lawrence his heirs, executors or assigns, the sum of twenty dollars [*later amended to six dollars*] for each and every gross of said Listerine hereafter sold by myself, my heirs, executors or assigns. In testimony whereof, I hereunto set my hand and seal, Done at St Louis Mo. this the 20th day of April, 1881 Jordan W Lambert (Seal)"

Simple. And by 1955, Listerine's maker had morphed into the Warner-Lambert Pharmaceutical Company, Inc. By the late fifties, they had already paid Dr. Lawrence and his heirs and charities over $22 million and were continuing to pay royalties at the rate of over $1.5 Million a year. (I guess this situation brings new meaning to the phrase, "Enough already!") And so Lambert, believing that they'd paid enough for the Listerine® formula tried again and again over the years to convince Dr. Lawrence's heirs and charities to allow them to stop making royalty payments. Those efforts consistently failed. Lambert hired smart lawyers, then smarter lawyers, who tried to "complicate" this simple deal the parties had made and to put an end to that deal. (From available records or lack thereof, we may assume that Lambert is still paying royalties today.)

Here's my dramatization of what might have happened, (but probably did not) – the epitome of "simple":

Mr. L: What do you want for the formula?
Dr. JJL: I'll take a nickel a bottle – you sell a bottle, you pay me a nickel.

Mr. L: Sounds fair. I'll have my lawyers draw up the papers.
Dr. JJL: Please, no lawyers necessary. It's a simple deal – sell a bottle, pay me a nickel.
Mr. L: Fine.

Then, in the late 50s, some new lawyers came up with some new "legal theories" and took the matter to court. First, they argued, the formula was no longer a secret, so Lambert should not have to pay. Second, "The Law" hates situations without a time limit; things "in perpetuity" get nixed all the time in court.[1] But alas, again the case failed; here are some of the Court's own words about this simple contract between Defendant Dr. Lawrence and Plaintiff Mr. Lambert:

> The plaintiff seems to feel that the 1881 and 1885 agreements are indefinite and unclear, at least as to the length of time during which they would continue in effect. I do not find them to be so. These agreements seem to me to be plain and unambiguous. . . .There is no ambiguity or uncertainty in this language. Nor can I ascertain any alternative or hidden meanings lurking within it. The obligation to pay on each and every gross of Listerine continues as long as this preparation is manufactured or sold by Lambert and his successors. It comes to an end when they cease to manufacture or sell the preparation. There is nothing which compels the plaintiff to continue such manufacture and sale. No doubt Lambert and his successors have been and still are free at any time, in good faith and in the exercise of sound business discretion, to stop manufacturing and selling Listerine. The plain meaning of the language used in these agreements is simply that Lambert's obligation to pay is co-extensive with manufacture or sale of Listerine by him and his successors.[2]

The Judge is saying just what the Agreement said as I've characterized it above: "You sell a bottle, you pay a nickel."

BLT #32-(a) : Notice that this legal protection of a trade secret has no time limitation unless it's built into the license deal. But if the deal is simply, "Sell a bottle, pay a nickel," – no mention of "secret" or any time limitation – that license deal continues indefinitely, even after the secret element of the trade secret (here, the Listerine formula) becomes public – ceases to remain secret. Creators and innovators and inventors should always weigh the benefits (and disadvantages) of trade-secret protection versus applying for a patent, design patent or whatever other government-granted legal protection for intellectual property is available to them.

KISS #2
Q: Who Owns the Superman Copyright?
A: That's Simple: The Assignee Who Bought It.

Let's now turn to the creators of Superman and their families' continuing struggle to get some more dollars for the then (at the time Superman was created) underestimation of the true future value of this character. As one judge described the struggle, "In this appeal, we address another chapter in the long-running saga regarding the ownership of copyrights in Superman—a story almost as old as the Man of Steel himself."[3]

The decades-long courtroom saga began in 1937 when the creators of Superman, Siegel and Shuster, signed on to produce comic strips for DC Comics. One of the cases describes the situation[4]:

> On December 4, 1937, Siegel and Shuster entered into an agreement with Detective Comics whereby they agreed to furnish some of these existing comic strips for the next two years, and further agreed "that all of these products and work done by [them] for [Detective Comics] during said period of employment shall be and become the sole and exclusive property of [Detective Comics,] and [that Detective Comics] shall be deemed the sole creator thereof...

Note how clear and simple these words are and, coming after the "boilerplate" copyright assignment language, which transferred all rights to the **assignee**; the assignee's (Detective Comics') rights were never in doubt.[5] The "KISS" point here is in the agreement quoted above and the later, 1938 assignment of rights. With the many cases that have come before any number of trial and appellate courts from 1947 to 2013 (and more to come?) – not one single judge has ever questioned that a complete transfer was intended by the parties and in fact took place when the creators of Superman "sold" that creation to Detective Comics. DC was not stupid; they kept it simple.

KISS #3
Back to Tale #2 : *The Hobbit* Gets Split Into Three

In Tale #2 you read about Miramax' licensing to Warner Bros. the movie rights to *The Hobbit*. The royalty: 5% of gross receipts from "the first motion picture." In Tale #2 my message was to look into the future, ask what could change, and then provide for it in your contract. But apparently Miramax couldn't easily predict that Warner would split *The Hobbit* into three installments and pay only on the first.

But here the focus is on clear and simple language, more particularly, Warner's agreement to pay royalties based on receipts from "the first motion picture." The dispute arose when Warner split *The Hobbit* into three installments and then paid only on the first. *The Hollywood Reporter* (November 14, 2014) story makes my point on straightforward, simple wording: Arbitrator Fried "ruled that **the first motion picture really means first** and that the Weinsteins [Miramax] are entitled to nothing." [my emphasis] KISS! You and I may think the arbitrator made a wrong decision and that Miramax was entitled to royalties based on all the installments of *The Hobbit*. Maybe so, but my focus in this Tale #30 is on using clear and simple language and, reading that report of the Arbitrator's decision [the decision itself is not a public document], makes the point you should take away from all these KISS cases. Clearly, the outcome of this case was not the royalty arrangement Miramax thought it had made – after all, "a *Hobbit* film is a *Hobbit* film, no matter how many installments you split it into," Miramax pleaded. But Warner replied succinctly, "After we made the first film, you got paid. The second film is *not* 'the first motion picture,' it's the second; and we did not agree to pay you on the second or the third, etc." And that's how the arbitrator ruled.

BLT #32(b) : I'm here recommending a style of contract drafting that I came to years ago, particularly where the parties' relationship and their deal has some "complications/complexities" and a degree of uncertain future circumstances. Use a "Preamble" or "Recitals" extensively – sometimes our more formal legal brethren begin those paragraphs with "Whereas…" A law partner once repeated the words of local counsel during a hotel deal in Tennessee: "When I expect a problem, I 'whereas' the paperwork to death." A preamble or recitals section is much like the factual/background summary you might present to a judge in court to help that judge understand the parties' relationship and their deal – the background and the respective rights and obligations each assumed when they signed their contract. Although such a Preamble/Recitals might not have avoided the Miramax problem – who could foresee that Warner would split the book into three installments? – it may well have given Miramax a stronger case. Without it, their case is destroyed by the simplicity of that fatal phrase, "the first motion picture."

Sometimes, the mere act of writing the Preamble or Recitals will bring to mind a possible scenario that hadn't occurred to you. Indeed, the Miramax-Warner contract (they called it the "Sharing Agreement" dated August 21, 1998), which was attached to the Miramax Complaint filed in the New York State court does not appear to begin with a Preamble or Recitals; it goes right into the deal terms. This device of the Preamble or Recitals allows you to tell the story in plain English and makes it easier for the reader (maybe a judge) to discern what the parties intend by these deals. I commend the technique in many contracting situations. And I believe a good Preamble might have helped Miramax win their case.

And remember: Keep It Simple, Stupid !

---

1 See, for example, Tale #21, involving the ancient Rule Against Perpetuities.

2 *Warner-Lambert Pharm. Co. v. John J. Reynolds, Inc.*, 178 F. Supp. 655 (S.D.N.Y., 1959)

3 *DC Comics v. Pac. Pictures Corp.,* 545 Fed. Appx. 678, 2013 U.S. App. LEXIS 23460, Copy. L. Rep. (CCH) P30,524, 2013 WL 6098416 (9th Cir. Cal. 2013).

4 Siegel v. Warner Bros. Entm't, Inc., 542 F. Supp. 2d 1098, 1106 (US DCt CD Cal. 2008).

5 There were other complications from later laws that Congress passed – extending the life of a copyright and the allowing such rights transfers before specified dates to be cancelled by the **assignor** – but we needn't go into these complications, which are unrelated to the "KISS" point I'm making here. Here's an edited/shortened sample copyright-assignment form to illustrate the simple clarity of such a sample assignment:

> ARTIST hereby irrevocably transfers and assigns to ASSIGNEE, its successors and assigns, in perpetuity, all right (whether now known or hereinafter invented), title, and interest, throughout the world, including any copyrights and renewals or extensions and the right to apply for and own all such renewals or extensions thereto, in THE ARTISTIC WORK, including, if available copyright registration number(s).

TALE # 31

STORE CHLORINE IN A RESIDENTIAL NEIGHBORHOOD – A CASE I'D NEVER TAKE ON TODAY!

I. The Client's Problem

C lient Gerry manufactured mothballs and other products to protect our sweaters and other woolens from the hungry little wool-eating critters. All products were essentially the same substance – paradichlorobenzene with a little perfume added to some of those products. Gerry's manufacturing process was essentially to chlorinate benzene; so you know right off the bat that he's dealing with "bad/nasty" and highly regulated stuff: Benzene is dangerous in the workplace and elsewhere and is highly regulated (think **OSHA, EPA, etc.).** And chlorine gas had been weaponized and used with deadly consequences in World War I (and maybe by Syria in 2014 and Iraq against Kurdish separatists). Not nice ingredients for any business.

Gerry had started in business many years before the 1960's, when I first met him. When he started out, his manufacturing plant was located in a desolate edge of an industrial suburban town near Boston. Over the years, however, the town had expanded and the plant now sat in the middle of a residential neighborhood. And so it was that Gerry's chemical plant came to the attention of the town fathers. More specifically, they were concerned (and rightly so!) about the three railroad tank cars of liquid chlorine stored on a rail spur/siding behind Gerry's plant – each tank car held about 30,000 gallons of liquid chlorine. The concerned Town officials proposed an order that Gerry remove the chlorine-filled tank cars and scheduled a meeting at the Town Hall on the issue. Gerry called me in a panic – this could be the end of his business, a business that was manufacturing and selling millions of dollars of moth balls, etc. around the country.

I went out to the plant. When Gerry told me the contents of the three railroad tank cars – liquid chlorine – I shuddered. 90,000 gallons of chlorine, scary and, well, creepy. "And what do I know about chlorine?" I asked myself. (Nothing.) "Wow, in gas form probably enough to wipe out five neighboring towns." I mentioned this concern to Gerry, thinking that the outcome of the hearing was a foregone conclusion – he'd lose and have to go out of business unless he found a location that would welcome the 90,000 gallons in their back yard.

Gerry insisted that I climb up a ladder on the side of a tank car and have a look at the liquid chlorine. These cars were apparently specially built multiple-lined railroad tank cars to hold the cold chlorine, compressed into a liquid with some of the stuff in gaseous form on top of the sloshing liquid below (if I'm remembering correctly). I looked at the stuff through a transparent lid under the steel cover of the tank car.

"It's not going anywhere and it won't hurt anyone," Gerry assured me. "And if by accident any of that liquid escapes," he said, pointing to a tall tank near the rail spur, "then the chemicals (caustic soda?) in that big tank are released and they react with the chlorine to form bleach, common household bleach." "Look," he said earnestly, "I wouldn't be exposing my brother and myself and my workers to any danger, but there is no danger. I've been making this stuff for years! Safely! You've got to do something at that Town Meeting." Gerry was trained and experienced: A brilliant MIT chemical engineering graduate who was called in as a consultant by some major U.S. companies. I believed in him, I trusted him and I could see how desperate he was. In the back of my mind were questions about any chlorine "incidents" in the past. What to do?

II. Toward a Solution

I needed an education, so I first talked at length with the people at The Chlorine Institute. I learned a lot from them and the printed materials they sent me. Government agencies had prescribed procedures in the event of a spill. I got safety statistics from them. And I learned about still more safety requirements imposed by the railroads for transporting liquid chlorine in those special tank cars. I learned that the only spills that had occurred were from crashes of speeding trains being derailed; not a single accident in the many decades this stuff had been used and chlorine was being stored at manufacturing plant railroad sidings all over the United States – not one accident! These data answered some of my doubts.

I asked Gerry to engage a well credentialed chlorine expert from The Institute to testify at the Town hearing on the safety matter. [Here, I was following one of my core concepts. "Synthesis," which shows up in some other Tales, like #2; #4; #12; and #15.] In many, maybe most cases, facts determine outcome. The lawyer must learn *all* the facts in order to prevail; and so I became a temporary and amateur chlorine guru. (Imagine that!) And so on the scheduled evening, Gerry, the chlorine expert and I headed into the hearing room at the Town Hall.

There they were, the Mayor, Chief of Police, Fire Commissioner, Director of Public Safety and other officials from the Town. I argued that there was no real safety problem, citing the decades-long history of no "incidents." I even brought in the fact that over 200 employees – mostly residents from this very Town – had been gainfully employed at the plant, some of them for many years. Several employees showed up at the hearing to support their boss. The chlorine safety expert testified on the safety issue from his long experience and emphasized the precautions Gerry had put in place. At the end of my presentation and the chlorine expert's testimony, the Town officials left to meet in private. After a while, one of the officials came back to the hearing room with a question for Gerry: "Can you do with fewer than three tank cars? How about just one?" Gerry whispered with his Plant Manager and responded:

"Yes, sir. We can keep a single tank car on site and just get more frequent deliveries. It may cost us a bit more, but that was not a real concern. So, yes, sir, one car is possible."

The meeting adjourned and the town officials took the matter "under advisement." Then came the "Permit" in the mail – it granted Gerry's company the right to continue to operate the plant, but limited the tank cars to a single one on his railroad siding at any one time. "Whew!"

Why would I not take on this case today?

Gerry continued in business for some years and then retired, leaving his younger brother, Shep, to run the business. The company was eventually sold and relocated by the buyer, but not before I heard about a problem from Shep (see Tale #32). But, you might ask, why would I not take on this case today? A couple of reasons:

1- Heightened public concern with matters environmental, and a lot more "activism." I think today this case would be a sure loser right from the outset. A lot of townspeople would show up at the hearing, maybe in the streets, banners, bull-horns and Internet. That would make it hard for Town officials to rule in Gerry's favor. But more to the point, my own personal beliefs (read personal ethical concerns) would constrain me. Today – more than 50 years later – my "inner voice" tells me that this kind of risk[1] should not be imposed on a community and others who might be affected. Sure, I still understand and, indeed, I had argued those safety statistics. But today, I would not accept the engagement; I would not want to live with the consequences of some unforeseen disaster (nor would I want to live near even a single tank car of liquid chlorine). This is one of those situations, discussed in the Prologue (Personal Ethics; Business Ethics; Legal Ethics: Don't Mix Them Up) where personal ethics come into play at the time of the engagement; and if the job conflicts with the lawyer's personal ethics, he'll turn down the job. Today I would turn down this job. Back then, I was ordered by my senior partner to handle this client's problem; I didn't think about it, and I had no choice.

2- Furthermore, I didn't *believe* in my client's cause, not enough to face up to the logical position of the opposition. And if I don't believe in the "rightness" of a client's position or at least believe that there's nothing harmful or illegitimate about the case I'm pleading, I would be doing a disservice to Gerry by taking on a case that would not get my complete focus and dedication. I'd probably urge Gerry to find an alternate location; maybe get some financial **SBA** or other assistance and move to a safer more industrial type of location. Or else get a new lawyer to handle the hearing. But this is now and that was then.

3- Finally, a matter of personal conscience. I know the safety record and all the arguments for how safe this chlorine-storage and handling are, but the "what if?" bugged me. I could not live with some unforeseen, unpredictable disaster killing and injuring people – and all because I had taken on and "won" some case. Sorry, Gerry – I would not accept this assignment today, some 50 years after the real event.

---

1 "This kind of risk" refers to a risk that's low and a price that's high. Here, the chance of something bad happening seemed remote, BUT if 30,000 gallons of liquid chlorine were, somehow released and the "bleach" protection didn't work, the casualties (to my untutored mind) could be horrendous. Not something I'd want on my conscience!

"I'll never forget that day as long as I live. I was in court, delivering my final arguments in a pesky little environmental case, and I actually felt my conscience leave my body!"

TALE # 32

WHEN THE REGULATORS RUN OUT OF THINGS TO REGULATE. A GOVERNMENT AGENCY MAKES THE RULES, BUT YOU CAN STILL WIN

There's no better way to start this Tale than to recall Supreme Court Justice Stephen Breyer's lecture at Harvard Law School in 1993, the annual Oliver Wendell Holmes Lecture. I was privileged to be present and later on to speak with Justice Breyer about what could be done about the "Problem" he described, in the words of his book:

> ...well-meaning, intelligent regulators, trying to carry out their regulatory tasks sensibly, can nonetheless bring about counterproductive results.[1]

Some of the problems he sees are mandated remedies that have outlived the ills they were supposed to cure. (Breyer cites the benzene regulations as an example of a very costly program to address what has become a very small risk.) Breyer proposes a new regime where regulation is ruled by people of science, not politics. And he writes that he does not believe that the people who now regulate risk are "out of control," or "wicked or foolish."[2] But in this Tale, the client was burned by those very scientists and you be the judge whether they were wicked or foolish. Indeed, in this Tale there was *no* problem until the scientist-regulators created one and then tried to force their solution on the client. So let's move on to Shep (from Tale #31), his tale of woe and how his problem was *SOLVED!* by my own Tale of Whoa!

I. Client's Problem

This Tale is more of a mini-horror show than a "Tale" that affected my mothball manufacturer client (check Wikipedia if you still don't know what mothballs are) – involved in Tale #31 about Gerry's company, the mothball maker, remember? – storing liquid chlorine on a rail siding at his plant. It began when Gerry's brother, Shep (who had taken over the company after Gerry retired), visited me and laid out on the table a few of its packages and, more to the point, an official notice from the United States Department of Agriculture (USDA). First, a little background:

The U.S. Department of Agriculture (USDA) was charged with enforcement of the Federal Insecticide, Fungicide, and Rodenticide Act when first enacted in 1947 (now under EPA jurisdiction). A registration system required anybody in the business (like this mothball manufacturer) to register – look and you'll find USDA registration numbers on pesticide packages. Later on, all states followed suit – more registrations and more numbers. The USDA notice to the client mothball manufacturer required that the package contain a new additional **Warning** "Irritating to the eyes."

We've heard that laughter is the best medicine, so beginning Monday we'll be regulating it.

Shep was clearly frustrated and sounded almost in tears: "There's no more room on this little box," he complained, pointing to "Keep out of the reach of children;" "Harmful if swallowed;" "Call physician or poison center immediately;" and probably a few more.

"You forgot the product label."

I couldn't understand how mothballs – which I remembered in use at home since I was a child – could harm the eyes. They are like small white rocks, just as hard, and they act by slowly evaporating a vapor that moths don't like. How they could possibly irritate eyes was puzzling, so I called USDA to inquire.

I was told that test reports had indicated this irritation and therefore they were imposing the label-warning requirement. I asked for and received from USDA a copy of their Test Report. That sheet of paper sent me through the roof. If there were ever a time when I was more exasperated, I don't remember it. The contents of that report had me boiling!

Your Tax Dollars at Work

USDA "scientists" (the test report form was signed by two Ph. Ds!) had ground up the mothballs (which are as hard as a rock) into a fine powder and sprinkled the resulting pulverized stuff in the eyes of six albino rabbits (Forgive us O' Lord for this outrage!), with six others standing by as "controls." After a time, the "scientists" noted that the affected rabbits' eyes seemed red and irritated, so they issued the new warning-label requirement. Can you understand how this made me nuts? I immediately got on the phone to the highest official I could find at USDA concerned with these labeling matters and identified their report and asked that he call me back when he had the report in front of him. Later that day the official returned the call.

When asked, he seemed to see nothing wrong and asked why I had called. I remember my words to this day:

> First of all, sir, know that I'm off the clock and calling you as a citizen and not as the lawyer of your registrant. I'm not earning any legal fees here. What you've done is taken a perfectly innocent and useful product, changed its form completely, creating your own USDA product – you ground up rock-hard mothballs into a fine powder – something that never happens. Consumers don't grind up mothballs. Then you find one of nature's most sensitive creatures, an albino rabbit, you go to the most sensitive part of this creature – its eyes – and you sprinkle this fine powder (a product which *your* people created, *not* the manufacturer) and then act surprised that the poor creature's eyes are irritated. So now the mothballs (*not* the product you used in your test!) have to be labeled "irritating to the eyes." Try sprinkling some other stuff into someone's eyes – maybe the eyes of the scientists, so-called, who engaged in this cruelty – how about talcum powder or maybe sugar or salt ground up – and see if you don't get the same irritation. Would you require the same warning on the talcum, sugar or salt packages? This is the most asinine and stupid piece of nonsense I've ever seen come out of a great and important agency, our U.S. Department of Agriculture which I know works hard to keep our food supplies safe. So as I told you, I'm proceeding as a citizen and not a lawyer on behalf of a client. You will be reading about these tests in [naming magazines

of the day, now almost all of them gone!] and the major newspapers in one week. One week! I hope I'll be hearing some sense from you before then, and the sooner the better!

The official asked me to send him something in writing, which I did by some fast mail or maybe even a telegram (look that up on Wikipedia if you don't know what a telegram is). Three days later came a letter of retraction -

"You may disregard Notice of Labeling Requirement No. XYZ".

Your (and my) tax dollars at work.

And so, gentle reader and fellow citizen, you *can* object to government regulations when they are mere nonsense, as was the case here. You have a more difficult problem when the agencies give you conflicting orders and you have to pick and choose!

"THE DEPT. OF AGRICULTURE SAYS YES, THE ENVIRONMENTAL PROTECTION AGENCY SAYS MAYBE, AND THE FOOD AND DRUG ADMINISTRATION SAYS NO."

Good Luck to US![3]

1 Stephen Breyer, *Breaking the Vicious Circle – Toward Effective Risk Regulation*, Harvard University Press (1993), at p. 11.

2 Ibid. at p. 11.

3 When the 10-year old son of an overseas-based banker tries to open a bank account and fails because of the Foreign Account Tax Compliance Act requirements, his father asks, "Should a fifth-grader be required to maintain personal tax records?" Op-Ed "A Boy's Allowance: Never Safe from the IRS," *The Wall Street Journal*, Oct. 18, 2016, p. A9.

TALE # 33

OFFICE BUILDING LANDLORD CONVINCES TENANTS
TO PAY A LANDLORD EXPENSE – HUH?

Adapting the Magicians' "Diversion Tactics" to Solve a Client's Problem

I. THE CLIENT'S PROBLEM

When you erect a building in a city's "redevelopment area," you're usually under the strict control of the Redevelopment Agency, which includes its Design-Review Panel (DRP). That was the case with Client Builder, who called and asked me to read through the things you couldn't do without approval from the Design Review Panel (DRP) – something like The No-No Ten Commandments times one thousand – all the things that "Thou Shalt Not . . ." Things like colors, shapes, structures, art, and on and on.

Client Builder (Landlord) and DRP were agreed on one major point: In order for the Building to look "good" from the exterior, Landlord had to exercise control over the office tenants' choice of curtains, at least the ones that could be seen from the street through the windows of the Building, which were numerous. The parties agreed on a neutral-color gauzy material which would let in light, but provide privacy for people in their offices. This would also provide the desired view of the exterior of the building – that clean, uniform look required by the DRP.

Landlord's Standard Form Lease, which I prepared in accordance with his instructions, gave Landlord total control over this curtain issue; it provided that the curtains remained property of the Landlord and forbade the tenants from hanging any other curtain or anything else visible from the street. The Building did, indeed, present a neat and uncluttered appearance, with all the windows having these identical, neutral-tone beige curtains.

As the second anniversary of the opening of the Building approached, it became clear that these lovely curtains had to be cleaned – people smoked in those days, and that cigarette smoke took its toll on the once pristine fabric. Client Building Owner called me about his problem: He was just informed of the cost of cleaning hundreds of pairs of curtains, *his* curtains!

"It's going to cost me over $25,000 (*in 1966 dollars* – in 2015, over $180,000) to clean those curtains. We never budgeted for that expense." Landlord clearly owned the curtains, but was totally unprepared for this huge unplanned-for bill for cleaning *his* curtains. I asked whether he ought to show the cost in his "Building Operating Expenses" and then bill the tenants under the **Operating Expense Escalation** provisions in the Lease. Landlord didn't like that idea – curtain cleaning was not factored into the Base Operating Costs. Also, a test calculation indicated that he would probably not recover anywhere near his entire cost going that route. He said, "Give it some thought. Come up with something if you can."

II. THE SOLUTION

"Have we got a deal for you!"

All I could think of was the magician's trick of diversion, distracting the audience while he did his "magic trick." And so distract I did; I sent Client Landlord a draft letter for him to send to all tenants in the building, something along the following lines:

Dear Tenant,

We hope you are as pleased being in this Building as we are to have you as our tenant; and that you are entirely satisfied with the level of services we provide, including nightly cleaning and our response to your repair and maintenance needs. As we approach the second anniversary of the opening of this Building, we want to assist you in maintaining the appearance of your offices, and, particularly, the periodic cleaning of the specially custom-fabricated curtains hanging in your windows.

Because of our purchasing power, we were able to obtain a very favorable price for this service. This will include, at a time convenient to you, the cleaning company's people removing the curtains, trucking them to their cleaning plant and then returning and rehanging the cleaned curtains in your offices. The per pair and total cost for your premises is shown below. And if you find it convenient, we can bill you in three monthly installments with no interest.

Please countersign the enclosed copy of this letter so we can book in the pickup dates as soon as possible. And always feel free to call me if you have any questions.

Sincerely,
Client Landlord

Agreed and Consented To:
Tenant_____   Date_____
          (name)   (title)
Hereunto Duly Authorized

The countersigned letters came in, all but one, and that one landed on my desk. The Real Estate VP of a major bank tenant (with whom I had negotiated their 3-floor space lease in this building) sent back the Landlord's letter with a large, bold red marker pen response: "BULLSHIT! They're your curtains – you clean them!– and say hello to your lawyer!" He'd apparently successfully guessed or skillfully deduced the authorship of Landlord's "curtain-cleaning letter."

II. THE END OF THE TALE

Landlord wanted to be able to honestly say that each tenant in his new building was paying curtain-cleaning costs, and so he made this arrangement with the Bank VP to achieve unanimity: Landlord and the Tenant Bank amended their Lease by reducing the rent by the amount of their curtain-cleaning cost; simultaneously, Tenant Bank countersigned Landlord's letter agreement and paid for their premises' curtain-cleaning costs. (Needless to say, the building's standard form lease was changed to reflect this curtain-cleaning arrangement.)

Thank you, stage magicians! Sometimes we need a diversionary tactic. Here, it was: "Have we got a bargain for you!"

TALE # 34

Hospital Tries, But Fails to Shift Responsibilities Onto Medical Device Supplier

Don't Let the Other Guy Dump His Responsibilities on *You*
(Especially When You're Not Equipped to Assume Them!)

Client, an overseas-based start-up surgical-device manufacturer ("SDM"), had invented and was selling its surgical-assistance equipment, a complex computer-driven electro-magnetic robotic machine – very large and very heavy. Installation of the machine often required additional floor bracing; and it had such large and powerful electro-magnets that the hospital's operating room where the machine would be used had to be totally "shielded". This process involved lining all walls, floor and ceiling with a material that prevented "leakage" of the powerful electro-magnetic energy generated when the machine was in operation (no pun intended). A few U.S. East-Coast and Mid-west hospitals had already bought the machine; and SDM was eager to open a west-coast market.

The required floor-load bearing capacity, shielding and other steps to prepare a hospital's operating room site for the machine were finely detailed in a set of plans and specifications for the hospital's use – a book the size of a small telephone directory. Each customer was required, prior to delivery and installation of the machine, to certify to SDM that it had prepared its operating room per those plans and specs. Only then would the machine be delivered, installed and tested before it was used on patients.

When the first inquiry came in from a potential west-coast buyer, ("Hospital ABC") a major hospital in California, SDM sent me the "Proposal" they'd received. They asked me to respond because the Proposal seemed to have some legal implications. They were right! The entire proposal appeared to have been written by Hospital ABC's lawyer. They indicated an interest in buying the machine, but Client SDM would be required to "do all things necessary to prepare ABC's operating room for installation of the machine including, but not limited to . . . etc., etc." In short, the Hospital expected SDM to do all the operating-room prep work described in SDM's Installation Manual.

Then there followed a broad **indemnification** provision: Client SDM would be responsible if anything – yes, *anything* ever went wrong in their operating room in any way related to Client SDM's machine. Client SDM was most anxious to open the west-coast market with this first sale to ABC, the leading hospital in the area. But Client SDM was concerned with the "lawyers' papers" they'd received from ABC Hospital. They were right to be concerned. The Hospital's lawyer was making a heroic attempt to shift *all* responsibility to Client SDM, and then make SDM the Hospital's "insurance company" with that **indemnification** provision. He was protecting his client's interests, as I was determined to protect my Client, SDM.

Although Client SDM, of course, remained responsible that the machine would operate properly once it was installed, they had always required that the purchasing hospital do the operating room preparation, floor-load capacity, wiring, shielding and the like. It was only logical that the hospital and its facilities manager, the ones most familiar with their building, the local contractors and conditions, and so forth were the best positioned to do the site preparation work.

George, the President of SDM was anxious to make this sale. He talked as though he were seriously considering accepting Hospital ABC's requirements. So anxious was he to open the west coast market that he appeared willing to have SDM assume full responsibility for the complex job of preparing ABC's operating room. And then there was that "total responsibility" shift over to SDM for *anything* that happened in that operating room under that broad **indemnification** provision.

I urged SDM to stand its ground. "First, cool down, George. This is their lawyer talking, not Hospital management. They know that their East-Coast and Mid-west counterparts have already bought and are successfully using your machine – you don't have to beg or go out on a 'liability limb' to make this sale. If a patient needs your machine and this West-Coast hospital doesn't have it, they could lose a major surgical procedure." I picked up then dropped the SDM Site Preparation Manual on the table; it landed with a loud thud: "This is *their* job not yours!" I told him, pointing to the Manual.

"Look, George, you are a surgical-device manufacturer, not a building contractor. You are totally unprepared to line up the people and supervise and inspect the work over 8,000 miles from your [overseas] headquarters; and 3,000 miles from your east-coast U.S. sales office. I don't want you to take on this prep work! And who's supposed to pay for it? Sounds like they may even expect you to foot the bill."

Hospital ABC was obviously trying to create a situation where, if *anything* ever went wrong, they could claim that whatever the cause (and, indeed, the exact problem might not even be known or knowable), no responsibility or liability could ever fall on Hospital ABC. The Hospital could almost never be liable because under their approach, ABC had absolutely nothing to do with any aspect of the installation of SDM's machine.

Furthermore – and this is important in many business situations – SDM would be creating a precedent. Once SDM took this route - clearly an exception to its standard operating procedure – word would get out in the industry and SDM would find itself in the contracting business in every major city in the U.S. where they sold their machine.

I kept at it with George: "Your initial business model at this early stage of marketing your machine is exactly the right one," I told the President. "Just look at your own Manual, this detailed book of plans and specifications in plain English that you provide to purchasers of the machines. Let the customers, the local hospitals that know their own buildings, deal with their local contractors or their own staff if they are big enough to have in-house capability. You cannot effectively manage, oversee, supervise and inspect this crucial site-prep function – a construction job! And you know better than I that site preparation is an important safety and operational component for your machine to operate successfully. Please", I implored him, "as they say, 'Shoemaker, stick to your last!' You manufacture a wonderful surgical device – don't try being a contractor in remote locations. One mistake and SDM's reputation for quality is gone – and that mistake does not even have to be yours."

I didn't even bother to mention the totally unacceptable broad indemnification provision in the Hospital's proposal. But I was not about to let the manufacturer Client become a de facto insurance company!

I explained to SDM's Sales VP (who had come into the room) and later to the CFO that hospital ABC's lawyer was obviously trying to shift all responsibility to Client SDM. I urged them that, as a matter of prudent business, SDM should be responsible *only* for its machine and its proper functioning – nothing more. Preparing the operating room site in cities across the United States (and each hospital building structure is different from the others) should be left up to each individual hospital customer. The original SDM business plan was sound and should not be changed, I urged.

After talking my little heart out to convince this guy who really wanted, needed to make this initial west-coast sale, Client SDM went along with me. And so I replied to hospital ABC that SDM's standard operating procedure had to be followed and it would not get into any hands-on involvement in operating room preparation. SDM had a construction consultant to answer specific questions relating to floor load-bearing requirements and all electrical and magnetic-wave shielding issues and the like. But each hospital customer was responsible for constructing the proposed site for the SDM machine to spec per the Manual; and the hospital customer had to provide that all-important signed certification that such prep work had been completed in accordance with SDM's Site Preparation Manual.

The sale went through and going forward, client SDM clearly understood that it must *never* get into the unfortunate position of allowing such a broad-scope of product and other liability exposure fall on them.

BLT #33: The lesson for you is similar to what Client SDM learned from my harangue: First, try to isolate the risks that you are willing to assume; ensure that you are capable of handling those risks; and take steps to avoid or minimize those risks – known and unknown! Avoid taking on responsibilities that you have no business getting involved in. Again: "Shoemaker, stick to your last."

Second, don't become, in effect, an "insurance company" which is responsible for *anything* that happens. Don't ever just skip over those boilerplate clauses labeled "Indemnity" or "Indemnification."[1] They've come back to haunt some unsuspecting signers of some "standard form," e.g. an oil company's gas station franchise agreement! And if you don't know what an indemnification provision looks like, check the footnote, below.

---

1 From the gas station franchise agreement: "**Indemnity**. Franchisees shall indemnify and hold Mobil harmless against all losses and claims (including those of the parties, their agents and employees) for death, personal injury, or property damage arising out of (1) the use or condition of Franchisee's premises or the equipment and facilities thereon, regardless of any defects therein, (2) Franchisee's nonperformance of this contract or (3) the storage and handling of products on the premises. Mobil does not warrant or guarantee any equipment or facilities." See *Hayes v Mobil Oil Corp.*, 930 F.2d 96 (CA1 1991), where the gas station operator was in for some unpleasant and expensive surprises that he had to remedy – cleanup of an unknown ground pollution situation not of his making.

TALE # 35

REFUSING CONSENT CAN BE "NOT REASONABLE," BUT ALSO "NOT UNREASONABLE." WHEN THE SAME WORDS CAN HAVE DIFFERENT MEANINGS.

I. The Fishing Buddies Invest in Vacant Land and a Tenant Appears

This Tale starts in 1950 when businessman Gerry and his fishing buddy, Samuel, decided together to buy some vacant land in their town, a suburb of a large city. They took ownership together, as **tenants in common**. They were trying to decide whether they'd run a farm or develop the land for residential or commercial uses when a broker for a restaurant chain approached them with an offer:

Restaurant Chain ("RC") would **net lease** the parcel of land for a long term and would pay Gerry and Samuel a fixed amount as "**triple-net rent**." This meant that RC would build and fit out its own buildings and pay all expenses including real estate taxes, all operating costs, insurance, etc. – in other words, nothing would be deducted from their monthly rent payments during the term of this long-term net lease. They all agreed on the rent and the fishing buddies, Gerry and Samuel, signed the Lease late in 1950.

The Lease had a 30-year basic/initial term; and then Tenant had four 15-year extension options – a term that could potentially run as long as 90 years. (These long terms are not unusual where the tenant is putting up its own buildings and all improvements at its own cost.) The Lease provided that rent would increase by 5% every 10 years. The net rent for the vacant, undeveloped land was, naturally, set at a fairly low number because Gerry and Samuel had nothing to do but sit back and collect rent checks.

Years went by and Samuel moved to the West Coast to live near his only son and his family. The years also brought inflation, which took its toll on the Lease's already low rent. Even with those 5% increases every decade, the annual rental was beginning to look disappointingly low. The Lease had become an incredible "bargain" for the restaurant-chain tenant, but for the owners, close to ridiculous in 2012 dollars.

II. Gerry and Samuel's Mistake, for You, a ...

BLT #34: The mistake Gerry and Samuel made was failing to provide for a more realistic rent increase (e.g., adjust [but only upward] to current market levels) over this potential 90-year period. Or they could have asked for more frequent increases or some adjustment derived from Consumer Price Index numbers – but they were apparently satisfied to get such a good return on their 1950 investment that they didn't think that far ahead or to ask for more. (In my experience, not an uncommon situation.)

III. The Years Fly By and . . .

Fast forward to the 21st Century. Over time, the two friends, who had lost touch with each other, died and the property was now owned by two groups: The Gerry Family on the East Coast and the Samuel Family out west, strangers to each other, but now co-Landlords of the net lease. The two groups owned the land just as Gerry and Samuel had, namely, as **tenants in common**. The restaurant originally built on the land had been renovated and enlarged from time to time, had changed hands a couple of times; but the owner was always another restaurant chain. Things were quiet until . . .

IV. The Entire Restaurant Chain – Including This Property – Is Sold to PEF

Enter Private Equity Fund ("PEF"), which bought the Tenant restaurant chain in 2012 (during the third of the four 15-year extension options). In order for PEF to take over legally as the new party Tenant under the Lease, PEF planned to have the current restaurant chain company **assign** the Lease to PEF, a step which required them to get Landlord's consent. The Lease provides, in the Assignment provision, that Landlord will not unreasonably withhold consent to an assignment by Tenant. At this point Gerry's son, Robert brought a copy of the Lease for me to review. "See what you can do about this 1950 rent number. We could be getting a rental double or more what they're paying for this property!"

Circumstances certainly do change over decades: What had been in the 50s a vacant, undeveloped parcel in the middle of nowhere, now had its own access/exit ramp off a major interstate highway; a new mass-transit station now sits across the street (the trip to the nearby big city takes just minutes); and commercial development had sprung up all around the restaurant. "Ridiculously low" is an apt description for the net rent for this property in 2012.

Robert showed me PEF's request for Landlord's consent to assignment. He also brought in some real estate title documents from the Registry of Deeds.

"We'd like some more rent," Robert said, "And we don't want to sign anything, not without some rent adjustment."

I explained, pointing to the Lease provision on consenting to an assignment by the Tenant:

"Your consent cannot be 'unreasonably withheld.' You've got to have some rational basis for refusing assignment that's 'not unreasonable.' And I just don't see it. PEF is a multi-billion dollar operation – certainly 'financially responsible.' And they already own a couple of major restaurant chains, which seem to be operating without a problem. What reason can you give PEF when you reply and tell them you're refusing to consent to the assignment?"

"You know what we want," Robert said impatiently. "More rent! Now that's not unreasonable."

I explained that once the rent and other terms are clearly stated in the Lease – as was the case here – it is usually considered unreasonable to withhold consent unless those agreements in the Lease are renegotiated. Renegotiating the Lease is not "reasonable." Robert grew impatient and said what I've heard from clients on other occasions: "Look, you're the lawyer. Figure it out. My family wants and some of us need more money from that property." I had my marching orders: I'm the lawyer and I'm now charged with finding a way to solve the low-rent problem. And this means Robert has got to have some rational and appropriate reason for refusing consent to the assignment to PEF, an action that may bring PEF, the would-be new party Tenant, to the bargaining table.

Summarizing Up to This Point: A Time-Line Chart of Events

1950… Samuel and Gerry sign the 30-year lease plus four 15-year extensions.
1980… The 30-year term ends; Tenant then exercises its first 15-year option to extend.
1995… First 15-year option period ends; Tenant exercises the second 15-year option.
2010… Second 15-year extension period ends and Tenant extends for another 15 years.
2012… Restaurant Chain is sold to PEF; they ask Landlord for consent to assign the Lease.

V. How Could Landlord Justify Refusing Consent to Assignment

I could come up with just one reason for Robert to refuse to consent to the Lease being assigned to PEF: PEF was not a restaurant operator. It was a multi-billion-dollar sophisticated investment vehicle that bought and sold businesses; and their sole purpose was to return profits to their investors. So I responded to the Tenant's request for consent to their assigning the Lease to PEF:

> Robert refuses to consent to the assignment because the proposed assignee is not an entity in the business of operating restaurants.

The Lease was originally signed with a dedicated restaurant operator, a genuine restauranteur. Previous assignments of Lease, with Landlord's consent, were always to other restaurant operators. PEF is not; it's an investment vehicle."

The expected reply came back from Tenant: PEF owns and operates two other chain restaurant businesses; so please sign and return the consent. "And, by the way," they told me, "the other party Landlord [Samuel's family on the West Coast] has already given their consent." I called Samuel's family representative on the West Coast and told them that Robert was refusing to consent and asked if they would be interested in joining him and sharing legal fees. Their response: "Not interested." I was told that they were all quite content to be getting their rent checks and didn't want to pay any legal fees. They had already given their consent and it stood.

So Robert, standing alone, would continue to refuse consent; I so notified the Tenant and PEF. We exchanged lots of emails and telephone calls with PEF's lawyer; neither party budged from their position. Apparently, as I learned from PEF's lawyer, most if not all Landlords of the other units in the restaurant chain that PEF had acquired weren't giving PEF any trouble and signing the consent and other forms. She also confirmed that the other owners (Samuel's family) had given their consent and "PEF was anxious to wrap up loose ends and move on." Robert was apparently the only remaining "loose end."

VI. Finally, a $ettlement Offer and Moving toward Closure

Finally there arrived the response I was waiting for – a settlement offer: "We'll increase the rent by 25% – first, last and final offer; no further negotiation, take it or leave it." I called Robert and he was quick to reply that this wasn't enough. "Look, the Lease rental is less than half of today's market rent rate. We can do better," he insisted. I reminded Robert that there was little, if any room for haggling when the offer is couched as PEF had – "take it or leave it." But Robert was adamant. The gap between PEF's offer and Robert's demand seemed unbridgeable. And again, the same old marching orders: "We have to get more rent. You're the lawyer. Figure it out!"

The only way to move toward Robert's target rent increase was to get away from the Lease and, more particularly, separate him from the other owner/Landlords, Samuel's family. After all, they had already given their consent; they were satisfied getting the present Lease rental rate; and they made it clear that they had no stomach for a fight with PEF and would not share in Robert's legal fees. That group of owners was not PEF's problem; Robert was. What to do? I had an idea, but I had to check with Robert first.

I asked him, "Robert, if I can get you a 50% increase in the rental you're now getting (which I thought was the most he could expect), would you accept that? Understand that we don't have an airtight case on your reason for refusing to consent to the assignment to PEF. If this thing ever went to court, . . ." Robert held his hand up, head down in thought, some slight hesitation, then, his short, reluctant reply: "Okay – fifty percent."

PEF's lawyer agreed to meet, but kept repeating her same-old/same-old: "Your client is not being reasonable…" I replied that this may be true, but that's not the standard. "He can't be unreasonable, *that's* the standard." I was prepared with chapter and verse:

> The law is that courts determine whether the withholding of con-
> sent to a transfer of a lease is reasonable by using objective criteria
> only. Subjective or arbitrary considerations are irrelevant, as are the
> mere whim and caprice of the lessor.[1]

"Robert is not being arbitrary or capricious – he's giving you a real reason and no court will rule that he is unreasonably withholding consent. He doesn't need to be reasonable or to have what you might consider to be a 'reasonable' ground for refusing to consent. All he needs is some rational basis for refusing consent; and his reason for refusing consent is 'not unreasonable.' Wanting a restaurant owner-operator to continue on as the party tenant operating a restaurant is not unreasonable."[2] It felt like I was making a legal argument in court before a judge.

I continued: "This property was originally leased to a restaurant and has always been run by a restaurant operator. Landlord believes that its best interests are served if their property continues to be operated by a restaurant operator and not a hedge fund or a private equity investment company which has its own agenda for its investors. And that," I insisted, "is not unreasonable. Maybe unwise; maybe foolish; maybe without a rational basis in fact; whatever – but it is not without reason. It is not unreasonable, and that's the standard for consent in the Lease. Why are we even talking about this? You've made us an offer – let's talk about that."

PEF's lawyer then reminded me that Samuel's family, Robert's fellow owners, had already consented and I replied: "Precisely! They are not your problem, Robert is. So let's take Samuel's family out of the picture and while we're at it, let's take the Lease out of the picture. We don't touch the Lease. We don't change or amend it or diddle with the rent. You want Robert's consent and are willing to pay to get it, so you pay Robert the amount you offered – remember, 'Take it or leave it!' – and we'll take it, all of it. You pay Robert an amount equal to 25% of the *total* rent due and you'll have your consent." I had prepared some numbers and spread them on the table for PEF's lawyer. [*Here's a simple example for my patient readers who have come this far:*]

Assume the total Lease annual rental was $192,000. Half went to Robert, namely $96,000. PEF had offered a 25% rent increase, which would amount to $48,000. And if this entire sum were paid to Robert, he would, in effect, be getting a 50% increase. This arrangement matched both (i) the amount PEF was willing to pay and (ii) the amount Robert was willing to settle for. These were the makings of a compromise, a settlement.

The Mechanics of My Solution

I proposed that PEF give Robert a non-interest promissory note in a face amount that represented the 25% increase in total rent to the end of the Lease term, assuming all extension options were exercised. The note was payable, starting out, at the rate of $4,000 per month or $48,000 per year – exactly the amount that PEF offered to settle the case; and the face amount of the note and the monthly payments would increase as the Lease rental increased (remember? 5% every 10 years). Furthermore, the note would run co-terminus with the Lease, so that if the Lease ended for any reason, the payments would stop and the note would be cancelled. PEF would be out of pocket the amount it offered in settlement, but that full amount would be coming to Robert. Payments would continue only as long as the Lease remained in force. And for this deal, PEF would get what it needed, Robert's consent to the assignment of Lease.

PEF's lawyer was slow to respond. "Well, I don't know about that . . .We've got those other owners, the Samuel Family, to worry about."

I interrupted: "There's nothing to worry about from them. You already have their consent. They're not your problem. Robert is. Your only problem – your one and only problem is getting Robert's consent. And you're settling your dispute with him by a payment of money to him – not unusual. It's as simple as that."

Again, the PEF lawyer hesitated: "Well, I don't know about that . . .I don't want them to sue us and maybe have to pay double." I asked to be excused and called Robert.

"What relationship do you have with any of the Samuel Family?" I asked him. "None," he immediately replied. "I don't even know those people, I've never seen them and no, I have no relationship. Why do you ask?"

"I'm proposing that PEF pay you the entire amount of the rent increase they're offering – a kind of side deal outside the framework of the Lease. Legally, I don't believe you owe the Samuel Family any **fiduciary** or any other legal duty in this situation – you're simply co-owners of the property, but otherwise strangers, right?"

"I told you, I don't even know who they are. They're certainly not family. I don't even know these people!"

"Robert," I said, "stay cool. PEF is concerned about being sued by the Samuel Family if they go through with my suggestion. So if you want this deal, you'll have to agree to indemnify them if they're sued by the Samuel Family. What do you say?"

Robert asked, "What if they learn about this side deal, what then?" I suggested that he and PEF would exchange some confidentiality and non-disclosure provisions – not at all unusual in any settlement. And, being "confidential," the terms of settlement were not to be disclosed to any other party by either you or PEF. (I was beginning to wonder how much more complicated this simple little settlement could get.) When Robert hesitated, I told him to think it over for a week or so and that I'd be back in touch with him then.

Robert called the next day and said he'd go along with the deal and if for some reason he had to end up sharing the money with the Samuel Family, he would. But he seemed satisfied that the confidentiality and non-disclosure would keep his settlement with PEF under wraps. I'm guessing he also got some comfort from my telling him that he probably (because there are few "sure things" in The Law) didn't owe his co-tenants-in-common any fiduciary or disclosure duty. The two families were geographically remote strangers who wouldn't recognize each other if they passed on the street. (If they had been negotiating together, jointly as the "Landlord team," I would have been a lot less certain about my no-fiduciary-duty conclusion.)

Furthermore, I intended to draft the settlement agreement so that PEF's performance of the confidentiality provisions would be a condition of Robert's agreeing to indemnify PEF if the Samuel Family sued them.[3] I assumed that PEF's right to be indemnified against a Samuel Family lawsuit would be weakened if it were a PEF person who violated the confidentiality/non-disclosure provision of the Settlement Agreement with Robert.

And so the papers were signed and the deal was done and Robert started getting his monthly checks with that 50% increase. A happy ending to a vexing situation!

BLT #35: Remember: If you get into one of those typical consent situations – "consent will not be unreasonably withheld" – you don't have to be "reasonable" within the usual dictionary definition of that word. That's not the standard. Your obligation is not to be unreasonable. And how the courts of various states interpret that simple phrase differs from court to court. Having a knowledgeable legal adviser is essential. And when you've got the definitional conundrum figured out (not reasonable while also being not unreasonable), call me – I've tried explain it in footnote 2, below.

And if you're the tenant and get into one of these long-term lease situations, you'll probably be happy with the kind of deal the Tenant, Restaurant Operator, made here – a mere 5% rent increase every ten years. But if you're the Landlord, your rule should be that (i) rent never goes down, only up; (ii) it goes up with market rates; and (iii) rent adjustments happen as frequently as you can get your Tenant to agree. Ten years can be painfully long in these dynamic times – five is better and three is grrreat.

---

1 Jacob L. Todres_ Carl M. Lerner, *Assignment and Subletting of Leased Premises: The Unreasonable Withholding of Consent,* 5 Fordham Urban Law Journal, Issue 2 (1976 Article 1).
2 Here I'm raising a conundrum, namely the same word having two opposing meanings: "I agree Robert is not being reasonable," meaning Robert's judgment is subject to criticism because PEF was, in fact, a seasoned chain restaurant operator and to reject them would be bad judgment and, in that sense, unreasonable. But soundness of judgment is *not* the standard for Landlord refusing to consent to Tenant's assignment to PEF; that standard is "not being unreasonable." The quoted definition in the text of this Tale, above, says it: Unreasonable as a piece of Lease terminology means having no rational basis and acting on whim or caprice. Since these same words – reasonable and unreasonable – have these two different meanings, I could well say, as I did to PEF's lawyer, "I agree Robert is not being reasonable; but his refusal to consent to assignment is not unreasonable. He meets the standard in the Lease for refusing to consent to the assignment." But the law varies from state to state. Some courts have interpreted the "not unreasonable" standard to require that the landlord be "reasonable." Just another reason for you to check your state's law.
3 An essential drafting tool for practicing law strategically is to effectively use the distinction between (i) a covenant (or promise) and (ii) a condition. To illustrate in this very case: I could have drafted the Settlement Agreement with PEF under (i) with two covenants or promises by PEF and it might read like this:

1- Each of the parties agrees to exercise and maintain strict confidentiality of this Agreement and all details of the dispute settlement between the parties [PEF and Robert].

2- Robert [the Gerry Family] agrees to indemnify and hold harmless PEF against and from any and all claims from the Samuel Family arising out of or related in any way to the matters covered in or related to this Agreement.

What I actually drafted read like this, utilizing a conditional indemnification instead of two independent promises:

Provided that PEF exercises and maintains strict confidentiality of this Agreement and all details of the dispute settlement between the parties [PEF and Landlords Robert/the Gerry Family], Robert agrees to indemnify and hold harmless PEF against and from any and all claims from the Samuel Family arising out of or related in any way to the matters covered in or related to this Agreement.

Let me translate and simplify this for the lay reader: If you, PEF, keep our deal secret, I, Robert, will indemnify you if the other owners sue. But if you breach confidentiality and the other owners learn of Robert's deal with PEF, I, Robert, owe you nothing. You can see the same approach in Tale #9. There, the Tenant's right to an early termination of its Lease carried a high dollar price. There, I did not want the Lease termination to occur and *then* have to go chasing after the Tenant for the termination fee. And so I drafted the early-termination provision making it exercisable by the payment of that money – in other words, the termination fee had to be paid in order for the termination to happen – it was a *condition* of termination happening, not merely a promise to pay the early-termination fee. If I can avoid it, I never rely on the mere promise to pay money after I have performed my obligations under the contract. Why? Because, as noted at the start of Tale #6, that promise to pay in that situation may mean that your claim may not be worth 100 cents on the dollar – you're subject to delays, refusal to pay, nuisance claims, and other bad faith actions by the party required to make the payment.

TALE # 36

LAWYER AS EMPLOYMENT COUNSELOR – ANOTHER PROBLEM SOLVED

I. The Problem: My Friend's Son-in-Law

Carl was a good accountant and a nice guy who had sent me some "interesting" clients. This tale is about his son-in-law. His newly married daughter was madly in love with Roger, he told me, and both sets of parents were delighted when their children became husband and wife. But the young man, Roger, having recently completed law school and passed the bar, was having no luck getting interviews, much less a job. Carl sent out a cry for "HELP!" to me, hoping we might take Roger into the firm. And so I met with Roger to see if I could help him, but really hoping to help my friend Carl out of this family problem.

I asked Roger to come in for a chat and bring his college and law school transcripts and any writing he may have done. It was not too long into the meeting when it became obvious that Roger would probably fare better as a model or actor – really a nice-looking young guy – but a middle-of-the-class graduate from, shall we say, not a top notch school. A little bit of conversation revealed that he'd taken this path because of pressure from his father: "You can't go wrong getting a law degree."

"And," Roger said, "Dad said I might even like and enjoy being a lawyer. And dad was willing to take care of tuition – no loans." (Now there's an incentive to choose a legal career!)

"Let me be frank, Roger," I said. "Boston is not the place for you. Too many lawyers from better schools with better records competing for the few jobs that are available. So don't waste your time in this town."

As we continued to talk and he responded to my questions, I learned that Roger enjoyed his law school experience; he liked knowing about "The Law" and was looking forward to becoming a practicing lawyer. What to do?

"Where will you be living?" I asked him; and he gave me the name of a suburb about fifteen miles from Boston. Both sets of parents were thinking of getting the newlyweds a "starter" house in the town as a wedding gift. I got an idea.

II. A Solution . . . Maybe

I went to my General Retail File (I had done a lot of retail chain-store leasing) and took out a map of Eastern Massachusetts and an old-fashioned school compass, the kind you use to draw circles: On one leg a pin that's fixed and on the other a pencil which would draw the circle. (I used this to illustrate the non-compete "radius restriction" that my client tenant-retailer would agree to – neither client tenant-retailer nor his store Landlord would establish a competing store within the set radius.)

"Roger, let's go to the library," and I led him to our firm's law library. Unoccupied (fine!) so we could talk without disturbing anyone. I spread the map on the large library table and located the town where the couple would be living.

"How far are you willing to drive to commute to work?" I asked Roger. He mulled it over and mused "A mile or two."

"Get serious, Roger. I'm trying to help you get started. Now give me a real number – maybe a 30-minute drive – would that work?" He nodded okay. Using my compass, I drew a pencil circle around the home town to be.

"So a job anywhere inside this circle would work for you, right?" He nodded yes. "Yeah."

I then showed him the Martindale-Hubbell legal directory volumes and we picked a town inside that circle on the map. "Now this is what I want you to do, and you can use this library, if you'd like." (I was thinking of Carl – I was really doing this for my friend, Roger's father-in-law.)

"We go to this nearby town in the legal directory, check the lawyers listed and look for a solo practitioner; and then find the oldest solo practitioner. You do the same for every town inside this circle. And then you prioritize them, but try to stick to the oldest. Maybe even one who graduated from your college or law school. Then the work begins." Roger was giving me a "Huh?" look.

"You call and make an appointment and work your way down the list. You tell your new boss that you're newly married and a new law school graduate and you'd like to go to work in your new boss' office. And here's the hard part, Roger, but you'll have to figure a way to make it work. You offer to work without pay until your new boss decides that you're ready to earn a paycheck."

Roger was clenching his teeth and looked worried. "Roger," I said, putting my hands on his shoulders and looking him square in the eye, "we're being realistic. This will give you any number of chances. If one doesn't work, just move on to the next name on the list. You'll make it!" He decided to start right then and there, so I left him with a yellow pad, the map and the lawyers' directory volumes. As I left I could see him begin listing the likely cities and towns inside that circle. A couple of hours later he returned the map to me on his way out.

"I'll work at the local library if I can," he said as we bid each other goodbye. I never heard from Roger again, that is not until eleven years later. Carl had long since moved to Florida for health reasons and we'd lost touch with each other. But now, eleven years later, our receptionist called me to the office lobby – someone wanted to say hello.

III. Success!

The face wasn't familiar and I certainly didn't recognize Roger until he identified himself – a little plumper than I remembered, but smiling when he cheerfully greeted me. He recalled our encounter eleven years earlier and told me that he had some business with one of our firm's lawyers. He looked prosperous enough and I naturally asked what had happened in the intervening years.

"Well, your plan worked. This solo practitioner took a liking to me and took me in. In fact it was only a couple of months before he started paying me a salary. In about four years he decided to retire and 'sold' me his practice for a dollar."

"So where are you today, Roger?" I eagerly asked him. He handed me his card – the firm was in his name "Roger X and Associates." He beamed: "Eleven lawyers and we specialize in personal injury, insurance claims and real estate closings. And," he took out his wallet to show me a photo of his family. "Two children!" My old friend Carl must have been a happy grandpa!

"So glad it worked out for you." He extended his arms and gave me a tight hug. "Thanks so much," he said in a quiet voice. It took eleven years and this chance meeting for this to happen, but what the hay – it all worked out for the best for my friend, the problem-solver turned vocational counselor. What a life!

TALE # 37

LAWYER AS DETECTIVE.
WAS I PERRY MASON, SHERLOCK HOLMES OR
INSPECTOR JACQUES CLOUSEAU?

T his caper began with a call from Jim, the department store owner, the Client in Tale #16 ("No Non-compete Ever Signed – But Departing Employee Can't Compete"). Jim had apparently asked for "the kid who took care of my Sonny problem," me, so I heard his new tale of woe.

Beside the great sporting goods department, Jim's store was known for its Oriental rug department. It was run by an old rug-merchant family ("Rug Merchants") and always had a stock of all sizes (some "palace size") of real Orientals from Persia, India and other great sources of these beautiful works of art. Theirs was a "leased department," meaning that they leased space within the store from Jim and operated their department in that space.

Jim's first words when I met him in his office were "Three Million Dollars!" That was a claim being made against his store for negligently causing a sprinkler system leak that flooded the rug department and ruined carpets worth $3 million. Apparently Rug Merchants had filed a claim with their insurance company, which was passing on its claim, against Jim's store for negligence. (The insurance company, when it expects to pay a loss becomes **subrogated** to its insured's rights.) The insurance company's letter claimed that Jim's employees' negligence was responsible for causing the break in the overhead sprinkler system and ruining this stock of valuable Orientals.

I asked Jim how they were claiming the store was negligent and he explained:

"The building has a wet sprinkler system, meaning the pipes hanging from the ceiling are filled with water under pressure at all times. The pipe gave way at a joint and the water just flowed out, flooding the [Oriental rug] department. The insurance company claims that one of our employees hit the pipe with one of those huge steel rollers on which rugs are stored and that this weakened the joint to the point where it gave way later that night. And they're saying there's evidence that the sprinkler system pipe was hit by metal – a steel rug roller they claim."

"What evidence?" I asked.

Jim said there was a mark on the sprinkler pipe showing where it was hit. I asked if he had the defective pipe and he said he did. He'd made sure to keep that pipe because he knew he might need it.

"I'd like to take that piece of pipe with me," I said, but Jim said it was too big to carry.

"It's wrapped up in my office. I'll have a truck drop it off." The pipe arrived that afternoon. I could see the screw joint that had popped and there was, indeed, a mark on the pipe. I called Jim to ask if I could meet briefly with the people on duty the day of the pipe burst and the next day I was back in the store with five of Jim's employees.

I explained that I wanted them to speak to me in confidence, one at a time, and that as the company lawyer, I would consider whatever they told me to be privileged and in any event, I promised to keep strictly confidential whatever they told me. I asked each one the same question:

"The rug insurance company is claiming that the sprinkler system pipe was hit by a steel rug roller and before I go off on some wild goose chase and waste a lot of time, I need to know – and this will stay with me as confidential information, not to be disclosed to anyone, even Jim – did any of you hit that pipe with a steel rug roller the day of the flooding?" Three of the employees said they hadn't even handled a rug roller that day; the other two were ready to swear on a stack of Bibles that they had not hit the sprinkler pipe.

"Hey," one of them said, "I've been doing rugs, rollers and all for fifteen years and I know how to handle them big babies. I never get near ceiling fixtures, lights, fans, sprinkler pipes, whatever. No sir! Never touched that pipe up there."

With those assurances I tried to figure out why that sprinkler pipe had given way and flooded the Oriental rug department. All I could think of was to have the pipe, now in my office, looked at by somebody who knows about pipes – a metallurgist! And so I called MIT, the Massachusetts Institute of Technology in nearby Cambridge, Massachusetts, and spoke to the Chairman of what is now the Department of Materials Science and Engineering. He gave me the name of their metallurgy specialist, who agreed to consult, but I had to bring the piece of pipe in question to his office. Jim arranged for a van and driver and at the appointed time the driver and I and the pipe arrived at MIT.

I explained our problem to the metallurgist and that we wanted to find out if the pipe had been hit and, if possible, what caused it to give way at the joint. After about a half hour, the metallurgist came back from his lab and said he had to do some more tests and needed some special microscope that wasn't available at the moment. "I'll probably have an answer for you in a couple of days," he said. So we went back empty-handed and waited. As promised, two days later he called.

I eagerly asked the metallurgist what he'd found out. "Good news for you," he said. "The sprinkler pipe was not hit by anything so close in time as to cause the joint to give way. And the reason the joint failed was that it was not properly installed." He explained:

"Of course, I'll send you a written report with copies of my test results, but that joint failed because it wasn't screwed tight enough. Normally, you need at least five threads of the screw to hold the water pressure in a wet sprinkler system. That's the plumbing code. This installation was tightened to less than three threads, and over time, it just gets looser and looser until the joint gave way and the water gushed out. This was just a bad installation."

"What about that mark on the pipe?" I asked him. "They say it was hit with a steel carpet roller and that's what caused the break."

"No way," he replied. "I checked the rust level at that mark on the pipe and a microscopic view showed that it's at least a year old – certainly not made within the last month," he said. "Nope, that break happened because of faulty installation – that pipe wasn't hit, at least not in the time frame of the pipe break." He promised me a full written report – it sounded like the problem was solved, maybe. Time to check the Lease that Jim's store had signed with his Landlord, owner of the store building.

There was a representation and warranty by Landlord that all building systems had been properly installed and required Tenant to keep them in good operating condition. We responded to the $3 million damage claim with the MIT Professor's report and that Lease provision. After a little bit of discussion – very little as I recall – that ended the problem for Jim. I heard that the rug insurer was making claim against the Landlord of the building. And he surely would pass that on to his liability insurer. So when I lost touch with the case, it ended as insurance company versus insurance company. But as far as client Jim was concerned, his problem was *SOLVED!* And really, it didn't take a Sherlock Holmes.

Part VI

A Bonus (Oligarch) Tale, Two Problems Unsolved – And a Bonus BLT

TALE # 38

THE GURU CLIENT AND A PROBLEM I COULDN'T
SOLVE. HE SOLVED IT HIMSELF, BUT CREATED
A NEW ONE.

I once represented a guru, a real-life guy who, how shall I say it? I mean, what can I say? I loved science fiction. I'd read about matters that transcend the material, enter the ethereal and get to the essence of existence – whatever. I'd read about the transformative experience of astronauts like Apollo 14's Edgar Mitchell who walked on the moon and looked back at the Earth, "hanging out there in space." In 1973 Mitchell founded the Institute of Noetic Science,[1] still going strong after 40+ years. But let me not get ahead of myself. The Guru story starts in maybe my second or third year of law practice, about 10 years before Astronaut Mitchell's trip to the moon.

The Guru Story – Chapter 1
The First Meeting
Client John (Tale #3) sent in this nice young man and his wife, let's call them Rick and Louise. They had moved from their farm community hometown – he from Texas and Kansas and she from Arkansas. They'd come East to pursue Rick's career as an engineer. Louise struck me as an intelligent, salt-of-the earth woman who helped support the couple by joining one of these so-called "multilevel marketing companies" selling household products. At our first meeting, after I assured her that I did not need any of the products she was selling, she put away her catalog and we got down to their problem.

They'd put money into some "investment company" or vehicle and were told that it was gone and would get nothing back – their life savings lost! I did some letter writing and made some phone calls and with this prodding got back most of their "investment." Given the circumstances, I took no legal fee – pro bono, as we say. But then, once again I had to say, "Thanks, but no thanks, Louise. I really don't need any of these products and you're very kind to offer them in lieu of a legal fee." That was the last time I'd heard from Rick and Louise until almost 20 years later.

The Guru Story – Chapter 2
The "Institute" and the First Donor

Rick called, he had changed his name and told me of his new name's historical origin and invited me to see a film that was showing at a local university. It featured him, now a Yoga Master, shirtless and wearing just some wrap around his middle. He went through a Yoga demonstration and I remember thinking the word "pretzel."

"An interesting new gig," I thought, "for a trained engineer who started out as an Arkansas farm boy, and now a Yoga Master." I met him and Louise after the showing; she was still pushing the products I really didn't need. I told Rick how impressed I was by his Yoga demonstration and what good physical shape he seemed to be in – at the time somewhere in his 40s. Then, my "So what's new" question brought news of the Institute he had formed and a major donor wishing to contribute.

"Could we meet at your office and finish the transaction?"

We did – I met with Rick (and this time, no Louise pushing "products") and a pleasant young man (Peter), the would-be donor. Some questions yielded the following information:

- Rick's Institute had been formed as a corporation, but did not yet have IRS "charitable" (Sec. 501(c)(3)) status. In fact, no application had been filed with the IRS.

- Peter had recently resigned as a student at a local major university (he was a senior) so that he could "study with Rick."
- Peter presented a personal check for $500,000 (yep, a half-million dollars!) made out to Guru's Institute. I passed the check to my secretary and asked her to call the New York bank on which it was drawn to verify the availability of funds.
- I asked Peter for some more "background" and he knew what I was driving at. "I'm the beneficiary of a substantial trust. I turned 21 . . ." "Happy Birthday," I blurted out" knowing what was coming. "And so I now have free access to the funds." He showed me an accounting report from the Trustee indicating a total trust fund in excess of $30 Million. Peter was named as sole beneficiary.
- Peter confirmed to me that he had already "sold a bond" to raise the money for his donation to the Institute. "See, there at the bottom of the list of assets, a UDC bond." "Helluva way to choose what to sell, just start at the bottom," I thought. But the bond had a value of something over $550,000, so maybe that was it – one asset sold and just enough money for this donation (and some "change" for "pocket money.")[2]
- I then asked each of them in turn to leave the room. I talked with the Guru first and then with Peter, without the other being present. Everything about Peter said "kosher" – but, you know, you get this feeling sometimes that a legitimate deal might be mischaracterized later on. The ingredients were there: A spellbinding personality espousing interesting and mysterious ideas and an immature and impressionable young lad with a lot of money at this disposal. My paranoia kicked in big time: I didn't want to become the tool of some scam. But this was only my own personal "sniff test," nothing more.
- When Guru left the room and I spoke with Peter, I asked him if he had a lawyer (if you recall, I don't like to take cases where the other side is unrepresented[3]). He did not, but his father's lawyer, their family lawyer would be available.
- Fine!

- My secretary returned and passed me a note about her call to Peter's bank: "The check is good. The bank person said:. . . , 'and there's a lot more where that came from.'"
- I asked Peter for permission to talk to his father's lawyer. He gave me a familiar name of a major mid-town law firm in New York City and their well-known litigator/partner lawyer. I called and reached him immediately – Wow – unexpected!
- After describing the situation, he confirmed what Peter had told me. I explained that there would be no charitable deduction and told him how much gift tax would be due – a six-figure number; the Guru's Institute was not yet a Sec. 501(c)(3) charitable organization. He asked to talk to Peter and then we spoke again. The lawyer said, "He doesn't care about the tax – he wants to make the gift now." I didn't need to explain to the lawyer that we might expedite the IRS process and get charitable status within weeks. No use. Peter wanted the Guru to have the money now and he'd pay the tax.

You can bet that after that meeting I made a detailed memo of every-thing that went on. If it ever turned out that there was something shady about this odd transaction, I didn't want to be accused of "aiding and abet-ting." But again, it all looked legitimate, and the contact with Peter's family lawyer gave me some comfort. But you should remember this memo for the finale of this Tale, coming in Chapter 3, below.

And so Peter delivered his $500K check to Guru Rick. Since you might wonder what a Guru and his Institute would do with the first half-million, here's the answer: First, buy a beautiful dark green Mercedes 450 SEL 6.9, *the* luxury-performance sedan of the day (early 1970s) with a price tag of almost $100,000. Second, the Guru bought two adjacent houses in the sub-urb that would be his Institute's headquarters. (Ah, for the "good old days" when you could get all those goodies for a mere $500,000!)

I recall sending a new associate out to the Guru at House #1 for the Purchase/Closing on House #2. The young man came back bug-eyed: "Your client was wearing a nightgown and beads – and sandals!" I explained that Rick was a Guru and a caftan (the nightgown) was standard guru gear.

It wasn't too long after that when Rick called to tell me about the next donors to his Institute: Two elderly "maiden-ladies," but they wanted to make a deductible charitable contribution and so we had to get going on the IRS Sec. 503(c)(3) application to become a charity[4].

I filled out the application form and sent it to the Guru to sign. He scratched out what I had put down for "Purposes" and inserted his own text. I couldn't understand a word! To a lay person – meaning one who did not understand the "mysteries of the universe" that the Guru was planning to explore – his text was pure gibberish; and I told him so.

"This will never pass muster with the IRS examiner! They won't under-stand what you're talking about," I almost shouted at him. "Let me try my hand at a rewrite and work in some of your stuff…" He interrupted me: "No way! Use my text!" There was no use in further discussion. "Rick," I said to him, shaking my finger in warning, "they'll bounce this. They won't understand it." Clearly it was no use – I had to walk into a battle that I knew I was going to lose.

And so up to the IRS I went, the appropriate division, for an "in-person filing" of the application for status as a charity. I watched the Examiner's face intently as he read through the form; and then he got to "Purposes." The crinkled brow, the puzzled look, the raised eyebrow and the look on his face all sent the message confirmed by his words:

"Ya gotta be kiddin', buddy." "Let me explain," I said, but his palm was in my face like a policeman stopping traffic: "Explain it here, buddy," he said, poking his index finger on the "Purposes" section of the application. "Come back when I can understand what you're all about," he said as he stood and handed back that flawed application.

I'd failed – this was a problem I was unable to solve. Client Guru wouldn't budge; IRS Examiner wouldn't budge; the latter was in control and I had an unhappy Client on my hands. I reported the result to the Guru and that may have been the last time I was in contact with him. Where he went and what he did I never knew. He completely disappeared from my radar screen and I went on with my more "normal" business-law practice. Sure, I knew what was coming up at the IRS – defeat was inevitable – but Guru had given me no choice and so, sadly, it was "Goodbye, Guru." But before we go on to Chapter 3, I want to introduce you to my late wife, Henny Bordwin, whose interaction with the Guru was, shall we say, interesting. Please indulge me.

Henny was a Dutch-born pianist, musicologist and music historian. In addition to her native language she had native-born fluency in German; and was pretty passable in French. She founded The American Schubert Institute (TASI) which successfully continued for 20+ years presenting recitals; symposia; a 3-day Summer Music Festival; and the ideas for two books written by NYU's Music Chair, Professor Martin Chusid. Henny was known for her open frankness, taking no prisoners when it came to some critical view she had. A favorite "Hennyism" quoted in the program of the Memorial Recital produced by her TASI performers:

Radio announcer: "Now, from a little-known composer, we'll hear a very rarely played piece."

Henny: " . . .and we'll hear why."

In my attempts at building client relationships, at one point I'd invited the Guru and wife Louise to a home-cooked dinner at the house, knowing and accepting the "risks" (which, of course, eventuated). I told Henny of our illustrious guest, he'd claimed that he had several Ph.D's and that he spoke numerous languages and, of course, that he was a guru. We were standing in our living room (a/k/a The Music Room) before dinner and the Guru went over to the harpsichord we had at the time. Maybe Henny even played a little Bach on it for us. He got a faraway look in his eyes as his hand slid smoothly over the top of the harpsichord case. He said something like "Oh, the sounds of the baroque past, those ancient tones that vibrate from this priceless, elegant instrument . . ." And he went on like that for a while, Henny giving me a funny look and me just smiling back. Then the "risk" eventuated when Henny said, "Rick: That's a veneer on plywood, a German instrument built last year. It cost $4,500." She took no prisoners.

When the subject of languages came up, once again my learned Henny spoke: "I'm sure you'd like to see this old family Bible we have," she said, striking a chord in the Guru I didn't even realize at the time: He was a lover of old books and this leather-bound brass-closured giant in the Dutch language and Old English style font from the early 1600s seemed to fascinate him. Henny opened this rare Bible, near the end of the Book of Genesis, I believe, and asked the Guru if he could tell what story in the Bible this was. Silence. Long silence.

"I'm hungry; let's get dinner," I said starting toward the dining room. Henny followed and when she faced me, gave a wry smile and a wink – no words, just a wink and a smile. Dinner was okay, but I knew I wouldn't be seeing Guru for a long time – and so it was.

One other incident related to the Guru and as weird as you might expect. It was a tradition in our family to invite people to our Thanksgiving dinner – usually foreign students far from home who were left alone on campus. I thought of ex-student Peter who'd said his folks were in Palm Beach, but he wasn't going to be with them, and so I invited him to our Thanksgiving dinner. He accepted and I started to give him directions to the house.

"I don't have a car," said the kid with the $30+ Million trust fund; and so I told him I'd pick him up (in my '51 Chevy). He asked if he could bring another student friend. Fine. On Thanksgiving Day I picked up the two lads and I could see that Louise's (the Guru's wife, remember?) marketing efforts had hit home with the lads. Each was carrying a gallon jug of one of her "products." This was, apparently, in lieu of the more typical bunch of flowers or bottle of wine for their hosts. When we got to the house I brought them to the kitchen and introduced them to wife Henny. Chatting, we learned that Peter-2 (he had the same first name as donor Peter) was the son of a very famous musical comedy composer and surely another "rich kid." They presented Henny with their "gift," the two gallon jugs they'd brought along – obviously some of Louise's "products."

Henny graciously said "Thank you" and the puzzled look on her face led the lads to explain the wonders of this universal cleaning product – they were bubbling over with enthusiasm. Peter grabbed a sponge off the kitchen sink, he opened one of the jugs and the two young men got down on their hands and knees and began cleaning the floor with this "product." I kid you not! Two young millionaires down there cleaning the kitchen floor and extolling the virtues of this universal cleaner. (This incident brought a new meaning to the phrase, "brain-washed.")

"This cleans everything, your hands and face. It's a great shampoo." Now I can't vouch for this, but I remember the oddest of the odd: One of our "floor-cleaners" said, "It's so pure you can even drink it – harmless and non-toxic – see?" And with that, he sipped from the open jug and swallowed the stuff. Henny gave me the strangest look I'd ever seen in all our years. "Please, please," she pleaded. "The floor is clean, so please get up and go into the dining room." (Translation, "Get the hell out of my kitchen, you crazies!") The dinner was uneventful after this odd beginning – no more memories of Rick, Louise or Peter and his friend, Peter-2.

The Guru – Chapter 3
Payback Time

Decades passed and then, sometime in the 1980s, I received what sounded like a frantic telephone call from the Guru. In a shaky voice, a lot less confident than what I remembered from our prior contacts: "Do you know a good trial lawyer?" Well, sure, we had a few in the firm. "You need defense counsel?" I asked. "Well, I'm the defendant and . . ."

"It's Peter, isn't it?" I asked. When the Guru affirmed that it was, indeed, Peter, I started a verbal auction:

"So he gave you more than that first half-million?" "Yes."

"More than a couple of million?" "Yes." "Five?" "Yes." I was hearing this, but not believing it. "Ten?" "Yes." I kept going – "Fifteen Million?" "More." Silence – I was actually at a loss for words. The Guru spoke:

"Eighteen Million." I gave him the name of our top litigator, but he ended up going to a much larger Boston firm and I heard nothing until one day his lawyer from that larger firm asked that we meet. Anticipating what he'd want I had the Records Department call back the old file on that initial $500,000 donation that Peter made. All I had to do was to provide a copy for the lawyer of that memo I'd made the day Peter gave the Guru the $500,000 check, explaining my call to the donor's family lawyer. I had no further involvement in the matter.

A case of this magnitude in the Boston courts, state or federal, would surely have been picked up by at least the tabloid reporters. But nothing showed up – this case was probably a sealed proceeding – no publicity.[5] In other words, a deafening silence descended over that lawsuit of Peter versus the Guru to recover $18 million. Silence followed by Settlement – which I understand is how over 90% of cases end – "amicable agreement."

I next heard from the Guru when a package arrived in the mail. It contained what looked like a large and expensive cloth-bound coffee-table book. It was actually the catalogue of a noted auction gallery – the Guru had assembled an incredible collection of art, artifacts and first editions of well-known books from all over the world and some items dating back centuries. The Guru had turned collector extraordinaire! The sale seemed to be a joint effort of the Guru's Institute and his first investor's (Peter's) entity. And if the luck of the rich continued, the auction probably netted a lot more than $18 Million for those treasures that the Guru had acquired.

Thus ended the saga of my client, the Guru and his problem I couldn't solve.

---

1 Noetic is defined as "inner wisdom, direct knowing, or subjective understanding." Astronaut Edgar Mitchell wrote about his experiences in *The Way of the Explorer: An Apollo Astronaut's Journey Through the Material and Mystical Worlds*, Revised Edition. His Institute of Noetic Sciences conducts research on such topics such as <u>spontaneous remission</u>, <u>meditation</u>, <u>consciousness</u>, <u>alternative healing</u> practices, <u>consciousness-based healthcare</u>, <u>spirituality</u>, <u>human potential</u>, <u>psychic abilities</u>, <u>psychokinesis</u> and <u>survival of consciousness after bodily death</u>. The Institute maintains a free database, available on the Internet, with citations to more than 6,500 articles about whether physical and mental health benefits might be connected to meditation and yoga.

2 I later appreciated Peter's sense of timing, probably accidental, but demonstrating the luck of the rich: The issuer of that bond, UDC, a state financing agency, was rumored to declare bankruptcy shortly thereafter and its bonds, as they say, "went into the toilet." Peter had sold just in time!

3 See Prologue, above, Part 3. (i) Personal Ethics; (ii) Business Ethics; and (iii), Legal Ethics.

4 To achieve tax-free status, the Institute had to have one or more of the following purposes: charitable, religious, educational, scientific, literary, testing for public safety, fostering amateur sports competition, or preventing cruelty to children or animals. It seemed Rick's Institute could be slotted into one of these categories from the general description. But Rick's stubborn sticking to his own unclear "purposes" caused my defeat at the IRS.

5 For a primer on sealing a court proceeding you might take a look at one of the websites that describe the process e.g., http://www2.fjc.gov/sites/default/files/2012/Sealing_Guide.pdf

TALE # 39

THE ONE THAT GOT AWAY: AN UNSOLVED!
PROBLEM – FOR 30 YEARS – FROM THE 60S TO
THE 90S! (JAKE'S TALE ABOUT THE BEST AUTOMATED
PARKING SYSTEM EVER!)

THE RISKS OF A PREMATURE INVENTION

This book would not be complete without this Tale – a problem that was *not SOLVED!* – the 30-year saga of the best (in all respects) mechanical car-parking system there ever was or ever will be: A system so impressive that the inventor was able to support himself and his family and cover business expenses out of investments from some of the smartest, most successful and wealthiest individuals in the Greater Boston community. And he assembled a team from the top tier of construction, financing and parking industries to serve as his advisors. This effort continued for more than 30 years, without ever taking in one cent of revenue. Time and again, a prospective investor would see the plans or the model and almost immediately they'd write a check – the system was that impressive. And yet it never took off, never became the commercial success that we all expected. (What a subject for a business school case study!)

Apparently, resistance to "new stuff" is part of our human makeup. Any entrepreneur trying to market a new idea reading this Tale #39 would probably benefit from Steven Overly's analysis in the *Washington Post* entitled "Humans once opposed coffee and refrigeration. Here's why we often hate new stuff"[1] and Calestous Juma's *Innovation and Its Enemies* (Oxford University Press, 2016).

"This really is an innovative approach, but I'm afraid we can't consider it. It's never been done before."

There's a lesson in this Tale, so let's start off with a **BT** – a Business Tip, because the genius mechanical parking-system problem involved no legal issues or disputes; just a nascent business that should have taken off, but never did. Putting aside the elements of luck and chance – which played a part in this Tale – here's what I've seen from my own experience why some innovations didn't make it to market:

BT #1: "A Great Invention Alone Does Not Always a Great Business Make."

Anonymous

I've seen this happen not only with this automatic parking equipment which, I believe, can never be surpassed in the features of speed; safety; modularity; volumetric efficiency; mechanical simplicity; dependability; environmentally beneficial[2], minimal labor costs and almost any other criterion you can think of. I've seen it happen with other worthwhile innovations, for example, great software code and programming in the areas of mapping/search of almost any physical area, indoors or out; business intelligence systems; screen-saver technology and more. Some were better funded than others; the technology worked and worked well and, just like the parking system, they also never got off the ground. Why? A few reasons for some situations I've seen – I'm sure you've seen them (and more) too:

1. **Timing** – Sometimes the new thing arrives ahead of its time. (Timing, as they say, is everything.) Have you correctly identified your market? And is that market ready for what you have to offer, or is it too soon?

2. **Execution** – A general term for the way the company executives develop a strategy and carry out a business plan and how effectively (or ineffectively), how prudently (or imprudently) they deploy their capital.

3. **Strategic Marketing** – Failure to identify the most promising and most immediate particular market for what you have to offer – a "rifle shot," as they say, not a shotgun. Failure to devise powerful responses to objections and negatives and focus on that particular application of your product/service that can most quickly start a revenue stream flowing. And retain that flexibility you need to change your course of action to respond to your market, competition and other changing conditions.

But let's get on with the Tale: This is the story of Jake, his magic machine and a series of problems that kept that machine from the success it deserved. Since it spans so many years, I'll label the episodes as chapters. Let's start at the beginning, Chapter 1, sometime in the late 1950s.

Chapter 1 – The Birth of an Invention

Jake and his wife, sitting in the car, in a long line waiting to enter a parking garage in the theater district, and it was almost show-time. His wife said the words she'd oft repeat in later years, because they changed the course of their lives, indeed all the way to the very end. She said, "Jake, if you're such a great engineer, why don't you do something about this way we're parking cars, sitting here, waiting, being late, driving around inside looking for a space. There's got to be a better way."

Jake, a graduate of Israel's Technion (their "MIT"), had been a competitive athlete in his youth and he took this as a challenge, and so his inventing began. Jake was a highly trained all-round engineer who had worked at the Dead Sea Works in his native Israel. He had been in charge of the machinery that moved the chemicals extracted from the Sea to a plant where they were processed and bagged for use in factories, on farms and for export. That machinery was essentially a giant conveyor belt built with wheels and gears and chains. So that's what Jake knew, conveyors, wheels, gears and chains. And, as a well- rounded engineer, he knew about the science of materials (metals), load-bearing capacities, and the like. (Indeed, he was probably a lot more rounded than many of today's engineers who, in this age of hyper-specialization, as it's been said, know more and more about less and less.)[3]

In the United States where he'd come to further his engineering studies at Massachusetts Institute of Technology, his day job was similar to what he'd done in Israel, but for a super-market chain. He was in charge of their materials-handling equipment – the conveyor belts that moved cases of goods around the warehouse and on and off trucks at the loading docks. More wheels and gears and chains and conveyors – the basic components of his invention to come: An automated mechanical parking system.

As he developed and perfected his invention, Jake came to know a highly respected patent lawyer, we'll call him Bob, who was also teaching at MIT. Bob was obviously impressed by the invention and became Jake's patent lawyer – and stuck with the project for the entire 30-year effort. In the early sixties, it was time to incorporate and get a business going and Bob approached my senior partner, Howard. He thought the "new kid" (me) could handle these details and Jake became one of my early assignments. And so I studied Jake's design, read Bob's patent application materials and took over the corporate paperwork of the entity that already existed. Let's call that entity "Auto-Park" (pretty original, right?).

Chapter 2 – The Early Days and "The Team"

Jake's initial financing came from two scions of old real-estate families, which seemed appropriate since a mechanical parking system would go into some building or a free-standing parking structure. Jake felt that he needed more diverse expertise from various fields and so he began to assemble his team. I continued to stick with this decades-long project largely because of the caliber of the people on this team and their decades-long faith in and dedication to Jake's invention. Calling this group impressive would have been an understatement. Some of the team members, all with their company headquarters in New York City, had names you'd instantly recognize as leaders in their industries:

- Howard, Chairman of one of the world's largest construction companies.
- Chet, CEO/Chairman of one of America's largest commercial financing firms.
- Bob, CEO of the Small Business Investment Company (SBIC) arm of a major American bank.
- Lou, Founder of one of America's largest parking operators.

And a few others. Jake had built a scale model of his device, measuring about 5'x3'x3', enclosed in a plexiglass case so you could see what was happening in his "underground" installation. It was a four-level automatic parking garage with little model cars on their individual platforms. Okay, it's probably time for me to describe the machine, so here's a quotation from the patent:

> **Abstract:** A novel delivery method and vestibule system for underground and similar conveyors, particularly longitudinally traveling conveyors carrying successive automobile-storage platforms, involving under an open vestibule floor area, conveyor loop structures that carry the platform upwardly into the open floor area for car delivery or removal, with automatic gating and walkway insertion to permit safe parking or retrieval of the car by the owner without attendant assistance, other than car platform selection and platform delivery command.
>
> **Filed:** December 7, 1987   **Date of Patent:** April 11, 1989

Some background on Jake's engineering principles and guidelines: He repeatedly used a phrase I cannot define authoritatively, as it appears to come from the field of athletics (and Jake had been a track star in Israel) – the phrase is *maxum maxumorum* (as best I can remember and spell it). His was the "fail-safe" approach: Each component of his machine was chosen never to break down; to give warnings when it was about to go so it could be replaced *before* it broke down; and to last a *very* long time.

And so

- If he needed a 100 hp electric motor to move, say, 25 cars on one conveyor unit, Jake specified a 200 hp motor.
- His "chains" were made up of links, each of which was a pair of ½"-thick steel plates joined to the next adjoining link by steel rods at either end.
- These steel rods were made of the same steel used for helicopter rotor shafts, the strongest tensile steel then available.
- If there were a power failure or the electric motor failed, there was backup power and finally, a gear arrangement that enabled a single person to move the chain by manually turning a crank – one way or another, the cars parked on the platforms could always be moved to the delivery vestibule.
- In the event of a breakdown, the vestibule gates and walkways could be operated manually so the car could be brought from the underground storage space to the surface, enabling the driver to get into the car to drive it away.
- A vacant platform would stop at the parking vestibule and the driver would drive onto the platform and park. After the driver left the car on a platform, electric eyes would confirm that the doors were closed and flush with the car. If not, lights flashed and an alarm sounded – doors had to be shut and flush with the body of the car being parked before the platform moved to make way for the next platform.

- At various points in the system, sound detectors could pick up any sounds coming from the car, maybe an animal or a child, and the sound would signal an attendant. (The jokers among us talked about "the-mother-in-law-in-the-trunk" warning device.)
- Fire/smoke alarms and bottles of fire retardant were installed strategically in the garage in the event of a car fire. In that event, all parking/retrieval operations would suspend; fire retardant would be sprayed on the affected car; and the conveyor would immediately move the affected car to the delivery vestibule.
- A ventilation system, common in garages, exhausted gasoline and other fumes.
- Space efficiency: Since there were no driveways or walkways; car platforms were close together (and one level of cars was only seven feet high), Jake's design would double and sometimes triple the capacity of a standard underground urban parking garage.
- Jake's design was modular, easily adaptable to a wide variety of sites. I saw designs where the conveyor holding the car platforms moved vertically, usually above ground; and the design for one particular site combined both horizontal and vertical movement of the car platforms.
- And, per my suggestion, he was investigating a bonding-insurance package that would cover damages to equipment or parked vehicles or persons on site and almost any mishap that could occur. I thought marketing would be facilitated by reducing or eliminating unforeseen risks.

I still recall all these details because I'd give the presentations to prospective buyers. Why? Because English was not Jake's native language; he spoke too quickly with a heavy accent and slurred his words and I could see that the people around the table were not getting what he was saying. And so after a few occasions when those people's facial expressions made me interject, "What Jake is saying is …" I told him either Patent Lawyer Bob (if present) or I would have to do the talking from then on. He agreed.

Chapter 3 – Getting Someone Interested in Auto-Park

The business problem was to get a real operating parking machine up and running and used by consumers – but how and where. We were never able to get a commercial unit into actual operation (we came close only twice) despite many efforts in many directions. A few examples of where the model was demonstrated:

1- Two Elevator Companies : Otis and Westinghouse
2- The Waldorf Astoria Hotel and Penn-Central Railroad
3- General Motors
4- U.S. Department of Transportation
5- A major New York Real Estate Developer Family

A couple of obvious prospects for Auto-Park naturals were the elevator and escalator companies, Otis and Westinghouse – they also worked with wheels and gears and chains and in some cases, conveyor-like equipment. But we struck out with these companies – talks and meetings, but no results.

Next: The Waldorf Astoria Hotel and the New York Central Railroad

I was in New York for a meeting at the Waldorf Astoria Hotel, the top-of-the-line hostelry back in the mid-sixties and I'd been working on Auto-Park for a year or so. What got my attention was a crew of young men jumping into cars and driving away very quickly, north on Park Avenue. This was the Hotel's way of handling their customers' cars – ferry them to some lot "uptown." It became obvious that they needed Auto-Park.

A little investigation led us to a steel door, at street level, to the right of and not too far from the main entry to the Hotel. When we checked it out, we found the door (amazingly!) unlocked. Down a long flight of metal stairs we went into what can only be described as an urban cavern. The broadness and ceiling height of the space made it immediately obvious that this might well be a ready-made space for an Auto-Park facility. Ready-made! No excavation! And Jake noted the obviously thick reinforced concrete walls and floor, more than enough to hold the weight of a major size Auto-Park System fully loaded with automobiles.

Inquiring of the Hotel people, we learned that this used to be a repair space for rail cars. (My guess is that this urban cavern was accessible by a rail spur off the railroad tunnel running under Park Avenue. And so rail cars needing work were simply shuttled over to this repair space.) But railcar-repair had long since ceased and the area was being used by the Waldorf to store dishes, glassware and linens. (There are other versions of what this urban cavern was used for, e.g., private access to the Hotel and an escape route should it be needed for U.S. Presidents,[4] although a "blue maintenance rail car has been spotted and photographed in this cavern.)

A meeting and demonstration with some Hilton Hotel people, who were then managing the Hotel, resulted in some real interest. If you saw that circus of these young men ferrying cars uptown and then running back to the Hotel, you would appreciate what it would mean to be able to store a large number of cars from just two or three drop-off points directly in front of the main entry. "But," we were told by Hilton, "you'll have to make your peace with the railroad. It's their space and we're using it because they moved their repair facility away from here." And so we trudged off to talk to the railroad people.

The New York Central Railroad gave us the names of two officials who had jurisdiction over the rail tracks and tunnel under Park Avenue, including this wonderful urban cavern, and so Hilton arranged for us to meet with them. The Waldorf (which was probably paying some nominal rental for their storage area) indicated a willingness to pay "a fair and reasonable rent" to use the space for parking.

We met with two elderly railroad men, one from the New York Central and the other from the Pennsylvania Railroad. The two were then in advanced merger talks, which eventually ended with the Penn-Central we know today. Our Auto-Park people were eager, filled with anticipation – after all, what a showcase – America's leading hotel on this major thorough-fare in the world's largest city! But the two railroad men were a lot less enthusiastic, they were downright hesitant and worse; they did not want to recommend that the space be leased out for parking. We probed for reasons and it finally came out: They were close to retirement and would not take the slightest risk that might endanger their pensions and a smooth transition to retirement. Nothing we said could convince them and they felt none of the excitement that our team felt at the thought of getting this site. "No dice." It became clear that we were wasting our time with these guys. And after trying, we found there was no place to go, nowhere to appeal – the use of some space formerly a rail car repair facility was small potatoes, no big deal, and these two had the final say. We revisited the matter at a later date, but it became clear that this was a closed matter – no deal on that urban cavern. We said a sad farewell to the Waldorf Astoria.

Next: General Motors – Truck and Coach Division
We're talking busses here, folks and an interest in selling busses as mass transit vehicles. Jake learned of their interest in running busses into the city from parking facilities off a ring-road outside the city. No rails, no right of way dealings, no tunnels – just Jake's machine. And so off we trudged to Detroit – Patent Lawyer Bob and I flew and Jake, as usual, drove with the model in a rented van.

At the huge, impressive GM headquarters building once again we put on our dog-and-pony show. There seemed to be interest, but the issue appeared to be the cost of the parking equipment as matched against creating vast parking areas or even parking structures. We returned home and that deal never got off the ground.

Finally, a Slam-Dunk! (Hardly) – a Grant from the U.S. Department of Transportation
The U.S. Department of Transportation announced that the Urban Mass Transit Administration (UMTA) would make grants to fund experimental technologies to improve mass transit. The government wanted to get commuters' cars off the roads and get commuters onto mass-transit facilities. Jake's system interested the staff and we were invited to make a presentation

at the DOT in Washington. Again, Patent Attorney Bob and I flew down; Jake drove down in a van with the model of his machine. DOT people were impressed and offered to fund a demonstration project at a number of "problem or choke points" in various states. One of those problem points was in our local Boston area and we chose to pursue that one.

Paperwork was next, which meant (i) an application form completed and signed by the local transit authority and (ii) approval by the Governor of the State. The project we chose was at an existing, but underused mass transit station located in the district of then Congressman and Speaker of the House of Representatives, Thomas P. ("Tip") O'Neill. His office reviewed the matter and promised full support. (How could we fail, right? Support from this great and respected legislator and a powerful man in Congress was a guarantee of success, right? WRONG!)

The first piece of paperwork was completed without a problem, quickly signed off by the local mass transit agency. But the Governor's form came back – he would not sign it because his own transportation official ("T-O") refused approval. When I contacted T-O he explained that he did not want this grant to affect the federal funding the state was getting: "I don't want to lose any dollars we get from Washington because of this grant."

I explained to T-O that this was a separate and distinct UMTA program and would not affect the federal funding he got from DOT. To confirm, I contacted DOT and they sent me a letter and I sent a copy, signed by a U.S. DOT Assistant Secretary of Transportation, clearly stating that federal funding to the state would *not* be affected by this UMTA grant. T-O still refused to sign the application for the Title VI grant, so I made an appointment to meet with him in person.

"What's your reason for refusing free money to try out a system that will help clear up the bottleneck at this choke-point in our system and promote public transportation on the existing already installed mass-transit rail line? DOT made it clear that your funding would not be affected! What gives?" His answer was one of the most bizarre I've ever heard from any public official:

"I don't think it's right for people to become millionaires using federal tax dollars for their startup." I was stunned and may have asked a question about his personal views, a question that probably contained the words "capitalist" and "communist." But he was unmovable – he would not sign the application for Title VI funding.

Since I knew the Governor from law school days and everyone knew he was a major proponent of mass transit – I'd often see him on the trolley line I took into work – I called for a meeting with him.

The Governor heard me out, and with furrowed brow, he gave me his answer: "Look, Milton, I rely on these agency administrators to do their job and T-O is an expert in this field. I take their advice and if I don't, I have to ask them to resign. And I'm not going to ask T-O to resign over this. Sorry."

That was the end of the road – no federal funding for Jake's machine.

A Major New York Real Estate Developer Family

None of the developers we approached were interested – "Too much risk." Or "I don't want to be number one" or "the guinea pig." Always the big question, "What if it breaks down?" All our engineering data and assurances fell on deaf ears. And there was also that unspoken, but universal concern with any innovation – timing! Some inventions are just ahead of their time and being too soon is as deadly to a project as being too late. In Jake's case, the idea of robotics, even as simple as his machine, was not yet in the public mind. Would consumers accept leaving their car, sitting on a platform, and then watching it disappear underground? Also, parking fees were not high enough in those years to support the extra costs of installing the Auto-Park system; today that would not be a problem. And I came to believe that until they could see an actual facility in operation, used by parking consumers and without a hitch, the real estate developers – the risk takers (up to a point!) – were not ready to take a chance, that was not until we met with Sam in New York City.

Sam Believes in Auto-Park!

Sam was one of New York City's major owners of apartment buildings and other commercial properties and he was then building a major office building at an important location – a couple of blocks south of Central Park between Fifth and Sixth Avenues. Sam had his own in-house staff of engineers who had checked out Jake's system in detail and gave Sam the go-ahead to install it in his new building. Jake's preliminary design required a small semi-circular driveway that would bring the cars right to the front door of the building and there had to be a sufficient turning radius for a car to enter and leave that driveway off the street. That turning radius was not possible on Sam's real estate parcel, but ... Sam said he'd buy the small red-brick building next door which housed a pizza restaurant – and he was ready to pay (overpay?) a million dollars to the owner of the building and the restaurant (over $5.5 million in 2016 dollars).

The owner was an elderly man who had come from Italy and was successful enough to buy the building and run his restaurant for many years. He did not want to sell, as Sam reported to us, repeating that building owner's words:

"Mr. Sam, what I'm gonna do with a million dollars? Sit home and look at the old woman? Here I got my work, meet my friends, make a few dollars. Maybe leave the kids something. No, Mr. Sam, I'm not gonna sell the building." Money was apparently not the issue – the owner loved *this* building at *this* location – and nothing would move him.[5]

Without expanding the footprint of Sam's parcel of land, Jake's system could not be installed. And so this second *real* chance was lost – another problem neither Sam nor Jake nor any of the lawyers could solve.

Chapter 4 – I Try Auto-Park On My Own Client!

An ironic incident occurred when my largest real-estate client planned a large waterfront project that would include a major underground parking garage. I learned that excavating for this underground facility at the waterfront for this multi-level facility would add $20 million to the construction costs and so I approached that client. I suggested he look at Jake's system, which would eliminate many feet of underwater excavation – remember, a two-level Auto-Park facility needed only 14 feet in height.

This new waterfront project was the biggest and most ambitious of all the work this client had ever done or would do – and a kind of first. He was himself an MIT-trained engineer, but Jake's high-level engineering didn't convince him. I understood that you don't take unnecessary risks on such a major project – that was unspoken – but what he said was: "What if it breaks down?" I explained the engineering decisions and that assembly-line technology (which is what Auto-Park was) is designed never to break down. It's just too costly for the assembly line manufacturer of automobiles or other equipment! No disagreement, "But what if it *does* break down?" And so this chapter ended – no sale! And then . . .

That grand new waterfront project opens – Offices; Hotel; Apartments; Restaurants and Retail Stores; Maritime-docking facilities; and a huge underground parking garage. When construction was about done, the hotel had opened for business and our law firm was the first office tenant to move in. That first day I drove down to the lowest level, parked and carried my two heavy briefcases to the elevator where I saw the sign: "OUT OF ORDER." I didn't know whether to laugh or cry! (Luckily, a construction worker exiting the garage gave me a lift in his truck to the street level.) Irony of ironies – "What if it doesn't work?"

Chapter 5 – The Full-Scale Model

At one point a major investor, totally convinced of the Auto-Park concept, decided that we should actually build a demonstration model, full-size and with real cars. Jake and the investor set out to find the right company to make the steel components and finally settled on a firm in western Massachusetts which fabricated, delivered and erected the steel components for the model. The Auto-Park company bought 11 used passenger cars (some the largest of their day to demonstrate the system's capacity). The cars were placed on the platforms/pallets in the system. Jake worked long hours on procuring and installing the motor and a smaller auxiliary motor. A close relative of this major investor, a computer and electronics expert, programmed the computer which flashed on the electric instructions to the drivers entering and leaving and the safety and other checks. We gave a number of demonstrations to possible buyers, but no deal was ever made. In hindsight, I guess a better strategy may have been to build that model on a site where parking consumers would actually use it – what do *you* think?

If Cost is the Issue, then . . .

Since we'd heard this complaint time and again, Jake began shopping for a manufacturer outside the United States. Somehow, he landed in the Czech Republic, City of Pilsen, and shop he did. He submitted plans and we got prices. Quality was a question but the supplier seemed to have a good reputation. But without a site for a real operating facility parking customers' cars – which, in hindsight probably would have been the best strategy – that matter died on the vine. Problem *not SOLVED!*

Epilogue
Jake Dies : My Eulogy

Jake was taken from us after a short illness – I sat at his bedside with his wife that last day. You can understand how badly I felt for this genius of an engineer not living to see his dream come true. At his funeral, I told the tale of another such genius, a man named Elisha Graves Otis, inventor of the elevator safety brake, an essential element if there were ever to be high-rise buildings with passenger elevators. That man faced the same sort of question that Auto-Park faced time and again, but as relates to the elevators which make possible our cities' skyscrapers today: "What if the cable breaks?" It was an obvious concern if you're in an elevator high up in a building – indeed, "What if the cable breaks?"

Otis argued that good, stout and strong cables don't just break. But he failed to convince concerned people. And so this brave man concocted a demonstration for the 1854 New York World's Fair. At the New York Crystal Palace, Otis stood on a platform that was hoisted high up in a tower and as he started to descend, on his signal, an axman cut the single rope holding that platform. The platform fell just a few inches before coming to a halt. The brake ("safety") was installed in a store building in about 1857, but Otis never lived to see his brake used for a passenger elevator in a skyscraper. He died in 1861 and New York's Equitable Building (reputed to be the first skyscraper) wasn't built until nine years later, in 1870.

Was Elisha Otis a failure? Hardly! And I'll always consider Jake as a success and not a failure, because his invention will, indeed it must become a reality, sooner or later as long as we have automobiles that have to be parked in dense, urban areas. As he once said in a cab trying to go cross-town in New York City, "These streets are meant for moving vehicles, not to store cars." I knew from personal experience that you could often walk cross-town faster than moving in a car – cars parked on either side and a delivery truck here and there – all reducing the 4-lane street to a single lane because cars were being stored on the street.

I'm at a stage of life where, like Otis and Jake, I will not live to see Jake's solution to the urban parking problem . . . or will I? Or maybe cities will become "Uberized" and there won't be so many private cars on the roads.[6]

---

1 *Washington Post*, 7/21/16, by Steven Overly, available at https://www.washingtonpost.com/news/innovations/wp/2016/07/21/humans-once-opposed-coffee-and-refrigeration-heres-why-we-often-hate-new-stuff/. And see Peter F. Drucker's *Innovation and Entrepreneurship*, Harper & Row (1985) and Michael Gershman's *Getting it Right the Second Time* (Addison – Wesley, 1990) – both listed in Exhibit D, Partial Reading List. On a lighter note, check out Ira Gershwin's lyrics to brother George's song, *They All Laughed*, which catalog just a few of the people with ideas that were new in their time: Christopher Columbus (the world is round, not flat.); Wright Brothers' airplane; Marconi's wireless; Whitney's cotton gin; Fulton's steamboat; and Henry Ford's automobile – bringing us full circle to the question, where to park!

2 Jake had calculated the gas wasted (not to speak of emissions avoided) by cars cruising searching for a parking space; and then the driving done inside parking garages searching for a vacant space). I remember being startled at the magnitude of that waste.

3 Bernard Gordon's speech to North Shore Technology Council. Gordon also once said something that pertains to Jakes' efforts; I'll leave it to the reader to judge how these words relate to Jake's efforts: "An engineering leader is the kind of person who takes the brilliant idea or invention, determines its worth, and carries it forward."

4 This was reported by *NY Times* in 2013 and by DAILYMAIL.COM in 2015: "The secret railway under the Waldorf Astoria: Siding used by Roosevelt to hide his paralysis found beneath New York hotel . . ."

5 A Google search indicates that in 2016, in that very building that Sam couldn't buy back in the 70s, there's an Italian restaurant called *Mangia*.

6 See, e.g., "Uber CEO Explains His Company's Highly Ambitious Goal to End Car Ownership in the World," by Alyson Shontell, available at http://www.businessinsider.com/ ubers-plans-to-be-cheaper-than-owning-a-car-2015-2.

TALE # 40

THE OLIGARCH BUYS AN AIRPLANE AND THEN ... HE NEEDS MONEY FAST, SO THE OLIGARCH SELLS HIS AIRPLANE.

Maybe My Strangest, Oddest, Most Fun Case(s)

I confess that there may not be much to learn from this tail-end Tale – you be the judge. But it was such a memorable experience for me that I wanted to share it with the patient reader who gets this far, so here's the Tale of the Oligarch and his airplane – my first aero-legal case:

———

My Russian client, also a lawyer, called and asked if I could handle an aircraft acquisition for a client of his, an "Oligarch." These kinds of calls are always a challenge; and I love to get them! I checked into what it takes to buy an airplane, concluded I could handle it and called him back for details. Thus began one of the strangest cases ever, involving a cast of characters that might make a good movie – or maybe just a short. And as they say, "Only the names have been changed to protect the innocent" (of which there were, at least a few).

Part One : The Purchase
Cast of Characters

Aircraft Broker	Like any sales broker, he puts buyers and sellers together and locates a buyer's desired property; or finds a needed buyer.

Aircraft Seller	In this case, a dealer in airplanes, located in Colorado, where the plane was hangared.
Client Buyer Oligarch	A Russian who'd apparently made his money when the USSR broke up and privatized its state-owned industries – in this case, steel.
Offshore Registry Agent	A division of a major international insurance company, these folks sit in a tax-free or tax-haven jurisdiction and register private jets. Maybe they had other functions, but that's not pertinent to this Tale.
Escrow Holder	A nice young lady located at the U.S. aircraft registry city, Oklahoma City. She takes and holds the deposit money and the full purchase price and, when title documents are delivered, she pays the Seller the sales proceeds and the Broker his commission.
New Buyer (from O)	As you'll read, the cash-rich Oligarch seemed to run out of money a year or so after his purchase and was in desperate need of cash, and fast! And so Oligarch returned for us to handle the sale of his new aircraft. Read on to see who the buyer turns out to be.

My first contact was the Aircraft Broker who'd found the plane the Client Oligarch wanted to buy. Like a car, the plane gets registered or licensed, in this case with the Federal Aviation Administration, Registration Branch, which is headquartered in Oklahoma City. Both Seller and his aircraft were located in Colorado. The plane was a large Brazilian Embraer executive jet with very few flight miles – apparently new and factory fresh – and with transatlantic capability. My first step was to engage local counsel in Oklahoma City to oversee the deal (and me!).

The price was $24 million for this private jet and Oligarch wired me the $3 million deposit. I learned early on that the market for this plane was "hot" – this Embraer model was then in great demand and there weren't enough of them to meet that demand. (But that market, like all markets, changed, as you'll soon learn.)

Negotiating the purchase was not difficult – just a matter of timing and some important details. Once the purchase and sale agreement was signed and delivered between Oligarch and Seller, I wired the deposit to the Escrow Agent in Oklahoma City. She would hold it and disburse it at Closing when title to the plane would be transferred from Seller to Oligarch.

While we were doing title checks and paperwork, the Seller called me. This was after a Purchase-and-Sale Agreement had been signed and that substantial deposit paid into the Escrow Agent. Seller asked, "I need to know if this buyer is for real. I've got another cash buyer who wants this plane and he'll pay me a million more – $25 million." I tried to reassure the Seller that the Oligarch/Buyer was, indeed, real. I reminded him that we had a deal all signed with the $3 Million deposit sitting with the Escrow Agent. But this Oligarch was a new person to me and so I couldn't give any resounding assurance that, yes, he's for real. But the deal sure appeared to be real!

When I got off the phone with Seller, I contacted Oligarch and told him what the Seller had said. I urged him to wire me another $3 Million as additional deposit, and there was no hesitancy. Within less than an hour I got a call from our firm's Accounting Department that the money had come in. We rewired the money to the Escrow Agent as "Additional Deposit." Then I called the Seller back.

"Money talks, my friend," I said to him. "We've just put another $3 million into the Escrow Deposit Account. Are you satisfied that this Buyer is 'real' and we can move to a closing?" Seller was reassured and we kept working toward consummating the formal purchase and sale.

One important detail when buying a plane – now listen carefully! Where do you close the deal – where will the sale take place? If the sale takes place in a state with, say a 6.25% sales tax (like Massachusetts), that tax could come to $1.5 million. So we were advised that the sale would take place and Oligarch would take delivery in an East Coast state that did not impose any sales tax on sales of aircraft. That meant lining up an appropriately licensed pilot to fly the Embraer from Colorado to our tax-free sales-tax haven – done! That's where the plane would be delivered and the sale would take place. And, of course, there's the matter of insurance, which the Broker helped us obtain to cover the Buyer's interest in the plane under the parties' Agreement. Done!

Another "detail" was where Oligarch should register his new plane. And again, what's least expensive? Advisers settled us on a "tax haven:" An ancient Western-European "dependency," inhabited since about 6,500 B.C. (Did their founders sign a "Declaration of Dependence" – and what was the "Declaration" written on? Makes you kinda wonder, right?)

The next step: Hire a transatlantic-qualified pilot and crew to shuttle the plane from its East Coast tax-free location (where the sale closed) to the tax-free place of registry (where the plane would be officially registered). Done! All these tasks got Done! with the fine assistance of the knowledgeable Seller; the Broker and our local legal counsel in Oklahoma City. Of the cast of characters (and I assure you, some of them were really "characters"), only the Escrow Holder had nothing to do – just sit on the now $6 million deposit – until the purchase-and-sale transaction closed in the east coast U.S. tax-free state. The deal closed; the pilot and crew flew the plane to the West European tax-free dependency for registration and all's well that ends well – but wait! It didn't end here.

Part II : The Forced Sale and Oligarch Loses $9 Million

A couple of years later and another call from my Russian lawyer friend – the Oligarch has got to sell the plane! He needs money and fast. The big problem: The market for this Embraer has now turned around. Apparently world markets are down to such an extent that there isn't that mob of buyers waiting in line for this beautiful aircraft. Instead, now there's a glut of these large Embraers. Where to find a buyer? They've already contacted the broker and his response is "Slim pickin's, but I'll try." Everyone tried, in Russia; in the dependency where the plane was still sitting (never having been flown in all this time!) and in the United States – maybe in other places I was not aware of.

Bargaining for price would be a tough task. Oligarch knew that he'd be taking a loss because of market conditions; I don't know if he was prepared for the size of the loss. But the message was clear: He needed cash and he needed it now and we had to close a sale of the aircraft ASAP!

We went through a few false starts – contacts that broke down with no deal made. Then came what appeared to be a real buyer, a wealthy oil man from a West African country. He meant business, he wanted the plane and he negotiated hard until the parties came to agreement on the price. He would pay $15 million; Oligarch would be taking a loss of $9 million on a plane he'd never even flown in. It had been sitting in a hangar (I hoped!) for more than 20 months! The deal was still in negotiations when the Buyer wired in a $2 million deposit to the Escrow Agent. One open item remained: How fast could we close.

The Buyer said he needed about 30 days. Oligarch was getting desperate. "I need the money *now*! Get him to move up the closing date." And he repeated himself: "I need the money NOW!" My call to the Buyer was one of the more "interesting" ones to emerge from this case. I asked if he could close in a week, hoping for maybe ten days or two weeks.

"Impossible. I won't have the funds for a month." When I pressed him, he explained: "Look, my tanker is fourth in the queue and unloading takes time – I'll work as fast as I can." When I told him how urgent timing was to the Oligarch (now Seller), the West African oil man went quiet, then said, "Look, I can get to the front of the queue, but I'd have to kill someone." I stopped him: "Please, do not kill anyone. Do the best you can to close sooner and I'll convey your situation to the Seller (Oligarch)."

The Oligarch seemed indifferent to any killing, but I told him I wouldn't hear of it. Oligarch then told me he had a Filipino buyer with cash at about the same price level. I argued with him. "I think you're wasting time and could lose a real buyer – he's already got a big sum on deposit. Just hang on, please, and let's not start a new deal all over again – and maybe, or probably a deal that will never close."

As time passed with everyone watching the calendar, nearing the fixed closing date, I got word from the Buyer that he was ready to close, but he wanted the plane to get a new set of tires. That was a new one on me! I called him and said that this aircraft had taken off and landed only about three or four times – the tires, like everything else, were practically brand new. The plane had been hangared since Oligarch bought it, and on and on I went. Response: "Maybe you don't hear me. I want a set of new tires on that plane before we close – and I am about ready to close. End of story!"

I called my Russian lawyer-client to report. I didn't want to talk to the Oligarch about this – his mental health was already hanging by a thin string and under tension to get the cash he needed to pay his debts. The Russian lawyer was also frightened about talking to his client, the Oligarch, and said, "Look, I'll pay for the [expletive deleted] tires and bill my client later. Let's just close the sale. We moved a little closer to a closing date when suddenly and oddly, this urgent matter of "the tires" receded into the background …

Out of the blue, Escrow Agent called and told me that she had received the balance of the purchase price; that she'd disbursed the funds; and the Registry Agents at the Western European dependency had transferred the title. My office advised me they had received our legal fee wired in from the Escrow Agent and a fax of the disbursement schedule. I thought this was now a done deal, but . . .

The disbursement schedule, apparently "dictated" by the Registry Agents in Western Europe, had taken an additional $75,000 in fees, deducting that amount from the Broker's commission. I began to do a boil at this dishonest grab and called the head of the office – nice and polite

English-accent fellow who heard me out. His underling had moved this money from the Broker to themselves. The Chief Registry Agent got the picture and then said (as if this weren't obvious), "Are you saying our Mr. XXX is a thief?" I didn't want to say it; I wanted the Chief to say it.

I asked him: "Sir, how would you label – what would you call – a so-called gentleman who, on his own and without checking with anyone else involved in the matter, particularly the person whose money he is moving into his own pocket – what would *you*, call such a gentleman?" No response. Silence. "I'll look into it." I thanked him; told him this was very serious business and trusted he could quickly straighten out a matter which might otherwise leave a blot on his parent insurance company's good name. Needless to say, that little transfer of $75,000 was reversed the next day. And within a week, I received a bottle of some very expensive champagne from a grateful aircraft broker in Colorado, the guy who, after all, did most of the work to get this deal done.

I'd cast the movie of this Tale, with some embellishments, but I'm betting that you, dear reader, could go back to the beginning of this Tale, above, and name the movie personality who could play each part. And so, as we say in Russian, *do svidaniya* –Goodbye!

———

A Bonus BLT:
#36 -- What to Do? In Negotiations – When to Interrupt and Talk,
and When to Be Still
and
If the other side's lawyer has instructions the opposite of
your client's instructions to you, what then?
Let's first clarify what I'm dealing with here and what I'm not, starting with the latter: Typically when you ask your lawyer this question about disclosing some "sensitive information," "Can I keep my mouth shut or do I have to say something?" you're talking about a legal duty – the duty of disclosure. That is *not* the topic now. (The Duty to Disclose is one of the "Nuggets" in my next book, *Nuggets and Gems : 25 Legal Concepts Everyone in Business Should Understand*.) What I'm talking about here is this situation:

You're in a negotiation discussion – and this has happened to me and maybe to you: I'm in a hurry to get done and move on, so when the pace is slowed by the other lawyer hesitating – seemingly searching for a word or something – I'd jump in and "read his mind," or so I thought. I said what I thought he was searching for. That lawyer's response guaranteed that this would be the last time I'd open my mouth on such an occasion. He said:

"Oh, I hadn't thought of that, but it's a good idea. Let's put that into the agreement." And then he goes on and finds what he was searching for. So much for my great "mind-reading" talent.

So my advice is to be patient, wait out the hesitant other party, because chances are better than even that what you think he's searching for is *not* what's on his mind. Wait patiently, but not in all situations – read on:

When to Interrupt and Talk
This actually happened to me in a multi-floor office lease negotiation with a major accounting firm represented by an experienced real estate lawyer (I

was lawyer for the building owner, the Landlord). The Lease provided for Operating Expense Escalation ("OEE"), which meant this: If the operating expenses for the Building exceeded the Base Year (typically Year One of the Lease), then Tenant would pay its proportionate share of the increase – a common provision in commercial office-space leases.

A number of tenants had asked for some cap or control on how high their OEE bill could go, but Landlord had given me my marching orders: "I will not be a guarantor against inflation!" – that was the firm policy I had to follow.[1] If costs went up, each tenant was expected to pay its share of the increase. And now, with this major accounting firm, the same issue arose. We seemed to be at a stalemate because apparently we each had conflicting instructions from our respective clients: Tenant wanted a ceiling put on OEE and Landlord's firm policy was not to give it. Time for me to interrupt the flow of our chatter:

"I think I know what concerns you, Willie," I interjected. "You're worried that Landlord will pad the payroll with friends and relatives and then call on tenants to pay the tab as OEE." (I knew this Landlord Client would never do this!) But I was offering the Tenant's lawyer a positive response, a way out – something I *could* give and which he could take back to his client accounting firm. And so I explained what I would agree to put into his Lease, asking that it remain confidential between us, to which he agreed.

I then proceeded to draft something that reflected this payroll-padding antidote I'd suggested, something like this: If Building Operating Costs increased over those of the preceding year beyond some threshold of increase – say 10% – and the Building payroll costs increased *more* than this 10% threshold, then Tenant's OEE would be reduced down to the 10% figure. This was, in a way, a cap on OEE.

"Yes, that's fine," he said; and we moved on to complete the deal, sign the Lease and see this Tenant move into their new quarters. I can hardly remember the details of what I'd drafted – but I had satisfied the tenant's lawyer with my suggestion and was more interested in moving on to complete the Lease, which we did.

Conclusion: Where the two sides have diametrically opposed goals in a contract, offer something positive that's within the other side's area of concern, but not the large, blanket concession they're looking for (and which you cannot give). This will often satisfy the other side and you can move on to other issues. Then, a strange sequel:

Fast forward a few years into the Lease term and what was a "mystery" to me at the time (and still is) happened: There was some occasion that required Landlord's CPAs to audit the books and review all the Leases in the Building. They called me to explain this special 10% limitation provision I'd put into the Lease in response to tenant's lawyer's demand for some cap or lid on his operating escalation costs. I did the best I could. But then came the "mystery" when the CPA said, "But such a set of circumstances – such a situation – could never happen." And that's the mystery – I didn't understand his comment then and I don't understand it now. Maybe it was just so unlikely that we'd have a 10% inflation rate in a single year and even less likely that Landlord's expenses to operate the building would *exceed* that rate, that the accountants concluded that the conditions described just couldn't happen. (I wish I had that old Lease available, but it's gone.) Then the CPA asked that I confirm with the Tenant's lawyer the effect of the provision – which to me was pretty simple, as explained above.

I called Tenant's lawyer and reminded him of this OEE-limiting provision and asked (and he agreed) that he confirm to the CPA how the clause was intended to work. The next day Willie, the lawyer, sounded exasperated when he called me back: "You SOB," he said, almost shouting. "You gave me nothing!" Apparently he read the provision just as the CPA read it. I thought it operated in a totally straightforward way. I protested: "But Willie, I gave you all I could give and exactly what you asked for." He repeated his angry words, "You gave me nothing!" and we parted "friends." I'll go to my grave not understanding why both the Landlord's CPA and lawyer Willie believed that the situation in that clause "could never happen." But back to the moral of this BLT:

When to "Open Your Mouth" and Say Something

Sometimes when the other side is fumbling, searching, reaching for something they want from you, or even when they're quite clear (as Willie was when he asked for a cap/maximum on OEE), and you can't give what they want, it may be time to interrupt and offer something that you *can* give. And when this satisfies the other side's need to bring back a response to their concerns, that may end the discussion.

So remember in your upcoming negotiations, there are times to be still and say nothing; and then there are those other situations where you ought to interrupt and say something and "give in." Only some experience "in the trenches" can help you distinguish one situation from the other. Good Luck!

Oh, and One Final Word: Beware the Typo Where Numbers Are Involved –

It Can Get Expensive – and It's a Mistake That's So Easy to Avoid!

In 1989, Prudential Insurance Co. of America, a unit of Prudential Financial Inc., sued three major law firms for a clerical mistake in loan documents that reduced an expected $92,885,000 lien/mortgage security to $92,885, according to *The New York Times.*[2]. More recently, a proofreading failure in 2013 proved even more costly, as reported by *Bloomberg*: "A Lawyer's Error Could Cost $1.5 Billion."[3] In that case, two judges' opinions differed: One would have corrected the error as obviously unintended – a mere mistake. But that trial judge was overruled by the appeals court which ruled that all the parties had reviewed the document and approved it and the court would not change the wording.

So much money and so easy to prevent the problem, just follow this 2-step procedure:

1-Go back to the old style of using *both* words and numbers. The law generally will enforce the words if the two don't agree, e.g., the Uniform Commercial Code provides:

UCC – § 3-114. CONTRADICTORY TERMS OF INSTRUMENT.

If an <u>instrument</u> contains contradictory terms, typewritten terms prevail over printed terms, handwritten terms prevail over both, and words prevail over numbers.

2- Proofread! And do it using different people multiple times, particularly in these big-dollar deals.

And again, Good Luck!

---

1 Indeed, we once walked away from a lease negotiation with a major insurance company in western Massachusetts. They insisted on having a cap on escalation because of their own internal budgeting needs. Client Landlord would not give in – no cap on escalation, ever! – and so we left. On the drive back to Boston, we stopped so that the Landlord partner I was with could call the other partner in Boston to report that this lease negotiation had failed. (No cell phones back then.) The partner in Boston responded: "They've already called me. They'll sign the Lease without any cap on escalation." That policy stayed in effect during my entire 30-year history with this client Landlord.

2 Available at http://www.nytimes.com/1991/10/04/news/bar-three-missing-zeros-brought-red-faces-cost-millions-dollars.html

3 Available at https://www.bloomberg.com/news/articles/2015-01-23/a-lawyer-s-error-could-cost-1-5-billion-business-of-law.

HOW THIS CAREER STARTED – A SORT OF MEMOIR AND THEN THE EPILOGUE AND A LITTLE EGO TRIP DOWN MEMORY LANE

Genesis : The Beginning of a Long Career

The very first problem I solved as a lawyer happened in the summer of 1957. I was starting my job at Harvard Law School and the Dean asked if I wanted to take on a research job for a small Boston firm – I did! That was the first time I met with my partner-to-be, Howard Rubin. His client, a candy manufacturer, had signed a contract to sell a sugar-processing plant in Cuba. The land and building were the only assets of a separate, single-asset corporation and the signed deal was a contract for the sale of all the common stock of that corporation – a stock purchase-and-sale agreement.

Problem: Before the deal closed, the plant burned to the ground and there was either insufficient or no insurance. Quite naturally, the Buyer assumed the deal was off, but Client candy-maker, the Seller, was anxious to sell.[1] The law on the subject? That was what I was supposed to research (at $3.00 per hour!).

At the time, the Cuban dictator, Fulgencio Batista, was in power and right after that fire, the local Cuban government arrested and jailed Client candy-maker's plant manager, a nice guy from Boston, charging him with arson (incendiario). Client then received an itemized "bill" for his release – $15,000, showing how much went to the local sheriff, mayor, judge and the national government for this "crime." (That $15,000 in 2016 dollars is almost $129,000). Client paid the "ransom" and the manager came home to Boston. But back to the legal problem.

I set out to research the legal question: Is a sale of stock of a single-asset corporation voided when that single asset is physically destroyed? My conclusion: No, as supported by case-law in about every jurisdiction in the U.S. I bound up my very long memo and authorities and sent it off to Howard Rubin. He called to ask if I'd like to sit in on "settlement talks." I did. I was anxious to see how "real lawyers" worked and how Buyer would react to my opus, that long memo.

When we met at the firm's conference room and everyone settled down and each stated their position on this sale-of-stock deal, Rubin said to the Buyer's lawyer: "We've got you dead to rights – in this state and your state (New York) and every other state in the union." And with that he flung my long memo, in its black binder (which I still have today!) on the table – it landed flat with a big bang. I was introduced to Buyer's lawyer as the author and proud to hear "Harvard Law School Faculty" after my name. The lawyer eyed me, picked up the black binder and read page one, the cover note, captioned "Conclusions," which supported Rubin's statement. I waited for some look into the contents, but all the Buyer's lawyer did was to riffle through the pages as though checking to ensure that they weren't blank. He closed the black binder, "Okay, let's talk." I remember the disappointment – nobody seemed to care what I written. The "Conclusions" on page one seemed to suffice! I could have copied the phone book!

But settle, they did, and so in August 1957 began my career as a business lawyer and, if you've read this far, sometimes as a problem-solver. What a beginning!

An Ego Trip Down Memory Lane

I end this book by going back to shortly after the beginning, after I began working full time at Guterman, Horvitz and Rubin (as Rubin and Rudman LLP was then known). This Tale combines a bit of a memoir with a problem I *SOLVED!* – and there's a BLT in there for you. So here is my last tale . . . for today, anyway:

I recently returned to The Bronx, the borough in New York City – a kind of "roots" trip – back to where I grew up from age 3 until I left for law school. While visiting my old Hermann Ridder Junior High School (a/k/a P.S. 98), our guide took us to the auditorium. I was impressed at what a large room it was and how broad the stage was. What I saw on that stage made me smile and then I burst out laughing. Responding to my companions' questions about what was so funny, I pointed to the very long ladder lying at the rear of the stage.

"That's what's funny," I said, pointing to the ladder, and explained: In our last year, ninth grade, we had a "Red-Letter Day Show." I guess you'd call it a comic romp. My friend (since first grade!) and classmate, Sol Friedman (now a corporate/securities lawyer in New York City) and I co-wrote the Show. We used a Greek-Roman mythology theme, part of our 9th grade English class curriculum. My name in the Show, which was to stick to me to this day among our group, was "Miltonus." Now this wasn't Mel Brooks or Woody Allen stuff – we were barely 14 years olds writing a comedy show. Here goes:

I walk across the stage, right to left, carrying a milk-bottle box, an old-fashioned wooden crate holding twelve glass milk bottles. Friedman asks me, "Hey, Miltonus, where're you goin'?" I respond: "I'm going to court; I got a case." [laughter?] Later in the show, I walk across the stage, this time left to right, carrying a ladder. Again, Friedman asks me, "Hey, Miltonus, where're you goin'?" This time I answer: "I lost my case, I'm going to a higher court." Recalling all this is what made me smile when I saw that ladder on the stage. But what made me burst out laughing? A sudden flash of memory.

Just 16 years after that "great" joke was performed I was, indeed, standing before Earl Warren, Chief Justice of the United States Supreme Court and the other eight Justices, arguing my case. I had arrived at that "higher court." Not a typical assignment for a second-year associate at a small law firm, but there, indeed, I was, nervous as hell. The case itself, which I'll briefly describe, is not nearly as interesting as what has happened *after* that Supreme Court decision in the decades following – and, indeed, to this very day and seemingly will go on happening.

The case (described earlier in this book) arose out of a claim by Ms. Foman, daughter of the deceased. Her father had made an oral promise to her that if she took care of her ailing mother, his wife, he would *not* make a will and she would inherit her share of his estate under the **intestacy** laws of Massachusetts.[2] The good daughter agreed and did her duty until her mother died. Soon afterward, father met and married another woman (Ms. Davis). He then did make a will leaving his entire estate to Ms. Davis and making her his **executrix.** When father died, Ms. Foman got nothing under her father's will, nor from Ms. Davis, so she engaged our firm to bring suit.

Massachusetts law (**Statute of Frauds**)[3] requires that a promise to make a will must be in writing in order to be enforced; at that time, the statute made no mention of a promise *not* to make a will. And an earlier case had ruled that in Massachusetts,[4] an oral promise *not* to make a will was ruled to be enforceable – it did not have to be in writing and was not barred by the statute of frauds. (One judge dissented – he believed that a promise *not* to make a will had to be in writing.) And so based on the majority ruling in that earlier case, our litigator partner, Henry, brought suit in federal district court to enforce the father's oral promise. He asked the court to award Ms. Foman what would have been her share of her father's estate under the **intestacy** laws. That's what her father had promised her; and she had fulfilled her part of the bargain by taking care of her ailing mother.

The U.S. District Court ruled against Henry – they didn't agree with that prior case that had ruled that an oral promise *not* to make a will was enforceable. Rather, it ruled that the dissenting judge in that earlier case was right: Although there was no mention of a promise *not* to make a will in the statute of frauds law, this U.S. District Court read that requirement into the law and dismissed Ms. Foman's claim on the oral contract. Verdict for defendant – case dismissed.

At that point, Henry filed a motion to amend Ms. Foman's Complaint by adding a count in ***quantum meruit.*** Under that approach, instead of asking that the oral contract be enforced, she asked that she be repaid the amount she had spent (at the request of her father) in caring for her ailing mother. Henry's motion to amend the Complaint was denied by the trial court (U.S. District Court). His appeal to the Court of Appeals affirmed the dismissal. That's the point at which Henry asked me to look into the matter.

It seemed clear to me that our client should have been allowed to amend her Complaint – after all, the procedural rules[5] expressly provided that leave to amend "shall be freely given when justice so requires." Both the trial (U.S. District) court and the appeals (First Circuit) court went through a convoluted rigmarole of legal detail and logic and various other of the Federal Rules of Civil Procedure.[6] They rendered decisions about a first notice of appeal; when it was filed; a second notice of appeal and when it was filed; what issues were being appealed and whether defendant had notice that plaintiff was appealing. To me, all this blather served only to obfuscate the real issue here: Once the lower court overruled a prior case eliminating one theory of recovery by plaintiff (breach of contract, namely the father's promise and agreement not to make a will), then it should have allowed amendment of the Complaint to ask for alternative relief, namely getting back the expenses Ms. Foman had incurred in caring for her ailing mother (**quantum meruit**). It struck me that the twists and turns in both the U.S. District (trial) Court and the Court of Appeals[7] about timing and what constituted a notice of appeal and doubts about what issue was the one being appealed were unnecessarily complicating a simple situation that was perfectly clear: When the lower courts ruled that Ms. Foman's claim based on the oral promise/ contract was ruled not enforceable, she asked to amend her Complaint to get back the money she had spent carrying out her part of the bargain with her father.

At this point, I have to recount Justice William O. Douglas interrupting my argument with a question that puzzled him about this little case, a claim for about $40,000 in a will contest: Sounding incredulous, he asked, "What's *this* case doing *here*?"[8] But sometimes cases with "small fact$" involve large legal principles and that's how "little" cases get to the highest Court in the land – there's a matter of principle at stake.

"Her landlord kicked her cat! How did this thing ever get out of Small Claims Court?"

Under Federal Rule 15, Client Mrs. Foman should have been given the opportunity to amend her Complaint, and I said as much at the conclusion of my oral argument at the U.S. Supreme Court:

> The Plaintiff, Mrs. Foman, is no lawyer and she will understand little of what has happened in her case so far. All we can tell her is that through the ingenuity of a federal judge, she has been denied her day in court for no good reason as far as we can see. If these decisions below are permitted to stand, they will constitute a travesty of justice and, in view of the modern development of the Federal Rules [of Civil Procedure], a long step into the past. Thank you for your attention.

Mr. Justice Goldberg, in what may have been his first opinion after being sworn in[9], with a unanimous Court behind him, reversed the lower courts. He wrote,

It is too late in the day, and entirely contrary to the spirit of the Federal Rules of Civil Procedure, for decisions on the merits to be avoided on the basis of such mere technicalities. . . .The Federal Rules reject the approach that pleading is a game of skill in which one misstep by counsel may be decisive to the outcome, and accept the principle that the purpose of pleading is to facilitate a proper decision on the merits.

Of course, the grant or denial of an opportunity to amend is within the discretion of the District Court, but outright refusal to grant the leave without any justifying reason appearing for the denial is not an exercise of discretion; it is merely abuse of that discretion and inconsistent with the spirit of the Federal Rules.

Years Later . . .

I'm driving with a fellow presenter to a Bar Association seminar and I asked what was going on in his practice and he mentioned a matter involving amendment of pleadings, just what I'd done decades before at the U.S. Supreme Court. When I recalled the name of my case, his eyes popped and he said in amazement, "*You* did Foman and Davis?" He explained that this was the landmark case in the area, something I checked in the textbooks when I got back to the office. Sure enough, it showed up in the index and "Table of Cases" quite a bit. Hmm, interesting . . . but . . .

More Years Later : Now The Fun Begins!

A year or two ago, a new automated search-engine service for lawyers was introduced by the Lexis-Nexis system and we were treated to a sales demonstration of its capabilities. One of those capabilities was to instantly find all the cases that had ever mentioned/cited a particular case since it was decided. I raised my hand and asked the speaker to check my old case, *Foman v. Davis*. She did and instantly came up with a high number, over 17,000 court opinions had cited the case since 1962 when the case was decided. I did a little quick arithmetic to see how many working days had passed since 1962 and then asked the presenter to demonstrate another feature of their search engine: Arrange the cases from oldest to newest and then reverse it; arrange the cases from newest to oldest. This is what I learned: Justice Goldberg was sworn in October 1, 1962; I argued the case to the Court November 14; Goldberg's opinion/decision is dated December 3, 1962 and the case was first cited by a court (the U.S. District Court for the Southern District of New York) December 27, 1962. It appears then to have been cited every single working day since then – a total of over 24,000 citations as of this writing. And whenever I check, the latest case was either yesterday or, on rare occasions, that very same day I'm checking. Now if that isn't a hoot, then I don't know what "fun" is. Given the broad applicability of the Federal Rules to all kinds of cases and the clarity and forcefulness of the Goldberg opinion, this little case may be the last word on the effect of Rule 15 of the Federal Rules of Civil Procedure and the right of litigants to amend their pleadings. If so, I suspect *Foman v. Davis* will continue to be cited by some court, state or federal, every working day into the future. Who'd a thunk it![10]

My Style of Arguing a Case to a Judge

Let's get back to those last few words in my oral argument, specifically these:

> If these decisions below are permitted to stand, they will constitute a travesty of justice and, in view of modern development of the Federal Rules [of Civil Procedure], a long step into the past.

I was engaging in the same tactic to win over a judge as in Tale #23, Case Two. That tactic is based on Lawyer Atticus Finch's three words to the jury in the film *To Kill a Mockingbird*: "Do Your Duty!" Judges have a strong sense of duty to come out with a just and right decision. And so, if I can cast my case, my plea to the bench, by asking that of the court, I will do so. Check Case Two, Tale #23 to see how I articulated this "do your duty!" approach in that Probate Court proceeding.

How Powerful is "Do Your Duty!" When Said to a Judge?

It's this powerful: The Probate Judge in Case Two, Tale #23 had very limited jurisdiction in this matter – his court was empowered only to allow the brother's will for probate or not. He had no authority to get into the matters I argued (and surely he knew that as well as I did). But I wanted to get this matter of the phony adoption into the record of the case at the earliest possible stage and "Do Your Duty!" seemed to do that.

---

1 This sounds like a classic "zero-sum" situation: Each party has a different interpretation of their contract and if that difference of opinion ends up in court, the case will end with one winner and one loser. (The "zero-sum game" is discussed in the Prologue.) But check out the case of the good ship *Peerless,* Case Three in Tale #2, p. 24. There the court decided that the parties had *not* entered into a contract – there was no agreement on a key element of their deal, namely, the date of delivery of the bales of cotton. But why is that different from this candy-maker's situation? Buyer assumed they were buying real estate; Seller assumed they were selling shares of stock. Are these two cases distinguishable because the stock sale was so clearly, by its terms – the words on the paper – a sale of stock; but in the *Peerless* case, there was nothing in the contract about shipping or delivery date – just the name of the ship and port of embarkation? So to repeat: The unexpressed intention will almost always lose out to the express words of the contract – say what you mean and mean what you say.

2 The Acts of 2008, Chapter 521.

3 Mass. G.L. ch. 259, sec. 5. (This was amended after the U.S. Supreme Court *Foman v. Davis* decision by Massachusetts Acts 1965, Ch. 560, Sec. 2, by adding to the categories of promises that have to be in writing to be enforceable "an agreement . . . to refrain from making a will."

4 Cleaves v. Kenney, 63 F.2d 682 (1st Cir. 1933)

5 Rule 15 of the Federal Rules of Civil Procedure.

6 What I call rigmarole (and what I had to cover in oral argument) is described in detail in Justice Goldberg's Supreme Court opinion: "The Court of Appeals reasoned that in the absence of a specific designation of the provision of the Federal Rules of Civil Procedure under which the December 20, 1960, motion to vacate was filed, the motion would be treated as filed pursuant to Rule 59 (e), rather than under Rule 60 (b); since, under Rule 73 (a), a motion under Rule 59 suspends the running of time within which an appeal may be perfected, the first notice of appeal was treated as premature in view of the then pending motion to vacate and of no effect. The Court of Appeals held the second notice of appeal, filed January

26, 1961, ineffective to review the December 19, 1960, judgment dismissing the complaint because the notice failed to specify that the appeal was being taken from that judgment as well as [371 U.S. 178, 181] from the orders denying the motions. Considering the second notice of appeal, therefore, only as an appeal from the denial by the District Court of the motions to vacate and amend, the Court of Appeals held that there was nothing in the record to show the circumstances which were before the District Court for consideration in ruling on those motions; consequently it regarded itself as precluded from finding any abuse of discretion in the refusal of the court below to allow amendment."

7 292 F.2d 85 (1st Cir. 1961)

8 Justice Douglas' question was quite understandable – a $40,000 will contest at the U.S. Supreme Court! He then answered his own question noting the jurisdictional basis for us being in federal court – **diversity of citizenship.**

9 Goldberg was nominated to the Court by President Johnson in August, 1962; confirmed in September; sworn in in October; I argued *Foman v. Davis* in November and the Court's opinion by Goldberg is dated December 3, 1962.

10 If I were ever to get a swelled head (I never would) about successfully arguing the U.S. Supreme Court at age 31, I'm sure my late wife (a Schubert scholar and founder/president of The American Schubert Institute – "our fourth child") would remind me that composer Franz Schubert died at age 31, leaving behind some thousand compositions, including over 600 songs *(Lieder)* for solo voice and piano; nearly as many piano pieces, some 150 part songs, some 40 liturgical compositions (including several masses) and around 20 stage works like operas and incidental music. His orchestral output includes a dozen symphonies (seven completed) and several overtures. Schubert's chamber music includes over 20 and several quintets, trios and duos. And he *died* at age 31!

APPENDIX A
GLOSSARY

Hint (as if you needed it): Google is a good source of many and more detailed definitions and articles on any of these terms.

Amortize; unamortized

An accounting term: Over a period of time, to amortize is to make back or recover the original capital outlay; and the unrecovered amount is considered unamortized. In this Tale #9, Landlord needed ten years to recover the costs of preparing this consulting firm's space – he could not do it in five (which is how long the consulting firm tenant wanted to stay in his building). A 5-year lease would leave Landlord with unamortized costs – expenses he incurred which he didn't get back from rentals.

Assign; anti-assignment provision

Assign is another word for transfer. The "assignor" is the party making that transfer and the "assignee" is the one to whom the transfer is made. Many contracts contain an anti-assignment provision or require the consent of the other party if one party wishes to assign or transfer the contract or some rights under the contract. Businesspeople usually like to know with whom they're doing business and don't like the prospect of suddenly finding themselves in a deal with some stranger, the "assignee" – hence, the standard-form anti-assignment provision or the limitation on assignment.

Boilerplate

Typically found toward the end of business contracts, these are "standard" provisions used in all kinds of contracts in order to cover many typical business contingencies. Examples are "attorney's fees," "jurisdiction," "waiver," "Force Majeure," or "warranties." In Tale #13, "Anti-Assignment" is the boilerplate provision at issue. Author Tina L. Stark has produced a massive collection of boilerplate provisions in her book, *Negotiating and Drafting Contract Boilerplate*, ALM Publishing (2003). (Bet you didn't expect a cartoon in the Glossary, right?)

"Four Boiler-Plate Specials."

Breakup Fee

When a company is buying another company and the seller backs out before the deal closes – with more detailed conditions and provisions – a so-called breakup fee, or termination fee, is required to be paid to the disappointed prospective buyer to compensate them for the time and resources used to investigate; negotiate; document and otherwise facilitate the deal. (Breakup fees are normally a small percentage – about 1-3% of the deal's value or purchase price if that has been determined or fixed at the time of seller's backing down.)

Class B Common Non-voting Stock

Typically, a corporation's common stock is voting stock, entitling the holder to vote at stockholder meetings. If you wish to give, say a valued employee, a share in the equity of the company, but you don't want them interfering with your exclusive control of your corporation, then you could issue another class of stock and designate it as non-voting. The thing to remember – and this may vary from state to state under their individual respective corporate statutes – is that certain crucial actions that affect these Class B shareholders may, under certain circumstances, require their consent. Thus, in some situations, on certain occasions/events, even the B-Non-Voting shareholder may have a limited voting right. So remember that "non-voting" may not be applicable in all situations. Check the terms of the stock issue itself and, of course, the corporate laws of the state of incorporation.

Close Corporation

…is a business organized as a corporation under the state's corporation statute with all the shares issued to just a select few individuals (usually family members or people involved in running the business, although some close corporations may have an investor who is not connected to business operations). A close corporation is not publicly traded on any stock exchanges and is, therefore, closed to investment from the general public. Some states have simplified the management structure, record-keeping and other requirements for entities that fit that state's definition of a close corporation.

Closing

If you've bought or sold a house, chances are you've been to a Closing. That's the event when the parties to the deal meet in person and sign the documents that make their deal firm and a done deal. Most real estate deals are not "done" until documents have "gone to record," i.e., recorded at the Registry of Deeds. Indeed, some closings occur right at the Registry. Many other kinds of legal transactions between parties are concluded when they meet this way to sign and exchange documents. Today, many transactions are "closed" via email or by other remote means of communication.

Collective bargaining agreement

The contract between a labor organization like a union and an employer of the members of that organization, usually covering basic terms, benefits, and the like of the employment relationship.

Counterclaim

A claim by a defendant opposing the claim of the plaintiff, possibly asserting a new claim of its own and seeking some relief from the plaintiff for the defendant.

Covenant

This can be a noun, meaning a promise or agreement to do or not do something. And it can be a verb, meaning the person who covenants to do or not do something is promising or agreeing to take that promised action.

Delaware

This is the favored state for incorporation because of the broad scope of freedom in setting up your corporation; the kinds of stock you'll issue; the officers and other personnel who will run the corporation; and all the other details of the business. The forms for making and filing changes are also simplified for ease of use by businesses. Many, if not most of the major American corporations are formed/incorporated in Delaware.

Discovery

Once a lawsuit is filed, each of the parties has the right to inquire of the other party about facts it needs to prosecute or defend its case. This fact-finding process generally takes place outside the courtroom and may proceed by face-to-face questioning sessions ("depositions") or by written questions ("interrogatories"). Although the kinds of information that a party can force someone else to reveal about matters related to the litigation is fairly broad, there are some limits. Discovery can be used to seek information not only from the other party to the lawsuit, but also from people and businesses that aren't involved in the pending legal proceedings, i.e., non-parties. Use of subpoenas is one way used by parties in a lawsuit to obtain evidence from non-party witnesses. A party can also use any of the discovery devices contained in the Federal Rules of Civil Procedure ##26 through 37.

Diversity of Citizenship

When all the parties plaintiff are from a different state from all the parties defendant, the lawsuit may be brought in a federal district court; the decision may be appealed to a U.S. Court of Appeals; and that decision may be appealed to the U.S. Supreme Court (which is what happened in my case, *Foman v. Davis*). It's more complicated, e.g., dealing with corporations and foreign parties to the law suit, so check it out if you need to know more.

Eminent domain
The power of a governmental unit, authority or agency (such as a City; State; Redevelopment Authority; public utility or railway corporation; etc.) to take ownership of real estate or rights (such as an easement for pipes/wires or a right of way for tracks) for a public purpose from the landowner and, in turn, pay the landowner fair compensation for what it takes.

Equity
When "The Law" was very formal and complex in Merry Olde England, they developed the Courts of Chancery or Equity Courts which could be more flexible. These courts could order people to do things (like specifically perform their promise to sell/transfer a parcel of land) or not to do things (like enjoin a trespass on their neighbor's property). Today, that branch of the courts has generally been merged into the court system, but we still refer to courts of equity when we need these special remedies (called "equitable remedies") or something that might be "right and fair," but not easily available from the law-courts side.

Fiduciary
The noun describes a person or company charged with protecting interests of another, as a trustee under a trust for the benefit of the beneficiary. The adjective, as in the phrase, "fiduciary obligation," relates to a duty to act in good faith with regard to the interests of another person or entity. A corporate director owes a fiduciary duty to his corporation; recent changes in the law provide that an investment adviser has a *fiduciary* responsibility to investors.

Force Majeure
Usually unforeseeable circumstances or events that prevent or delay performance of contract obligations, such as a severe storm that delays construction completion beyond the projected finish date. Some contracts use "act of God" phraseology; but it's usually a good idea if you use these terms to give examples to clarify your intent. For example, "conditions of supply and demand" may prevent essential materials arriving in time for completion of work under a contract – a phrase that any particular court may or may not rule as being covered by "force majeure" or "act of God."

Indemnify; Indemnification

To indemnify another party is to compensate that party for some described loss or damage that has already occurred. Indemnification can also operate going forward so as to guarantee under a contract to repay another party for loss or damage that may occur in the future. A liability insurance policy is an example of such an indemnification: The insurance company, as part of an individual general liability insurance policy, agrees to indemnify the insured person for losses that person may suffer as the result of accident or property damage for which the insured person is legally liable.

Indemnification can be inserted into many other kinds of contracts. For example, in the construction industry, a subcontract will usually contain the subcontractor's agreement to indemnify the general contractor for any losses incurred or claims made against the contractor based on something the subcontractor had caused. Those losses or claims might result from a suit filed against the general contractor for failure to adhere to contractual terms, or because of personal injury suffered at the job site by a worker's or some other individual's negligence.

Initiative

A procedure whereby some required minimum number of voters may propose a statute, constitutional amendment, or ordinance, and then compel a popular vote on its adoption.

Inter Alia

Latin phrase meaning "among other things" and is usually used to indicate that a listing is not intended to be complete or all-inclusive. For example, "Mr. A will perform his obligations hereunder in all kinds of weather conditions, including, *inter alia,* rain and snow."

Intestacy Laws

These laws, which vary state-to-state, provide for how a decedent's property/estate will be distributed if that person dies without a will. Thus, there is usually provision for a surviving spouse and children, grandchildren, etc.

and moves down to more distant relatives if none of these close relations survive the decedent's death.

IPO
Abbreviation for "Initial Public Offering" – the occasion when a privately owned corporation registers its shares for sale to the public and offers them for the first time on a stock market such as NASDAQ or New York Stock Exchange.

Irrevocable Bank Letter of Credit
A document issued by a bank in the form of correspondence, a letter that promises payment of a specified sum of money under the terms of the letter (used frequently to pay for goods or services being purchased by the individual or entity, referred to as the applicant, that requests the letter of credit from an issuing bank). An irrevocable letter of credit cannot be canceled or in any way modified, without the explicit agreement of all parties involved (in this Tale #9, that would be the Tenant, client Landlord and the issuing bank).

Leased department
An arrangement for providing a variety of departments in a large store and frequently used during the height of the "discount store" era which began in about the late 1950s. A department store, rather than owning and operating all the various departments in its store, would have a leased department. A defined area of floor space within the store would be leased to a department lessee, creating the appearance that it is part of the department store, but actually run as a separate business by the leased department operator, usually under a minimum-rental plus percentage of sales financial arrangement between the store owner/operator and the leased department operator.

Liquidated damages
When a party to a contract doesn't perform their obligations under the deal, it is sometimes difficult or impossible to measure the damage that the innocent party will suffer (e.g., the loss of some market advantage). In those types of situations, a liquidated-damage provision included in the contract

is a useful tool. It provides for payment by the breaching party to the innocent party to the contract of a specified dollar amount or other fixed or formula-determined sum. (In the case of a debt instrument, like a promissory note, for example, liquidated damages is sometimes stated as an interest rate applied to the amount owed and unpaid. And in a lease of real estate, liquidated damages might be described as "additional rent.") Courts will usually enforce this pre-agreed amount of damages unless, for example, (i) damages can easily be calculated *without* the use of a liquidated-damage provision, or (ii) if the amount is excessive. (Liquidated damages are excessive if the amount is grossly disproportionate to the probable *actual* damage that would be suffered by the non-breaching (innocent) party.) And if a court finds the liquidated damage amount "excessive," then it will refuse to enforce the liquidated-damage provision, dubbing it "an unenforceable penalty."

Author's Note on Liquidated Damages: I don't want to leave this explanation without emphasizing why I like to use a strong **liquidated-damage** provision whenever possible. Since I always tried to stay out of court, having a fixed amount stated right in the contract not only gets rid of that aspect of any litigation, but it provides an incentive for the other side to perform their obligations under the contract; and a disincentive against their doing what they should not be doing under the contract.

Motions
In a pending litigation, when one of the parties wants the judge to take some action, for example, to dismiss the plaintiff's case or render judgment in favor of the plaintiff (or defendant), that party, "the moving party," will file a motion with the court requesting a judge to issue a ruling or order on a legal matter. Motions can cover a wide variety of matters in the course of a trial.

Motion to strike
A request by a trial lawyer for one party that the judge eliminate something in the other party's pleading or evidence (which is deleted from the record of the litigation); and if there is a jury, they are instructed by the judge to disregard the stricken material. Procedural rules provide, for example that

material in a plaintiff's complaint may be stricken if it contains "any redundant, immaterial, impertinent or scandalous matter," or any "irrelevant, false, or improper matter inserted in any pleading."

Motioned

A motion is a pleading a lawyer files in court and this use of the word connotes a Motion to Dismiss the plaintiff's case. If there is no legal basis for the Complaint (the pleading filed by the party plaintiff to begin the lawsuit), the party defendant would file this Motion to Dismiss and, if granted, that case would have been motioned out of court.

Net lease

In a typical "gross lease" the Landlord pays for the costs for property taxes, insurance, maintenance of the structure and sometimes other expenses relating to the property. All these costs and expenses are deducted from the gross rent which Landlord receives to arrive as his net rent. In a net-lease arrangement, the tenant picks up all these costs and the rent which Landlord receives is net to him, no expense deductions, since they are all paid by the tenant under a net-lease arrangement. (Sometimes called a "triple net lease" whereby the tenant pays "triple net rent," "triple" referring to taxes, insurance and maintenance.)

Nominal damages

In some lawsuits, the plaintiff presents a strong and winning legal case against the defendant, but the court finds that the defendant suffered no real monetary loss. For example, defendant made a false statement about the plaintiff, committing defamation (libel or slander), but plaintiff suffered no real monetary loss because of the false statement. And so the plaintiff may win his case against the defendant, but the court would award an insignificant, symbolic sum, like six cents, which is called "nominal damages." The 1970 Leon Uris novel, *QB VII*, involved a defamation claim being tried in an English court. While the court found that defendant was defamed by defendant's statements, the judge awarded the lowest amount it could as damages, one-half penny, nominal damages.

1- Non-competition; 2- confidentiality/non-disclosure agreements; 3-anti raiding; 4- non-solicitation; 5- non-disparagement

Modern employment agreements, typically in the hi-tech sector, contain provisions under these headings. They are sometimes also used when an employee leaves the company – sometimes in exchange for a severance payment. Typically,, the employee is asked to sign an agreement promising not to: 1- Compete with his former employer for some fixed period of time; 2- Disclose his former employer's "confidential information," trade secrets and the like; 3- Try to hire away employees of his former employer; 4- solicit or even contact his former employer's customers; and 5- bad-mouth or disparage his former employer.

Operating Expense Escalation

Usually found in multi-tenant office space leases, this is a provision requiring the tenant to pay its pro-rata share (usually based on square footage area of the premises) of increases in the building's operating expenses over those expenses in a base year (usually the first year of the lease term). (Where real estate taxes are not included in operating expenses, then this same arrangement will pass on to the tenant its share of increases in real estate taxes over the taxes in a base year.)

OSHA – EPA

These are Federal (and in some states, state-level) agencies regulating a broad range of Occupational Safety and Health (OSHA) matters and Environmental Protection Agency (EPA) issues.

Penalty

See "Liquidated damages," above.

Phantom Stock Plan

A contractual agreement between a corporation and recipients (usually officers and employees in lieu of actual shares or a cash bonus) providing for book entries of phantom shares (with *no* voting rights) that bestow upon the grantee the same economic benefits as if they owned shares in the company that established the plan. Thus, the person holding these rights will receive a benefit which increases as the stock price rises in a registered public company, or as the book value of shares increases in a close corporation. Some plans provide a vesting schedule that delays actual ownership until, for example, the employee has been with the company some minimum number of years. Tale #24 illustrates a simple such Plan in a close corporation situation.

Probate
This is the judicial process that authenticates ("probates") a decedent's Last Will and Testament. The word also describes, in some states, the branch of their court system that handles family law issues like those arising under wills, trusts and estates. In some states it has other designations, for example, what is called the Probate Court in Massachusetts is called the Surrogate's Court in New York,

Publicly Listed
When a privately held or close corporation registers its shares in an **IPO,** it becomes publicly listed on some stock exchange where members of the public can buy and sell its shares.

Race to the Courthouse – "Forum Shopping"
When litigation is imminent and one of the parties can spot some advantage in being in court in State A rather than some other state that might seem more "natural" for the parties, that party may engage in "forum shopping," i.e., finding the court that they believe will rule in their favor. If that party can find some basis for that preferred state to have jurisdiction over the case, they might "race to the courthouse" and file first. Usually, but not always, the court in which that case is first filed is the one where it stays. Later filings in other courts may be dismissed or held in abeyance until that first case is disposed of. A prime example is the Pennzoil-Texaco-Getty case in the late 1980s.

Referendum
In government, this principle or practice, once a legislature has passed a law, refers that law to the voters for their approval or rejection; and that referendum determines whether the law remains in effect or is rendered null and void.

Representation and Warranty

A representation is an assertion as to a fact relating to some present or past matter; and an assertion that the fact is true at the time it was made. Representations are usually given to induce another party to enter into a contract or take some other action. A warranty is a promise of indemnity, that is, to pay the injured party for damages sustained if the assertion is false.

Restatement of the Law of Contracts

The distinguished judges, scholars and lawyers who make up the American Law Institute have produced "Restatements" of various branches of the law: Contracts, Torts, Trusts, Product Liability, and many more. These treatises attempt to state the general principles of each of these subjects as ruled on by American courts and are relied on by lawyers in their arguments to courts and cited by judges in deciding cases.

Right of first refusal (and right of first offer)

Often used in real estate transactions, these methods for securing desired rights to get property show up in other industries, media, movies and publishing, for example. The right of first refusal (ROFR) is triggered when the property owner receives an offer (from ABC) he'd like to accept. Before he can accept the offer and make the deal, he has to give that same offer to the person holding the ROFR; and only if that person turns down the deal, can the owner go back and make the deal with ABC on the terms of ABC's offer.

A right of first offer (ROFO) requires the owner, when he decides to sell or make some other deal, to first go to the holder of the ROFO and first offer it to him. Understand that lawyers can and usually should take pages and pages to express the operation of these two "simple" concepts and procedures in sufficient detail so as to avoid disputes and lawsuits – this is just a short explanation.

Both the ROFR and the ROFO are "weaker" than an outright option or right to purchase, lease or make the movie from a book or other right not conditioned on an offer being made or contemplated. Such an outright right is the "option."

Sale-and-leaseback
This is a financial transaction used in both real estate and personal property (e.g., equipment) transactions. In the real estate area, it is used instead of a mortgage to provide funds to the property owner. The owner of real estate sells it to the financier-lender and then leases it back, usually for a long term and usually on a triple-net-lease basis (lessee/tenant pays all expenses; taxes, maintenance; insurance, etc.) One version may include the lessee/tenant's right to buy back the property at some negotiated or nominal price once the amount of the financing/loan has been repaid by the rentals. A similar arrangement is used for personal property, e.g., factory equipment financing.

SBA
Abbreviation for Small Business Administration, a Federal agency with a menu of financial and other resources for small businesses. They maintain an extensive website at *https://www.sba.gov/* and offices in most major cities.

Scrivener's Error
The legal principle that a typographical **error** in a written contract (or in map-drafting) may be corrected by oral evidence if the evidence is clear, convincing, and precise.

Special Damages
These are the damages that the aggrieved party (plaintiff in a lawsuit) has suffered that may not be obvious, clear and apparent to the defendant. In Tale #10, the expiring-lease tenants are not expected to know all the harm and costs they cause to Landlord by not getting out of their space when their lease expires. For a plaintiff to collect any damages from the defendant, those damages usually have to be foreseeable. To put it another way, to recover for this harm, the plaintiff must prove that prior to the breach of contract occurring, the defendant knew or reasonably should have known of the special circumstances leading to such harm. If these are not obvious to the defendant (tenant in Tale #10), then Landlord must inform the tenant of their exposure to special damages by giving a notice of special damages. This notice is illustrated by the 3-letter procedure described in Tale #10.

Statute of Frauds
Each state has a law requiring certain types of contracts to be in writing for them to be enforceable in a court of law. Examples are sales above a certain dollar amount; many real estate transactions; agreement to make a will; and more. Whenever you're relying on some oral promise, check and ensure that it's enforceable and not a promise that you could not enforce in a court.

Subrogated
The most typical type of subrogation occurs when an insurance company pays its insured for a loss that was caused by a third party; the insurance company then steps into the shoes of its insured and owns the legal claim against that third party who caused the loss. More generally, subrogation is the substitution of one person in place of another with reference to some legal claim or right. The right of subrogation can also arise when A pays the debt of B to B's creditor, C; A can become B's creditor under certain circumstances and within certain limitations. This is just one of several business situations where a right of subrogation can arise.

Subsidiary corporation
A corporation that is owned or controlled (i.e., more than 50% of its stock is owned) by another corporation. The owner or controlling corporation is called the "parent corporation" or "parent company."

Tenants in common
The relationship of concurrent and shared co-ownership, usually of real estate, where each of the tenants in common owns an undivided share of the property. Thus, for example, in Tale #33, each of the two owners owned an undivided one-half interest in the property they'd bought together. But the shares can also be of unequal size, as when two tenants in common own a 70% and 30% interest, respectively. This form of ownership can usually be sold or transferred and passed by inheritance when one of the co-owners dies. Typically, each of the co-owners has the right to use and occupy the property they own as tenants in common.

Triple-net rent
See "Net lease," above.

Unjust enrichment

This happens when one enjoys some benefits at the expense of another, but the one getting the benefits chooses not to pay for them. The recipient of that benefit, the law says, has been unjustly enriched and should, in fairness, pay for that benefit. A common example might be a contractor hired to build a house for landowner and proceeds to excavate and put in the foundation. Landowner changes his mind and halts the work, refusing to pay for the excavation work and foundation already done. He has been unjustly enriched and a court would be expected to award restitution to the contractor for the benefit his work and materials have bestowed on landowner.

APPENDIX B
LEGAL SUBJECTS/SPECIALTIES INVOLVED IN THE TALES

Accounting: (#10

Advocacy – Arguing a Case to a Court: (#22; Postlogue.

Arbitration: (#1.

Constructive Trust / Resulting Trust: (#15.

Condemnation / Eminent Domain Taking: (#21.

Contracts – How to write a "good" one: (#1; (#29.
    Interpretation (What do they mean?) (#1; (#2; (#4; (#22.
    Formation – The Mailbox Rule: (#14.
    Recitals/"Whereas". . . – Very important! #29.

Corporate: (#24.

Deferred Payment Arrangements (#7; (#8.

Environmental Laws/Regulations: (#16; (#30.

Administrative Agencies: (#22; (#30.

"Fun" Tales: (#6 – KDL Tale; (#34 and (#35.

Insurance (Product Liability): (#12.

Law and Ethics : How do they relate? (Prologue

Lease – long-term with options to extend: (#23; (#33.

Margin Regulations (Borrowing to buy securities): (#18.

Minority Shareholder: (#24.

Negotiations – A Tip (#33); Obligation to negotiate in good faith: (#17.

Non-Competition Agreements: (#25; (#2; (#3; (#11; (#15.

Non-Legal or Extra-Legal Remedies: (#25.

"Not to be unreasonably withheld . . ." – Typical condition to granting consent: (#33.

OSHA Rules/Regulations: (#16.

Product Liability: (#19; (#26.

Real Estate Issues: (#16; (#21; (#23.

Risk-Shifting: All Part II Tales; (#32.

Rule Against Perpetuities: (#20.

Sales, Licensing & E-Commerce: (#28.

Statutes – Interpreting (what do they mean?): Tax (#4; ObamaCare (#4.

Sublease / License: (#5.

"Synthesis" – Lawyer learning client's facts points to solution to problems: (#2; (#18.
Taxes (Federal Corporate Tax) (#4)
Tricks of the Trade: (#31
Troublemakers – Spot'em and avoid'em: (#27; (#28.

APPENDIX C
SAMPLING OF INDUSTRIES OF
MILTON BORDWIN'S BUSINESS CLIENTS SINCE 1957

(I Served as Outside General Counsel (OGC) to 15 of the Following:)

- Advertising Agencies [OGC]
- Automobile Dealerships
- Banks and Commercial Lenders
- Broadband/Spectrum Ventures/ Investors
- Candy Manufacturer
- Chain Store – Household Goods/Discount (OGC-IPO-SEC work)
- Chain Store – Hardware, Home, etc. Paper Goods (OGC)
- Chain Store – Toys (OGC – No SEC)
- Chain Store – Women's Apparel
- Chemical Manufacturer (OGC)
- Clothing Stores
- Commercial Bakery (OGC)
- Commercial/Office Landlords (1 OGC)
- Computer Systems Manufacturer
- Construction Company
- Cyber Security (Supply Chain and Critical Infrastructure)
- Dental Office Chain
- Department Stores (OGC)
- Fine Jewelry Store
- Food Processing Equipment Distributor (OGC)
- Furniture Stores (Retail)
- Furniture / Stereo Cabinet Manufacturer
- Furrier (Manufacturer and Retail Stores)
- Guru / Mystic / Yoga Master
- Hi-Tech Optical Inspection Eqpt Mfr (OGC-no SEC)
- Hotels
- Insurance Brokerage / Claims Agents

- Internet – E-Commerce/
  Merchants
- Inventors

- Medical Device Manufacturers

- Nano-technology Scientist

- Packaging Machine Distributor
  (OGC)
- Paper Box Manufacturer
- Pharmaceutical/Bio-tech
- Public Relations Agency
- Research Laboratory
- Shiatsu Studio
- Shopping Center Developers

- Turbo-generator Manufacturer

- Woolen Mills

- Interstate Trucking Company

- Leased Dept (Dept. Store)
  Major Appliances
- Meat processing/pkng machin-
  ery distributor (OGC)
- Multi-Family Housing
  Developers (OGC)
- Non-profits: Theatre; Music
  Institute; Suicide Hot Line
  (some OGC and all pro bono)
- Paint Manufacturer

- Paper Goods Wholesalers
- Printing Company (OGC)
- Real Estate Developers
- Restaurants
- Shoe Manufacturer
- Software Developers – Various
  (Business Intelligence; Telecom
  services; knowledge manage-
  ment; search engines; anti-copy
  protection; etc.)
- Wireless Transmission Static/
  Interference Filter Mfr

APPENDIX D
PARTIAL READING LIST

These books in the author's business/law library have been important and useful in practicing law and in the writing of "SOLVED!" I am grateful to all these authors.
  (In alphabetical order by author.)

—

Paul Adams, *155 Legal Do's (and Don'ts) For the Small Business,* John Wiley & Sons, Inc. (1996)

Paul Allen, *How to Keep Your Company Out of Court: The Practical Legal Guide For Growing Businesses*, Prentice-Hall, Inc. (1984)

The American Bar Association, *Legal Guide For Small Business* (Random House reference) (2010)

Ken Auletta, *The Highway Men-Warriors of the Information Highway*, Random House (1997)

Bagley and Savage, *Managers and the Legal Environment*, South-Western Cengage Learning (2010)

Constance E. Bagley & Craig E. Dauchy, *The Entrepreneur's Guide to Business Law (2ⁿᵈ Edition)*, Thomson (2003)

Louis Brown, Richard S. Gruner, Anne O. Kandel, *The Legal Audit: Corporate Internal Investigation*, Clark Boardman Callaghan (2005-2015)

Carl T. Bogus, *Why Lawsuits are Good for America,* New York University Press (2001)

Steven Brill, *Trial by Jury*, American Lawyer Books/Touchstone-Simon & Schuster, Inc. (1989)

Louis M. Brown, *Lawyering Through Life*, Fred B. Rothman & Co. (1986)

James L. Buckley, *Saving Congress From Itself*, Encounter Books (2014)

Thomas F. Burke, *Lawyers, Lawsuits, and Legal Rights*, University of California Press (2002)

Daniel Burrus, *Flash Foresight*, Harper Business (2011)

William D. Bygrave, *The Portable MBA in Entrepreneurship*, John Wiley & Sons (1994)

Paul F. Campos, *Jurismania*, Oxford University Press (1998)

Clayton M. Christensen, *The Innovator's Dilemma*, Collins (2006)

Clayton M. Christensen and Michael E. Raynor, *The Innovator's Solution*, Harvard Business School Press (2003)

The Council of Better Business Bureaus, *How to Protect Your Business*, The Benjamin Company, Inc./Prentice-Hall (1992)

The Court TV Cradle-To-Grave Legal Survival Guide, The American Lawyer/ Little-Brown and Company (1995)

Catherine Crier, *The Case Against Lawyers*, Broadway Books-Random House (2002)

Colleen DeBaise, *The Wall Street Journal Complete Small Business Guide Book*, Three Rivers Press (2009)

Dawn-Marie Driscoll and W. Michael Hoffman, *Ethics Matters-How to Implement Values-Driven Management*, Center For Business Ethics – Bentley College – Waltham, MA (2000)

Peter F. Drucker, *Innovation and Entrepreneurship*, Harper & Row (1985)

Kevin Dutton, *Split-Second Persuasion*, Houghton Mifflin Harcourt (2011)

Martin Eskenazi and David Gallen, *Sexual Harassment*, Carroll & Graf Publishers, Inc. (1992)

Diane Fassel, *Working Ourselves to Death*, Harper Collins (1990)

Roger Fisher and William Ury, *Getting to Yes* (Houghton Mifflin (1981)

H. Scott Fogler and Steven E. LeBlanc, *Strategies For Creative Problem Solving*, Prentiss Hall, PTR (1995)

Richard Foster, *Innovation*, Summit Books (1986)

Monroe H. Freedman, *Lawyers' Ethics in an Adversary System*, Bobbs-Merrill (1975)

Morton S. Freeman, *The Grammatical Lawyer*, ALI-ABA (1979)

James C. Freund, *Smart Negotiating*, Simon & Schuster (1992)

Lon L. Fuller, *The Morality of Law*, Yale University Press (1964)

Michael Gershman, *Getting it Right the Second Time*, Addison – Wesley (1990)

Malcolm Gladwell, *The Power of Thinking Without Thinking*, Little Brown (2005)

Malcolm Gladwell, *Blink*, Back Bay Books (2005)

Jerome Groopman, M.D., *How Doctors Think*, Houghton Mifflin Harcourt (2007)

Andrew S. Grove, *Only the Paranoid Survive*, Currency Doubleday (1996)

Bertram Harnett, *Put the Law on Your Side*, Harper & Row (1985)

Chip Heath & Dan Heath, *Made to Stick*, Random House (2007)

David R. Henderson and Charles L. Hooper, *Making Great Decisions in Business and Life*, Chicago Park Press (2006)

Philip J. Hermann, *The 96 Billion Dollar Gain You Are Losing*, Legal Information Publications, Inc. (1993)

Phillip Howard, *The Death of Common Sense*, Publisher?, Date?

Peter W. Huber, *Galileo's Revenge*, Basic Books-Harper Collins (1991)

Robert Hughes, *Culture of Complaint*, Oxford University Press (1993)

Lee Iacocca, *Iacocca: An Autobiography*, Bantam Books (1984)

Lee Iacocca, *Talking Straight*, Bantam Books (1988)

International Franchise Association, *What You Need to Know to Buy a Franchise* (1988 1999)

Jathan Janove, *Managing to Stay Out of Court*, Berrett-Koehler Publishers, Inc. (2005)

Lewin G. Joel III, *Every Employee's Guide to the Law*, Pantheon (1993)

Ronald L. Jones, *Practice Preventive Corporate Law*, American Law Institute-American Bar Association (1985)

Ronald L. Jones, *How to Counsel Corporate Clients*, American Law Institute-American Bar Association (2000)

Daniel Kehrer, *Doing Business Boldly*, Simon & Schuster (1990)

John F. Landrum, *Out of Court-How to Protect Your Business From Litigation*, The Headwaters Press, Inc. (1992)

David Lebedoff, *Cleaning Up*, The Free Press – Simon & Schuster (1997)

Dorothy Leeds & Sue Belevich Schilling, *Smart Questions to Ask Your Lawyer*, Harper Paperbacks (1992)

Theodore Levitt, *The Marketing Imagination*, Free Press-MacMillan (1986)

Karl N. Llewellyn, *The Bramble Bush*, Oxford University Press (2008) (11th printing)

Dr. Frank Luntz, *Words That Work*, Hyperion (2007)

Harvey MacKay, *Swim With The Sharks Without Being Eaten Alive*, Morrow (1988)

Massachusetts Continuing Legal Education, Inc. (16 Legal Practitioners), *Things a Corporate Attorney Needs to Know*, (1991)

Mark H. McCormack, *The Terrible Truth About Lawyers*, William Morrow (1987)

Larry McFadin & Beeler Gausz, *Cashing the Prevention Check*, iUniverse, Inc. (2005)

Walter K. Olson, *The Excuse Factory*, The Free Press (1997

Walter K. Olson, *The Litigation Explosion*, Dutton (1991)

Vance Packard, *The Hidden Persuaders*, Pocketbooks (1968) (35th print)

Lynn Sharp Paine, *Cases in Leadership, Ethics and Organizational Integrity*, Irwin (1997)

Henry H. Perritt, Jr., *Your Rights in the Workplace*, Practicing Law Institute (1993)

Sumner Redstone, *A Passion to Win*, Simon & Schuster (2001)

Barbara Kate Repa, *Your Rights in the Workplace*, Nolo Press (3rd Ed.) (1997)

Cliff Roberson, *Business Person's Legal Advisor (2nd Edition)*, Liberty Hall Press (1991)

George H. Ross, *Trump-Style Negotiation: Powerful Strategies and Tactics for Mastering Every Deal*, Wiley (2006, 2008 [paperback ed.])

Martin J. Ross, *Handbook of Everyday Law*, Harper & Row (1975)

Douglas Rushkoff, *Coercion – Why We Listen To What "They" Say*, Riverhead Books (1999)

Steven Mitchell Sack, *From Hiring to Firing*, Legal Strategies Publications (1995)

Steven Mitchell Sack, *The New Lifetime Legal Guide*, Book of the Month Club (1998)

Robert W. Schachner & Marvin Quittner, *How and When to Be Your Own Lawyer*, Avery Publishing Group, Inc. (1993)

Joan Schneider & Jeanne Yocum, *New Product Launch: 10 Proven Strategies*, Stagnito Communications, Inc. (2004)

Thomas A. Schweich, *Protect Yourself From Business Lawsuits*, Simon & Schuster (1998)

Martin E. Segal, *Preventative Law For Business Professionals*, Thomson (2005)

Larraine Segil, *Intelligent Business Alliances*, Times Business-Random House (1996)

Phillip F. Seidman, *Legal Aspects of Selling &Buying*, Magraw-Hill (1983)

Nate Silver, *The Signal and The Noise*, Penguin Press (2012)

Bert Spector, *Understanding Your Business Clients*, American Bar Association (2013)

George Stalk and Rob Lachenauer, *Hardball, Are You Playing to Play or Playing to Win?*, Harvard Business School Press (2004)

Peter B. Stark, *It's Negotiable*, Pfeiffer & Company (1994)

Paul N. Strassels & Robert Wool, *All You Need to Know About the IRS*, Random House (1979)

Gordon R. Sullivan & Michael V. Harper, *Hope is Not a Method*, Times Business-Random House (1996)

Donald H. Sweet, *A Manager's Guide to Conducting Terminations*, Lexington-MacMillan (1989)

Charles J. Sykes, *A Nation of Victims*, St. Martin's Press (1992)

Noel M. Tichy & Warren G. Bennis, *Judgment*, Portfolio (2007)

Michael G. Trachtman, *What Every Executive Better Know About The Law*, Simon & Schuster (1987)]

Michael Treacy and Fred Wiersema, *The Discipline of Market Leaders*, Addison – Wesley (1995)

Donald J. Trump, *The Art of The Deal*, Warner Books (1987).

Stephen Tumim, *Great Legal Disasters*, Arthur Barker Limited London (1983)

U.S. News & World Report Books, *What Everyone Needs to Know About Law*, 1973

Kenneth J. Vandevelde, *Thinking Like a Lawyer*, Westview Press (2011)

Donald H. Weiss, *Fair, Square and Legal,* Amacom (1991)

James Q. Wilson, *Moral Judgment,* Basic Books-HarperCollins (1997)

Richard Wincor, *Contracts in Plain English,* McGraw Hill (1976)

Michael J. Wolf, *The Entertainment Economy,* Times Books-Random House (1999)

Charles E. Wyzanski, Jr., *Whereas – a Judge's Premises: Essays in Judgment, Ethics And The Law,* Little, Brown and Co. (1965)

Philip F. Zeidman, *Legal Aspects of Selling & Buying* (1983 plus supplements)

APPENDIX E
CARTOON CREDITS

**Thanks to the cartoonists and the two licensing agencies,
Condé Nast's Cartoon Bank ("CB") and Cartoon Stock ("CS")**

Aaron Bacall and CS, pp. 185; 187; 328

Mike Baldwin and CS, p. 116

Charles Barsotti and CB, p. XLIII

Brenda Burbank, p. XXXVI

Dave Carpenter, pp. 65;196

Leo Cullum and CB, pp. XL; 222

Roy Delgado, pp. XXII; 44; 131

Fran and CS, p. 168

Sam Gross and CB, p. 62

William Hamilton and CB, p. XVIII

Sidney Harris, pp. XLV; 70; 283

Kes and CS, p. 105

Robert Mankoff and CB, p. 16

Henry Martin and CB, pp. 25; 40

Theresa McCracken and CS, p. 50

Mike Mosedale and CS, p. 228

Tim O'Brien and CS, p. 125

Everett Opie and CB, p. 362

Doug Pike, p. 280

Harley Schwadron, p. 320

John Singer and CS, p. 279

Peter Steiner and CB, p. 59

Andrew Toos, pp. 9; 161

Bradford Veley and CS, pp. 181; 278

Robert Weber and CB, p. 143

Chris Wildt and CS, p. 368

Gahan Wilson and CB, p. 21

Jack Ziegler, p. 225